VIDEO GAME DESIGN REVEALED

GUY W. LECKY-THOMPSON

CHARLES RIVER MEDIA
Boston, Massachusetts

Publisher and General Manager, Charles River Media: Stacy L. Hiquet
Associate Director of Marketing: Sarah O'Donnell
Manager of Editorial Services: Heather Talbot
Marketing Manager: Jordan Casey
Senior Acquisitions Editor: Emi Smith
Project Editor: Karen A. Gill
Copy Editor: Barbara Florant
Technical Reviewer: Dan Whittington
CRM Editorial Services Coordinator: Jennifer Blaney
Interior Layout Tech: Judy Littlefield
Cover Designer: Mike Tanamachi
Indexer: Valerie Haynes Perry
Proofreader: Mike Beady

Charles River Media, Inc.
25 Thomson Place
Boston, MA 02210
617-757-7900
617-757-7969 (fax)
info@charlesriver.com
www.charlesriver.com
http://www.courseptr.com

This book is printed on acid-free paper.

Guy W. Lecky-Thompson. *Video Game Design Revealed.*
ISBN-10: 1-58450-562-1
ISBN-13: 978-1-58450-562-4
Library of Congress Catalog Card Number: 2007939357

Printed in the United States of America
08 09 10 11 12 TW 10 9 8 7 6 5 4 3 2 1

Charles River Media titles are available for site license or bulk purchase by institutions, user groups, corporations, etc. For additional information, please contact the Special Sales Department at 800-347-7707.

This book is for my sister Nikki.
You see, sis, there's more to playing games than meets the eye!

Contents

Acknowledgments

First and foremost, I want to thank my wife, Nicole, for putting up with the occasional rant as I went through the final drafts of this book. Sometimes, we creative types just need to get it out of our system, and it's the nearest and dearest who tend to suffer.

Once again, I owe a debt of thanks to the painstaking work of the editorial team, and in particular Karen Gill for her tireless efforts in coordinating my rough prose into something more readable. Thanks also to Emi Smith and the rest of the fine publishing team for making the book a reality.

Finally, a special note of thanks and respect to Dan Whittington, the technical editor for this book; we didn't always see eye to eye, but I think we both got the result we were aiming for.

About the Author

Guy W. Lecky-Thompson is an experienced author in the field of video game design and software development, whose articles have been published in various places, including Gamasutra and the seminal *Game Programming Gems*. He is also the author of *Corporate Software Project Management*, *Infinite Game Universe: Mathematical Techniques*, and *Infinite Game Universe, Volume 2: Level Design, Terrain, and Sound.*

Introduction

Welcome to *Video Game Design Revealed,* in which we first dissect the history of video games—from their beginnings to the most recent—to learn why certain games work, why others do not, and how to turn an idea into an actual game in a box on a shelf. There are many approaches to making games, as many as there are would-be game designers and creators. This book tries to point the way for as many game designers as possible—from those heading up entire teams of designers, artists, programmers, and sound engineers, to the one-man band, bedroom game builder, or freelance entrepreneur trying to tap into a very lucrative market.

Lucrative it might be. Safe it is not. Most games fail to recoup their implementation costs. Some safe bets never pay off. Many studios go bust and fail to make any money at all, leaving investors with large holes in their pockets.

Once in a while, however, a game will take off in a blast of glory in a way that even leaves the brains behind the game stunned and scratching their head. *DOOM* was one of those successes; one has to wonder if the creators had any idea that it would spark an entire genre of its own.

So, in learning why these games are successes, we can hope to understand how they can be replicated. Chapter 1 runs through video game history, covering arcade cabinets, home gaming systems, computers, and consoles. The aim is to equip the reader with an understanding of how video games have evolved and show where technology has driven this evolution.

With these basics in mind, Chapter 2 shows how important video game design is—how we take an idea and turn it into a game, based on the genre, market, game style, subject matter, and other impacting factors. Having read these first two chapters, the budding game designer should start to appreciate how his hit game will take shape.

Having looked at the theory, the practice of video game design is covered in Chapter 3, with vital coverage of information management, documentation, and planning. Some of this chapter might seem a little "dry," but it is all necessary if a successful game is to be produced from the design.

The design contains the embodiment of the idea, as well as how that idea will be realized, with an emphasis on how the game design is fleshed out, documented, and shaped. This naturally includes the project planning, and what to do if things go wrong.

Chapter 4 then shows what various platforms and technologies are available to implement the game. The design put together in Chapter 3 is, of course, a perfect game, but it will be limited in part by the choice of the technology used to create it and the platform for which it is intended. The platform choices made might also cause the design, itself, to take a new direction, provided the design document is fluid enough to support this kind of evolution.

Another step forward is taken in Chapter 5, where we consider the importance of sound, music, and graphics in the implementation of the game. Again, the platform choices might also have an impact on the design; they will certainly have an impact on how the game will look and feel. These may also be covered in the design document, and some tough choices will likely have to be made along the way.

Chapter 6 introduces a topic that takes the design as close to actual implementation as possible without knowing what choices the designer has made on platform, technologies, and overall game creation. It is not possible to address actual implementation in this book; object-oriented game design practices will be presented to help game designers as much as possible.

Following on this topic, Chapter 7 then takes a high-level view of the actual game mechanics that could be implemented. These are the rules of the game universe. In essence, it is the application of game mechanics to the game universe that will make the end product unique, interesting, and fun.

With all of the above decided, we then take a short look, in Chapter 8, at how the game *could* be implemented. There are several choices for the developer:

- Take an existing game and create a modification (mod) for it.
- Implement the game as a series of scripts inside an existing engine.
- Create a whole engine from scratch.

Having made that decision, the actual game creation can begin; and since this is a book about design, we leave the implementation details at this point, and look at how the nuts and bolts of the game can be put together. This begins with a discussion of the user interface in Chapter 9, in which we see how it can be best implemented to serve the game design.

We follow this with a detailed examination in Chapter 10 of how the difficulty curve should be laid out and how best to break down the game into playable chunks (Levels and Missions). This is further elaborated on in Chapter 11 when we look at vehicles and objects as distinct from in-game characters (non-playing characters, or NPCs).

Chapter 12 (the final chapter dealing with actual mechanics) covers video game AI (Artificial Intelligence) design. This is an important part of the mix, and it could be a book on its own. Nonetheless, it is necessary to have an appreciation of how various techniques can be used for good effects within a video game, and how intelligence can be designed into the game, rather than bolted on at the last minute.

At this point, with a good appreciation of the topics related to actual game design, we then introduce in Chapter 13 the concept of the entire Design Document—the blueprint from which the game can be made. Whether the reader is intending to implement the game himself or contract it out, or even seek funding to create a studio with this game as the first project, an Official Design Document will be required.

The document serves as the reference point for creating the game, including milestones, layout, mocked-up artwork, box designs, and so on. In today's distributed implementation environment, where it is no longer necessary to have a "brick and mortar" office, it is even more important that communication between parties is done using a tried and tested approach.

In Chapter 14, we look at how funding can be obtained to help realize the designer's dream. From venture capital companies to banks and angel investors, there may well be someone who can help you build a solid studio or just invest in a single, good title.

Income can come from other streams, also, including sponsorship, advertising, and technology licensing—all of it necessary to take a game from paper to reality. The goal of Chapter 14 is to look at where the money comes from and, more important, where it will be going—that is, how best to spend it.

Much of the game designer's life will be taken up with all of the above, but it is also worthwhile to do some research into the tools and technologies, and to keep current on gaming news. The Appendix presents a list of reliable sources for this research and is a great starting point for both would-be video game designers and professionals in the industry.

The accompanying Web site (http://www.courseptr.com/downloads) also contains live versions of these links, along with an FAQ to answer specific questions about the book and video game design and development. Any errata will also be available here, as will a list of links to additional resources such as download points for tools and utilities for video game design and development.

1 A Brief History of Video Games

In This Chapter

- In the Beginning . . .
- Arcade Systems
- A Timeline
- Technologies
- Home Entertainment

Video games have been around for a long time—much longer than the casual observer might give them credit for. There is some contention over where the first video game came from, just as there is contention over the "inventor" of the computer: Do mechanical counting machines qualify as true computers? There has been plenty of academic debate since the acceptance of computer study as a true science. The video game culture, though, has not yet had that chance.

It is a strange twist of fate that without video games, there is every chance that many different branches of computer science might not exist. Of course, in the murky academic world, there are those who would disagree and state, with a hint of aloofness, that it is, in fact, the other way around; but since video game science is not yet an accepted part of academia, the argument will probably not even surface.

On the other hand, academics cannot argue with history, and a close look at the evidence suggests that the first use for a commercial, digital computer was to play a game. They also cannot deny that video games present the most challenging, real-time systems that computers deal with. They have to react immediately, display a complex result (along with audio support), and offer (rudimentary) support for artificial intelligence. Make no mistake about it, video game development is a science.

Of course, we shall be approaching the subject from the design point of view, and since designs are largely dependent on the complexity, availability, and cost-effectiveness of technology, we will only touch on game development as it relates to restricting or enabling game design. This is not a textbook; we will avoid using "high-tech" phrases to describe what a piece of hardware can do, except where the phrase has already entered the popular scientific vocabulary.

This first chapter looks at the evolution of video game design—what has been done and when, and why some of the advances took so long. If you think that you know your video game culture, then you might be surprised by some of the historical facts that have been dredged.

In the Beginning . . .

So, let's begin with some name-dropping: Bushnell, Atari, *Pong*. These should ring bells with anyone interested in video gaming as either a science or just for recreation. Especially the last two—everyone has heard of Atari, right? These names are linked by one of the singularly most important and misrepresented facts in video game culture:

> Nolan Bushnell created the first-ever video game, *Pong*, for his company, Atari, in the 1970s.

This phrase is fraught with historical inaccuracy, much of which would have been resolved long ago had video game design and development been accepted as a science; and it all began in 1958. Much of the information in this chapter is the result of research in reading, verifying, and following links from the excellent article by Sylvain de Chantal, "Who's the Real Father of Videogames" [Chantal01].

Here is a name that you probably don't know—Willy Higginbotham. Higginbotham was a physicist with a penchant for games, and he created a tennis-style game that, according to the Brookhaven National Laboratory, used logic that was implemented by vacuum tubes (even though transistors existed at the time), and which was more sophisticated than *Pong*. On the other hand, the game would never have survived commercially due to its immense size. But it was, technically, the first "modern" computer game. Higginbotham later worked on atomic weaponry research.

At the time that pinball was attracting people to amusement arcades in droves, a Massachusetts Institute of Technology student, Steve Russell, created *Spacewar!* while working on Digital Equipment Corporations' PDP-1 computer.

The game was based on a simple premise. Two spacecraft orbit a star and try to bomb each other. The only real complexity was that the physics were entirely accurate. The bombs curved around the gravitational well of the star, and the backdrop of star systems was scientifically correct. This was in 1961 on a machine that cost $120,000. Customers who purchased the system were given a copy of the game *for free*. Commercially speaking, it would never have taken off, since you could buy quite a few pinball machines for the price of one PDP-1; plus, it would have taken up too much space—all of which led Russell to the conclusion that a copyright or patent was probably not a viable proposition.

Which was a pity, because as we all know, the size and cost of digital computers were about to plummet, leading to the creation of the first home video game system in 1971. In those 10 years, the technology behind video games improved to the point that Ralph Baer, while working for a military contractor, devised a machine that allowed people to play games on their television sets. This idea was sold to Magnavox, who decided that instead of building a $20 device that could play tennis, they would make a fancier version with 12 games (all variations on tennis) and try to persuade people to part with $100 for the dubious privilege of owning an Odyssey home-entertainment system.

The obvious mistake was that they rejected Baer's vision of putting cheap video game technology into the hands of the general population. Magnavox, instead, turned the video game into a luxury device. Later on in the history of home video gaming, this would be rectified; but in the meantime, attention turned to the amusement arcades. Made popular by the pinball machine, arcades are still with us today, but the dwindling prices of home entertainment systems that can outstrip arcade machines is leading to a slight lull in their popularity.

So finally we come to Bushnell. Having been immersed in the *Spacewar!* experience while a student at the University of Utah in 1962, Nolan Bushnell came up with the idea of creating a cabinet with a machine inside that was capable of playing a single game. Most of his peers at the time were experimenting with computers that played multiple games, but Bushnell saw the commercial advantages of the single-game system—the electronics would be cheaper, smaller, and more than capable of rivaling pinball machines in the amusement arcade.

His first attempt, a *Spacewar!* clone called *Computer Space* was a complete disaster and sold around 1,000 machines. The fledgling Atari was formed shortly thereafter, and their first product was a game called *Pong,* which was based on the *Computer Space* electronics. Bushnell had seen the ill-fated Odyssey at a trade show and communicated the gist of his idea to an engineer, Al Alcorn. Subsequently, a two-player variant of the tennis game was installed in a cabinet in a California bar.

Having installed the machine and left the premises, Alcorn received a phone call from the owner of the bar, stating that the machine had broken down. Alcorn responded and found that the only real problem was that the paint can used to collect the coins had overflowed, causing the coin-drop mechanism to jam—or so the myth goes.

Whether this is entirely accurate or not, it is a documented fact that *Pong* resulted in the first-ever video game–related court battle. Many other companies attempted to put *Pong* clones on the market. Magnavox (once associated with Baer and who held patents in the video game arena covering *Pong*-style gaming) successfully sued Atari for approximately $700,000. Undaunted, 10,000 units of *Pong* were manufactured in 1973 and installed in various locations worldwide.

Still embracing the "one machine, one game" principle, Atari released a home *Pong* system in 1974, a simple affair and brainchild of Alcorn, Harold Lee, and another engineer, Bob Brown. Not surprisingly, given the dire sales record of the Odyssey, retailers were reluctant to carry the Atari Home Pong machine—that is, until Bushnell met Sears representative Tom Quinn. Several meetings later, 150,000 consoles were purchased and duly stamped with the Sears Tele-Games logo, just in time for Christmas 1975.

With such a large outlet, Home Pong made it into the hearts, minds, and living rooms of hundreds of thousands of Sears customers, and by January 1976 had not only achieved commercial success, but was also being imitated. Programmable consoles that played multiple games were not far behind, and by 1978, *Pong* and its clones had become something of a historical curiosity.

Naturally, Atari was ahead of the competition; in 1977 the Atari 2600 was released, a system hailed as a classic home game console by video game enthusiasts the world over. Amusement arcades were also filled with Atari classic games that more or less guaranteed that Bushnell would forever be known as the inventor of the video game, despite the fact that only game he actually invented, *Computer Space,* was something of a flop.

The key (and a point that should not be lost by any video game designer) is that Bushnell and Atari saw the commercial opportunities in what they did, in the same way Bill Gates and Microsoft saw the opportunities in partnerships with IBM in the early days of the personal computer. They share one thing in common—popularizing the technology that caught their imagination.

Arcade Systems

Throughout the history of video games (at least up until the mid-1990s), the arcade (or coin-op) machine has been a behind-the-scenes, stalwart gauge of the pace of technology. In 2003 it looked as if the arcade game had had its day; the hardware available to home users seemed to have overtaken the classic arcade cabinet systems.

It also heralded a social change. With the advancement of high-power, low-cost hardware used for home entertainment consoles, people preferred to club together, visit a friend's house, rent a copy of a multiplayer console game, and play in the comfort of their own homes. While interconnected machines in the arcade environment were one of the big advances for racing games, such as those created under the Sega license, the advent of Internet multiplayer games (both console and PC) has more or less killed the concept of playing against your friends down in the local amusement arcade.

But people still bemoan the apparent death of the amusement arcade experience. Broadband (ADSL) connectivity means that you can connect a console to a server hosted on the Internet and play your favorite first-person shooter, such as *Unreal Tournament 2003*, against players from all over the world as if they were sitting next to you. You can even "shout" at them, using a clever piece of "headphone plus microphone" equipment.

The reason for this change is quite simple. Arcade cabinets are fantastically expensive to produce, install, and maintain, and the per-play cost increase required to offset fixed costs means that people are less willing to play, driving the break-even point even higher; it is cheaper just to buy a console and rent the game, and play in the comfort of your own home. Also, console hardware production is cheaper than trying to satisfy the amusement arcade demand, so we have a typical Catch-22 situation. As *EDGE* magazine points out:

> "Once mastered, a classic coin-op game could keep a skilled player occupied for hours on one ten pence piece alone . . . Now, simple economics mean that the 50 pence, three-minute-play maxim is the only language coin-op manufacturers and amusement arcade owners understand." [EDGE01]

From the manufacturer's point of view, arcade cabinets are no longer profitable, and from the player's point of view, a console or PC is simply heaven realized—you can play a variety of games at home without even needing to purchase them. Video rental outlets now stock games for almost every platform, with the exception of the PC (it is just too easy to pirate PC games—despite the attempts of publishers to invent ever-increasingly subtle ways to protect the media).

Of course, at traveling fairs, bars, and other places where people congregate for relaxation, or where there is a need to relieve boredom (for example, long trips on ferry boats and in airports), there will always be a fairly lucrative source of revenue for arcade cabinets, as long as the investment in the equipment can be cost-effective—a concern that seems to have nullified any advances in the area of arcade cabinets.

There are exceptions, and the Japanese in particular seem to have bucked the trend toward home video game playing. There will always be a market for the video game arcade cabinet, but it is shrinking due to the success of home (and even mobile) entertainment.

Bearing this in mind, new paradigms, designs, and approaches are being used to try and woo the players back. There are two areas that seem to be of interest, with two entirely different cultures—the casual gamers who do not even *own* a console and use a PC purely for practical tasks, and the hardcore gamers who will play (in a group) anytime/anyplace. This latter group is important, because hardcore gamers represent a market that will own a console, play in the privacy of their own home until they have perfected their art, and then go out to the amusement arcade to show off to their peers.

The barometer of video game culture, at least in Europe, is *EDGE* magazine, and they recently reported on this phenomenon in October 2002 [EDGE02]. The game was *Dance Dance Revolution* (*DDR;* in Europe, *Dancing Stage Euromix*). There were others, but this appeared to be the most popular and accessible, and it was also available for home consoles.

The idea was deceptively simple. You dance, cued by the music and arrows on the screen. Your score is a reflection of the accuracy with which you follow the arrows and music. It is not, however, the score that counts as much as the way in which it is achieved. People who have never danced before in real life, but who play video games, are lured onto the stage and have the showperson in them set free to kick and scream.

The point is that this is social gaming revitalized. The players show off to their peers, invent new ways of playing the games that the manufacturer (Konami, in the case of *DDR*) probably never even dreamed of. The graphics are simple, the sound is exquisite, and the experience is earth-shattering. If anything will save the traditional amusement arcade experience, it is this kind of game.

It is no coincidence that these games embody the music/dance culture that has grown up around the advent of techno music and the club culture of the 1990s. They appeal to hardcore gamers and casual gamers, alike.

On the other hand, games that appear to have been conceived purely for the casual market are also springing up, usually in the guise of sports simulations. Snowboarding, skiing, canoeing, even hang-gliding have all appeared as bar-arcade novelties of late. They, too, represent gaming in a social context, with wide screens that show your every move to a growing crowd of onlookers.

So, this is the situation today. Amusement arcades (and arcade cabinets in particular) appear to be in trouble, at least until the next big attraction. Dance and sports simulations will just have to suffice until then. Of course, this chapter is supposed to be about history, and it never hurts to get a bit of background under your belt to beef up your gaming lore, so let's take a look at the high points of the past 30 years of arcade video game history.

A Timeline

For convenience, we have divided our potted timeline into three decades, leading up to what we might think of as modern gaming as we know it. The divisions are artificial, but we need to try to separate the phases in relation to the kinds of experiences that technology and theory allowed.

1970s

The first cabinet, *Computer Space* (Atari), was a bright yellow affair that stood two meters tall, with curvy lines and protruding controls—an oddity and a failure, as we have already seen. The internal hardware was created especially for the game, and the fledgling company urgently needed to garner some success, so they developed *Pong*. *Pong* was a resounding success and needed only some reworking of the cabinet so that it resembled a contemporary television, right down to the wooden cabinet.

Incredibly, the shape of the traditional stand-up-and-play cabinet barely seems to have changed over the past 40 years. It is ridiculous to imagine that, had the original *Pong* cabinet been shaped differently—for example, included a seat or some such innovation—this would probably still be true today. Fashion, it seems, does not extend to cabinet design.

Between 1971 and 1979, there was only one other game of note—*Asteroids*. It was a simple, line-drawn, monochromatic affair, but *Asteroids* started a craze for shooting things that began in 1962 and is still with us today.

1980s

This was the boom decade for the arcade industry. In the top-100 arcade games of all time, chosen by the editors of *EDGE* magazine for a feature about arcade emulation on home computer systems [EDGE03], there were 75 games made in the 1980s, 1 in the 1970s (*Asteroids*), and the remaining 24 in the 1990s. They were usually sprite-based affairs, with two notable exceptions: *I, Robot*, which in 1983 brought fully shaded polygons to the arcade world for the first time; and *Star Wars*, also in 1983, which relied on simple, four-color wire-frame graphics.

Sound also changed over the 1980s, evolving from beeps and white-noise explosions to expansive musical background tunes and the catchy pumping beats of games such as *OutRun* (1986). The 1980s also saw the advent of multiplayer gaming, with cabinets such as *Super Sprint* (1986), which boasted three sets of controls, a top-down, sprite-based view of four-color racing vehicles speeding around a variety of different tracks.

This was also when the big names in video games started to become known. Sega, Konami, Atari, SNK, Nintendo, and Taito, among others, were all formed in arcade ventures of the 1980s—except, of course, Atari, which in the opinion of many failed to capitalize on its position as the "first" arcade cabinet manufacturer.

Always at the forefront of cutting-edge software, it seems, Sega released the first-ever isometric arcade game in 1982, called *Zaxxon*, which pushed the hardware available at the time to its limits. Largely hailed a classic, *Zaxxon* has also been turned into a board game by Milton-Bradley.

The isometric view started a trend that saw, in 1984, the release of other titles using this design technique, such as *Paper Boy*, *Marble Madness*, and *Pac-Land*, the successor to the unfailingly popular 1980 classic *Pac-Man*. In fact, several titles stand out from this era as embodying what would later become accepted genres:

Pac-Man	1980	Top-down puzzle
Tetris	1988	Blocks falling from the sky
Yie Ar Kung-Fu	1985	Martial arts fighting game
Defender	1980	Side-scrolling shooter
Donkey Kong	1981	Platform game

There are other games that stick out in history, but these five started genre revolutions whose repercussions can still be felt three decades later.

1990s

The tail end of the revolution will be best known for fabulous and ever more impressive fighting games of a genre that was started by *Yie Ar Kung-Fu*. The big three, *Street Fighter II* (1991), *Mortal Kombat* (1992), and *King of the Fighters '94* (1994), continued a craze for pitting two fighters against each other, and letting them loose with a myriad moves, combinations, and unusual "specials," such as the finishing moves in *Mortal Kombat*, which allowed the player to rip out the beating heart of his opponent—not a game for kids.

Still, it wasn't all violence. There was a great basketball simulation in *NBA Jam* (1993), a magnificent puzzle game that required the player to pop bubbles in *Uo Poko* (1998), and the 1990 hit *Smash TV*, which required the player to look in eight directions at once to avoid being nailed by an advancing ring of robots. This last game also introduced the concept of firing and moving simultaneously in different directions.

Technologies

One way of seeing how the video game industry has changed over the years is to look at the change in arcade (coin-op) game technology from the heady 70s, through the boom of the 80s, and into the high-tech, low-cost 90s. It is often possible to declare a game "dated" without actually playing it—perhaps from a feeling cultivated by years of experience, or perhaps because of a recognition of the technologies used during its time in video game history.

This is important, since one of the sure-fire ways to fail in game design is to ignore what has come before. Some games have been "over-done," such as the *Street Fighter II*-style fighting games—for example, look at the recent versions of *Mortal Kombat* and the reviews that they garner. Other genres, such as those that stem from *Tetris*, are always fun to play, but they lack the novelty of the original.

If the designer ignores history, he may well end up designing a game that evokes the inevitable comparison with some other game (and maybe one that the designer has not even had heard of). On the other hand, some failed games made use of techniques and technologies that can be combined with an original idea to make a good game great.

This was the original driving force behind *Street Fighter II (SFII)*. One-on-one fighting games had been done before (perhaps even over-done), but *Capcom* managed to become accepted as one of the top-10 games of all time by introducing something from *SFII:* "combos"—devastating combinations of impossible moves that add bonus points and decimate the opposition. (Historical note: These combos were actually inspired by a programming bug, which illustrates another reason for extensive play-testing.)

Tabulating the top-100 arcade games of all time reveals that there are certain elements that enable the trained eye to spot whether a game has a dated look or not. It pays to remember that eye-candy is an important factor when a player decides whether to pay money for the experience that the game offers. This is not a hard rule, since certain games, like *Dance Dance Revolution*, do not really need advanced graphics; they rely on bizarre peripherals, great music, or other design "tricks."

The first indicator is the style of graphics on the screen. Early games used simple, line-drawn, or block graphics. *Pong*, for example, used two solid bars and a square ball, separated by a dotted line (see Figure 1.1).

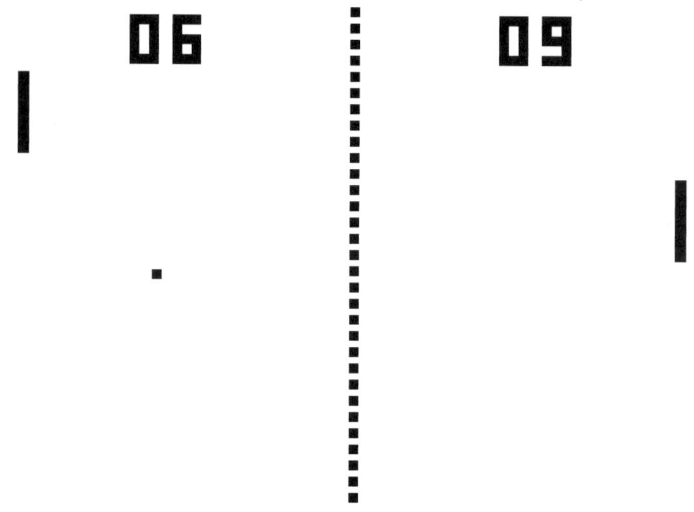

FIGURE 1.1 *Pong* artist's impression.

The other aspect of this game that makes it look dated is the fact that it is monochromatic—displayed in one color. If we were to add some colors, then it would immediately begin to look more like a game that had been released with the advent of mass-market color television, which is another indicator that video game technology has generally followed consumer technology over the years. Currently, though, video game technology has become a part of, and is driving consumer technology.

In Figure 1.2, we can see what *Asteroids* might have looked like with monochrome, line-drawn graphics, giving it a somewhat dated look. The step up from these kinds of graphics was to add two aspects: color and sprites. A sprite is simply a collection of dots arranged in such a way as to suggest a shape that can be associated with an object, either real or imagined.

One of the first games to use sprites was *Space Invaders*. It simplified the job of the designer and programmer, since each sprite had a set number of possible places that it could appear on the screen, as well as a predefined sequence. All that the programmer needed to know was which version of which sprite to display where, and the underlying hardware took care of the rest.

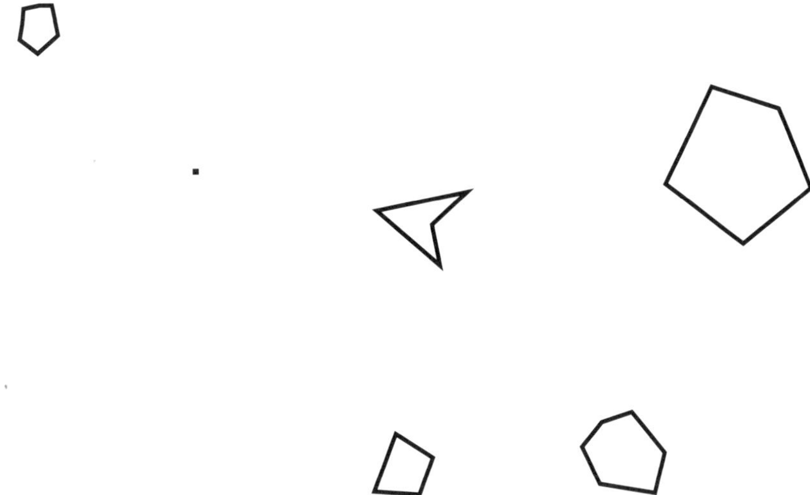

FIGURE 1.2 *Asteroids* artist's impression in monochrome.

This also meant that, unlike previous arcade game hardware, one circuit could be programmed to display different sets of sprites, even to the extent that essentially identical hardware could be used for a number of different games. Because of memory restrictions, though, only one game could be stored in the machine at a time; once it was manufactured and delivered, it was a *Space Invaders* machine and only a *Space Invaders* machine.

Over the years, colors have steadily been added to the palette available in arcade systems, and these days, intricate shading and visual effects can be achieved in cabinets capable of displaying thousands, sometimes millions, of different colors.

Sprites have given way to cartoon-style characters with animated faces and fast-paced, high-color graphics set against static or scrolling backgrounds. The advent of 3D and pseudo-3D graphics means that if the game has a background that scrolls at a different speed, or if the line-drawn graphics display a scene that has "depth," then it is likely to have originated in the 1980s.

Shaded polygons were a breakthrough in 1987 with David Branen's *Zarch*, but they were not really used to their full extent until later, when racing games such as *Daytona* and some Sega-licensed variations on the Formula-1 theme appeared. Bright primary colors and simple, blocky polygons dates a game to the late 1980s, while detailed, multi-polygon, high-definition graphics tend to place a game in the 1990s.

The perspective from which a game is played is also a good indicator of age. Top-down games have always been prevalent; however, side-on scrolling with sprites or cartoon-style graphics place a game as being more contemporary than the line-drawn, simple sprite action of *Defender* (1980). In addition to the design, some game genre reveal much about their age:

- Action games are easy to place, because the fast pace means that processor time is at a premium. Often, graphical complexity had to be sacrificed in favor of reaction speed.
- Puzzle games are slightly more difficult to date, and closer observation of the colors and *resolution* of the sprites is the only real clue. The more color and detail, the more recent the game (generally speaking).
- Sports simulations are easy to date by virtue of the amount of detail that the principle characters have in their rendering, as well as the backgrounds. Animated, seemingly varied crowd movement will place a game in the early 1990s, while static crowd backdrops and blocky, sprite-based athletes tend to point toward technology used in the 1980s.

We have based our brief excursion into the history of arcade gaming on the 100 titles chosen by *EDGE* magazine. Clearly, to do justice to the subject, the budding video game designer needs to do some time-consuming research before considering himself an expert. It helps, however, to have at least a small understanding of the evolution of arcade games, which this section has hopefully instilled.

Home Entertainment

With all this talk of technology and the limits imposed on video game designers due to the lack of sophisticated hardware (by today's standards), we might be forgiven for thinking that home entertainment began with the advent of the PC. However, the first home entertainment units appeared right after their arcade counterparts in the mid- to late 1970s.

We will look at consoles (dedicated gaming systems) in the next section of this chapter, but right now let's turn to the other aspects of home entertainment—the home computer. For those who lived through the birth period of the home computer, names such as Commodore, Sinclair, Oric, and Acorn, as well as Atari, will bring back nostalgic memories.

PC Gaming

It seems that nowadays, every home has a computer, and we take for granted that it has always been so—or that is the way history likes to present itself. The reality is that home computers were simply overpriced calculators until the arrival of 8-bit computing. The 8-bit home computer revolution brought us machines such as the Commodore 64, BBC Microcomputer, and Sinclair Spectrum. These were followed in the mid- to late 1980s (and into the 1990s) by machines that boasted improved performance, including eight-channel sound, hundreds of colors, and a whole half-megabyte of memory, such as the Atari ST and Commodore Amiga.

At the same time, another breed of computers was becoming prevalent—the personal computer (PC)—which was styled as a serious machine for the home, and as such always lagged slightly behind the traditional home computer market, since they came bundled with advanced gear, such as printers.

Home computers, with their limited architectures and nonstandard operating systems, eventually became a footnote, since it was clear that the original IBM PC architecture could outstrip it. The reason was that the business market was very lucrative, and the sale of advanced PCs could drive the investment in technology required to make them ever more powerful. This spilled over into the home PC market and brought high-technology systems at a price that was competitive enough, by the year 2003, to make them commonplace.

One of the principle reasons that the home computer was so popular in the 1980s was that enthusiasts could learn to write programs for them themselves. Or, if they were too lazy or just didn't have the time or inclination, they could type in programs from magazines. This also meant that people could, from their homes, write games for the video game market, and be successful at it.

Home computing changed the face of video games forever. People still played games in their local arcade, simply because the arcade games were always technologically one step ahead of their humble home-system cousins. On the other hand, publishers quickly became adept at pushing this technology further and further, and so made ever more complex and innovative games.

At the same time, gamers realized that they could, if they chose, alter the way in which the game reacted to their play style, and even enhance their own character. Cheating and hacking (in the video game sense of the word) was born. Codes were typed in to give a player's characters infinite lives, infinite energy, or limitless power-ups. This was something that couldn't be done with an arcade cabinet; there was no access to the underlying machine.

While gamers were playing around with the code that drove their favorite games, they were also learning more about how those games worked. Many of the programmers who entered the fledgling video game industry in the early days learned their trade by playing around with a home computer and trying out new techniques, copying other peoples' techniques, and generally using their hobby to further their own education at a time when college courses failed to offer practical skills other than staid "computer science"–style offerings. Designers were also being herded back to the arcade industry, since there was potentially more money to be made there and certainly more recognition in producing a glittering, high-tech game for *Taito*, *Capcom*, or *Konami* than a home computer title—at least in some people's eyes.

These days, computers are far too powerful in the vast majority of cases for one person to harness the technology alone. In addition, the market has become so well developed that it is almost impossible to enter the market without the financial backing required to make a truly eye-catching game. With the level of realism offered by games such as *DOOM III* or *Unreal Tournament 2003*, and even *SimCity 4*, it is unlikely that any one person has the exact mix of skills required to put out a real contender.

This is a shame, since it raises the barriers to entry to the point that it simply becomes too expensive for small teams to create viable games. There is the shareware route, which generally rewards smaller game studios for putting out a limited version of a game in the hope that those downloading the game will pay for the full version.

This is how id Software started, of course. Shareware is still a good route, since it removes the need for a publisher, at least in the early stages of a studio's life. All too often, however, a publisher with big ideas and a wallet to match will come along and turn a studio comprised of a group of friends (who began their dream in a bar) into a 20-person team; and along the way, the intimacy and character are lost. Such an approach can be necessary, especially if a game is in sequel mode or is just too big for three or four people to deal with, but it can also stifle the initial creativity from which a good game might emerge.

There is a way out for game designers who wish to retain the intimacy of a small studio, play-test their idea, and only contact publishers at the last moment to get the cash needed to create better sound, better graphics, and get the game into the market. The key is in the increased power of home computing. PCs are now powerful enough that a free software package containing the underlying engine for a game—the beast that handles the chores of getting input from the player and dumping graphics on the screen—can be combined with a scripting language (which is closer to natural language than machine code) to enable the designer to be both a programmer and artist.

Many games come with built-in editors, too. They can be scripted to the point that the entire game is altered, which is how many of the "new" variations of games, such as *Capture the Flag*, have come about. Even top-flight games such as *UT2003*, *Quake*, and *Half-Life* have the option for user-created "mods." Gamers have become game developers, making what was good even better—and in some cases, even perfecting an otherwise flawed release.

Such is the power of home computing.

Consoles

The console market is the most cut-throat of them all, and here is the proof: there are only three major manufacturers of home consoles—Nintendo, Sony, and the relative newcomer, Microsoft. What is more, there has never really been more than a handful of console manufacturers in the market at any one time.

While Atari has not been able to replicate the success of their early arcade cabinets, and has bowed to the likes of Konami, Nintendo, and Sega, they have not been dormant in the industry, especially when the home market is taken into account. They have put out some very successful cartridge-based home entertainment units (consoles) over the years, such as the Atari 2600, but they have also failed to turn this line into a long-term proposition.

The only manufacturer to stay ahead out of the current three market leaders is Nintendo, and their dominance is through a combination of hardware technology and the licensing great games. Until recently, rival Sega also managed to keep their console dream afloat, until Sony came along with the PlayStation and later the PS2. Sega now restricts itself to great games, and Atari has disappeared from the scope entirely.

The evolution of consoles has more or less followed a similar evolution in the arcade industry. In fact, the technology that drives both arenas is more or less common. That is, they share some of the vital components, such as graphics, and a push forward in one platform tends to spill over into the others, usually because the manufacturers work in harmony.

Single-Game Systems

In the beginning, 1976, one machine meant one game or several variations on a theme. These systems plugged into the television, and were cheap and popular. The limitation of only being able to play a single game didn't dissuade people at first, since there was simply nothing else on the market. There were tennis-based games, soccer-based games, and shoot-em-ups.

Then manufacturers started to put screens on the systems and make them self-sufficient, with their own power supplies, such as transformers for about-the-house gaming or batteries for pseudo-mobile gaming. Of course, the systems were far too bulky to enable them to be played everywhere, but for a time, it was every child's dream to be able to play *Space Invaders* in the back of an automobile.

The LED (at first green and black, but then color) screens used in these models relied on the fact that when lit, they were visible, and when not lit, they weren't visible. If this seems a little obvious, remember what we said about early arcade games. The principle behind many sprite-based systems was the same, and these were truly one-game-only systems. There might have been different levels and even different speeds, but the graphics were *predetermined*. More to the point, the screen was manufactured as a set of cells that could be powered in such a way as to display an image comprised of subcells. Look at an LED watch or calculator and try to imagine how many different numbers can be displayed.

This legacy, which has been carried through to cheap electronic games that are still available in supermarkets worldwide, has remained until today and will remain for a long time to come. These machines are cheap—not nasty, just limited—and can be played via television or on the move. Then came Nintendo.

Mobile Systems

Nintendo will always be famous for bringing us mobile gaming. The Game and Watch machines were great. They used a pure-black and not-black LCD display in which, if you looked closely, you could see the figures etched into the plastic underneath. The definition of the individual cartoon-style "sprites" was incredible, for the time.

They worked on the same principle as LED sprites, but because a liquid was used inside the screen, the curvy lines required by the cartoon-style graphics could be represented. The whole package was slim and fitted nicely between two teenage-size hands, thumbs on the controls that were lighter, smaller, and more aesthetic than most controllers used for modern gaming systems. On top of that, they had a watch and alarm, so parents could claim that they were valid household items.

Still, they were single-game systems like all those that had come before, and Nintendo obviously felt that improvement was necessary; and another legacy was invented—the GameBoy. Yes, GameBoy cartridges can still be bought today. The system is so robust and brilliant that developers are actively creating games for them, even 10 years later. The trick is that they use an LCD screen comprised of pixels (small dots) and use an easy-to-program sprite system that takes much of the graphical work away from the developer. Simply design some sprites, tell the machine where to put them, and you're on your way.

The original GameBoy now comes in GameBoy Color and GameBoy Advanced flavors, too. GameBoy Color has color, instead of black and backdrop-brown, and the GameBoy Advanced has a wider screen, high-color graphics, and great sound. The principle, though, remains the same—portability and great games.

Atari tried to muscle in with the Lynx, a system that did not take off in the same way, probably because everyone already had a GameBoy in their back pocket, and Sony revamped their original PlayStation to fit into an almost-portable version, complete with color LCD screen and an almost acceptable battery life. The jury is still out on that last one.

The next big thing on the horizon, supposedly, is mobile telephone gaming, now that screens have reached acceptable sizes and definitions. They come with their own restrictions, however, and as a developing market is perhaps not the best first port of call for the budding video game designer.

If you can overcome the technical challenges, on the other hand, it is a good platform to consider developing for. Most of the tools and technologies (such as Java) are readily available and reasonably standardized. Exchange (publishing) is also easy, from downloads to peer-to-peer sharing of the game.

Cartridges, CDs, and DVDs

Where home console manufacturers really started to take gaming seriously was with the invention by Atari of the game cartridge (cart). Carts were the medium for distributing games and contained a certain amount of real gaming logic, as well. It is worth taking note of a little bit of history before we consider the power of the cart.

Computers need something to execute (a program) before they will do anything interesting. This program needs to be entered into their working memory in some way. The program can be typed in, but when the power goes off, everything that was typed in is lost. In the first computers, cards were used; the programs were encoded as holes punched into them.

For the early mass market, such as Commodore, audio cassettes were used to store the programs, which were then loaded into the computer. If you had spent your entire afternoon typing in a game from a magazine, you could save the program to a cassette, which was practical. What was not practical was the fact that loading a commercial game often took somewhere between 5 to 10 minutes.

With the advent of game consoles, manufacturers were acutely aware of the impracticality of having to spend as much time loading the game as playing it, and were mindful of the impact that the ease of copying cassette tapes would have on their sales. So they decided that the games needed to be delivered some other way; and the game cart was born.

From the start, carts were meant to be left in the machine while the game was being played. There was no more loading of the entire program from cassette before the play session could begin. What had to be loaded could be done at high speed, since there was no "media" to contend with, just electricity.

Plus, the cartridge was difficult and expensive to copy, and thus kept piracy rates down. All in all, console gaming needed the boost of the cart, because it also meant that memory inside the system could also be kept to a minimum at a time when memory was expensive. This meant that other game aspects, such as sound and graphics systems, could be bolstered with the extra cash.

In time, however, it became clear that the cost of electronics was always going to outweigh the requirements for space. A CD can hold 700MB of game data, while a cartridge is restricted to about 32KB (in the first cartridge-based systems) to 2GB (in the case of the Nintendo DS).

Cartridges, of course, are more expensive to produce, but they rule the roost in the handheld market despite this, being smaller and requiring less power. In the mobile market, where multifunction telephones are combined with a gaming platform, miniaturization is key, which drives the cost up even further.

At the same time, platforms such as the PSP (PlayStation Portable) make use of the UMD format, presumably offering a better storage capacity–to-cost ratio than a big cartridge.

These days, with the advent of the DVD (which uses similar laser technology to the CD and often, somewhere between two and four layers), even more game data can make its way onto the media. Much of the data remains on the disc, with only the bare minimum entered into memory. Of course, the decrease in memory cost means that much of the game mechanics can be loaded into the console, leaving only the graphics, sound, and other fancy bits on the media itself.

Of course, both CDs and DVDs can be copied, which presents something of a challenge for manufacturers of both formats. The answer for game consoles lies in the hardware; most off-the-shelf consoles that support DVD as the media format have made some security advances that should help mitigate the worst excesses of pirating. For example, the PlayStation 2 (Sony) contains specific hardware to prevent it from playing non-Sony DVDs. The PS3 contains similar technology. At first, Nintendo did not even support generic DVD playback on their platform, meaning that movies could not be played, and therefore games were harder to pirate.

The Xbox and Xbox 360 (Microsoft) adopt similar tactics. Naturally, most platforms also have so-called mod chips available that will allow the owner to play DVDs and copied games. Installing these not only voids the warranty, but there are also reports of some legitimate games that will work on "chipped" consoles.

A recent trend also supports hard drives as an extension to the console—the Xbox 360 and PS3 both ship in versions with hard drives. The upside to this is that the games can use the disk space, gamers can use the disk space, and service providers can use the disk space for all kinds of entertainment-related tasks. The downside is that games will inevitably be shipped that *require* a hard drive. Inevitably, there will be console owners who bought the console package without a hard drive.

Note also that the hard drive pushes the price of the console up, and to remain competitive, manufacturers must create two versions—one with and one without. Those who buy the version without the hard drive lose out—for example, buyers who shop by price without necessarily appreciating the additional value, or who don't realize the constraints they are placing on the platform.

SUMMARY

The aim of this chapter has been to take the reader through the past 30 to 40 years of video game history so they can appreciate the immense changes that have occurred. The pace of change makes any other industry look sloth-like by comparison. It has often been said that if the automobile industry had moved as fast as computers, then you would now be able to buy a gold Mercedes-Benz that ran forever on garbage and was able to park on a pinhead.

The technology driving the computer industry has made things possible in the video game world that would have been unthinkable even 10 years ago. Gamers can now develop games, and the average person on the street can dream of designing the next great video game—which is why this book exists, and also why it never assumes that the reader is an industry professional. Technology has put the power to create into the hands of the general populace; the overnight success of the Internet and World Wide Web only proves the point.

The next three chapters build on this introduction and lead the reader through a crash course in video game design, a look at the platforms and technologies available to turn the dream into reality, and also how the process works in the real world. Like it or not, although the technology has advanced, attitudes have not—or rather, they have, but in a direction that requires a cash injection for success, a degree in computer science, and knowing the right people at the right time.

The antidote is, as is so often the case, the Internet—specifically, the shareware world. Distribution has never been easier, and there has never been as large a test market available as there is today. People will download the game if it has been properly marketed (and email marketing is so much cheaper than regular mail), regardless of its proven track record. They will play-test the game, and if it doesn't meet their expectations or they discover a bug, they will often tell you.

On the other hand, even if the game contains errors and is graphically inferior to other available games, your good idea will lead to good commentary, constructive criticism, and general, widespread support for the independent developers. It is a good time to get into the video game industry.

REFERENCES

[Chantal01] Sylvain de Chantal, "Who's the Real Father of Videogames?"
[EDGE01] *EDGE,* No. 115, October 2002, "The Mame Game."
[EDGE02] *EDGE,* No. 115, October 2002, "Rhythm Nation."
[EDGE03] *EDGE,* No. 115, October 2002, "The Mame Game."

2 Introduction to Video Game Design

In This Chapter

- Gaming Perspectives
- Genres
- Perspectives
- Markets
- From Idea to Design
- Stories and Narrative Elements
- Descriptive Elements
- General Design Issues

Chapter 1 covered what was essentially a condensed history of video game culture over the past 40 years, so the reader would be forgiven for wondering when the video game design discussion will begin. We have looked at the technology changes that have fueled the video game industry, but they were driven by the ideas of creative minds, and implemented by engineers.

The creation of video games relies on a mixture of hardware and software tools and technologies, all coming together to produce a platform upon which dreams can be realized. The bottleneck will always be the hardware platform—and rarely the software tools or ideas that are implemented.

Designers are always trying to push the envelope and create games that stretch the limits of available technology. It might not seem so to the casual observer, but *Pong* was such an achievement. The game took the highest available technology of the day (televisions were still in early commercialization) and combined it with electronics (which had barely made it out of the laboratory) to make interactive entertainment machines complete with logic, sound, and visual experiences.

Each cutting-edge game, from *DOOM* to *Grand Theft Auto*, took the available platform technology one step beyond what designers and players had previously thought possible; it is a trend set to continue. Like all history lessons, the learning experience is a valuable one.

Now that we know what has gone before, we can begin to plan for the future and first consider such questions as: If *Pong* were released tomorrow, would it still sell thousands of units? A good idea, after all, remains a good idea. The proliferation of *Breakout* clones might suggest that single-player *Pong* remains a concept that will sell to even the most technologically aware consumer.

For the uninitiated, *Breakout* consists of batting a ball toward a wall of cubes that disintegrate when hit, creating an ever-changing wall against which to bounce the ball. If, on the other hand, there was an identical paddle on the other side, controlled by the machine, and which unfailingly hit the ball back in ever more impossible angles, would this be as popular?

The answer is probably, "no." The reason for this is simple—single-player games work best when the player has the illusion that they are up against a fallible opponent. This can be the player himself, as in *Breakout*, or it can be marauding aliens, as in *Space Invaders*. On the other hand, playing against an opponent that always makes the right decisions gives the player the impression that it cannot be beaten. Plus, single-player *Pong*, with a player-controlled paddle against a machine-controlled one, lacks the essential fun factor.

Plus, there was a certain novelty attached to *Pong* as both a single- and potentially two-player game, which has been outdone by other games since. After all, games such as *Top Spin* (tennis) are just *Pong* dressed up in different clothes. *Need for Speed* is just *Outrun* with fancier cars. *Big Mutha Truckers* is *Elite*, but with trucks. At the very basic level, even the most original RPG is just another version of "explore the dungeon and stab anything that moves." The key to making these games attractive to the consumer is to add a special twist that makes them unique and more fun than what has gone before.

One point will be stressed continuously: A good gameplay idea will make a good game, even if the graphics are low on the technological curve, but the best use of available technology cannot make a bad game idea sell. There are many abject failures that look very pretty—the latest *Spiderman* games, for example—and some games that, despite the graphics, just work—for example, *DefCon*.

This chapter will deal with various aspects of styles (genres) of games that have been well received by the playing public, along with hints as to what the ingredients are that make them saleable as ideas, even before they are implemented as actual products for sale to the general public.

Gaming Perspectives

A video game genre reflects the core ideas of the designer. The term "genre" is used freely here—for example, as in works of "fiction." What is more, it seems that there are now some core genres, subgenres, and extended genres. New genres are invented with almost every new game that comes on the market.

The descriptive name of the genre takes into account the game's goals, the protagonists, and the perspective offered to the player—that is, how their character interacts with the gaming universe. One such genre descriptive name is the First-Person Shooter (FPS). The genre communicates what there is to know about the game—it is played in the first person (through the player's eyes) and involves shooting at things. We instantly know what the game is about and how it will be played, and in a certain measure, what gameplay will look and feel like.

By reducing the game to its genre, however, we miss some vital ingredients, such as the exploration aspect, which doesn't do the game justice. So, we need to look beyond the basic description and actually play some of the genre games before we can really know what it describes. This is as good an excuse for playing games as the reader is likely to come across—it is research. Beyond knowing the genre of a game, we need to know what it is that makes it tick, beyond the various prescribed features that the genre will suggest. Cross- and mixed-genre games often end up as genre classifications of their own.

Take *Grand Theft Auto (GTA)*, for example. What kind of a game is it? Is it a shooting game? No, but you will do some shooting. Is it a driving game? Not really, but you can do some driving if you choose. Is it an RPG? Again, not exactly, but it does have some elements of RPG mixed in with the shooting and driving. So it's a simulation (sim) game, like *SimCity* or the *Sims*? Sort of. Almost. But again, not really. It is *GTA*, and other games will draw comparisons in the future and be stamped with the genre "*GTA*-like."

Putting this kind of conundrum to one side, a discussion of genres is a good starting point in understanding what kinds of games have been built in the past, so that the budding game designer can borrow on ideas that have worked. There is no point in building the best game in the world if it is not recognizable to the gamer; it will be too hard to get into. For example, Japanese-style RPGs have never made it in the West. The genre fails to match the market, and understanding why is necessary for creating a popular game.

Genres

The market has long been segmented when it comes to computer games. We tend to put games into little boxes—genres—which seem to fit the way that they look and feel. Like so many artistic categorizations, these will often be artificial, sometimes inaccurate, or just hopelessly subjective.

However, it makes it easier to talk in general terms about video games if we can have categories that work for the vast majority. With this in mind, the most common genres are presented in this section.

Action Games

The games on the very first entertainment systems to arrive in the home were basically copies of existing arcade machines, such as with clones of *Pong*, *Pac-Man*, and the ever popular *Space Invaders*. This first game genre has become known as the arcade or action genre. The game's emphasis is on split-second reactions, intense concentration, fast-paced action, and, of course, an intense fun experience. Previous restrictions on graphics and processing speed also meant that the interfaces were fairly basic, giving rise to some instantly recognizable characters—for example, *Pac-Man*—which were built from block graphics.

Since arcade machines were designed to take your money, customers had to feel that they were getting the maximum experience for their money, and manufacturers needed to make the machines pay. Hence, arcade games were geared toward short, intense experiences.

While technology has moved on since these classics, the overall emphasis on intense experiences has not—arcade games still need to achieve a high usership to recoup the cost of developing and installing the machines. We are now treated to a highly immersive, reality-intensive experience in the arcade, but more importantly, this experience is now being transferred to home consoles and personal computers, too. The difference is that, in this market, the player's attention needs to be retained for more than a matter of minutes; after all, we have already spent our money, and we want to feel that it has been a worthwhile investment.

The advances in technology, coupled with new paradigms for computer entertainment, have led to the birth of new genres, as well as enhanced the existing action/arcade (twitch) gameplay experience. As Marc Saltzman points out:

> "Action games are arguably the most popular genre for both PC and console systems. But there are many different flavors of action games. *Half-Life*, for example, is a 3D shooter but adds a deep, involving, story element." [Saltzman01]

Free from the necessity to make fast money, the home gaming industry is able to indulge many different genres and subgenres that involve cerebral involvement at a higher level, rather than just shooting anything that moves. The action genre is not dead, however, and many great games have been written that require only that the player have the reflexes of a cat. More often, though, the action portion is merged with something deeper, which has resulted in some more-refined gaming genres.

As a brief aside, the advent of platforms such as Xbox Live Arcade might bring back a resurgence in arcade action gaming. Each game is delivered online through a system of credits that can be used to buy playing time. The idea is very similar to the arcades of old, with the social interaction substituted by the ability for live chat with other gamers, thanks to the power of the Internet.

The architecture of Xbox, coupled with some great support from Microsoft for part-time hobby developers, makes it possible to put games together and share them for money in a way that only the PC has allowed. Perhaps the reality is not as easy as this might sound, but the thrust of Microsoft's strategy is clear:

> "Coupled with XNA Game Studio Express, the XNA Creators Club opens up video game development to untapped creative minds, enabling anyone to affordably build and play amazing game ideas on Xbox 360 systems for the first time ever." [MICROSOFT01]

Certainly, Sony and Nintendo should take notice of this developer-friendly approach, as it will probably gain momentum in the same way that the original home computers did in the arcade era.

Of course, the benefits of the Xbox architecture are what makes it possible—being close to a PC and thus susceptible to open development in a way that Sony and Nintendo's systems are not. The upside for Sony and Nintendo is that their systems are reasonably backward compatible.

Simulation Games

One level above pure action games (for example, "shoot-em-up" classics like *Space Invaders*), simulation games arrived in the arcades under two guises. The first was the racing simulation (rally cars, motorcycles, Formula 1 simulations), which retained some of the fast-earning features of the action game while boasting a more competitive style. The key difference was that in the action game, it was always the player versus the enemy, with both sides bent on the other's destruction.

Racing simulations introduced the concept of the player versus other players, who may have been computer controlled, but who were striving toward the same goal. This paved the way for multiplayer sports simulations in which some of the drivers were actually controlled by real people.

Increases in processing power also meant that actual simulation became possible, making for a more realistic experience all around. There could be more independent opponents with their own choices, rather than the prescribed, preprogrammed movement, as in action games.

The second simulation style again harkens back to the player-versus-enemy theme—this time in a realistic war style, and includes classics such as *Steel Talons*, which was later ported to at least one home console. The idea behind these games is that the player is immersed in a cockpit mock-up of a helicopter, tank, aircraft, or even an oversize mechanoid, which is designed to resemble, as much as possible, the real and/or imagined world. This meant that the control possibilities are no longer restricted to up-down-left-right; more-complex and sophisticated control systems are introduced. In the case of helicopter gunship simulations such as *Steel Talons*, this includes controls for adjusting the speed, and angle of the blades, which in turn affected both altitude and forward speed.

Coupled with these new control systems was the need to understand the physics behind both the simulated machine and the world that it inhabited. Again, simulation was being made possible by investment in the underlying technology; home gaming systems could not yet compete with the arcade experience.

Of course, these gaming advances meant that the quick-earning philosophy of the arcade was slowly being eroded, because it took ever more coins to actually master the machines. The players, however, kept on coming back and spending more in their attempt to exert control over the games.

Amateur psychology aside, it seemed that either players were becoming more refined or the game-playing audience was getting larger, or a combination of the two. After all, if a market becomes larger, it is likely to include consumers of varying sophistication, and tastes. Whichever element was causing it, the manufacturers were quick to capitalize on the phenomenon and moved into a third genre—the sports simulation.

Sports Simulations

People have different views on what constitutes a sport or a sport's simulation. This author tends to lump them all together, so that fighting games are considered as much a part of the sports genre as football or tennis. When trying to disagree with this opinion, many people have found it difficult to separate the genres effectively, since the lines between the subgenres are very blurred.

Perhaps the most influential beat-em-ups to date have been *Street Fighter II* and *Mortal Kombat*. In a bizarre parallel and as an example of franchising (which we shall cover later on), both *SFII* and *Mortal Kombat* have been adapted into successful films; classic franchising (or licensing) usually happens the other way round, with the film first.

A beat-em-up is to the sports genre what the shoot-em-up is to action arcade games. They rely more on reaction time and predefined moves than do simulated sporting events. Simulation games have the same quick-earning, coin-guzzling philosophy; unlimited lives are allowed as long as the player has the money to spend.

At the other end of the sports simulation spectrum are the ball games, including baseball, golf, tennis, football, and soccer. The excellent NeoGeo multigame arcade machine had many of these, and since then, the technology has moved into ever more-realistic simulations, recently culminating in the modeling of extreme sports such as snowboarding and skiing, and even a kayaking simulator . . . No sport is going to be safe.

The question is, how do we separate these from racing games? Surely, rally driving and Formula 1 simulations can be considered sports simulations, even more so than *Street Fighter II*. The answer is that lines have to be drawn somewhere, and sports simulations conjure up different images to different people. A better /*-+answer is that sports simulations are usually based on humans controlling nonmechanical vehicles, including themselves, and this sets the games apart from those based on controlling a mechanical vehicle, such as an automobile or aircraft.

Many of these games actually made an appearance in the home before the arcades. There may be many reasons for this, but one explanation might be that the games were based less on one-coin, one-play, and more on strategy. The fact remains that while these games could be found in the home on personal computers and consoles, the arcade machine manufacturers were, at the same time, perfecting the art of short-attention-span, maximum-profit gaming; but in the home computer world, a different style was fast becoming popular.

Sports Management Simulations

Sports in the real world require managers to help run the team (the crew, squad, and so on). They make important decisions with respect to player capability, position, and even the business side of the team. Sports management simulations have several advantages that made them extremely popular on home computers with limited power and resources.

First and foremost, they typically require very little processing power to display the actual game. Indeed, most of the player's time will be spent accessing plain-text interfaces (perhaps through graphical menus), trading players, doing deals, and looking at statistics. Those that simulate the actual game at all usually do so in a reasonably abstract way, largely due to the huge quantity of processing power eaten up by the Artificial Intelligence (AI) actually deciding the outcome of the game. This typically leaves much less processor available for the graphical output.

Even the games themselves and the planning of the in-game moves usually take place on a stylized, low-level graphical content interface. Player-manager simulations aside, most of the actual real-time game interface is below the curve of contemporary graphics (for example, *Premier Manager*).

However, this does not make the games any easier to create. The low-level graphics expectations simply mean that the rest of the game has to shine. Usually they do; and in any case, this unique fan base is quite apt to buy the game even if it does not shine in all respects.

Technology has changed in recent times. Game systems can now create, render, and replay complex 3D scenes involving all aspects of the particular, defining moment in a match, session, or race . . . meaning that the bar will continue to rise. Nevertheless, this genre remains one in which it may be easy for the right game to do very well, providing it offers something unique and captivating.

ADVENTURE GAMES

While pictures are largely believed to be possibly the most important form of sensory input in real life, at the time when personal computers became affordable enough to be used as game machines, they simply were not capable of producing an image quality that was better than the richness of text descriptions. Hence, early adventure games were based purely on text, both printed to the screen and as a form of input by the user.

Based on exploration, puzzles, inventory management, and general strategy (plus a pencil and paper for making a map), adventure games drew the gamer in and made them think. These games were unsuitable for the arcade; they were huge in scope and took hours or days to complete, but they really caught on in the home market.

Part of the attraction is linked to why people often prefer books over films, sometimes to the extent that they will say the book was *better* than the film. The human imagination's ability to create images from words is often more powerful than the display of graphics. Some people, however, just do not have this level of imagination and prefer their images served to them on a plate . . . No criticism intended, different people enjoy different media.

Some of the more impressive games include *Sphinx Adventure*, which came into being on the Acorn Electron home computer in the early 1980s. What was really remarkable about *Sphinx Adventure* and the host machine, itself, was the amount of detail and sheer number of locations that were persuaded into 16k of memory—that is 16,384 characters, or roughly 2,730 words, for both the code needed to manage the game and the descriptions for the locations within the game.

With an emphasis clearly on exploration, text-mode adventure games were quickly extended by the advent of the Internet and online Multi-User Dungeons (MUDs). Role-playing games had also been played in the "real world" on a tabletop; a team of players would attempt to thwart the obstacles put into their way by the Dungeon Master (DM). Possibly, the most popular of these games was *Dungeons & Dragons* (*D&D*). MUDs were the online versions, with a computer as DM, and contributions by players made up many of the various quests.

In due course, as the technology caught up with game designers, text-mode adventure games gave way to text-and-graphics versions (such as *The Hobbit*, a computer game adaptation of Tolkien's book), and finally to games in which graphics played a larger part than text. These included entertaining parodies that were popular for years, such as the *Leisure Suit Larry* franchise marketed by Sierra Online.

Finally, with intense gaming experiences like *Myst*, the adventure game genre moved to purely graphical interfaces. These replaced typed-in phrases, such as "EXAMINE BOOK," with clickable hotspots on the screen. These enabled the player to react to the game universe in a more intuitive and proactive way. Now we have gone beyond even this; a combination of the real world and online gaming has taken the adventure genre to a new level.

This culminated in 2007 with the first winner of an adventure game called *Perplex City* that combined game cards, the Internet, and real-world locations to solve a variety of clues to find the *Receda Cube*.

Not only could the winner keep the treasure, but they also received a cash prize. The entire two-and-a-half-year-long game was extremely popular, and the creator is going to do the whole exercise again, but make it episodic next time around, so players can enter at different stages. They no longer have to be in it from the start to have a chance to win something.

This is the real-world equivalent of a genre that takes simple adventuring and adds twists to it—the role-playing game.

Role-Playing Games

One step up from adventure games are role-playing games, which we have already briefly encountered, earlier. The key attraction for many RPG enthusiasts is the ability to assume the persona of a specific type or class of character (the avatar). No longer is the player expected to rely solely on raw weapon power, such as swords and guns. Magic and spell casting, and other types of attack mechanisms can also be used to further the progress of the player in the game.

Coupled with this is the possibility to advance through the game by solving particular problems (quests) while gaining experience with each successful solution. Racking up experience points leads to advancement within the class chosen by the player. Depending on the game, this might mean advancing up numerical levels or a slightly more complex, title-based hierarchy. With each new level comes enhanced powers that can be used to defeat enemies or gain experience points in other ways, which in turn increases the player's level. All of this is played against a backdrop that maintains a constant theme throughout. This is another facet of the RPG world: The characters and backdrop remain true to the storyline, and the mixing of specific times, places, technologies, and races is often frowned upon.

Borrowing on MUD-style technologies and concepts, a more recent innovation is the Massively Multiplayer Online Role-Playing Game (MMORPG) genre. Put simply, these are games in which there are many participants, and each player falls into a specific category. Rather than one player striving to save the world, these games take place on a central Web server, and client software displays the immediate game universe. The user interface is usually graphical, due to the large amount of information that needs to be manipulated.

There are, of course, subgenres that tailored to specific markets. Japanese RPGs for example, require a level of concentration, skill, and micromanagement that Western audiences just do not have the patience for. Many other game genres also mix in some RPG elements to enhance gameplay.

Multiplayer Action Games

Many single-player games, such as *Soldier of Fortune II: Double Helix* or *Quake,* also have multiplayer modes that allow a connection to a central server in much the same way as an online RPG. However, these tend to be aimed more at team-play style (with the exception of death matches), with the main emphasis being placed on pure action. Hence, they are usually played at a specially designed or well-known, packaged level, with very few puzzles or traps.

From a design point of view, many games start out as successful single-player implementations and are then extended to a multiplayer platform. This is as true for PC games as it is for console games (whose the ability to connect multiple machines is in its infancy). Of course, in the PC world, machines have been furnished with modems, broadband, or classic telecom lines for a long time. Games consoles, on the other hand are only recently being equipped for reaching out into the cyber world.

Puzzle Games

As was mentioned earlier, many action games were centered around reaction gaming, with little or no puzzle solving required. This is not to say that they lacked a strategic element, but simply that the strategy was so entwined with the action elements, there was very little space (or time) left for the decision-making process that defines traditional puzzle solving.

The general format for traditional puzzle games often includes a problem that needs to be solved, followed by some kind of subtle scenario change, followed by another puzzle that needs to be solved in order to gain points or move up a hierarchy of levels. Examples include games like *Repton*, *Knights Lore*, or *Castlequest*. Each of these follows the general format of problem solving and level advancement.

In *Repton* (and the game *Boulderdash*), the puzzles involve the manipulation of earth and rocks in order to gather diamonds before the player escapes to the next level. Rocks are placed in cunning places, so that if a player fells one by accident or in an incorrect sequence, then the level is rendered impossible to complete. Rocks follow specific game mechanics, and later levels include monsters to crush under rocks and keys to unlock safes, among other interesting mechanisms.

A different kind of puzzle is presented in *Knights Lore*, which revolves around pushing blocks around a series of three-dimensional, square, prison-like caverns. These blocks form a path from the entry point to the exit. Some blocks support the weight of the player, while others do not and sink down toward the bottom of the cavern when the player steps on them. The player moves from one room to another, and more-intriguing (and seemingly impossible) levels are encountered.

Yet another puzzle style is apparent in *Castlequest*, in which the player is presented with ways to manipulate the environment and the objects it contains to access other items/parts of the game universe. Inventory management plays a large part in *Castlequest*, and the end goal is to find the way out of the castle. Different objects can be used to solve specific problems, and sometimes the player has to carry them for a long time before their use is apparent.

Also in the puzzle genre are the brain games. These began with *Sudoku*, a game based on allocating numbers in a grid, and has been taken further by a partnership between Professor Kawashima and Nintendo on the Nintendo DS handheld gaming device. The aptly named *Brain Training* series of games challenged the player with tasks that must be completed.

A unique aspect of these games (which almost places them in the non-real-time gaming genre), is that the player is only allowed to play the game for a certain length of time per day. The game itself restricts the player, based on the theory that repetition is more valuable to the learning experience than trying to complete it all in one session.

Non-Real-Time Games

There are a number of games that are not played in the real-time environment, but which follow a slightly more disjointed playing pattern. Some of the most prevalent are known as Play By eMail (PBeM) games, a variation on the old play-by-mail enhancement to *Dungeons & Dragons*, where large groups of geographically diverse individuals could play and follow a turn-based scheme.

Of course, this has largely been made obsolete by the advent of the Internet, since it is now possible to have real-time gaming, but the genre remains quite popular. The main problem with recent RPGs, for example, is that combat remains turn-based, which can be somewhat disconcerting when combat sequences start and the tempo changes. In the multiplayer world, this disjointed feeling is enhanced, which is why some people prefer PBeM, which is entirely turn-based. Then again, some machines cannot cope with the rigors of full, multiplayer games due to insufficient processing power or modem speed; whereas almost every machine that can connect to the Internet is capable of supporting email.

Although one might believe that only strict RPG-style games lend themselves to play via email, there are a couple of other styles that are worth mentioning. The first is an implementation of the classic Commodore 64 (C64) game *Chaos*, which was released in the heady days of the home computer (circa 1985).

For the uninitiated, *Chaos* is based on a card game, and each player is dealt a number of cards that can be used to cast spells. The C64 version is much the same. The player is pitted against the computer, each trying to outdo the other with spells that range from confusing their enemies to spawning armies of mutant rats.

There is a deep element of strategy that underpins the tactical action that takes place on a square battlefield. The game's author realized that this strategic twist would make for an extremely addictive real-time game (and also an excellent PBeM variant), where each move lasts a mere 10 seconds of game time, but can be thought about offline for hours. A handy replay tool is also available that shows the various moves to date.

The second kind of game is aimed more at budding developers and proponents of artificial intelligence. It involves a battle between computer programs that are constructed using C language. Battles take place in the memory of a simulated SUN machine, and each opponent can drive a virtual tank, scan for enemies, and fire bullets. They begin with an energy level of 100, and each shot that lands near them does a proportional amount of damage. When the energy reaches zero, they are dead.

The entire game runs very fast, and the aim is to gain entry to a top-20 list of computer programs, known as the Hill. Thus, this "survival of the fittest" style game is known as King of the Hill. It is an intriguing concept, and a great training and testing ground for AI used in computer games to control enemies.

Other Simulations

Games such as *SimCity* and the more recent *The Sims* are an attempt to get ever closer to reality, where the player makes decisions regarding a city and the ways in which its various aspects are connected, on the one hand, and on the other hand must consider the lives of people living under the player's control. This is not a terribly new idea; the "god-games," like *Populous*, also carried this kind sort of theme.

In fact, *SimCity* and *Populous* are very similar. They are based on building up a civilization and reacting to various problems that are thrown their way, including famine, floods, war, and fire. In *SimCity*, a city being manipulated; in *Populous*, it is an entire race.

On the other hand, *The Sims* is more a case of micro-management of individuals, be it families or individual people. The others deal with crowds and not the whims of individuals. Situated in between the two are games such as *Megalomaniac*, which deals with individuals in terms of fighting, but larger groups of people when it comes to mining, development, and mob-warring.

There is another form of simulation that centers around buying and selling goods, as well as fighting. *Elite*, for example is a space trading simulation (buy low and sell high) coupled with fighting—be it bounty hunting or just simple defense of an innocent trader. Later incarnations used a mission-based structure, where the player was able to make money by carrying out assassinations or taxi-style courier operations.

Other games in this genre are the recent *Big Mutha Truckers* and the ever popular *Dope Wars*. These revolve around trading, but against slightly different backdrops and with their own specific hurdles and obstacles.

Perspectives

The playing perspective is a combination of player's position in the game universe coupled with the way that they are allowed to perceive that game universe. It is partly about the mechanics of the game design and partly about the story that unfolds as the player plays the game.

Some genres seem to use the same playing perspective, whereas others use diverse perspectives, while still delivering a game that works. Choosing the perspective and control style can make or break a game; always bear in mind that most games will find a niche somewhere—they will simply sell less copies. This is because there will always be a small part of the market that is so enthusiastic about the concept that these players will put up with less-than-perfect controls or playing perspective. The general market is not so forgiving; gamers may well pick up and drop a game based on an imperfect camera or quirky controls.

Even the seminal *Super Mario Sunshine* contrived to mix both of these two flaws in a single decision to map the camera to a control stick and then leave it to the mercy of the player. When it disappears behind a wall, effectively blinding the player, it's very hard to get it back again. Luckily, the rest of the game is so well presented that this is more of a petty complaint, but it does show that sometimes, even the best get it wrong.

If the game had not been so good in other respects, this flaw might have caused it to fail. Of course, it didn't, and arguably, Nintendo made sure that the rest of the game was almost perfect, and it decided to let the camera issue go.

The 2007 *Odin Sphere* (PlayStation 2) was not quite so lucky, with frame rate slowdown painfully apparent at times, and *Monster Madness* on the Xbox 360 suffers from an odd decision to map jumping and dodging to twin analog sticks, somewhat counterintuitively.

Often, the control style and player viewpoint will be dictated by the designer's choice of perspective for the player in the game universe.

Playing Perspective

The first component we shall discuss is the perspective offered to the player as the hero of the game. For example, in some games, the player represents an individual. This individual can be viewed in either the third person or the first person.

The distinction between the two may seem obvious, but it is important to realize the psychological differences between the two. It is often much easier to get involved in a game if it is viewed from the first-person perspective, but sometimes the player might feel restricted by the fact that the screen can only show a very small portion of what he would be able to see if he really was inside the game. Third-person views often compensate for this by showing more of the surrounding game universe to the player.

Some examples of first-person games include classics from id Software: *Wolfenstein 3D*, *DOOM*, *Quake*, and also games like *Soldier of Fortune*, and more recently *Operation Flashpoint (OF)*. The reason *OF* is mentioned here is because it digresses from the classic first-person action genre epitomized by games of the *DOOM* ilk, in that it does not revolve around the single player, but around a team that the player is either a part of or is in charge of. This is subtly different from the survival-instinct approach of *DOOM*, *Quake*, and *Soldier of Fortune*.

First-person games view the game universe through the eyes of the hero, while third-person perspective tends to view the world from a viewpoint that is distant from the player's character. These include both three- and two-dimensional implementations. Two-dimensional variants often range from old-style platform game side-on views, as seen in *Sonic the Hedgehog* and *Super Mario* (which changed in 2002 with the release of *Super Mario Sunshine*), to top-down views as in *Ravenskull* and *Asteriods. Pac-Man* could also possibly be considered a top-down-view game. The important difference is that the player is able to see all around the character, as well has have a decent view of the immediate game universe, which is often not the case in first-person perspective games. (*Red Faction* is one of the worst offenders.)

Linking the two perspectives is the *Tomb Raider*-style, "over-the-shoulder" viewpoint, which is a strange mixture of first and third person. In fact, many arcade-style beat-em-ups, such as *Street Fighter 2,* also use a zoomed-out version of this type of playing angle, as does *Blade* and games like *Resident Evil.*

Many games also offer the possibility for the player to select between first-person and third-person views; the key difference for games like *Tomb Raider* is that a first-person perspective would make it much less visually appealing. In these games, the over-the-shoulder view is an integral part of the playing experience.

Playing Angles

In the 3D arena, there are also different angles at which the game universe can be viewed. This applies to group hero-style games as well as single-character hero games. A brief discussion is worth entering into at this point to note the difference between the two.

A group-hero game typically centers on either the manipulation of a large number of individuals who react as a crowd (as in some of the combat scenarios from *Megalomaniac*), or one in which the player manipulates a set number of individuals, as in *The Sims.* A single-character hero game is distinct in that the player controls a single entity that never changes; therefore, the game designer does not have to work quite as hard at getting the player to build a rapport with their in-game incarnation. More important, multiple- or group-hero games often cannot be played in first-person style.

So, our focus here is mainly on third-person games. The most common playing angle for 3D games to date has been isometric. This is a 45-degree view of the playing area, which has been used to great effect in *SimCity 2000* and *Railroad Tycoon*, among others. It enables a good view of the player and surrounding game universe, not to mention any other nonplaying characters that might be involved in a specific scene.

We have already mentioned the over-the-shoulder view, which is a close-up form of the classic isometric view and brings into play the issue of camera work. In this context, "camera" refers to the way in which the player sees the game universe, and more important, from where, in relation to the character, that universe is seen. Isometric game views tend to use a fairly static or user-controlled camera, whereas (true 3D) games such as *Tomb Raider* take over the manipulation of the camera and try to always give the player the best view—without wandering around too much and causing the player to have motion sickness.

Often, camera angles are the first and easiest part of a game to be criticized, simply because they can be so hard to implement well. The issues center around how to make the camera follow the various changes in character posture and position so as to give the player the best possible view at all times, without morphing through walls or focusing from one side to the other so fast that the player loses track of what they were trying to achieve.

Markets

The intrepid game designer also needs to decide which of the possible markets they are aiming for when designing the game. The decision is dictated by many different factors, since the object is not to satisfy a particular niche, but to approach as wide an audience (or market) as possible. For example, simulation games like *SimCity* have a larger fan base than just would-be city planners, and *Tomb Raider* was probably conceived to appeal to both the traditional fighter- and exploration-oriented players, rather than just one market or the other.

Attention Spans

In the heyday of the arcade machine, and even back to the original pinball arcade, the gaming experience was finite. The player was limited by the amount of money that they were willing to spend. One coin gave them between three and five balls to play. After that, they had a choice—walk away or put in more money. The game designers had to work hard to ensure that the players parted with as much money as they had in their pockets.

With the advent of arcade-quality game systems for the home, as well as in the traditional arcades, the gaming experience has become somewhat less time-limited. Publishers no longer have to try and ensure that they get the maximum amount of money from the player. Games can go for hours on end; there is no financial reason for quick endings.

On the other hand, console gamers are split into two camps: quick fix versus hardcore—that is, those who just use gaming to unwind after a hard days' work, and those who are willing to play the game until they complete it, respectively. PC gamers fall into similar camps, but arcade gamers tend to be a special breed. They probably own several consoles just so they can play the same games at home as they do in the arcade. Dance-oriented games like *DDR* are a great example of this.

Violence

The topic of game violence has to be mentioned. Mazzi Binaisa, writing for *Game On: The History and Culture of Videogames* (produced in conjunction with an exhibition of the same name at the Barbican Centre in London, U.K., in 2002), puts it like this:

> "*Street Fighter* and *Mortal Kombat* were the precursors to the gut-wrenching *Unreal Tournament* and *Quake*. Whereas with games of the *Street Fighter* ilk, I could chuckle at the implausibly high kicks of Chun Li. . . . with *Unreal* and *Quake* I can now only look away." [Mazzi02]

Clearly not a great fan of abject violence and gore, Mazzi Binaisa opines that there are people who do not rejoice in the glorified killing that is the first-person shooter. An increase in reality has led to an increase in gore, and there is a market for it. Mazzi Binaisa goes on to elaborate slightly: "The surprise factor in playing games has faded over the last 20 years."

Even *Halo* and *Turok Evolution* have failed to put the spark back into a genre that sells to a market that views violence differently—where reaction times are more important than planning strategy. Make no mistake, it is a very lucrative market, but many game journalists tend to view them as a poor examples of video games that *should* be available.

The two recent *Manhunt* games take in-game violence to a logical conclusion. The first game was attacked in the nonspecialty gaming press and largely condemned. Even the gaming magazines found it hard to ignore the glorified cold, calculated killing, which was just one step removed from murder. The second *Manhunt* game was quickly banned from sale in many markets. While the first was tolerated as being innovative, the second was treated as commercialization of the kind of human behavior that fell short of being acceptable.

Violence for the sake of violence might sell, but it is also distasteful to many people. Even innovative violence will garner a reputation for the game creator that might be less than desirable.

Puzzles

It is often said that games sell consoles, and that to really be successful, a console needs one good game. On the basis of that one good game, when a gamer buys the console, they will continue to buy games for it. Of course, as the price of technology drops, this becomes less important, but if there is one franchise that repeatedly sells consoles, it is the Nintendo *Super Mario* series.

The hit *Super Mario Sunshine* sold GameCubes for Nintendo; of that there is little doubt. It is a puzzle game, intrinsically nonviolent, and the first full-3D rendering of the *Super Mario* series. These puzzle games, such as *Tetris,* among others, tend to appeal to a special kind of market.

Many games contain puzzle elements, while others are totally puzzle oriented. For example, take a game such as *Brain Training* for the Nintendo DS. This is a game that relies on the player's wish to have his brain "trained" for periods at a time. The game shows logical puzzle after logical puzzle, which the player must solve within a certain time span.

Arguably, this sort of game will appeal to a certain mentality, and yet advertising for the Nintendo DS quite clearly shows a family of four battling it out, using the wireless connectivity offered by the DS. The inference is that the whole family is into DS just for the sake of playing one game, together.

Puzzle games are, indeed, a genre where the appeal is more or less universal. In addition to games such as *SingStar* or certain rhythm action games, puzzles are great party games. They promote social collaboration, making for an interesting genre with plenty of crossover potential.

MULTIPLAYER

The Internet can be blamed for many things—above all, the antisocial behavior that is the multiplayer death match. This is many parents' points of view, of course. Gamers look at it as a chance to socialize with like-minded acquaintances . . . and then kill them in a variety of interesting ways.

Then again, there have been a multitude of online games that do not involve killing, beginning with card games such as hearts and evolving to entire worlds with vibrant economies, such as *Everquest.* Trading characters and information on the Internet in return for in-game currencies adds to the entire experience, as does the possibility to visit other peoples' game-universe creations.

This may sound like we are talking exclusively about PC gaming, since that is the platform that is associated with modems and connectivity. Consoles are also frequently being fitted with modems, too; broadband access leads to wonderful games, such as *Animal Crossing* for the Nintendo GameCube, in which the player's character lives in a world that can be shared with others. This game also heralds the arrival of another submarket aimed specifically at people who will play for a few minutes (or hours) at a time, and are then forced to stop. Time passes at the same rate as it does in the real world, and often the player has to either hang around waiting for something to happen or take this opportunity to attend to chores in the real world.

So, the multiplayer market is one that will buy a game just because it is multiplayer, in the same way that the violence FPS market will buy a game just because it is laced with gore. The same goes for driving games and crossovers, such as *Crazi Taxi* and *Grand Theft Auto*, which achieve violence on the road.

Finally, the possibilities offered by competitive sports also open doors to the multiplayer market, something that has not been wasted on the creators of *Unreal Tournament*, who have added "game" modes that involve all kinds of strange twists on the original, such as deathmatches.

From Idea to Design

Bearing all of the above in mind, there comes a time when the game designer needs to translate an idea into an actual game. The planning that goes into the creation of even a simple game should not be underestimated. The simplest games still need advanced planning, otherwise the implementation process will be long, tedious, or never actually completed. Proper planning, while preventing poor performance, also forces the designer to think more carefully about what he is trying to get across to the audience, just like in making a good movie.

The Idea

There is no hard and fast rule about what constitutes a good game idea or how to come up with one. In most books, the approach taken to creative ideas is very simple: either you have them or you don't. This is where cloning takes over. For those who have difficulty coming up with an idea that is truly original, they should first try taking an existing idea and adding a new twist. This twist becomes, what David Perry of Shiny Entertainment and the designer behind titles such as the *Earthworm Jim* series, calls a hook. According to Marc Salzman:

> "A good hook means that you can describe your game in one sentence. For *MDK [Murder Death Kill]* it was, 'He has a weapon so accurate, you can shoot your enemy in the eye from a mile away.'" [Saltzman02]

While David Perry did not invent the idea of shooting enemies, the hook above offered "sniper mode," something that did not really exist on the market until *MDK* was released. A twist on an existing theme, it offered a unique hook. So, if a game designer wants to clone an existing title, they should find an aspect that they can sum up in one sentence, which will make their game different from other games in the same venue.

Those lucky people who routinely have ideas, and can afford to pick and choose which idea to flesh out into game designs also need to take a step back and filter out those ideas that are merely copies of existing games. The problem is quite often that, in playing many games, we have a tendency to "re-have" ideas that already exist. Spotting that they are simply cloned ideas of games that we have previously played is a tricky business, but it is essential. Developing the idea into a game design forces us to take this step back.

Also, those people who do routinely have new, unique, creative ideas should also find a hook phrase for the game; they are not exempt from this stage simply because the game idea is unique. The hook phrase is quite often what will make the game sell.

In addition to having a hook phrase, something else is key to creating a good idea (something we can all relate to): Play games—play many, many games. If you cannot afford to buy them (not surprising, considering the retail price of most commercial games), then play all the demos you can get your hands on. Seriously. This is not just an excuse to play games. By playing them, you get a chance to take a look at the current level of technology and how the game was put together, and decide what you find appealing about it. This will also give you, the designer, a chance to see what has already been done, so that you do not simply repeat an idea, but enhance existing game ideas that have found commercial success.

Similarly, retro gaming (playing games that have had their day) is also a must, as it is a rich source of ideas. Play classics like *SimCity* or *Prince of Persia*, and get a feel for what makes them still playable, despite their looking a little dated. Try to imagine how you could extend or enhance these golden oldies to bring them up to date, such as the jump that Maxis made from *SimCity* to *SimCity 2000*, or the novel innovations that Bullfrog made when they brought *Theme Park* to the market. It is sometimes difficult to find retro games, let alone play them on today's hardware, so most retro gaming will either have to be done on second-hand consoles, home computers (perhaps with emulation), or simply by going to car boot sales and buying old games magazines.

It is well worth the investment in time, and if downloading demos becomes too expensive in communication costs, new games magazines can also be a great way to learn about the latest releases. A good multiplatform gaming magazine such as *EDGE* (U.K.) fits the bill perfectly. The reviews need to be to the point and seriously impartial, something that single-format magazines can occasionally fail to produce.

Although nobody can claim to actually be able to tell you whether the idea will make a game that sells, we can at least try to emulate success by learning from previous releases. What is important is that the designer gets a feel for how gaming has evolved, and is evolving, to try to learn how the idea that he has might look when translated into a game.

Refining the Idea

Once you have a clear idea, it needs to be refined. Even if the hook seems to be perfect, it is only a summed-up version of the core driving force behind the game design. A document has to be written; putting the words down will aid the process of refining the idea into something that is more concrete. Even a modification to an existing game (such as a *Quake* mod) will need to be shaped, even if it seems like the core idea (i.e., the idea behind *Quake,* itself) has already been hammered out.

One of the most famous modifications to *Quake* has been the *Capture the Flag (CTF)* mod made by Dave Kirsch. It was so popular that id Software incorporated it into the *Quake* engine. The idea behind *CTF* is very simple. The hook might be summed up as "Two teams fighting it out to defend their own flag and capture their opponents." Obviously there is a multiplayer option involving an open level (i.e., one with no doors or keys), with two teams wearing different colors so they can be told apart, and liberal weapon and health caches laid out on levels that are fairly symmetrical so that neither side has an advantage when it comes to starting position or flag placement.

So from one simple idea, we begin to enhance the core and establish some basic rules of play, and also design restrictions for the levels themselves. It is this process of looking deeper into each area of the prospective game that refines our idea. Some key areas include level design, dynamics, placement of weapons, ammunition, health boosts, and so forth—and whether or not to include nonplayer characters.

Game Characters

One of the most important aspects of the game are the characters—and most important, the lead character, be it the hero or the adversary. Also, the main character (possibly the one that sparked the idea in the first place) need not be the hero (or player-controlled character). The entire game could revolve around the traditional adversary.

A common principle applies to all of the characters: They should have depth and a role to play in the game. The exact amount of depth that they have will depend on the game itself, and in some cases (such as *Mario*), it can take years to fully flesh out a game character. In fact, in the recent Nintendo release, *Super Mario Sunshine,* the underlying plot and game idea revolves around a new adversary, nicknamed *Shadow Mario.* This new character is the enemy and reveals himself at many points in the game. In fact, the whole game revolves around him and not, as in previous *Mario* games, the good guy.

This kind of approach should not be confused with using an anti-hero as the main character when the anti-hero is a player-controlled character. An anti-hero is usually associated with the opposition, but is also used as the hero in a given scenario. This does not necessarily make the anti-hero a "good guy," after all. Taking *Raiden* or *Sub Zero* all the way to the end of *Mortal Kombat* leads to success for the player, but the characters that they represent are associated with an entirely evil background.

This takes us to the core of character development—having a set of facts that stick out in the player's mind, which are called to mind as soon as they see that character. Keeping the background information rich but simple means that the character's persona can be called up instantly. This will help the player during the game, as they can quickly make a decision from a visual cue.

The player should also be able to relate to the characters in the game. If they do not care enough about the hero, then they will find it difficult to react as that hero in a way that is required to win the game. In addition, should the enemies not seem to be threatening enough, then the player might not feel like defending their hero against them.

There may not actually be an on-screen character. Puzzle games such as *Tetris* do not actually have a lead character or even enemies. The idea is to beat the machine, which becomes the "enemy." The blocks falling from the top of the screen, and which need to be arranged in order to complete lines and thus win points, can be seen as enemies or heroes—you can be either with them or against them, depending on your point of view. Puzzle games rely on a recognizable screen layout, the game environment, and its dynamics to achieve success.

THE ENVIRONMENT

In addition to the characters, there is the game environment which they inhabit. While "character development" might not apply to some types of games (we used puzzle games as an example of games without characters), the "environment" applies to all games. Even games such as *Tetris,* which do not have a discernable character beyond the blocks that fall from the top of the screen, have a game environment that is instantly recognizable.

Incidentally, in the case of *Tetris*, the environment is a hollow, U-shaped container with a score panel to the right of the screen. Even without the colored blocks, most people who have played *Tetris* for any length of time will recognize this specific layout. A chessboard offers the same, instantly recognizable game universe. There are many others, both in the home and arcade arenas, including the textured walls of *Wolfenstein3D* or the curving track of the arcade classic *Daytona*, or the pressure mats of *Dance Dance Revolution.*

This last example indicates a slight deviation in that there are also games in which the game environment extends beyond what is seen on the screen, to that which is used to control the game. Games such as *Tekki* also have a very unique environment, which is illustrated by the unique set of controls that it sports.

Game Dynamics

Game dynamics relates to the way in which the characters interact with the game environment. The speed at which the cubes fall in *Tetris*, for example, is a part of the game dynamics that help to shape the overall game experience, and is key to the way in which the game, itself, works.

The fact that the speed increases over time as levels are achieved is also an example of the game dynamics. By way of comparison, there are many clones that differ slightly in this implementation, for example, by not allowing the shape to slide once it has touched the nominative ground. The original game allowed the player to move the shape once it had touched down, thus opening up a kind of corrective measure for certain isolated cases where the player had previously made a mistake. Excluding this "out" in cloned versions might alter the game dynamic in such a way that would not be acceptable to some players.

If the game dynamics are flawed, then the game will be, too. No amount of eye candy, special effects, or cuddly characters can help poor game dynamics. However, game dynamics, by themselves, can quite easily make a very popular game without any graphics, sounds, or special effects; just ask the hundreds of thousands of players of games like *Drug Wars* or *The General*. Neither have graphics to speak of, but their game dynamics are breathlessly well implemented.

Stories and Narrative Elements

Everybody likes a good story. Even people standing in a crowded shop, reading the back of a CD case, and sweating in anticipation can be captured by the story that encompasses a good game idea. While it is no substitute for a game idea or any of the game design principles that we have already touched on, a story can be the glue that holds the entire illusion together.

Some games (such as puzzle games) do not need a story at all. Others, such as text-based role-playing games, cannot survive without a storyline. Usually, though, the story is a backdrop to the rest of the game. As such, it is important that the game appears to grow out of the story, as this is the key to maintaining congruence between the characters, backdrop, and game dynamics.

Back Story

Each character needs to have their place in the tapestry that is the story. In this way, they will begin to flesh out, as opposed to remaining two-dimensional representations. A character with a history is much more likely to attract a gaming enthusiast. Part of the attraction of *Wolfenstein3D* was the illusion that the player was chasing a real enemy that had caused suffering, and the desire to make that enemy suffer in turn. History gives a sense of urgency and, ultimately, a goal to the game.

Some games, such as *Max Payne*, are all done in a semi-movie-like setting. The movie influences are used to draw the player into the game, forming a storyline on top of which the game is placed and integrated with. It is the story that gives the player a reason to continue. It makes them care what happens to both their character and those being hunted.

The recent *Soldier of Fortune II: Double Helix* follows a similar theme, using a developing storyline to push the game along. The first mission involves rescuing a professor who has been locked up in an Eastern Bloc hotel in a desolate town that seems entirely in the grip of the army. The player is compelled to care about the professor, although we are helped by a sentence in the mission brief which runs along the lines of:

> "Guard the doctor. If any harm comes to him, the mission is a failure."

This line might seem a little over the top, emotionally, but it is important that the game designer realizes the emotive power behind "hooks" like these. It is not just a collection of words that set the scene for the game; it is also a clue to how the current task can be achieved, or a key to what constitutes a game-oriented error.

Narrative Elements

There are also narrative elements that can be liberally spread throughout an adventure world, but they will probably seem very out of place in a simple shoot-em-up or puzzle game. Narrative elements provide more than just the story backdrop to the game; they give depth to the various situations that the player finds himself in.

Narratives help to tell the story as the player makes his way through the game, as opposed to the marketed storyline that is intended to help sell the game. On the other hand, these narrative elements do need to be prepared beforehand and placed where the player will either stumble upon or be directed to them.

A recent game example includes some of the exploration that is required in *Max Payne*, where the player is guided by an ongoing story, but needs to use a little lateral thinking to advance through the plot. There are guns, too, and the entire effect is more like a movie than a video game. Techniques used are "borrowed" from movies such as *The Matrix*—for example, bullet time; the action slows down when the character fires a particular weapon.

Another example of narrative is present in the *Empire Earth* tutorials, which are based on real history, but which use narrative elements to guide the player through situations they are bound to come across in the game proper. Then again, *Mafia* uses an ongoing story to teach the player what is and is not possible inside the game world, while also introducing the player to the world he will inhabit during his play sessions.

The narration itself can be performed through speech, pictures, or text. There are a few guidelines that need to be respected, however. As a general rule, if the narrative is of any real importance, then it should be delivered via either semi-permanent text or voiceover, or both. The text should linger on after the voiceover ends, in case the player missed the vocal instructions. (There is nothing worse than trying to trigger the voiceover again simply because we forgot the exact instructions.)

Even semi-permanent text should also be accessible via a scrollbar for future review. The simple truth is that if the game requires 100% of the player's attention and punishes them during the *tutorial* for missing a beat, then a certain portion of the anticipated market will be alienated—that is, the players that don't want to pay 100% attention during a game's familiarization period.

We have already mentioned the need to trigger narrative elements, and this is fairly important. There are several ways in which this can be accomplished, and it is up to the video game designer to decide which way to use. Some common ones use points along a prescribed path, and these points trigger instructions as to what to do next, or even objects that, when picked-up, evoke a section of narrative.

The designer also needs to decide what happens when the player passes over the trigger a second time; should they get the same result or a different one? Imagine that the player is told to shoot at cans (as in the *Mafia* tutorial), manages to knock them all over, and continues shooting. Should they then be penalized (or at least shouted at) for continuing to fire when all of the cans are already down?

Descriptive Elements

If characters and places have narrative cues to prompt the player, then objects have other mechanisms, such as descriptive elements that indicate to the player the object's worth, age, or use. Of course, the primary descriptive element is the shape of the object. This may sound obvious, but the only way that the player knows what the object is for, or even what it *is*, is by its shape.

For those objects that have a real-world equivalent, the chances are that the player will recognize them. After all, look at how parents can recognize a picture that their child has drawn, even if it is not a perfect copy of the real-world object that it depicts. What about objects that have never been seen in the real world? A video game is a reflection of imagination, and indeed, quite often there are certain objects that are invented for the game.

Video game objects will probably fall into categories: vehicles, weapons, people, things, tools, or even food. They should be recognizable for what they are, even if the player has never seen them before. This might sound a little difficult. What does a "weapon" look like? Usually, weapons, like guns, have a right end and a wrong end. No matter what the gun, it can be recognized as such.

Vehicles are also pretty recognizable, they have wheels or wings, and cab/cockpit that the pilot looks out of or sits in. Tools can also be recognized by certain facets of their appearance, but what about food? Or furniture? Or even, people?

Texture and Color

The key to recognizing some elements is by their texture. Skin looks like skin, and a moving thing that is covered with a skin-like surface is probably an animal or a person. Texture also helps us to tell wood from stone, or metal from plastic (although this last case can be quite a difficult prospect; some plastics are made to look exactly like metal).

If texture fails to evoke the correct reaction, then maybe the color will give additional visual clues. Pink metal blades, for example, might not be appropriate, so the player may be able to use color to tell the difference between a saber and a large feather. (This is a fairly weak way of telling one material from another; they can always be painted, so it cannot be relied on, except in very obvious cases.)

Sound

The use of sound is not limited to the environment. Objects can also have sounds associated with them, and not just explosions and shots. Paper rustling, for example, can help to distinguish between serviettes and handkerchiefs. Maybe this last example is far-fetched, but as an extreme case, it indicates how the sound of an object can define an object.

The current technology that drives video games lacks two important facets that humans use to indicate their immediate environment: touch and smell. The player cannot feel the objects, which might come in handy when trying to find one's way through a darkened labyrinth.

Sound replaces the sense of touch to a certain extent, since it offers the player aural clues to both the environment and the objects that they encounter. It is all part of the descriptive tapestry that makes the gaming experience more realistic.

This does not necessarily translate into fun. Some games are just too realistic, which, strangely, makes the games less fun. Imagine being subjected to the full sound of an automatic weapon chattering incessantly in your right ear; it would be quite unbearable. Fun games usually take the realism just so far, and then pull back before the realism turns the game into something less than entertaining.

General Design Issues

Finally, there is the meat of the game structure. The budding game developer needs to set out the structure of the game within the parameters of the genre, story, and game dynamics, while paying attention to the environment and characters. There are an almost infinite number of possibilities, but some key issues are linked directly to the game style.

Hardware Controllers

We will discuss this again later on, but the recent spate of unique hardware controllers to hit the market has created some interesting game designs. It is tempting to say that it all started with the PlayStation 2 DualShock controller (which vibrates, has analog and digital directional control, and eight buttons), but in truth, most controller designs date back to the arcade era.

Joysticks have evolved. Then again, the machines have too—enter *Tekki* and the $150 price tag, with a control deck that numbers tens of buttons, twin joysticks, pedals, and a range of authentic-looking dials. All of this has been made possible by a jump in machine capability—the ability of the machine to take all the input variables, map them to the game dynamics, and feed back into the game and to the controllers, appropriately.

Other games, such as *Dance:UK* or *Dance Dance Revolution*, require a dance mat, a joystick that the player can jump on. Then there are the various pulley and wire arrangements that allow the player to swing a club, bat, or other sports appendage to get a more realistic playing experience for golf, tennis, or even baseball simulations.

Enter the Nintendo Wii with its unique take on motion-sensing control, which was swiftly followed by Sony's PlayStation 3, also boasting a similar technology. These gave rise to even better gameplay in that they extend the joystick experience.

However, some games use truly one-shot hardware. *SingStar*, for example, requires two microphones and an adapter that plug into the PlayStation 2. They are used to relay the player's voice to the machine, but are useless for any other game. It was a gamble that, five variations later, seems to have paid off. As has the decision to make a game reliant on four oversized buttons reminiscent of quiz show buzzers. Indeed, *Buzz*, now has several variations to it's name, and is another party, trivia quiz game that encourages participation of the whole family.

Then there is EyeToy, a camera-based motion-sensing game input device that has spawned various games based on its motion-capture technology. Again, while there are specific games that use it, EyeToy is useless for anything else.

Interestingly, there are a few exceptions—*Guitar Hero*, for example. The game is designed for a special controller (a guitar), but the player can equally use a standard analog controller to play, too. Of course, most people want the version with the guitar so they can "rock out," but making both versions equally accessible was probably a good design move.

Scoring

Players need some way to measure their success. The first-ever video game, written in 1966 and entitled *Space War!,* was based on a simple premise: kill or be killed. The arcade classic *Space Invaders* also borrowed on this premise, but added the new dimension of an incremental count of the number of alien invaders killed, bonuses collected, and a multiplier of this *score,* which was linked to the collateral damage inflicted by the bombs unleashed by these invaders.

The game also introduced the idea that the difficulty should increase once successive waves of aliens were vanquished. We take these key features for granted these days, but at the time, there was no real concept of terms such as a *high-score table* or a *perfect score*. Kudos is attached to a perfect number of points in *PacMan*, for example. Reaching the end of the game is not enough for true hardcore gamers; there is the additional goal of reaching that end while making zero mistakes.

On the other hand, there are situations in which a score is not realistic, or in which the success of the player is not measured by actual points, but by something else—such as *money* . . . money to purchase improvements to one's spacecraft, as in *Elite*, or more recently, money to customize race vehicles.

When a direct score is not in line with the game's style, genre, or general storyline, there needs to be another way for the player to gauge how well they have performed. Enter the *mission* concept.

Levels and Missions

Increasing difficulty levels can be coupled with a score-keeping system to add a different dimension, as discussed above. Recent games, such as *Soldier of Fortune,* revolve around completing tasks in order to fulfill missions. Points are not scored for killing enemies; rather, the player progresses simply by not being mercilessly slaughtered and not failing in certain tasks. Other games, such as *Quake,* do give a nominal score—time taken to complete a mission, number of enemies killed, or secret rooms found—but it is not an integral part of the game in the way that it is for other first-person shooters.

We shall look at equating levels, missions, and scoring later on in this book, in chapters that are dedicated to such matters, but for now it is enough to try and attach some kind of structure to the game. Try to imagine what is most in line with the game's genre and style, while also giving the player something concrete to aim for. This will ensure that the player feels that they are constantly achieving goals and gives them something to look forward to, thus increasing the chance that they will persevere to the end of the game.

Lives

Again, we step back in time to games like *Space Invaders* or *Defender*, which also removed the consequences of failure to a certain extent. The game begins with a nominal number of lives (three seemed to be the standard), much like the number of balls in the video game predecessor: the pinball machine. Each life (or ball) gave the player one chance to succeed (i.e., score as many points as possible).

Death decreased the number of lives and success granted extra lives, something that was definitely borrowed from the pinball era. When there were no lives left, it was "Game Over" and "Insert Coins to Continue," both in the video and pinball game industries. In the home console/PC era, "Insert Coins" is a meaningless proposition, hence the "infinite continue" concept was born, usually as an introductory level of difficulty.

The idea has been refined over the years in a number of ways. The first is the "savepoint"—a feature by which the player is returned to a certain moment in the game to continue from. Then there are "savegames," where the player is able to decide at which point a game should be saved, usually after defeating a particularly gnarly task, hard-to-overcome level boss, or when levels of armor and health are particularly high.

Armor and health are the final refinements to the *lives* concept. They are ways of extending the game experience; one can recover pieces of strategically placed armor, power-ups, weapons, or ammunition with which to defend oneself, or negate at least some of the effects of enemies' bullets. In some games, medical kits or food allow the player to replenish lost lives (energy), so that being shot is much less of a handicap than in the original video games, like *Space Invaders*, or *PacMan*.

The exact mix of these features is, again, a genre-based selection. Some will fit better than others, and it is up to the game designer to decide exactly how they need to be used. These features will also be coupled with the way in which the level, mission, or score structure of the game is organized, often to the point of foregoing certain features, such as automatic savepoints, in order to increase the overall difficulty of the game. This will let players boast to their fellow gamers, for example, that they completed the game in one session with savepoints off, over a period of three hours, and with armor and health restored to 100%. This appeals to players' competitive nature and is a sign that the game has, in itself, succeeded in garnering their favor.

Unlockables

Finally, there is the possibility to unlock features. This is a relatively new innovation and is particularly effective when a game is backed by a license holder, such as an automobile manufacturer that is offering their line of supercars for use in a racing game.

The theory is that if the player manages to excel at mastering the game, he should be rewarded by features that are not available to the casual player. This extends the game for casual players and, hopefully, converts them into hardcore gamers.

An interesting aside is the use of subgames in which players can unlock features of the main game by excelling at a specific task in a strictly condensed game universe. The Sega classic *Sonic the Hedgehog*, for example, had subgames that allowed the player to recover rings in order to gain an extra life. This style of approach gives the casual gamer another opportunity to extend their experience beyond simply scoring enough points to get extra life, while also encouraging hardcore gamers to get not only all of the standard goodies, but also all of the goodies offered in the subgames.

Summary

This chapter was designed to give the inexperienced video game designer a few pointers on how a typical video game is put together. It showed the various elements that make up a video game and the assets that are needed to convey the gaming experience to the player: sound, graphics, and textual elements.

In addition to these assets, we have also seen that there are some typical game styles that use them. Each specific genre or style goes hand in hand with a particular market, and it is very important that the designer knows in advance how the game is going to be sold. The idea behind the game is only the seed, and that seed grows into a product that mirrors the market and genre for which it is destined.

Some designers might look at this as being slightly cynical—that is, it might suggest that the same idea can be turned into a multitude of different games, depending on the whim of the publisher. To a certain extent this will be true; the publisher might intervene in the design of the game in order to make it more attractive to a target, lucrative audience. In such cases, the designer needs to decide how they are going to react. They have a choice—adapt or stand firm. Standing firm might actually mean that the publisher will drop the product because it doesn't "fit" with their specific needs. Perhaps the game has been so long in the design stage that the original market has disappeared or changed beyond the publisher's ability to retain the original idea.

Having a good design prepared in advance will help. If the story and textual samples are in place, this will also give the designer the confidence that they need to make sure that the publisher, once approached, will be more likely to remain with the project until it comes to fruition.

So, the perfect world view means that the designer needs to keep a finger on each of the elements that will make up their game. In reality, this is not going to be possible. A single person (even if they are the one that holds the vision) simply cannot be expected to deal with every possible angle.

The next chapter will show how the designer can rein in their responsibilities to the point that they are only overseeing and planning the project. In the beginning, this is all that will be needed. Details can be left to other, more-specialized people, such as graphic designers and the all-important programming staff.

References

[Mazzi02] Mazzi Binaisa, *Game On: The History and Culture of Videogames.* Laurence King Publishing, p. 45, 2002.

[Saltzman01] Saltzmann, M., Game *Design: Secrets of the Sages.* BradyGames, 2000.

[Saltzman02] Saltzmann, M., Game *Design: Secrets of the Sages.* BradyGames, p. 18, Year 2000.

[MICROSOFT01] Microsoft "Creators Club" founding statement, http://msdn2.microsoft.com/en-us/directx/Bb219592.aspx.

3 Video Game Design in Practice

In This Chapter

- Information Organization
- Planning
- Documentation

This chapter also avoids describing video game design proper, but is as vital as Chapter 1 and Chapter 2 for describing the parameters with which the video game project can be actually realized. Now granted, some of the topics covered in this chapter are not really going to instill a sense of excitement in even the most enthusiastic video game designer, but we shall try to convey this information in such a way that learning does not become a chore.

Many people believe that a good video game is simply the implementation of a great idea communicated by the designer to the engineer and shipped in a pretty box. In the *Pong* days, this might have been true, but designs have moved on since then at about the same pace as the technology that supports the designers' dreams. When post-*Pong* games were created, engineers drove the vehicle and put on their designer hat when game designs were needed.

By this we mean that the ideas behind the early games were simple, but the technology required to implement them was inaccessible to all but the engineers. High design was not required, and games could have simple rules; the machines were a miracle of engineering and the designs as simple as the instructions on the Atari *Pong* cabinets:

"Avoid missing ball for high score."

The initial conversation between Bushnell and Alcorn (designer and engineer, respectively), had it been recorded for posterity, might have gone something like this:

Designer: What I see is two players hitting a ball with paddles, batting it across an invisible net.

Engineer: When does the game end?

Designer: Give them three chances to miss the ball, and the one with the most number of hits wins the game. The best player gets the high score.

Engineer: How do we represent the paddles and the ball?

Designer: Hmm . . . three blocks in a vertical line for a paddle, and one floating block for the ball.

In the 70s this was akin to rocket science—real-time interaction between players and the machine, pitting players against each other or the machine, a high scorer (implying memory), and increasing difficulty levels that make it harder to score. You could fit the entire design on one page of paper, including all the rules, and the basic paddle and ball designs. There was probably more-formal documentation along the way—engineering documents, probably—but the Design Document for the game itself was probably not much more detailed than it was in the initial conversation.

This is pure conjecture, but it illustrates the point that arcade games in the early days used technology that was cutting-edge—not merely in programming circles, but with respect to all the elements, such as cabinet, controllers, screen, and sound system. Now the hardware technology that underpins video games is better understood.

Programming the hardware remains a complex and hard-to-understand-and-accomplish feat of ingenuity; but we probably understand a lot more about the actual hardware and the way it works than the early engineers did. This enables hardware manufacturers to put together excellent consoles, cabinets, and platforms for the game designers and programmers as well as provide more technical support than in the early days of video game creation.

There are still advances to be made, otherwise many research engineers would be out of a job. If you wanted to create, build, and sell a *Pong* machine these days, the only intellectual investment needed would be the game design. This goes for most designs, be it an arcade machine or a home console; the technology available now is more than capable of handling whatever the designers can throw at it.

This means that the success of a unit depends on the game design and not necessarily the technology that drives it. Like anything else, there are advantages and disadvantages in taking this approach. One key disadvantage is that those in the industry (publishers, for example) who want to do something new need a vast quantity of money to do it, and they have to make sure that the sales will justify the investment.

In other words, platforms are uniform, with known limitations and strengths. Game creators are invited to build games for particular consoles, rather than the other way around; game designers don't fit the console to a particular game. Any extensions to the hardware that enable a game require a suitably large investment, but games can be created within the existing known technology that, with good design, will sell to all owners of that technology.

As a brief aside, the cost of developing new technology is prohibitive enough that it becomes unfeasible to try to create the game first and the machine second. In the early days this was attempted, such as in the first-ever arcade game, *Computer Space*. Of course, we know that it was not a resounding success. *Pong* grew out of the necessity to find a game that would enable the manufacturers (the fledgling Atari) to recoup their investment.

Hence, despite the many games that are on the market, all are based on principles that are fairly similar. Console game systems (for the home entertainment industry) also share common hardware design principles, and the constant battle between vendors revolves not around the hardware, but on the games available for the platform.

For example, *Sonic the Hedgehog* was one of the principle selling points for the Sega Mega Drive (Genesis) system, and the rival was the SNES (Nintendo), with the key title, *Street Fighter II*. The two consoles had similar principles, different capabilities, but one could not have been said to be vastly superior to the other, except in the games that were available for them.

In the U.K., the two consoles were sold side by side, one package was *Sonic* on the Mega Drive, the other was the SNES with *SFII*. Many of the decisions made by would-be consumers revolved around *Sonic* versus *SFII*, as opposed to Sega versus Nintendo. The GameCube (again from Nintendo) owes a lot of sales to *Super Mario Sunshine*, while the Xbox (Microsoft) is largely thought to have not yet found its "key selling point" title (with the exception of *Halo*).

(From a development point of view, there is another great selling point. The Xbox and Xbox 360 are closer to PC technology than any other console platform.

This ought to make it easier to move from the development environment to the platform itself, and lead to better games.)

The Nintendo Wii has a unique controller as a great selling point, and consumers will probably buy the console for the sports-simulation options that it offers as much as for other applications of this new technology. The Wii promotional video makes excellent viewing, and highlights the "family and friends" social gaming that the natural-motion-sensing controller allows.

PlayStation 3 (Sony) also sports motion sensing, while the Xbox 360 (Microsoft) has (as of this writing) entered the current generation of console technology with better graphics, connectivity, developer support, and options list. Sadly, it has no motion-sensing controller, but with games such as *Project Gotham Racing,* which offer mind-bending, graphical realism, the Xbox 360 doesn't need motion-sensing right now.

All three platforms are standardized, and have their limitations and strengths. The game designer has few options for altering the hardware beyond the addition of unique plug-in controllers—microphones, cameras, and such. Keep in mind that the console owners have already made a substantial investment and do not want to pay an additional premium for games that need hundreds of dollars in additional investment just to play them, like *Tekki.*

In short, there are no more one-trick ponies. Consoles now do much more than play bat-and-ball games, and there is little profit margin in manufacturing single-shot game systems, despite the resurgence of plug-n-play games in the retro market. You have to choose a platform and make your game for it, rather than the other way around.

On the plus side, today's system technology makes it easier for would-be video game developers to create games. However, market competition also means that video game designers need to take special care to ensure that their designs result in efficient implementations of first-rate games.

Information Organization

Video game design will always result in a large amount of information. Even simple games, such as *Pong, Tetris,* or *Space Invaders,* are quite complex systems that have all manners of detailed nuggets that need to be written down and organized in a manner that makes them easy to absorb. Put another way, a video game is probably the most advanced form of real-time control system that programmers can create. It will test the skill of the programmer and designer, stretch the hardware platform, and be a challenge to implement *at all,* let alone on time and within a given budget.

All of the details involved in moving a bat around the screen, detecting when the player wants to move it and where to move it to, as well as keeping track of the score, game universe state, and position of game objects within it are pieces of information that need to be identified, cataloged, and written down.

This is important because a design needs to be complete, and missing details are easier to recognize by looking at the information set. It is impossible to expect one person, even the initial designer, to be able to retain every single little detail in his head and understand the whole system in such a way that the design will be complete in all aspects.

The game *Space Invaders*, for example, has many facets. The original design was for an arcade game, and the hardware was created for the sole purpose of supporting the game, itself. Therefore, the designers had to be aware of the screen dimensions, control system, height of the cabinet, and cost per game, *as well as* the gameplay mechanics, themselves. Their initial design outline probably focused on ensuring that, when placed in an arcade setting (bar, club, or student dorm), the game would give the player a sense of mastery as quickly as possible and *keep him coming back*, hopefully challenged to score more points or go further in the game the next time.

Video game developers will have different reasons for consulting this preproduction information, depending on their roles. Even when a game is the brainchild of a single person, he will look at the information from different angles, depending on whether he is checking the game design, feasibility, cost, or expected revenue. These factors will be different for arcade games, console games, or even mobile or Internet games, but all information needs to be fed into the design; it is necessary to make game design decisions. Bad information management will certainly reduce the chances for good (correct) decisions.

Information Trees

The human mind has difficulty coping with information in short-term memory. Numerous studies have tried to estimate what the optimum retention rate is. The accepted norm is that the average human mind can cope with about five pieces of discrete information, held and understood in short-term memory, at any one time. This means that the average video game designer will probably only be able to deal with five issues at once. (Of course, some of us might be able to focus on 7 to 10 discrete pieces of information any one time, but 5 is a safe average.)

We also organize information internally; we can "dig down" at will to discover new levels of complexity and push what we've already digested into long-term memory, a feat usually achieved by repetition. Familiarity bred over time also helps us retain the information that is needed.

Reading, rereading, tweaking, and working with the information will help ensure that it becomes cemented in long-term memory, increase the ability to focus on new information, and compare how it relates to other information in the system. In other words, new information can be held in short-term "focus" memory with longer-term "learned" information; and we can juggle between these memories in order to make the most optimal decisions.

Wonderful as the mind is, it sometimes messes up; pieces of information "fall out" and are forgotten, which is why we need to get as much information down on paper as fast as possible. Brainstorming is the best way to start. Write down everything that seems to be connected with *the idea* on a scrap of paper, electronic or otherwise, and worry about the organization of the information later.

When it comes to organizing the brainstormed information, a *tree* is a good way to create a map of the initial design. Because of the previously mentioned short-term memory capacity, this tree should have no more than five branches at each level. (Actually, it is more like the root system of a tree, since it is usually developed in a top-down fashion.) The kind of information that winds up in the tree depends on the game's specific genre. For a classic shoot-em-up, we might begin with something like the tree shown in Figure 3.1.

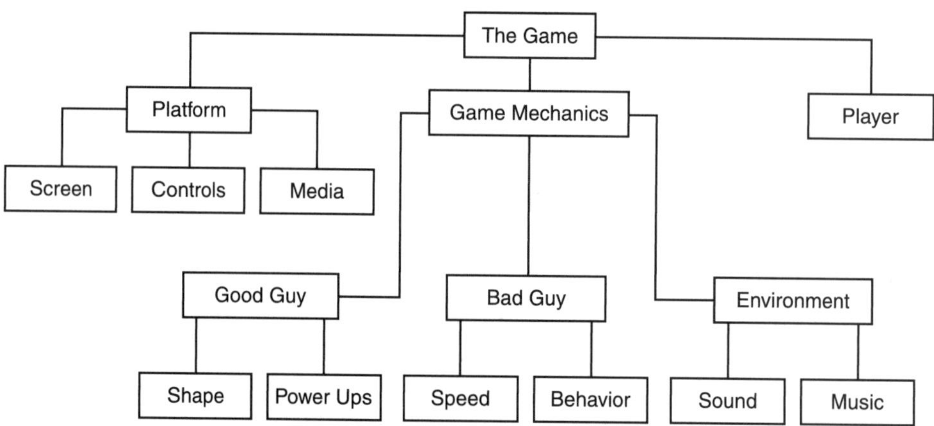

FIGURE 3.1 Simple information tree.

Of course, the information in Figure 3.1 is not complete by any means. It just illustrates how the initial idea can give rise to many different branches of information that otherwise would be impossible to focus on all at once. As each branch is developed, new offshoots/nodes will sprout and lead the designer down avenues that need development in order to gauge the scope of the whole design project.

The rules are simple: Each set of nodes should be related to the parent, and there should be no more than five nodes at any level of a given branch. Ideally, no branch should be deeper than five levels, either, which means that the designer will end up with a tree that should fit on a single page and contain no more than 5^5 items. This represents up to 3,125 separate pieces of information that need to be organized for the largest design that one person is capable of managing. We call this the "Rule of 5s."

Again, this is simply a guideline. Projects can be more or less complex, but the Rule of 5s in building the information tree at least gives us a good idea of the eventual complexity of the project. Now, a lot of the complexity could be eliminated simply by choosing a platform that is not constrained by arbitrary design considerations and ignoring the "Platform" branch. Similarly, we could ignore the "Player" completely if the game is not targeted to a specific market.

A good tool will serve the reader well in this kind of exercise. There are many brainstorming tools available under Open Source licenses and some commercial ones, too (see the Appendix).

The tool needs to be able to present information in two ways: as a "bubble cloud" of interrelated/interconnected items that can be expanded to include new concepts, and a tree view of the same information (something like an expanded table of contents). These two abilities make creating the tree easier, and also provide a formal layout that is easier to annotate and share with others.

INFORMATION NETWORKS

The Rule of 5s has an important aspect: We need to be able to follow a branch down through its sub-branches, and across each branch's nodes in order to see what the links between the nodes are, if any. This will enable us to create an *information network* that illustrates the tree as a whole and helps us to see if there is anything missing.

Unlike the tree, drawing the network requires a lot of patience and a big sheet of paper. The term "*network*" here is merely symbolic. The actual rendering of the information network will likely take the form of a table in which we try to associate each node with another node on a different branch.

To do this, we might start with the Speed of the Bad Guy in Figure 3.1, and decide that it is linked with the Music on the Environment branch. In other words, the Music being played is dependent on the Speed of the enemy (Bad Guy).

Think of the movie *Jaws*, for example. In it, the music is driven by the presence of the shark. Implementing that as a game idea would entail networking the position of the shark (with relation to the player character) to the music. It adds atmosphere and gives the player an audible clue as to what state the game universe is currently in.

We would not, however, link Bad Guy to Good Guy, or Platform::Media to Platform::Screen—for two reasons: One, it doesn't make sense; and two, we are not allowed to because they share the same immediate parent. Linking BadGuy::Behavior with GoodGuy::Shape may or may not make sense, and we are allowed to do it because the immediate parents are different.

As was mentioned, the network is probably only going to be symbolic, and the embodiment of these linked pieces of information will be a series of tables that associate nodes. However, there is a third option for using a structured brainstorming tool.

Hyperlinking allows us to create a document that is "clickable." In other words, the presentation and navigation of the information tree/network becomes easier to create and follow when using hyperlinked nodes, the backbone of the Web. Most structured brainstorming tools provide this option: export to HTML.

We can also create hyperlinked documents ourselves by either editing the HTML manually or using a word processor. The process remains the same. Identify two nodes in the tree that are linked by some kind of relationship and create a text link that explains that relationship.

The resulting hypertext document has its good points and bad points. A good point is that it's easy to navigate. A bad point is that it cannot be printed out without losing the key reason for hyperlinks in the first place—to have a dynamic document. This makes the hypertext document difficult to share. So, the tables of relationships between nodes will still probably be necessary.

Information-Naming Conventions

An important ingredient in managing and organizing information is the way that we refer to individual pieces of data. They should have names that identify them as uniquely as possible, without having more than five parts. Three parts is probably closer to the ideal, but if we have adhered to the Rule of 5s and have 3,125 pieces of information, then five parts will allow us to uniquely identify each piece of information as well as its position in the tree hierarchy. This system will enable the designer to keep in check all the document's pieces of information and eliminate the possibility of confusion. The actual convention chosen is not necessarily as important as ensuring that it exists and is adhered to as strictly as possible.

Granularity

The granularity of the design refers to the level of detail that is needed to express concepts that the designer feels are important. Some information is not as important from a design point of view. For example, the screen width of the chosen platform might not be relevant in the design stage—only in the implementation stage.

However, the granularity will also change depending on the target audience. For some members of the design team, a piece of information that contains the screen width might be vital to their decisions. For example, if the graphic artist is trying to work out how big to make the sprites, it will be necessary to know how wide and high the screen is, as well as how many sprites are expected to be on the screen at once.

On the other hand, a coarser-grain representation of the information will be needed if the document is being reviewed by a possible investor. He might not care how the developer intends to use the screen real estate, but will be very interested in how the game mechanics make it stand out from the crowd so that the game/studio will bring in a return on his investment.

So, granularity is about the representation of the information network or tree, rather than about information collection. Of course, the finer the information store's granularity, the more pieces of information will need to be managed. It might be more appropriate to state that a screen has certain properties, and leave it at that level of granularity, rather than have the screen width represented by its own piece of information.

Planning

A large studio can afford to hire people whose sole role in the project is to plan it, and who have access to the tools and techniques needed to create detailed plans. More important, these planning professionals have the mindset that enables them to not only perform a competent job, but they actually enjoy it—and a job is much more likely to be done well if the person enjoys doing it.

Smaller, independent projects require planning, but this is often accomplished without employing additional staff or purchasing software. It is up to the (often meager) resources of the team and its members to accurately plan and direct the project from design through to the product's release.

The independent game developer, working on his own and creating a game for sale on the Internet or though a channel such as Xbox Live Arcade, will need to direct his project, or the way will quickly be lost. Part of the problem is that creating a video game is so complex that it is easy to get sidetracked into tasks that do not directly advance the project. To avoid this, it is necessary to plan the project's resources and actions around what is to be achieved, when it will be achieved, and by whom. This is standard practice for any project, of course, but tighter control needs to be applied in the case of software design/implementation—and doubly so for real-time systems, including video games.

The Team

Before considering how and where the project will go, it will usually be necessary to establish a team with responsibilities for each aspect of the project, and someone who is nominally in charge—that is, not someone who is "above" the other team members, simply a coordinator who will ensure that the vision is taken from plan to completion. Often, the coordinator is the person who had the initial idea; he will call upon others who have the necessary skills (which he doesn't possess) to carry out the execution of various phases of the project.

The strength of having a coordinator, rather than adopting the usual hire-and-fire hard-line project manager, is that it increases the sense of team spirit. The project manager, whoever it is, will have the last word and might not be the person holding the original vision. This person will, however, need to be able to take a strong line with the team, as he will be responsible for keeping to financial and time constraints.

A one-person video game studio operating out of a simple office will often need to outsource certain aspects of the implementation. Someone will need to be in the position of knowing who is doing what at any given moment in time. Small studios need to make sure that the teams are correctly led, and larger studios with more ambitious projects will likely have many such points of coordination within the project team. It is important to view the coordinator as not simply another cog in the machine—everyone has equal responsibility and seniority in independent game production.

In a commercial team, the work is divided into areas of responsibility: artists, musicians, audio designers, programmers, those who script the various dynamic parts of the game, and the all-important level designers—and each may also contribute to different parts of the final product.

A project that uses existing, well-understood technology will probably consist of a prewritten engine that has several thousands of lines of code to be maintained, extended, and implemented—and probably some scripts that, themselves, might account for up to 80% of the game mechanics, supporting artwork, and audio. If you are lucky, a minimal team will consist of one or more people who perform the functions that maintain each of these separate departments, but there must still be a generic planning/management role.

The reality is that for many projects that are either the first for a game studio or represent a project that is purely independent, these roles will be spread among multiple people. That is, a team might consist of a programmer, an artist, a game designer, and one member who takes overall responsibility for planning and project execution.

Of course, it is also possible that the game will require no underlying engine modifications, and the entire game can be implemented using scripts. A minimal team, therefore, will consist of two or three people: the programmer and game designer, and the artist—although if you are a programmer with artistic tendencies, even those two roles can be merged, thus reducing the team to one person. The upside of this, perhaps, is that you only have yourself to blame if the project fails. An obvious downside is that there is no one else to bounce ideas around with.

Usually, a team will revolve around the design, programming, and core creative staffs, and each of these staffs should have a head (coordinator). This model will scale efficiently, especially if larger projects are treated in terms of subprojects of the main effort, with the project coordinator at the top.

From the perspective of video game design, it is important to understand that the team should be in place even before the overall Design Document is fully completed. This will help in the latter stages of the design, since having people with different skills to draw upon will keep the design in line with the technology being used to create and implement the game, even if that goal seems a long way down the line.

The initial team will include "the person with the idea"—someone not badgered by the requirements of others, and who has the flexibility to organize what has to be done when. It can be pretty lonely being the only one on a project, but if you skimp on planning (even in a one-person team), the project will likely never see the light of day. So if the reader is just starting out, take pencil and paper to hand—the next section is quite vital.

Timing

The most important aspect of a design plan is the project's timeline; if there are no other external factors to consider, such as publishers' desires, the project leader has to establish some guidelines for the project's timeframe so that the team members do not lose track of the final destination.

Part of defining the timeline is knowing what the series of steps are that will lead the project to completion; this will depend largely on whether the design is destined for another game-development house, or whether the game is going to be written by the designer, himself. Without a concrete timeline, there is no way to measure progress (or the lack of it). It gives us a way to gauge how the project is going (or not going). Good intentions are simply not enough.

First Steps

So, grab a spreadsheet program or (if you are lucky enough to have Microsoft Office 2007) Microsoft Project or its equivalent. List all the steps are that needed in order to put together the project, in qualitative terms and from beginning to end.

Maybe you will dedicate a month of spare time to rounding out the idea on paper so you can try to convey (to a team member or publisher) what it will be like to play the game.

Then you will need to refine the idea, add documentation, and try to round out the ideas that came to mind along the way—and create your timeline. Since it is your idea, this should be quite easy. At this point, it is not important that these time milestones be accurate; what is important is that a timeline exists that can be followed.

For example, when this book was written, the author had a good idea of what the deadlines were—and he also needed to know if he was about to miss one. The book had a spreadsheet that was used to monitor the progress of each chapter—broken down in pages, number of words, and parts complete—and that chapter's relation to the book as a whole. This organizes the mind and serves as an early warning system.

An early warning system is important; writing a book and designing a game are similar projects, and the human mind has a tendency to jump from one topic to another. It gets bored if it has to concentrate on one topic for too long. There is also the temptation to do the interesting tasks first and neglect the milestones for less-entertaining work, leaving them short on the attention that they deserve/require.

The book-game parallel also illustrates another aspect of game design: The author is alone in the first stages of creating the book. Later on, the book's publisher will likely add editors, technical reviewers, designers, layout artists, and so forth, and take over managing the project to the final production of the book. For a video game designer, the same path might be followed. The initial idea will take on an independent life once others become involved, and the designer may have to decide whether to continue serving as head of the entire effort, or farm the project out and relinquish some control.

The fact remains, however, that planning is needed to make sure that the design is correctly created and implemented. Whether this plan is mandated by a publisher with substantial investment in the game or book, or whether it is self-imposed, we need to make sure that a plan exists to follow, and we know what to do if we can no longer honor that plan.

Planning for Failure

Assuming that we adopt a three-stage approach to video game design—the idea, design, and development guide—with appropriate timelines of say, one month, three months, and five months, respectively, we need to consider what to do if the complexity of the original idea grows and the original timeline becomes unachievable. Due to circumstances beyond the designer's control, the project might suddenly look doomed.

This is not a bad thing; it just means that under-estimation has led to the project falling behind the original target milestones. It happens all the time, and this is one of the key reasons for measuring the actual time that tasks take, compared to the expected time. It lets us spot when the venture is heading toward failure.

Clearly, it is better to recognize this sooner rather than later so that steps can be taken to adjust the original plan in a way that the milestones become realistic. Some designers become agitated at the prospect of "failure"—which is a bad choice of words, because it demoralizes the team, even if it is just a team of one.

So, it is important to plan for failure. (This is not the same as planning to fail, since no one in their right mind would plan a project that had no chance of success.) There needs to be a recognition that failure is possible, and that we should try to safeguard against it as much as possible.

One great way to build safeguards into the planning process, is to over-budget. For example, we can over-budget time constraints. Unlike money, time is finite, and is lost once it is spent. The few moments that you, the reader, spent reading the previous paragraph are gone forever. Money can always be replaced. In the video game industry, there is usually money to be found for the best ideas, but time is less easy to come by.

Creative time, programming time, design time, and promotion time cannot be replaced; often, missing a certain milestone can have consequences. If we miss a promotion milestone—failing to have a demo ready by its designated date, for example—the consequences could be disastrous and have an impact on the amount of confidence that the investors have, even to the withdrawal of funds.

Adding 50% to initial timelines will ensure that there is a margin for error. It is also an accepted fact in development circles that programmers have no concept of time; they routinely underestimate the time required to complete a project. Doubling the estimated effort is not unreasonable and will give you a safeguard.

For less-critical team members (for whom the creation of a video game is less of a business than it is a hobby), planning can be a little looser. However, they still need to be sure of where they are going and how long it will take; otherwise, they run the risk of never getting there.

As the project takes shape and gains momentum, the timeline might start to take on an importance over and above the original idea. The moment that the designer shares the idea with someone else (be it professionally or informally), he will start to realize that he has a responsibility to complete the project. If plans were not structured enough in the beginning, then suddenly it might start to look as if that responsibility is being shortchanged, and the designer is not taking the project seriously. At this stage, despite not having built in any safeguards, we can still do some *replanning* to try to address any issues.

Replanning

If the original plan looks hopelessly unachievable, then it is time to replan, and take into account the work done to date and the actual percentage completed. For example (using arbitrary figures), take 25% away from the estimated completion level and add 50% more time to the project phase under examination. It is up to the designer to assign percentages that, using actual progress and experience as a guide, lead to a meaningful and realistic new plan.

In Figure 3.2, we see an alternate, formal approach to replanning a specific project phase. It is applicable in a variety of different circumstances and will work for any project that requires measuring elapsed time, and each segment's success or failure, and planning for eventual completion.

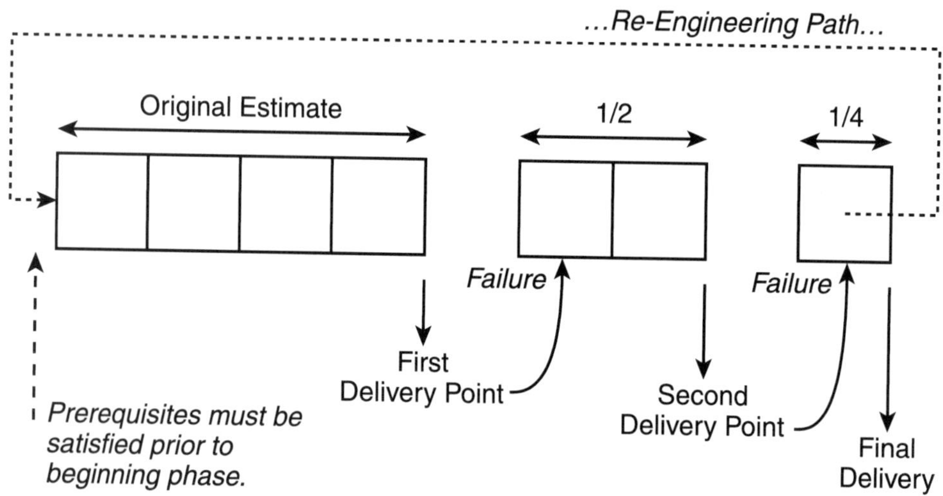

FIGURE 3.2 Replanning guide.

The guide in Figure 3.2 has three "Delivery Points," or chances to arrive at the successful delivery of the completed work. Should the Final Delivery not be achieved, then it is assumed that the piece of work needs to be re-engineered. In the process, we have added 75% more time than originally budgeted to the overall timeline.

One of the reasons that the process might fail is that the project's prerequisites have not been correctly identified and created. These might be the result of another phase, which means that we not only need to re-engineer the current phase plan, but also the previous phase; suddenly the plan is in disarray. It is important to realize that a project might need to be 'done twice' before the result is perfect.

Let's be realistic for a moment. If you are lucky enough to snag a publisher and be involved with the planning *at all*, then remember that the publisher has a deadline. The publisher of this book, for example, has a deadline to stick to, and the author has to respect that. There is very little scope for replanning in either industry.

Dealing with this is simple enough in theory—plan for failure. Make a plan that allows for replanning in the first place. If it turns out we don't need to replan, then that's great; maybe we can use the time to make the product even better. If not, then at least we have that buffer, which is far preferable to turning out something that is thrown together and below par. The paying public *will* notice.

This is the dry theory behind planning and timelining a project. If it all seems too complex or "overkill" for your project, then focus on only the relevant parts. Take away from this section as much or as little as fits your immediate needs; this information is provided as an insight into some of the techniques that have worked in the past and will work in the future. Let us now move on and see what we are actually trying to plan *for*.

DOCUMENTATION

If our discussion on the details of planning seemed at first a bit dry, at least it had the benefit of being vaguely entertaining in terms of creating a visionary team, using a spreadsheet to create a nice project plan, and talking about resources and money. All of these issues are interesting and game-related.

Documentation—writing it, reading and reviewing it, and formatting it—can also hold all the fascination of watching grass grow. Of course, some people (like botanists) enjoy watching grass grow. This is not meant to sound sarcastic. In the same way that grass-growing rates are central to lawn management, documentation is central to designing, developing, and selling games—and *selling* is essential if the developers expect to get the game professionally published and make money in the traditional markets. There is substantial money to be made through electronic distribution, but it does not pay to neglect the fact that *most* people still prefer to buy a boxed product.

In the end, like the biologist and his grass, the development team has to find one person who has enthusiasm for writing documentation, coupled with coherent writing skills. This person will be nominally in charge of documenting the project—likely the person with the widest skill range; they will need to understand everything from the technical aspects to the artwork and sound.

Although game designers can be used to document the work in progress, they will need to have the correct skill sets to carry it through. The documentation in question here is the actual development documents that trace the realization of the designer's original dream. A good writer-designer-developer will be able to create those documents that will make reworking or fixing errors that much easier.

While this person may or may not actually write all of the documentation, he will at least be able to rewrite the rantings of hyperactive developers and generally ensure that the whole package retains the same tone. Writing coherently is a skill that should not be wasted; a good technical writer can organize and distill mounds of disconnected information into a coherent whole.

Programmers might not create coherent development documents. Development documents are necessary to share information both with the designers and with programmers going back over pieces of the game already created, and trying to fix, adjust, or enhance them.

Everyone will benefit from the all-important, all-encompassing, and entirely necessary *Design Document.* College students who have taken programming, software engineering, or even game-development courses will already have standard course outlines and plenty of notes to go with them.

Even though it's great that the academia are attempting to lock horns with the real world over these issues, you should never forget that these courses will try to be all things to all people, in all situations. Without forgetting what has been learned, because it is extremely useful, when you hit the ground (running to keep up), the rules tend to get a little bent.

The practice rarely, if ever, matches up with the theory. The theory is like a pen knife: It contains everything from toothpicks to that special tool for getting stones out of horses hooves. In practice, we usually just want to cut something up. In the same way, there will always be a need for a multipurpose software design course, because some people will end up needing some of the more esoteric concepts.

The same goes for video game design; we need a usable Design Document (outline with notes) with which to base the implementation of our game. The game-design process is complex enough without over-designing it, so we need a workable, practical template.

Enter The Oracle. Hosted by God Games (Gathering of Developers). The Oracle was a forum where industry hopefuls asked questions that were answered by industry experts who actually produced games—practical answers to practical questions on game design and development.

Among other key resources, The Oracle also posted what it called a Standard Design Document Form. This was an attempt to reconcile the perfect-world theory (taught in college) with the high-pace, cutting-edge industry where 18- to 20-hour days merely result in the impression that there is *never* enough time to actually develop a dream.

The Standard Design Document offered by The Oracle was complete and worthwhile to experiment with. Sadly, the site is no longer in existence, the developer having been taken over in the meantime. So, what follows is derived from the original and stands on its own as a (hopefully) useful update of what was an excellent attempt to standardize a nonstandard process.

It is especially important if a document is needed to pitch an idea to a publisher, without investing too much money into the proposed game. Usually the document will be created before going to a sponsor for financial help. Even if this is not required, going through the motions will help you get a better idea of what is on the table, give you a better starting point when the actual development begins, and also let the sponsor know that you are serious about the project.

Before we take a look at the document itself, it is worth noting the observations of Luke Ahearn:

> "For the most part, the game design should be done on paper first, but there are many benefits to doing functional prototypes first. . . . With so many game engines available and the similarities among technologies, obtaining and using the technology to create a functioning demo is a very doable goal." [Alhern01]

So, document first, unless the technology is available to play around with a prototype of the ideas. The important point to note is that, prototype aside, the document comes first, even if it is not as formally structured as the one we are about to examine. Even a text file with basic ideas and background is better than nothing.

The Treatment

The original creator of the standard design document, Drew Haworth (Terminal Reality, Inc.), breaks the task down into three pieces. The first is the *Treatment,* which covers everything in a bird's-eye view. The Treatment is designed to capture the imagination of the reader, such as a team member or possible team member, publisher, or just an interested third party visiting the game's Web site.

There are three guidelines for the Treatment, which amount to the following: short, broad, and focused. There are also 13 elements of the Design Document (most of which were covered in Chapter 2 in an informal way). We should add a one-sentence hook to the list of document elements, since this will help capture the reader's attention. Here is the list of elements in full, with comments, in italic:

1. Game title . . . *and hook phrase.*
   The title and hook need to capture the reader's attention immediately.
2. Game genre.
   Discussed in Chapter 2, choose wisely; it should be either an existing big-selling genre, or a new one that comes with its own challenges, but which offers the possibility that your project will be unique.

3. Brief story description.
   Important in laying out the game universe, it also spells out interesting features to attract potential players' attention to the game.
4. If applicable, main character or units description (including general actions).
   Remember Tetris? How can the game's characters be described? Take another look at the hook phrase for clues.
5. Brief description of settings and scenarios.
   Depending on the genre, this may or may not be linked to the story and hook phrase. In role-playing games, these links are unavoidable.
6. Overall look of the game.
   Again, this will probably be linked with the genre.
7. General computer AI description.
   Ranges from simple, physics-based Pong*-style AI to complex RPG interactions.*
8. Minimum recommended hardware specifications.
   The game might become tied to the engine being used. This should be checked before development begins. Bear in mind that over*-specification may limit platforms, but* under*-specification may limit the game.*
9. List of necessary development tools.
   For commercial engines, these are well defined.
10. List of team members and skills required to produce game.
    Independent developers have less choice in this; usually the team will be comprised of like-minded people who share "the dream." Attracting more team members may also prove difficult with little or no money budgeted for wages.
11. Estimated completion/release date.
    Again, independent teams are at a slight disadvantage. For many team members, the game will take a back seat to their day jobs.
12. Similarities to other genre games.
    Unless, of course, this game represents a new genre, pointing out similarities to existing games may prove dispensable.
13. Standout features—that is, "competition killers."
    See 12, and also the hook phrase. In the world of independent game design, this might not matter.

Although this list was targeted toward seeking a contract from a publisher, and hopefully you will enter the commercial area with a hit game, most designers will try to realize their dreams without commercial backing. But in any event, a list similar to the one provided will help to give the project focus.

Consider the following Design Document for a new fictional game. Read through the document, and see if you can relate it to any games you might have played:

Text Invasion

Shoot the marauding aliens while they try to bomb your cities.

"Text Invasion" is a classic 2D shoot-em-up, with a top-down non-scrolling view point, where alien ships drop bombs on the players' cities. The player has to shoot back, whilst avoiding being destroyed by the attacking craft, using weapons that can be upgraded by collecting power-ups.

The player controls a simple ship, which can be expanded with power-ups, and fires directly up the screen at the attackers. Various weapons can be employed, ranging from simple bullet style, through to one shot lasers and smart bombs.

The game is cunningly rendered in ASCII characters, which makes it ideal for lesser platforms, such as mobile devices. The retro look is in line with recent re-releases of hit games from the past. Keyboard support is restricted to the number keypad, which also makes porting to mobile devices (including telephones) an easy prospect.

The level structure relies more on increasing the speed of descent of the invaders, as well as an increase in the frequency of bombs that fall from them. There is rudimentary AI, based around the ability of the aliens to drop their bombs around the immediate vicinity of the player. In addition, they are moving, usually away from the bullets fired by the player, however, they retain an entirely predictable movement from side to side.

The development can be easily handled by a small team, due to the simplistic, ASCII-based artwork, which also reduces the hardware requirements, and required development tools. Naturally, with this reduced complexity, the project timeline to completion is similarly reduced.

Being a retro product, there is very little competition on the market, however, there are several features which make it stand out from the crowd, especially the classic *Space Invaders* game around which it is based. One such feature is the availability of power-ups, which extend the players' firepower.

Even without playing the game, would its description convince you to buy? Or, as a publisher, would you consider investing your money to put it on the shelves for the masses? If the answer is "yes," then why? If the answer is "no," then why not? What is wrong with the *document,* itself (not the actual game idea)? If these questions can be answered, then the you, as a game designer, have learned something. Granted, our opinions on what does and doesn't work in a game Treatment is entirely subjective; different people will look for different things, and ideas are very often presented to several publishers.

The Treatment makes sure that we can present the key features of the game succinctly—a check that it is as good as we think it is. It is a review of the game concept, how it looks and feels, when it will be ready, and what sets it apart from every other game in a similar genre.

Now we are ready to create the game's actual foundation: the Design Document. Keep in mind that this is a book about design, not development, but that the two worlds interact frequently; they are interconnected by the need to share information constantly and consistently.

The Design Document is just a starting point; all manner of influences from outside the designer's own sphere of influence may cause the design to change through the development process. So, the interaction between the design and development tasks will be reasonably high throughout the development of the game and had better have a good foundation upon which to build.

The Design Document

This is the second section of the previously mentioned Oracle Standard Design Document Form. What is presented here might seem a little sparse and watered down, because the original document was overkill for a small team or the individual designer. On the other hand, if you are going to try for a commercial game your first time out the gate, then treat the following as a guideline, and try to encompass as much of the game concept as possible when overhauling it for presentation to a publisher. So, advice aside, we shall proceed:

A. Overview/Story

This is where you let your creative inner self take over. Describe the game universe, the style, the plot, ambiance, and any artwork that has already been put together. Capture the essence of the game, like in a movie trailer.

B. Characters/Units

Put down the background stories for all the principle characters—their likes and dislikes, how they react to their place in the game universe, and what kinds of abilities they have, along with how these affect their dealings with each other and the rest of the universe. The background, nonplayer characters also need to be placed in the general context of the game universe, as well as the various weapon types that can be found within it.

C. Level Description

The game's universe and mechanics need to be broken down into pieces that can be described using a minimum of words. These become levels. Each level has a description; and some may need a name, an immediate environment, whether there is a backdrop, or a foreground. Maps, if they are needed, should also be included, along with the stated goal of the level. (Of course, some of these will not be needed. It would be hard to actually name Pac-Man *levels.)*

Along with this information, we also need to know what the music style will be, if it changes, how it relates to the central story, and what characters and enemies occupy each level. Any items that are used to increase the power of the player character also need to be listed, along with any accompanying sound effects.

Some games will need more detail than this, others will require less. The key is to try and define the general game idea in the terms of these three issues. This Design Document is the bare, minimum description of what the game is about. Combined with the Treatment, it should be a complete description of the game and the experience it will offer.

However, this is only a starting point. The Official Design Document (see Chapter 13) extends each section with subsections; the designer can refine it as necessary for use in a real project.

THE SCHEDULE

Finally, the design needs a place reserved for the schedule. When we discussed planning in this chapter, looked at how the project can be planned in a qualitative way. The scheduling part of the Design Document attempts to make these plans more concrete.

The schedule presented here is a watered-down version, because a perfectly planned project requires many resources available only to commercial ventures, but, it is necessary when attracting team members to know what kind of commitment they are going to be making. They, too, need to be able to measure the project's progress.

If you set yourself up to design a game with the expectation that it will be developed "at some time in the future," you will be tempted to get on with it and abandon attempts at rigidly scheduling the work. Besides being a good habit to get into, accurate scheduling will also avoid the project's death due to overburdening. Scheduling and planning will help the intrepid designer keep everything in perspective and achievable.

1. Technological development milestones.
   Traditionally, this allows a substantial amount of time for actually creating the engine and tools. Of course, when using commercial engines, we can reduce this to a bare minimum. However, two things always need to do be done: Look at how long it will take to implement the gameplay mechanics; and see if an engine update is scheduled and whether we need to apply it.

2. Art and nontechnical content development milestones.
   Actually, this needs to be worked in with the previous schedule such that the artwork is ready when the programmers need it. Otherwise, there will be bottlenecks. A guide for the indie developer: Have the artwork and models ready before development begins. Lone designers still need to have a handle on this, even if it is simple, ASCII artwork.

In the original Design Document, Drew Haworth assigns real values to these milestone points—one year for the engine and another for the game proper, along with 8 to 10 months for each technological addition, with the art and other nontechnical aspects ready by the end of the first year. Following these guidelines, using a commercial engine could potentially save a whole year of development work.

Again, this loose description is a placeholder for the more-detailed planning and scheduling points included in the Official Design Document (see Chapter 13). Milestones help us know where we are and where we need to go.

Documentation Tricks and Techniques

The method described in the previous section will work in most situations, but the rigidity might not appeal to many game designers or developers. At the end of the day, independent game designers just want to turn their idea into a game and the game into money (which is also sometimes optional; imagine asking id Software how much they had *planned* to make out of *Wolfenstein3D* or *DOOM* at the start of these projects).

By the same token, there are some tricks that can usefully serve an independent team—especially a team that is geographically diverse. The Internet is a wonderful medium for getting a top-quality team together; it puts people in touch with each other who would otherwise never have the opportunity to meet.

The chance that your home town has enough talent to start a successful game-production studio is fairly remote, unless you are lucky enough to live in New York or another large metropolis. Even then, what is the chance of finding that one in several million people who can share your vision?

Unfortunately, you will probably find that your dream team is composed of a designer from the U.S., a graphic artist from Australia, a couple of top-notch programmers from India, and a systems analyst from Europe. This poses a few interesting questions. One thing is for sure; they most likely have day jobs and are working on the project during their free time. Telephone conferences are probably out of the question, especially considering the different time zones.

Peer Review

Enter a technique called "Game Design Peer Review." This is a deceptively simple concept that can be executed in just a few stages. First, get the team together. The team can be either local or remote. This technique will work whether everyone is sitting in the same room or if they're located on separate corners of the planet (though tasks will be completed faster if everyone is in the same place at the same time).

With the team set up, the coordinator should draw up a simple text document that has an outline of the original vision; or, if the coordinator is not the person who started the machinery in motion, then the person with the original dream should create the document. This document needs to have the sections A, B, and C, as noted in the Design Document section of this chapter.

Next, make a list of all the people in the team. This list will include everyone and their proposed areas of responsibility. Cut the list into entries, shake them up so the names are in random order, and paste the list to the beginning of the document under the heading "Distribution List." Locate the entry for the author's name, place the author at the end of the list, and send it to the first person on the list.

When each person receives the list, he has two duties. First, take his own name and put it at the end of the list, in the manner of a chain letter. Second, review the entire document, add entries if necessary under each of the sections (and initial the additions), but remove nothing. (Admittedly, a certain level of trust must exist in those entering information, that nothing will be deleted; but the team member may make entries indicating that something, in his opinion, should be removed, and why.)

Once edited to his satisfaction, the team member sends the entire document to the person who is now at the head of the list. In this way, everybody gets involved with the design process, which (aside from massaging the collective team ego) makes for a complete view and ensures that no ground-breaking ideas are missed. The result is a living document that can be edited until the team leader is satisfied that it represents an achievable, yet sufficiently diverse goal.

There are a few pitfalls. The first is, to avoid a document that stalls because one member takes weeks to forward it; there should be a time limit placed on the exercise. This can be as much a problem with a local team as it is with a remote one. The project leader needs to have the authority to step in and kickstart the process if one member is taking too long to record his views.

For this reason, some team leaders may wish to send the Review out to everyone at once and expect them to reply within, say, a week. The downside to this is that it misses the *Peer Review* aspect, which is the core strength of the exercise. Either way might not work for every team, but it represents a very good start and cures the "blank page" syndrome, which typically makes any documentation difficult to start. Finally, the actual Treatment can be attempted, and with a fuller view than any one person working alone could ever hope to produce.

Summary

The book started on an informal, theoretical, and easy-to-read note. This chapter has, inevitably, been a little more formal. The topics are not very far up on the budding video game designer's list of priorities, and might be considered boring—but they are necessary. At the very least, some nuggets of information presented here will hopefully be useful to the general game design. If only two or three of the sections apply to and help the reader, then this chapter has been worthwhile.

It also gives a good idea of how video games are designed in the real world, and what tricks and techniques have been successfully applied over the years by the best game designers. For those who believe that the way to design a video game is to write about the idea and then run off and make a best-selling game, this chapter will probably have been a bit of an eye-opener. The industry reflects a relaxed, *laissez-faire* image of software creation. Not so. Hopefully that myth has been shattered. Success can only be achieved if the design is well organized.

The industry—through various mediums, such as the Garage Games Web site, journals like *Game Developer Magazine*, and many newsgroups dedicated to the art of creating coherent and useful game Design Documents—highlights the fact that too many people pay mere lip-service to the topic of organization. It is important not to view video game design as just another "sexy" industry; hard work is sometimes required. In short, there are three main aspects to real-life video game design as either a hobby or profession:

- Information organization
- Planning the design documentation
- Writing good design documentation

Without all three aspects, the project will just be a collection of (possibly great) ideas. Even simple games have their unique aspects, but there are probably thousands of "the best game around" that never make it beyond the designer's imagination for lack of a proper Design Document.

References

[Alhern01] Luke Ahearn, *Designing 3D Games That Sell.* Charles River Media, 2001: p. 114.

4 Platforms and Technologies

In This Chapter

- Platforms
- The Design Platform
- Technologies
- Special Cases

Now that we know how to shape our idea into a video game design, and how to plan and execute it, one small concern is left: the platform. Is it going to be an arcade game, a console game, or do we lever the power of the personal computer? Will it be aimed at the handheld or the mobile (telephone) market either now or in the future? Is it a single- or multiplayer game?

Does our game need special controllers—such as motion-gesture technology, microphones, or a little TV camera—and does these limit the platforms that are suitable? Above all, is there enough support to develop the current state of our game for a closed platform (console), or do we need to go with an open platform, like the PC, to generate some income and valuable industry kudos?

These are all questions that need to be answered before development begins—preferably addressed before the design phase. The game genre will dictate the platform choice to a certain extent, and the platform choice, in turn, will have a direct effect on the sound and graphics that the game will be able to take advantage of, so it is an important decision. There are also nontechnical considerations, such as marketability and the all-important sales value of the platform choice. This chapter is designed to ensure that the budding video game designer makes the right decisions.

After all, the designer has a vision that might or might not align with a specific platform. Consider, for example, the failed *Computer Space,* or the Odyssey machine. They failed because the designers did not properly take into account the effect that platforms have on the marketability of a product. (Imagine, if the creators of *Spacewar!* had tried to convince customers that $120,000 was a small price to pay in order to play a great game in the comfort of their own homes, they would have been laughed at.) Magnavox failed to recognize that their Odyssey machine was overpriced with respect to the games that could be played on it.

These days, single-game machines are still around, usually cheap gizmos that are either given away or sold to the pre-teen age group. Recently, there have also been some retro releases of classic Sega games, devices that plug directly into the television and come loaded with one or two vintage games.

The purpose of this chapter is to help the reader determine what effect the platform choice will have on his game design, and how the game design might dictate the platform choice. Economic realities will also need to be taken into consideration. For example, basing a game on the Nintendo platform is such an expensive and complicated process, many start-ups would not be able to afford to embark on such a project.

We shall, as always, make references to history and speculate on the future, where relevant, in an attempt to help the reader make an effective choice concerning the target platform for his game idea. Some games naturally lend themselves to a certain platform—there is a synergy between the platform and game. For example, inexpensive devices are the perfect platform for games that use popular cartoon characters aimed at the pre-teenage market, but the synergies can also be more subtle. In many cases, it may be obvious to the designer that the game requires features that are only available on one or two platforms.

Apparently, *Blinx The Timesweeper* used the hard drive of the Xbox to provide time-manipulation effects, when hard drives were not standard console add-ons. Some puzzles in *Blinx* were solvable only because the player can be in two places at the same time. The hard drive was instrumental in this, allowing the game to record up to *x* seconds of the player's actions. (In case the reader is wondering about the success of this particular game, the answer is: negligible. By and large, *Blinx* did not deliver on the advertising hype that indicated only the Xbox provided technology to support innovative gameplay.) The gameplay, itself, was innovative and enjoyable, but unfortunately, *Blinx* did not meet with universal acclaim, despite the innovative use of the Xbox hard drive.

Platform manufacturers took note, and hard drives are now standard console add-ons, along with wireless controllers and network connections. More recently, motion-sensing controllers have also been added, and most consoles have games that ship with modified controllers—from *Singstar's* microphones to *Guitar Hero's* guitar, and the *Tekki* super-controller.

The platform choice is a difficult one, indeed. Publishers also have a say, and if you sell your game to a publisher that favors a specific platform, it will be hard to get the publisher to change that. So, if you are choosing a platform for hardware reasons (internal or external), then you will limit the publishers that you might want to present the game design to.

PLATFORMS

In the video game industry, there are many different kinds of platforms, each with their own capabilities and limitations. Every platform has a reason for their individual technology, which is sometimes a trade-off between nontechnical aspects (such as portability, as in mobile gaming devices) and price (like in the console market). Sometimes manufacturers simply want to release a new technology that is so perfectly engineered, it will be irresistible to the gamer, such as in the arcade cabinet market.

Regarding arcade cabinets, we have already discussed the decline of the arcade industry. Portable, high-quality, multigame devices became more common as the console market expanded into almost every household. The point that has not been made explicitly is that arcade cabinets these days often cater to the captive market—such as airport departure lounges and long-haul ferries. The player has the option of putting his money into a wide variety of gaming machines, each sporting its own particular brand of entertainment. Shooting games will be displayed next to racing games, simulation games (such as skiing and snowboarding, which have a certain novelty value), and the ubiquitous fighting games, like *Street Fighter II* or *Mortal Kombat*. This means that two aspects (other than price) will draw the players: graphics and sound. Eye candy and aural stimulation, plus an intriguing cabinet design, will pull in the cash. As *EDGE* magazine notes:

> "Atari's decision to put speakers in a 'boom-box' on top of the cabinet was one draw; the absolutely compelling gameplay was the other." [EDGE02]

The game was a 720-degree, state-of-the-art skateboarding video game, and the leader of the pack until *Tony Hawks Pro Skater* arrived on the scene. The cabinet was appealing, but if that had been all, then the game would have only pulled in one-play gamers looking for a novelty. It was the gameplay, itself, that kept them coming back.

The main reason for buying a gaming console is the variety and quality of games that are available for it. The technology behind the console, conversely, will draw developers to create games for it, and the amount of support that the manufacturer is willing to give the developers is also a factor. But games sell consoles; ask anyone who's chosen between the Sega Mega Drive (Genesis, U.S.) and the Super Nintendo Entertainment System (SNES) in the 1990s. The former was bundled with the cute *Sonic the Hedgehog,* the latter with the (then) ground-breaking *Street Fighter II.* Hardcore gamers probably bought both.

Every console, if it is to survive, needs that one game or franchise that will push the platform to the top of the consumer "wish list" and keep them coming back for more games for the system. Sony has had many such titles; *Wipeout*, for example, probably sold countless PS1s. Nintendo has *Mario*, and the Xbox has *Project Gotham Racing,* among others.

Doubtless, *Halo 2* has sold some Xboxes over the years; where initially it was thought that Microsoft might have difficulty competing in the console arena, the games have led to the current situation, which is pretty favorable. They are competing, and, in some cases, surpassing the traditional players.

In any event, these are all very different systems, as we shall see, and are currently in their second or third generations. All have some great games, some okay games, and some poor games. Gamer are still hard pressed to choose between them, and games are more often becoming multiplatform, including those for the venerable PC.

Before we look at all available video game platforms in detail, note that the PC does not suffer from the game-sells-the-platform problem. This is because PCs can do anything—not just play games. The PC market is captive in that many people already own a PC and will not be enthralled with the idea of buying another gaming system. The casual gamer will be content with downloading demos and only pay out real money for a game that is demo-proven.

MOBILE DEVICES

We will start our discussion on platforms with mobile devices, the smallest platform, and one in which innovations have been the most recent. What began as a lowly communication device has grown into a true gaming platform with the advent of operating systems such as PalmOS and Mobile Windows. Mobile telephones used to come with tiny, monochrome LCD screens, but now they boast full color, high resolution, and Internet-capable Windows-style interfaces.

Mobile devices are multifunctional (the buzz-word for the twenty-first century). Third-generation mobile phones have arrived with extra-high data-transfer rates; a phone is now more than just a communication device, and this attitude will become more widespread due to several reasons: price, convenience, and the ability to consolidate multiple devices into a single unit.

Due to this convergence of technologies, the consumer now has the choice of buying into the mobile device platform for one additional and very obvious use, as a gaming platform. The designer needs to remember that the game alone is not going to sell the device. Mobile device are, on the high-price/high-tech end, designed for professional or semi-professional use. At the other extreme, they're designed as fashion accessories—low price and medium tech—which Nokia understood early on.

A full convergence across product ranges has yet to become affordable for the average person—the main market for video games. Affordable, in this case, is around $450 for the mobile telephone and $200 for a PDA (Personal Digital Assistant), and there are the basic diving forces behind models.

Most phones that are available to consumers can run Java applications, and some are smart-phone mobile operating systems. Applications and games can be downloaded for these platforms at reasonable cost, and are aimed at the casual market.

One key point is that many of these phones also have Wi-Fi and Bluetooth communications abilities, making them also good for local multiplayer games, or even Internet-based games. Players are not going to spend hours on such small screens, however, unless they're stuck on a train, so this market remains fairly casual.

There are other options, such as using the text-messaging capabilities of the phone to communicate with a server for a high-tech, text-based RPG. Other games revolve around text messages, and these also lend themselves to the lower end of the mobile telephony market.

PDAs have taken a bit of a bashing with the arrival of the smart phones. However, Palm still rules the roost to a certain extent, with other manufacturers close behind. Palm development is very well supported, though, with plenty of official and unofficial information available to potential developers.

There are differences between these devices, and some that use operating systems that have their roots in other platforms. One such example is the Windows Mobile operating system (Microsoft). It looks and feels like a trimmed-down version of Windows 95, and is available on a variety of devices. The big plus to using these systems is that video game designers and developers who are just starting out might also have experience in the PC development industry, and therefore can apply many of the techniques that they are already used to.

There are advantages to using the PDA as a gaming platform (or a converged PDA/telephony platform): The screens are typically larger, and the sound system is more sophisticated. Consumers prefer a larger screen on a multifunction device, and pure-telephony units tend to provide sound through a speaker that also carries voice; therefore, the sound quality will be slightly lower than the separate, dedicated speaker offered in PDAs.

However, this is a very fast-moving market. A game released on the mobile telephone platform will not have a very long shelf life. Added to this is the fact that consumers change their phones quite regularly as new technology becomes available, so games tend to take the form of gimmicks or freebies that come along with the phone.

To counteract this, Web-based game developers can make their product available to the bare-bones Web browsers used by both phones and PDAs. Consumers can change their platforms at will, and can still play the games. As the cost of Internet connectivity through cell phones decreases—for example, using high-speed mobile data services—Web-accessible gaming for mobile devices will become more prevalent.

Pocket mobile computers such as PDAs, on the other hand, are changed less frequently by consumers. Therefore, they are a viable target platform for a potential developer. Bear in mind, though, that they are also rather pricey, so this market is quite restricted. Still, they do represent a platform with a very low technology barrier and could be a good starting point for a small game design studio. Games can posted for sale on the Internet very inexpensively, and the underlying technology is both well understood and well documented. Some of the development tools can even be obtained for free.

There are also other revenue streams that can augment basic sales. They range from advertising and other inline revenue, to upgrades and mission packs. Part of the sales model could even include distributing a free version, and allowing the user to buy "play credits," or level and mission packs.

Mobile Consoles

The main difference between a mobile device and a mobile *console* is that there is less emphasis on multifunction PDA-telephony and more emphasis on pure gaming, with few other uses for the device. Something of a price war is currently (as of this writing) in progress between the major manufacturers of mobile consoles, namely Nintendo, Microsoft, and Sony.

Sony, for example, pushed their PlayStation 1 console onto the mobile gaming market by substantially reducing its size and adding an LCD screen as an option. In addition, the PlayStationPortable (PSP) is a genuine, made-for-mobile gaming entry into a market traditionally dominated by Nintendo.

This prompted Nintendo to combine the GameBoy Advance and GameCube into a similar kind of gaming system. In typical Nintendo fashion, they came up with the Nintendo DS, which has dual screens, one of which is a stylus-controlled touchscreen. With some clever games, such as *Brain Training*, they have managed to hold on to their market position, somewhat.

Sony, on the other hand, also bolstered their niche by adding a new piece of technology to their existing Clié handheld device, called the "Clié Gear," which boasted a host of buttons that offered as many controller options as a typical controller unit, attached to the Clié, itself.

Microsoft, already involved in the full-console market price war, has yet to enter the mobile-console market with anything more substantial than their existing Pocket PC and Windows Mobile platforms. At the time of this writing, the market seems to be cornered by Nintendo with the GameBoy, GameBoy Advance and DS lines. The original GameBoy surfaced in the late 1980s with a monochrome, 160 × 144-pixel screen.

Games were delivered as cartridges, and it was possibly the first portable device to offer multiple games. Up until then, Nintendo had been supplying a hungry market with the one-game-per-machine Game & Watch LCD-based toys. With the GameBoy, still LCD and still monochrome, gamers now had the possibility to use the same unit to play multiple games.

Amazingly, GameBoy is still one of the most popular systems on the market, even though it's undergone a few minor changes over the years, such as a smaller unit size and the introduction of a color-screen version. As late as 2004, there were still mainstream games being sold for GameBoy Color systems.

More recently, and something of a departure from the original "low-tech, low-end" Nintendo product placement, is the GameBoy Advance, which boasts increased screen resolution with 32 thousand colors and 240 × 160 pixels. It still runs GameBoy and GameBoy Color cartridges, but also offers additional memory and power (15 hours on two AA batteries).

GameBoy Advance (GBA) hasn't lasted quite as long as the original. Despite some revamps—smaller size and a clamshell version—in 2007, stores had already ceased stocking GBA titles in the U.K. This has been largely thanks to the success of the DS, which has taken gaming to new heights—opening it up to all generations, and promoting cooperative play through built-in wireless connections and "brain-tease" style games.

All of these platforms are dedicated mobile-gaming units, built for portability and durability. Casual gamers might play the odd game on their phone, but serious gamers will spend hours locked in virtual adventures on the DS, even if there is a game console (and probably more than one) sitting in the corner of their living rooms.

Developing for the dedicated gaming market has its inherent advantages, such as increased game-specific performance (graphics and sound) and the excellent support for game programming (much of the complex screen- and sound-handling work is lifted from the programmer's shoulders); but there are also distinct hurdles that need to be overcome.

It seems that Nintendo, ever anxious to retain their quality line of gaming products, have guarded their cartridge specifications closely, which means that only those games that pass the "quality test" will ever make it onto the shelves. None of them use "industry standard" media. This is a pity, because the process of certifying a game is so expensive that smaller studios cannot compete.

On the other hand, it is worth noting that PCs and Pocket PCs (devices that support Java and standard operating systems), and some consoles do not require this quality-check procedure—which opens them up for the general market, but also means that lower-quality releases will make their way onto shelves. PC owners are well aware of this, but mobile telephone owners might find this objectionable, especially since downloading mobile games is expensive compared to downloading PC games from the Internet via a standard modem or broadband connection.

Another point to note is that even though consoles (except Nintendo) use standard media, a special development kit is required (as an additional purchase) in order to unlock the power of the gaming system for the programmer. The only platform that remains totally open to date is the PC.

Consoles

Until recently, the console market read like a who's who of video game excellence. Looking back over history, however, we can see just how cut-throat the industry is. The key casualties to date have been Atari (failing to capitalize on their 1600/2600 series) and more recently Sega, with the sad demise of the Dreamcast unit. Three manufacturers remain: veteran Nintendo, relative newcomer Sony, and most recently, Microsoft.

Of these, 2006 sales figures show that Microsoft is managing to push more Xbox 360s down in rank than equivalent offerings by Nintendo or Sony. However, Sony is still largely on top thanks to the continued success of the PS2. There is still life in that console, and remarkably, still some excellent games for it.

Typically, consoles are custom-built devices, which makes them quite expensive to produce, although the Microsoft does base their system's architecture on that of the PC. This is no doubt because Microsoft has a good understanding of the synergies that can be exploited through judicious use of off-the-shelf components.

In addition, it makes the porting from the development environment to the actual platform much less painful. Indeed, with the advent of XNA (Microsoft's game creation middleware) and the December 2006 release of the XNA Game

Studio Express, PC owners can create Xbox games without the need for expensive development kits.

While each console is different, they all share some common features. These features will no doubt be extended and expanded on in the future.

First, these devices use the television monitor as their screen, so consumers have come to expect both high resolution and color depth. With the advent of high-definition television, console manufacturers can also begin to address some of the shortcomings that may have restricted TV monitor technology.

Behind the scenes, all the complex functions required to support realistic graphics—such as smoke, shading, glass effects, and a whole host of filtering functions—are available at the hardware level, and at native speed (around 150MHz). This means that the programmer does not need to write these functions into their gaming software.

The sound system will likely mirror that available in the television/DVD world—Dolby Digital quality with 5.1 surround sound. Provided the player has a good speaker system, this will add to the game's realism by offering true 3D sound.

Controllers have also advanced over the years. Console manufacturers offer increasingly more buttons and more opportunities to extend the basic controller. The most recent innovation has been wireless motion-sensing controllers. The Nintendo Wii and Sony PS3 both offer these features.

Individual game developers are also not afraid to add their own twists. *Guitar Hero* (PS2, PS3, and Xbox 360), for example, can be played with a mini-guitar that serves as the controller. The Xbox sports a pair of drums for a series of games, and *Buzz*, the quiz show game, comes complete with four big, red, game show buzzers.

Other peripheral connectivity options include USB (Universal Serial Bus), which allows other things to be connected to the system. On the PS2, perhaps the most interesting is the *Singstar* microphone. There are numerous other unique peripherals, including dance mats and little USB cameras (EyeToy). More-recent gaming platforms now have network connectivity and the option to add a hard drive. Microsoft has also rolled out a networking concept called Xbox Live Arcade, which provides games to consumers in a pay-to-play format.

True to form, and greatly helping the success of the Xbox and Xbox 360, Microsoft supports independent developers more than the other two manufacturers. In fact, the level of information-sharing between Microsoft and independent developers is quite remarkable. It is quite easy to develop for Xbox 360 Live Arcade (likely a deliberate choice on the part of Microsoft). Contrast this with Sony (closed development kits) and Nintendo (prohibitively expensive acceptance process), and it is evident that console development is not for the faint hearted.

All in all, game development for the console market is probably out of reach for the designer who is just "cutting his teeth" in the industry. It is, though, a market with high penetration. In essence, there will be gamers who own a console or even two, but who have no PC games or even a PC in their house. Then there are gamers that would rather buy a new console than upgrade a PC for gameplay.

So, consoles are mainstream with high penetration and acceptance. People understand that they are gaming systems, and the sales of console games tend to be reasonably buoyant.

Add to this the fact that, despite the differences between console models, the developer is guaranteed a certain minimum level of technology. If he develops for a console, there is a guarantee that each console is the same as the developer's, and probably will not change. This is a big advantage, as we shall see when we take a look at home computers.

Home Computers

Before we begin, let us state the obvious: The PC is the easiest platform to develop for—and also the most difficult. It is the easiest because it has the best-supported knowledge base and tools, but it is the most difficult because each system is going to be slightly different with varied processor speeds, graphics cards, and sound peripherals. That means there is no such thing as a standard PC.

On the other hand, PC hardware is standards-based. For example, there is a guaranteed minimum level of multimedia support, and (thanks to the niche nature of the market) only two processor manufacturers, and a handful of graphics and sound card suppliers. This means that, by and large, two machines built to similar specifications will have similar capabilities.

There is large variance, however, in motherboard and memory types, and these will rule out a minority of systems. The chances are, however, that gamers know what makes a good PC gaming platform—that is, what is needed in terms of processor speed, RAM, and hard disk space.

Over the years, the PC has really taken hold in the home as much as in the office, thanks to the substantial price wars that have made the PC quite affordable in the marketplace. In the past 20 years, the performance of the average PC has also evolved at a very fast rate, though it is now slowing as the architecture nears its maximum performance ability.

Unlike the other platforms, there is really very little else to say about the PC. Most people are already familiar with terms such as processor speed and memory, and are even acquainted with the capabilities of graphics cards. The top end of the processor market is currently represented by two manufacturers, Intel and AMD. Their top clock speeds at the time of this writing are between 2GHz and 3GHz.

Memory sizes considered acceptable for gaming are roughly 512MB to 1024MB, while game-centric graphics cards tend to have a lot of onboard memory.

Although there might be several different manufacturers of graphics cards, an industry-standard set of components and chipsets are used, which are supplied by one of the leading manufacturers, and this keeps specifications in line.

Part of the reason that little discussion is needed here is because of the nature of the PC; the biggest difference between them will be the operating system and device drivers employed. (We will touch on this later, under Technologies.) There are essentially only three kinds of PCs in homes today.

Windows-based PCs are most common. Something to remember when designing for the Windows platform is that the operating system soaks up a lot of processor power by itself. It will provide a solid base for the developer; he can write the code on one system, execute it on that system, and be able to have a pretty good idea of how the game will run on *all* similar machines. Be aware, however, that especially in the graphics market, certain cards have capabilities that not supported on all PCs.

Microsoft dominates the PC market, and supports gaming and multimedia enhancements in each variation of their Windows operating system. Linux systems exist, and their numbers are growing, but games written specifically for Linux do not tend to win universal support. Nobody is going to buy a PC and put the Linux operating system on it just to run your game.

Developers should avoid using tricks that circumvent the operating system when creating their games. For example, many Linux users will readily buy a Windows game that they can run through an application called Wine. This is a package that translates Windows system calls to Linux, enabling Windows software to run under Linux, provided Windows best-practice programming has been followed.

One of the nicest things about Linux systems is that the processor is not overburdened by the operating system, itself. This is because Linux is incredibly lightweight and offers huge potential for the gamer in the way of good performance from slightly less-powerful hardware. Some might even say that you get more "bang for your buck"; a Linux system can cost half as much as a Windows-based system and offer similar performance.

Finally, there is the Apple Macintosh. All Apple machines come with the same basic premise: they are all built alike. Unlike PCs, where customization is the name of the game, Apple have closed their architecture to the point that user upgrades are frowned upon. Apple does everything in its power to make upgrades impossible.

The upside is that, like a console system, all machines of a similar specification will respond the same, and the developer does not worry about certain features not being available, such as the standard graphics card being replaced by the gamer for another made by a different manufacturer. It simply doesn't happen. Porting from

Windows to Apple is a tried-and-tested, reasonably well understood and supported process. It can be expensive (using a cross compiler) and is intensive in man hours, but it is definitely achievable.

Key to the decision when developing a game for the home-computing platform will be its familiarity. The home PC is, in fact, perfect for a first-time designer or studio. It is low cost, with easy delivery channels (the Internet), has mature technology, with very well-supported development platforms, and benefits from an open technology. As a video game platform, the PC is a good place to start. The developer can code and deliver on the same platform, without needing costly development kits and QA processes. It is also easy to get the product to market (even if it might be a bit limited) without any help or hindrance from manufacturers, and often without a publisher. Shareware games have a rich heritage and were arguably made possible by the PC platform.

Arcade Cabinet Systems

The last platform that we are going to look at (briefly) is the classic arcade cabinet. Designing games for these systems is a very difficult proposition for the first-timer. They are even more difficult than the console platform by virtue of the fact that they are, essentially, single-game systems—that is, each cabinet must be manufactured to support a single game, making the whole process very costly.

The cabinet, itself, serves in part as advertising for the game and as brand recognition. This means that it has to be designed separately from the game, but also in accordance with the support needed for control systems, the sound, and the screen. If the game is to be a simulation, such as skiing or snowboarding with a pair of skis or board, then a different style cabinet will be required than for a driving or fighting game.

Obviously, there is no point in designing the next best video game to hit the arcade, only to find that the window dressing that makes up the cabinet is so large that it will not fit inside the arcade, itself. On top of that, many systems will need to convert into formats that fit into trailers for traveling fairs. They must also provide income comparable to the four classic stand-up cabinets.

These are the downsides; so there must be upsides—and of course there are, but they are not immediately apparent at the design stage. When we dig deeper, we find that, like the console market, there are very few hardware manufacturers that create workings to support features required by specific video games. In the beginning, each circuit board needed to be created specifically for the game under development, but these days the trend is toward a good, all-purpose arcade system board.

These all-purpose boards can be reloaded with different games, too; and if the game is designed to be placed in a stand-up cabinet with a standard controller, then there is no reason why it shouldn't be introduced on existing systems. All it takes is simply reprogramming the main board and changing the decals on the outside cabinet.

The arcade is also a potentially lucrative market, since each system will have more "owners" over its lifetime than will a console; the game will get more exposure, and if it is good enough, the revenues from it will be high. Add to that the fact that the classics become crossovers—reworked for the PC, console, or handheld market—and the potential earnings are enormous. Of course, it is also an easy market in which to lose all of your money more or less overnight.

A final note on the subject of arcade technology: It is a fast-moving market. Manufacturers try to come up with ever-more ingenious ways to prevent arcades from disappearing completely. There is now even the ability to save games onto memory cards that the player can take from machine to machine, or even from arcade to arcade. Other innovations in the future will probably include online gaming that links machines all over the world, advanced control systems (such as gloves or bodysuits), and tie-ins with mobile, console, or PC technology in an attempt to pull in those gamers who prefer to play at home.

These innovations are on the table because an arcade cabinet is much more expensive to produce and purchase than a home console. Being a one-game system, it can be endowed with technological wizardry that would be out of reach for the consumer. This expensive platform is, in effect, being paid for by multiple owners (players) over a significant length of time.

The Design Platform

Before we look at the technologies that are available to the video game designer in the production phase, we should take a look at the platforms that can help us in the design process. To this point, we have considered the final product and how it will be executed—in other words, the target platform. However, during the design phase, it may be necessary to try to test out various techniques; and in order to do this, the video game designer needs to be aware of exactly what tools are available. Bear in mind that the designer may not be a programmer himself (which is actually quite common). There are tools available that enable the designer to play around with techniques that will be used to write the actual game, and with very little programming involved.

The platform for doing this is the PC. Not only are there tools such as Game Maker that can be used to create games visually, but there are many emulators available that can mimic handhelds, consoles, and even arcade systems.

Even if prototyping in this way is considered out of reach for the designer, simple Microsoft Office tools, such as Excel, can be used to examine the logic behind a game's design. All Microsoft Office tools are backed by Visual Basic for Applications (a macro language), with which the designer can even add some interactivity to prove that the design ideas will actually work—and all before the expensive programming phase begins.

As an added note, real games can be built with tools such as GameMaker, and they can also be distributed royalty-free. There are certain things that these tools cannot do, and their performance is of slightly lower quality than games that have been programmed from the bottom up, but they provide a great introduction to video game programming as well as design. The trick is to use the correct tool for the job: Game Maker for platform games; The Games Factory or GCS for 3D games.

The Development Platform

The platform that the game is developed *on* is likely to differ from the platform being developed *for* unless the target platform is the home computer. Therefore, an emulator is used to mimic, as closely as possible, the behavior of the target platform on the development platform.

In some cases, the target platform might not even be in production; certain games will be designed to ship at the same time as a console to drive demand. It is the games that will sell the console platform, and not the other way around, so it is logical that development has to start about two years before the console is released. Subsequently, the choice of the development/design platform may well have a bearing on the target platform. There is no use trying to design and develop a game for a PS3 if there is no money available to buy the tools required.

As we shall see when we look at ways in which a game can be developed, this is only the beginning of the issue; games can also be developed as parts of or modifications to existing games. For example, *Half-Life* can be altered to include new graphical objects, logic, and environments, thereby making a new game.

Id Software, in particular, has been open to this process, as long as the derived games were only playable with their full versions of games, rather than the shareware editions. Valve's *Half-Life* has also been used as the basis for commercial offerings, such as *Counter Strike*, which started out as a mod, or modification, and turned into a game.

Copyright laws dictate that commercial games cannot use other people's ideas, artwork, sound, code, or other assets that have not been explicitly licensed. *Counter Strike* made it into the commercial mainstream thanks to the publisher and the fact that the original mod needed a full *Half-Life* install to work in the first place.

So, for those designing a next-generation first-person shooter, this route might be desirable. We then need to know what the limitations of the platform will be (PC only, probably) and the design/development environment—that is, scripting, objects, and so on. As long as they stay within the law and realize that there is a risk inherent in that the publisher might not pick up the mod and turn it into a commercial offering (the odds are probably against it, in fact), designers can now take existing games and derive works from them.

Having done this, we might find that part of the design makes the game impossible. We will have to decide whether or not to change the game, the genre, the platform, the technologies, or the design/development process, itself.

Technologies

There are always ways to improve the basic platform system. This can be broken down into two distinct areas: hardware and software. Hardware technologies include the peripherals that make the gaming experience more intense, while software technologies include the operating system or gaming environments that can be loaded onto the platform in order to give your game life.

While hardware technologies can be universally applied to any system, it is unlikely that all systems will be able to change the software aspects of the platform. The only platforms that allow software technology to intervene are the PC and handheld markets. Ways that gamers can customize what lies behind the scenes, so to speak, include upgrades to operating systems, new device drivers, or simply pieces of software that work with the hardware to make a game easier, more difficult, or more enjoyable.

As always, an interesting little sidebar in the software technology discussion is the rise of the Internet and the ability to share data over landline and wireless networks. Gamers are encouraged to design and distribute their own levels for games (mods) over the Internet for free—or even charge for them.

New levels could also be made available from the manufacturer (provided the platform allows it), and at the same time the parent game is purchased. Platform advances often complement these possibilities, and vendors are often quick to capitalize on them.

Hardware Technologies

The first hardware technology that can be part of the design process is the controller unit. Console systems used to come with one or two controllers, which was considered standard. Now they often come with controllers that put the joysticks of yore to shame; two sets of four buttons (one directional) and two analog joysticks provide the player with an often overwhelming choice of actions. There are also a couple of "shoulder buttons" thrown in for good measure and the ability to make the control unit vibrate in the player's hands. This "Dual-Shock" joystick technology has allegedly caused medical problems, however, because of the combination of the vibration effect and the weight of the controller.

Then there are wireless motion-sensing controllers that add a new element of realism and immersion to the gaming experience. Sometimes this is not well received. Extreme-gore games such as *Manhunt* are already super-realistic, and adding the ability to slice the victim with a gesture might just be a step too far.

The game design has to take into account all of these issues. A game that uses all of the possible control options will raise the barrier to entry; the casual player might feel that it is simply too complex.

Usually, mainstream games restrict themselves to camera movement in cases where the angle becomes unplayable or weapon control that can be directed independently of the main character. Where game designs call for the use of many buttons, they need to be logical and natural, or the player will be overwhelmed.

If the video game designer is thinking of creating a joystick controller specifically for the game that he has in mind, it always pays to carefully consider the effect that this will have on the desirability of the game, the cost to the consumer, and the development cost as the game goes through untold trials and the inevitable concept changes.

Custom peripherals and control units are not the norm in the gaming industry; they are exceptions. Most common among standard inventions seems to be the steering wheel, accelerator, and brake pedal that were created especially for driving games. They even come complete with little Ferrari-style emblems where the horn would normally be, in the center of the steering wheel.

These controllers can be used for almost all driving games, and are sold separately. They are usually also available for PC and console platforms, alike. At the other end of the spectrum is the special controller unit created for the game *Tekki* (*Steel Battalion* in the U.S. and Europe), which boasts two joysticks, numerous buttons, and even a plastic, shielded ejector button—the cover must be flipped before pressing it to respond to an emergency. This controller pushes the price of the game up to the $200 mark and cannot be used with any other game. Furthermore, it is *required* to play *Tekki*, the game for which it was designed. Available for (only) Xbox, *Tekki* gamers control a sophisticated "mech" with numerous weapons systems and absolutely gorgeous graphics, sound, and gameplay. Since the game costs almost as much as the console that it runs on, whether it will prove popular is another question entirely.

What has proven to be a popular addition to the console environment are the dance mats that accompany games such as *Dance Dance Revolution*. The inclusion of the mats, designed to be put on the floor and danced on, do not overly increase the price of the game, either at the manufacturer's or consumer's level, and adds a dimension to the game that involves coordination, and is extremely entertaining. It is the kind of game that leaves the player exhausted, but encourages them to keep going.

Recently, games such as *Guitar Hero* have added collectible and inexpensive simulated guitars as optional extras. It is possible to play the game without the guitar controller, but using the guitar is "cooler" and is easier—if the player buys one.

This synergy of hardware technology and the gaming unit in the video game concept is a good example of why it pays to introduce new technology that supports a single title. It may not work every time, but when it does, it can be a goldmine.

Take, for example, the microphones shipped with *Singstar*. In this karaoke-style game, the machine scores the players. The microphones are required; it cannot be played without them. There are at least five *Singstar* series titles in circulation, and more in the pipeline, which are sold at standard retail prices or bundled with microphones at a higher price point. The game can only be played on the PS2 platform and is phenomenally successful, despite the hefty price tag.

So for consoles, the only real options are: provide an innovative controller that plugs into a standard port, find a platform with a controller that fits the design needs, or find a way to take advantage of any expansion additional ports (USB, network, and so on) on the hardware platform.

More recent consoles offer wireless peripheral control; the Xbox 360, for example, has wireless headsets for in-game player-to-player communication. This trend will likely continue. However, except for controllers, there are very few games that currently seek to extend the capabilities of their target platforms in non-standard ways.

In the portable gaming market, hardware extensions are much less commonplace. This is largely due to the nature of the platform, itself; it just does not lend itself to being expanded (to be portable means to stay small), and any additions would not enhance gameplay. There have been games that provide cartridge modifications, however, such as *Boktai* (GameBoy Advance), which has a solar sensor. These cartridge modifications must first pass the Nintendo quality board, of course, before they can be manufactured. This is fairly common practice, the theory being that if a cartridge is manufactured by a third party, which then damages the unit, the original equipment manufacturer cannot be held liable under the terms of the guarantee.

The owner is unlikely to have recourse if the unit is rendered unusable because of a device that is not officially supported. Of course, there have been exceptions, but the manufacturer of "uncertified" peripherals had better make sure that their equipment doesn't cause damage or conflict with the original hardware.

The most extendable platform is, of course, the PC. Almost anything that the mind can conjure up can be attached to a PC, but to date there have been very few attempts to go beyond the previously mentioned steering-wheel attachment. This is a real shame, because the average PC has USB ports galore, as well as serial ports for innovative controllers. A potential growth market for the future exists, if only the game is good enough to warrant the additional expense.

Software Technologies

The easiest extensions to the gaming device are those that are made through the operating system or underlying software technology. As previously mentioned, only those devices that support custom software can be upgraded in this way.

The principle advantage is that there is no additional production cost when software technology is added to a video game, but the game, itself, can be sold at a premium, simply by virtue of the fact that it contains some clever software technology.

The original *Creatures* (PC) boasted "contains digital DNA," announcing that there was some clever programming at work inside. This is an example of extending a game through software technology, as is the inclusion of the ability to tap the unit's graphical subsystem, which can then be used to enhance other games—for example, an extended version of Microsoft DirectX video technology.

Aside from these simple examples, there is very little else to say. The obvious uses for software technology are, of course, Internet access to provide multiplayer support, new levels, or the ability to share levels with other players.

Special Cases

This last section details some of the most recent innovations that the budding video game designer cannot afford to ignore when considering using a particular platform or technology. These current/emerging trends can be used to good advantage in order to create a game that has an edge over the competition.

Quite often, a good game idea can be made into an excellent, genre-busting implementation, simply by the inclusion of some technology that is perhaps not obvious. One of the most famous examples has to be the combination attacks in *Street Fighter II*, in which a piece of soft technology (or design) evolved from the discovery of a bug in the original system code.

JAVA

One of the most important cross-platform innovations in the past 10 years has been the SUN Java language, which works on a very simple principle. Java programs can be compiled to run natively on a given platform, using the free SUN Java SDK (Software Development Kit), which is available for many different platforms (from Linux to Windows to ARM-based portable devices).

Java can also be compiled to bytecode, which is only executable by a Java VM (Virtual Machine). This has the advantage that many devices, from PCs to mobile telephones, can contain Java VM chips. These chips are capable of running applications built with the Java SDK; therefore, one game can run on multiple platforms, with very few changes to the code.

The user interface is probably going to differ between platforms, as will the screen resolution, but by and large, if the game design is done intelligently, very little will need to change. A big plus is that the Java bytecode can also be downloaded from the Internet or even run in a browser.

STRICT MULTIPLAYER

Strict Multiplayer is a technology that has grown out of the natural human need for interaction, and it also enhances certain game experiences. Recently, Internet technology has advanced to the point where two people can play a game over the Internet, across the globe, and in real time.

Games such as *Unreal Tournament 2003*, for example, allow up to 64 players at a time to compete against each other in a number of games—from all-out death matches to pseudo-sports. Today's high-speed connections mean that although the game is fast paced, there is almost no lag between a player's commands and their execution on another player's machine. This is very different from the "old days," when people would log on to a server and chat in text mode, and there was always a discernable pause between typing a message and receiving a response.

There are some things that the video game designer needs to remember when designing a multiplayer game; the amount of data that needs to be exchanged in order to coordinate the game must be minimized. This is important, because even with the extreme speed of today's networks, we need to be aware that there might be someone out there with a slow modem who will not be able to take full advantage of the game simply because his connection cannot keep up.

This is why the designer should try to synchronizing the entire gaming system so that no one suffers (if at all possible). The usual way to do this is to connect systems together via a server, and let the server decide on the flow rate of information. The designer will need to provide for a client-side piece of software as well as an application to manage the server side.

Web Multiplayer

While Strict Multiplayer is possible via the Internet, it is more common for games played through the browser to use an asynchronous approach. This means that a player makes commands that are sent to the server, but which do not directly affect another player (who may not even be connected).

The reason for using an asynchronous design is to release players from the need to be continually connected to the server while the game unfolds. They can play for a few minutes at a time from any Web browser, be it on a PC, Apple, Linux, or handheld device. The only platform that will be left out of these kinds of games will probably be portable or pure consoles.

There are ways to connect consoles to the Internet, but these will usually be Strict Multiplayer, as opposed to asynchronous games. Exceptions abound, as usual; more recently, *Animal Crossing* allows players to use the multiplayer option for visiting other people's creations or sharing trinkets acquired during play sessions.

When designing a Web-based multiplayer game, the client-server paradigm, again, needs to be respected. In addition, there will be an HTML-style interface, or possibly a Java applet, so the designer needs to be aware of what specific constraints this choice will entail. On the other hand, it is sometimes the perfect trial ground for the mechanics that will be used in the real game, and the technology can also be used to generate interest in the eventual game.

Web games that use HTML and some clever server programming will be cheap to implement and potentially open to the entire Internet-based gaming community—not to mention that the Web provides the perfect feedback tools: message boards, email, and newsletters.

Finally, there is a whole series of games that work in an even more asynchronous way than those we have just discussed. For example, PBeM games let players send messages to an email server that contains a virtual environment, and the commands contained in the email can affect the virtual game world. The results are then collated and sent out to all players on a predetermined schedule, such as weekly or monthly. Sometimes these email messages contain full programs that orchestrate battle in the virtual environment set up by the server. Often, competitions are run as KOTH (King of the Hill) tournaments. This means that only those programs that can defeat the others remain in the game (on the hill). This sort of gaming is not for newbies, however; designing such games can prove complicated for those without programming experience.

SUMMARY

This chapter was intended to arm the video game designer with information that he will need to choose the platform(s) that will be used for a proposed game. It is the final abstract chapter—that is, the last in which the scenes are. From here on, our discussions will be more concrete, and cover specific techniques and design issues that help the video game to take shape.

So this is a good place to stop and take stock of what has been learned. For example, the game idea should now be tailored to a specific implementation. While the designer does not need to address specific coding requirements, he does need to be aware of the capabilities of the chosen platform. The designer should also have an idea of what kind of software will be used in the design process, since at some point, the abstract idea will need to be turned into something that is a little more concrete.

The actual choice of platform, if not limited by the game genre itself, can be based on either commercial or technological concerns. In addition, a platform can be used to test a simple implementation of the techniques that are required by the game design process; that is. The end design need not be implemented, just a "prototype" to allow the designer to "get a grip" on the design process and prove that the concept works.

REFERENCES

[EDGE02] "The Mame Game," *EDGE*, No. 115, October 2002.

5 Sound, Music, and Graphics

In This Chapter

- Sound Effects and Music
- Graphics
- Concept Art and Sound

In the video game world, communication occurs in much the same way as it does in the real world—through the eyes and ears of the player. Of course, the all-important sense of smell is left out of the experience, and until recently, so was touch. (Chapter 9, "User Interface Design," will deal with the sense of touch in video games.) Nasal trickery will have to wait until technology catches up, as will stimulating the sense of taste.

Trickery, of course, is what it is all about: visual trickery—making a two-dimensional screen display a three-dimensional representation of real life (in the case of television programs) or a designer's virtual dream (in the case of video games). The representation is in two dimensions, yet appears to be three-dimensional. The player is convinced of this illusion for the time that they are playing the game if, of course, we have done our job well.

In the same way that a novel persuades the reader to temporarily enter a different reality, and a movie (however unbelievable the premise) convinces the audience that its plot really could happen, the video game needs to be able to pull off this "suspension of disbelief" more than any other media. Done well, the result is a smooth playing experience; done badly, the suspension of belief can be shattered in the blink of an eye. All too often, poorly implemented graphics can break the spell and hurt video game sales—*if* it gets that far. Bad technology can kill the developer's dream just as quickly as bad sales figures can bankrupt the studio.

The effects that create the illusion of a universe different from the one inhabited by the player need to be thought out in advance and implemented as part of the overall design, not bolted on afterward. There are many parallels made between video games and movies—some valid, others less so—and the trend of placing movie-style cut scenes between action segments has only encouraged the comparisons.

Both art forms share roots in the escapist nature of the experiences they provide. This may sound a little highbrow, but the truth is that whether watching a movie or playing a video game, the audience tends to forget about the real world—if the product is well implemented. Otherwise, they start looking at their watches and rustling their candy wrappers.

The principal difference in the beginning was that arcade games provided a quick fix for the fraction of the cost of a movie ticket, even though a movie lasted an hour and a half to two hours. Since the advent of the home video game console and home computer, the arcade gaming experience became extended. In the past, if you didn't like a game, you stopped putting money into the slot. Today, if you had invested $40 in a console, you would feel obliged to play the game for a while, even if the game is terrible.

From the consumer's point of view, this means that the public is more discerning about what they spend their money on. They rely on good reviews to guide them—well, not necessarily good as in "blockbuster," but honest. Consumers respect honesty more than they do lip service to games that obviously are not all they are cracked up to be. If they purchase the game on the advice of a review and find that they have been duped, then it reflects badly on the magazine, studio, and label.

This little discourse serves to highlight the fragility of the gaming environment and to illustrate the point that good video games, like good movies, are built on a subtle blend of music, sound effects, and on-screen graphics. All three are required. Remove one and the structure is lost, so these features need to be present from the onset—the design, just like in the movies.

Sound Effects and Music

We shall open this topic with a great quote from Matthew Johnston, audio lead at Microsoft:

> "Rarely does anyone design game audio that has any use." [Saltzman01]

He attributes this not to the sound engineers, themselves, but to a misunderstanding that the purpose of audio in a game is to provide sounds for the graphics. After frequently being called in at the last minute to provide audio for a game, Johnston became cynically aware that there was never enough importance attributed to game audio. Bob Rice, CEO of Four Bars Intertainment, a U.S.-based management company for game audio designers, is quoted in *EDGE* magazine:

> "Our mantra is this quote from Steven Spielberg: 'Sound and music make up more than half of communicating a story, even more than what you are seeing.'" [EDGE01]

For example, consider a player walking through a concrete jungle with a rifle cradled in his arms. Assuming that there are no other sounds, how would he be able to tell if someone was behind him? As animals, we rely on our hearing (one of our five senses) to give us information beyond that which is delivered by our eyes.

Our eyes give us a view that is fairly wide, but we cannot see beyond our field of vision or behind us, unlike some creatures with compound eyes. Some fish, like sharks, for example, have an even narrower viewing angle than we do, plus they are fairly short-sighted and therefore rely on other senses for information, such as smell.

Sharks, then, back up their eyesight with smell, and humans usually back up their sight with sound. This facet of game audio gives us an additional dimension that prepares the player for things that are about to happen. This is called an "audio cue," but it is not, however, the only way in which game audio is used.

Sound can also be used as a way to create atmosphere—that is, sounds that are not a direct consequence of the player's actions, or the actions of a game object or non-player character. For example, music or a distant heartbeat can add substantial atmosphere to a game. Movie directors, composers, and musicians have long understood that emotions can be manipulated with sounds. There are happy tunes, sad tunes, eerie tunes, or frightening tunes.

Even with our eyes closed, we can discern the meaning of a scene just from the music that is being played. We may not know the actual plot or storyline, but we know what kind of scene is being played out. (Note that music can also be used ironically; some filmmakers include musical interludes that are in opposition to the nature of the scene being played. However, other audio cues would probably help the viewer determine what was going on.)

The industry is taking note of the fact that the musical score behind a game is important—even to the point that synthesized music is being phased out in favor of entire orchestras. However, Richard Jacques, interviewed for *EDGE* magazine, has a cautionary note for future game audio developers:

> "I hope we don't get into a scenario where publishers believe that if they get an orchestral recording it will provide them with a great soundtrack. It won't." [Jacques01]

The orchestra is just one ingredient in the mix that produces fine game audio. Granted, a large orchestra will make the game sound better, but there is no point in spending a lot of money to record a soundtrack that is not cued properly. Even a MIDI track that is correctly cued will offer more power than a badly cued orchestral track that has nothing to do with the on-screen action, and which stutters as the machine struggles to keep up with the hardware demands.

A MIDI track will also be several orders of magnitude cheaper to produce, easier to manipulate, and less resource-consuming. An orchestral score will require much more technological wizardry than a simple, electronic MIDI track, so the underlying technology is also important.

Having set the scene, we shall spend the remainder of this section looking at exactly how audio can be used to enhance the game experience and, more specifically, how game engines deal with audio, and how to design good game audio.

One last anecdote before we pursue the theme of this section—the game *Dance Dance Revolution* (*Dancing Stage Euromix* in Europe, which probably describes the game better) is about dancing. It started out as an arcade game and proved so popular that it was adapted for consoles, thus making *DDR* the ultimate copycat dancing game.

Controllers in *DDR* include pads on the floor, which you try to hit with your body. Knees, hands, elbows, even your head can be used to match the musical rhythms of the pulsing arrows on the screen. The game eventually becomes the music, with the arrows merely serving to guide the player.

Audio in games is important. In games like *DDR*, the focus is on the music once the player has become adept at following the arrows; the game is only about dancing to a beat. Most games do not use audio to this extent, but *DDR* is just one example of how we can use audio as a game vehicle that is often as important, if not more so, than the visual cues that make up the gaming environment.

In case you think this sounds a little dated, in 2007, *DDR* was upgraded and a new version released that takes advantage of the advances in technology. The ongoing success of *Singstar* (karaoke with points awarded for musical accuracy) and *Guitar Hero* (air guitar with points awarded for following the tune) also prove that sound supports ongoing gaming excellence. Obviously, audio and its manipulation are paramount to the success of these games. They are all about the audio, and the quality of that audio goes far beyond what is necessary in a generic game, because the player has an advantage—they already know the music.

The music has to be correctly segued; the feedback to the player has to work perfectly so that the player has a chance to correct their approach to improve their score, and the backdrop has to be simple enough that the maximum resources are available for managing this complex relationship between player and game. On top of all of this, getting the music tracks will likely be a long, drawn-out, expensive licensing process. When it works, however, it is fantastic—a mixture of "I can do that," an intimate familiarity with the music, and the wide party appeal that these products have. Music can continue to fuel a market comprising, potentially, at least two generations of gamers.

Bearing this in mind, we will cover different kinds of music as well as sound effects, without concentrating too much on rhythm action games (which occupy a niche market that could take a whole book to explain). Quality sound effects are often more important than orchestral scores as a backdrop. Even so, sound effects recording quality sounds can eat up the budget as fast as hiring some professional musicians, but they will probably be a better use of financial resources. From recording the sounds of a Formula 1 car on a test track to simulating gunfire and other incidental sounds, creating this soundscape could prove to be an expensive necessity. As we shall see, sound effects are necessary to maintaining the suspension of disbelief that we are asking the player to invest in.

One of these sound effects is simple enough in theory: the spoken voice. But as in radio plays or movies, spoken audio performs a delicate balancing act, especially since a good voice actor is horrifically expensive, and a bad do-it-yourselfer *will* break the gaming spell.

Spoken Audio

Many games will not only need sound effects, they will also need spoken audio. It helps to tell the story. For example, the player will react much better to a "talking head" than he will to text that is read from the screen. Games such as *Mafia* also have a tutorial section that makes up the first 10 to 15 minutes of gameplay, instructing the player on how to control the game.

In *Mafia*, this comprises basic walking, running, and jumping, to picking locks, obtaining and using weapons of various types, and driving cars. The player is taken through his paces by a disembodied voice that tells him what to do next. Usually, these voices are a pastiche of what they are supposed to represent, such as the grating voice of a mob boss.

Lately, however, the quality of voice acting has increased substantially. Voice adds a dimension to the game that is guaranteed to make the whole experience more like a movie and less like a traditional video game.

Games such as *Enter the Matrix* use the actual actors from the *Matrix* movies to provide the voiceover behind the gaming action. This was only made possible by tying the projects together in such a way that the game and the second movie were created in parallel; it contains about an hour of additional movie footage that serves to steer the player through the game. The game is an interactive version of the movie, down to the characters' voices and soundtrack.

Naturally, licensed properties such as *The Matrix* also have a financial advantage working for them (in addition to the possible opportunity to have the stars record the audio). Most games will not have this luxury. Often, the audio will have to be pared down as far as possible to minimize expenses while preventing costly mistakes.

Spoken audio takes a variety of different forms, many of which can replace other facets of the video game interface, such as status indicators and events. Examples include a suit that speaks to the player, telling him that there has been damage sustained as a result of battle, or a ship that tries to warn the player of impending doom.

One such technique is used in *Empire Earth*, where it is used in three different ways. The first is to instruct, and the audio works in conjunction with on-screen textual instructions. The text leaves the screen quickly enough that the player is left wondering how to get them back. But the audio lends a personal experience, and the player is grateful for spoken prompts that take the place of the more-explicit textual pointers. In other words, the text comes and goes, but the audio reminder is easier to recall and serves as a constant reminder of what the player should be doing. These voice-overs can actually vary in quality—there is no reason at all why the vocals cannot sound artificial and bland. Even a voice synthesizer could be used in these cases.

The second way in which spoken audio is used is to inform the player of changes in the immediate environment. It might be the arrival of enemy forces or clues to information on events that the player has set in motion, such as the completion of a building (this becomes indispensable when the player has created a town that exceeds the screen's viewing area).

It is worth mentioning that *Empire Earth* is a mixture of a traditional war RPG and a *SimCity*-style world-building game. It differs slightly from games such as *Civilization* in that there is more emphasis on mixing politics and war, and it lacks the *Civilization*-style "build up an army and go to war" process. Instead, the game uses the longevity associated with the *Sim* franchise.

The available property in *Empire Earth* expands quickly. Each area is also quite vital to the player's success, and so audio cues are helpful in enabling the player to keep track of the whole area, without necessarily having to divert their immediate attention from the task in hand. We can often simultaneously monitor background information, maintaining an internal to-do list based on audio messages, while we handle more-immediate gameplay.

The third way in which the voice-over can be used is to chide the player when they have done something wrong (the "advisor"), but it can also *inform* (at least in tutorial mode) and coach the player in how he might have dealt with a situation better.

It pays to think about how the game design can make use of spoken audio, both at the global level and the personal level—the words spoken by various characters that the player will encounter. The responsibility of the game designer is to try and second-guess the use of spoken audio in the initial design, so that the complexity of the game filters through to the reader of the inevitable Design Document.

There is a fairly logical and direct correlation between voice-acting quality and the nature of its delivery. At one end, if the speaker is an actual in-game animated person, then the voice-acting should be delivered by an actor—that is, a real, live person. At the other end of the spectrum, if the speaker is a computer, some leeway in vocal style is possible.

In the middle there are various possible grades of audio quality, including the guttural roars of animals, and the beeps and trills of vocal alien life forms. Some of these will fall into the scripted audio category—an effect that is as important as a spoken line in a movie or play.

Scripted Audio

The game universe will be made up of sounds, and each object and event in that universe will probably have a sound associated with it. The object and its sound will eventually coincide in events. For example, an automobile contributes to the general tapestry of sound by making a particular noise when it is driven and another noise when it hits a brick wall. (The wall, prior to the accident, was probably silent.) These sounds are temporal. They start, have a specific duration, and then end. The "driving" sound would not overlap the sound of the vehicle hitting the wall; it would seem that the engine was still running after the impact had rendered the vehicle unusable.

The way that these sounds are cued is called *scripting*. The designer will need to make a list of these scripted sounds in order to plan how each object's sound will react to other objects in the game universe. In addition, there are sounds that occur in conjunction with specific events, especially those that result from natural causes. Drops of rain may not, in themselves, make a noticeable noise, but rainstorms probably will—usually the sound of water splashing against a window, accompanied by wind and thunder.

A player looking at a window during a light rain can be greeted with a generalized dripping sound, without linking the sound to each and every drop of rain hitting the window. On the other hand, if the imagery used when the player looks out of the window indicates heavy rain, there is no point in using scripted audio that suggests a mild drizzle.

One of the most frequent uses of scripted sound is with weapons. The noise that a weapon makes should reflect its power—for example, if a 20-foot-long plume of fire leaps from a weapon's muzzle, it should not be accompanied by the pop of a cork gun. Audio, particularly scripted audio, is very important.

Recording the sound effects is limited only by the amount of money the game producer has available to spend. There are many areas of the game design and development process crying out for investment, and it is very tempting to skimp on something like sound effects as being an area in which we can make do with whatever resources are left at the end of the day. This is a big mistake. Sound effects are important, and while there are a good many sound-effect CDs that can be used in games, nothing beats getting an original sound together. Allowing the creative team to think laterally, make mistakes, and spend time getting it right will prove beneficial in the end.

Licensed titles have a responsibility to use licensed materials in their works. In other words, if Alfa-Romeo has sponsored a game—*S.C.A.R*, for example—then the developer has a duty to record the sounds of various Alfa-Romeo cars. Otherwise, the cars will not sound authentic.

Another reason to spend time recording sound effects is that you can make sure that different embodiments of the same object or event can be distinguished—pistol versus shotgun, thunderclap versus explosion, and so on. Also, possible copyright issues can arise from using commercially available sounds; licensing them could be expensive.

Generating sounds is also an option, and if the game budget is tight, some effects can be created by simple synthesis. These kinds of sounds used to be restricted to the tinny chirps and whistles of the older generation of games, before processing power was good enough to produce complex sounds. However, with more-sophisticated software, we can now generate all manners of sounds and tinker with them in real time. Even an amateur sound engineer can have some success—although, (as with voice actors) it pays to get a professional to shape some unique sounds for the game. They will sound better.

Nothing, however, beats recording real sounds, and this is true for musical instruments as it is for the sound of thunderstorms. Also, remember that a collection of instruments playing together can produce music that provides an additional layer of control over the "scheduling" of the musical score. This could entail slowing it down or speeding it up, altering the tone, producing alternate melodies, or generating the music in real time during the play session. The scheduling is powerful, because it allows us to immerse the player and adjust his actual progress through the game.

Music

If the previously discussed cacophony of sounds is not enough, a game should also (like a good movie) be accompanied by a soundtrack. This soundtrack should add to the mood of the scene being played out on the screen. It should also tie in with the experiences of the player in the immediate game universe.

If things are not going so well for the player—for example, if he is limping along a dark corridor, bleeding from several bullet wounds—there is little point in playing an uplifting dance track. It will clash with the current state of the player.

The music needs to follow the experiences of the player and the course that he has chosen throughout the game. This approach ties in with the idea of scripted audio that we looked at in the last section. The general idea is that the game has, in its implementation, a series of possible soundtracks that can accompany the player as he tries to make sense out of the game universe presented the play session. In addition, the music can adapt to the game universe in a dynamic fashion; a particular musical track, played at several different tempos and modified slightly each time, can be used appropriately when things are going well or when things are going badly.

Apart from the general musical theme that accompanies the gameplay, there should also be some specific scores that complement scripted cinematic sequences. If you get the chance, play a game like *Severance: Blade of Darkness*, in which there are several points at which the gameplay stops, and the character looks around. These are almost like cutscenes, except that these little interludes reveal some of the surrounding objects and characters. The background musical track provides a clue to the events that are about to unfold, as well as painting an audible environment in which they are about to take place.

The combination of animation and audio track creates a sixth sense; the player is able to get into the right frame of mind to confront the next part of the gaming experience. This augments both the enjoyment and ease with which he can enter the game world and take on the role of the character.

Take, for example, the incredible cinematic sequences in the movie *Far and Away*, which were performed by the well-known artist, Enya. Set in Ireland, the movie contains many sequences of rolling hills and cliffs against a rough sea. The music that accompanies these sequences is always perfectly chosen to bring the majestic atmosphere to the viewers in a way that the fine imagery on the screen can only partially convey. The movie is the next best thing to actually being there.

This is the purpose of music in some video game sequences. Only so much can be conveyed by graphics alone, but a human being can listen to the music that accompanies a movie and, without seeing the screen, have a fairly good idea of what is going on. For example, as this chapter is being written, there is the sound of a television program in the background—a cartoon, and certainly involving the legendary Tom and Jerry duo. We can tell this just from the unique, upbeat tunes associated with this kind of cartoon.

Next most important in creating a believable, realistic, and immersive game universe are the graphics. It is natural to put the emphasis on the graphics, but this author is a firm believer in the atmosphere that music and sound can inject into a game; and if there are any doubts about this, go back to the beginning of this chapter and reread the quote by Mr. Spielberg.

Graphics

Artwork gives a game visual appeal. There is little doubt that the graphic representations of violence depicted in games such as *Soldier of Fortune*, *Quake*, and *DOOM* are (for some people) the basis of the games' appeal. This does not detract from the supreme leap forward that the genre (created by id Software) represents. The visual aspect is just one very important ingredient.

It is important to understand the way in which graphics have changed over the years—not just the quality of images or textures used, but also the way in which graphics are perceived, both in terms of the platform and the gaming genre. This section will look at the various types of graphics technologies that exist today, as well as a historical rundown of how they were born. Many of the techniques that originated in early games are still in use today, and it is always useful to know not only where we are, but also how we have arrived there.

No book on game design or development would be complete without a look at some of the fantastic eye candy that is possible with the graphics cards available on the market. At the same time, however, we should not neglect the fact that visual representations within a game are achieved through a synergy of hardware, graphics driver (Application Programming Interface, or API), and clever game programming.

Working our way up from the hardware, we start with the actual graphics card, itself. In a handheld or console, this is a dedicated piece of circuitry that cannot be altered once the system has been released to the market. In a home computer, and especially in the IBM PC clones, the graphics card is treated like any other expansion card.

Expansion cards, including graphics cards, can be removed, replaced, and upgraded with a better model. This sets the PC industry apart from consoles. To change the graphics capabilities of a console, you must purchase a whole new machine. Keep in mind, too, that design and development technologies move with incredible speed within the games industry. Therefore, it pays to offset the impact of aging graphics subsystems with clever preparation at the development stage of the video game.

So, the hardware and software are tied together in development, but there is an additional piece to the jigsaw puzzle. To enable the game, the hardware and software need to communicate with each other in a reliable and efficient manner.

This is where the next layer comes into play: the API. The piece of software that connects the graphics card to the operating system is called a "driver." The driver is backed up by a special set of libraries, the API, which implement many important routines for graphics manipulation. The driver and API, together, represent a unique, system-specific combination, meaning that no two PCs are ever really the same. The API knows how to communicate with the driver, but the programmer knows how to communicate with the API and what it can do for him.

In the console market, the graphics subsystem will be well documented and understood. This means that, in essence, following the guidelines provided by the manufacturer will lead to a dependable design. We should be clear on this point; it relates to the choice of platforms and technologies that will be available to our video game design.

What is achievable on a PC, a console, or a handheld machine varies enough that the designer needs to be aware of what the proposed target platform can do, as well as his ability to alter the game to fit the platform. (Of course, the designer can switch platforms if the game design becomes too restricted by his first choice, but this would undoubtedly entail a massive overhaul.)

Remember, too, that although development is usually carried out on a PC (some say that development is *always* carried out on a PC), getting a good emulator is half of the battle toward targeting a given platform. If a switch does need to be made, unless it is from a high-definition console environment to a mobile phone, or graphics to text, then it will be expensive, but largely possible.

So in the design phase, we can ignore *how* the graphics are displayed and concentrate instead on *what* we would like to see displayed. There are many constructs inside commercial game engines and libraries that will help us to display the graphical elements of the game, as well as controls for rendering text and buttons. We will deal with these in Chapter 9, when we look at the graphical user interface; here we are more concerned with the main game graphics.

Sprites

The first kind of artwork that ever existed in computer games was the sprite. A sprite is a recognizable shape that moves around on the screen. Sprites can be animated or static. Typically, an animated sprite is either animated on the spot or uses sequential movement; as the sprite moves to a new position, its shape alters to give the illusion of animation.

Sprites were fairly typical of a series of machines produced by Nintendo, called Game & Watch. They had an LCD screen with a number of shapes on them that lit up, depending on the current game state. The technology stemmed from digital timepieces, where a series of segments could be lit to represent numbers.

Imagine taking this a step further on a large screen that contains many segments, each of which is shaped like a particular game element. The LCD Game & Watch units were based on static graphical stencils, but which were activated in accord with the in-game action to give the illusion of animation. The player-controlled character was limited to a zone at the bottom of the screen where there was a row of, say, 10 segments, each a slightly different shape. As the player pressed the left or right, button, the different segments would light up and give the impression that the character had moved from one side to the other. The fact that they were all slightly different also gave a reasonable illusion of animation.

You might even have some games that use this kind of technique in your possession; it is still widely used for handheld game devices, because it is cheap and effective. However, it is really only used for single-game devices, since the shapes cannot be changed. Of course, a more refined version is currently used for the Nintendo GameBoy series.

In the GameBoy world, the LCD screen is composed of a series of dots (pixels), each of which can be lit up as required. In this way, a sprite can be created from a series of pixels, and when viewed from a comfortable distance, the sprite appears solid. Of course, if the player holds the GameBoy up close to their eyes, the pixels are apparent.

Each sprite can be animated by turning pixels on and off. The machine allows for a limited number of sprites in memory. Animation can be achieved by displaying each a little differently, showing them one after the other.

A slower way would be to animate the sprite by altering its data. In this case, the programmer reclaims a certain amount of control, but some of the inherent speed of the machine's hardware is lost to dealing with the sprites.

The GameBoy Color extended the standard LCD screen with a set of four colors, and the most recent GameBoy Advance and DS models use a very high-resolution LCD screen with many colors. As recently as 2000, however, games were still being produced for the GameBoy, and GameBoy Color, simply because of the popularity of the system.

Sprites were also used in the console world. Starting with the Atari 2600, to the Nintendo Entertainment System, the Sega Mega Drive (Genesis in the U.S.), and the Super Nintendo Entertainment System (as well as other variants), a sprite interface has almost always been offered as an option for programmers. These interfaces meant that the programmer did not have to worry about displaying sprites; it was simply a matter of telling the machine where to move the sprites. There were very rigid standards in these machines, which differed from one system to another, and which dictated the exact format of the sprites, so that no matter what the sprite looked like, it was more or less guaranteed to follow the same format as all the others.

Sprite engines are also widely available for most gaming environments. Management libraries exist that free the programmer from the responsibility for sprite storage and manipulation, something of a blessing for game studios that are just getting to grips with the rest of the design and development process.

Other platforms, such as mobile phones, despite having sophisticated cameras and multimedia players on board, also rely on sprites for gaming applications. They are easy to draw and can convey a large amount of information in a small resolution.

Drawing sprites, however, is not always straightforward; they need to be an abstract version of what they represent. Larger game entities can be built by combining sprites or parts of sprites, of course, but the designer has to be very conscious that they are, in the end, just a collection of dots with static dimensions.

WIREFRAMES

Whereas a sprite is essentially a piece of artwork, of varying resolutions and color depths, that can be moved around programmatically, a wireframe is a slightly different approach to video game graphics. The wireframe technique takes an object (say, a spacecraft) and renders it as a collection of connecting lines.

Imagine, for a minute, a cube. If we were to draw it on a sheet of paper, we would start with the face, and then we would extend lines beyond and connect them to make the rest of the outline. What we do not draw, however, is the hidden lines. This is a wireframe of a cube, and any shape can be rendered this way, with varying degrees of resolution.

In the home-computing world, automatic interfaces, such as the built-in sprite handlers of the GameBoy and consoles, were not always present. They did often reprogram standard ASCII characters so that little eight-by-eight-character sprites could be created. The versatility of the home computer meant that built-in sprite-handling functionality has never really been on the top of the feature list. Software developers were expected to provide the graphical interface, themselves. Of course, with each successive generation, sprite handling was made simpler, the reliance on assembly language, which epitomized early gaming development, was also eliminated. This applied to almost any kind of video game system.

The story begins with a short look at how graphics are displayed on a computer screen. Typically, in the first home computers, an area of memory was mapped to the screen display. This was known as the "video memory," and altering the data contained in the video memory directly affected what was displayed on the screen. The problem was one of speed; it takes a long time to loop through each possible position and update the screen.

This was partially solved by using "pages" of memory—either an on-screen page (displayed) or an off-screen page (not displayed). At a given moment in time, the machine may need to update the display, and does so in the off-screen page. Once the page has been completely updated, the computer swaps it with the on-screen page so that the new page is displayed. The reason this is more efficient is because writing to the off-screen memory is much faster than writing to the on-screen memory; it does not need to be displayed immediately. The hardware's ability to swap the off- and on-screen pages is far faster than altering the value for each and every pixel in memory while directly updating them on the screen. To put simply, it is faster to create a new page in memory and display (swap) that page all at once, rather than paint-and-display, paint-and-display pixels one by one on the screen.

Understanding this leads us to the way that many game engines handle sprites, which is by having three screens. One is the "off-screen" display, a second is the "on-screen" display, and a third screen exists as pure memory; it has very fast access and contains the desired state of the screen to be displayed (we will come back to this). The final resource-saving trick is to compare the on- and off-screen, and only display those items that have changed. In addition, we can compare the actual display with the desired display and only post the changes to the off-screen page.

The pure memory screen is basically an area of memory that is directly mapped to the display. In pre-PC home computers, the video card was part of the motherboard, and there was no such thing as "compatibility" across systems. So, programmers exploited the architecture by directly reading from and writing to screen memory, often much faster than would be possible via conventional methods built into the programming language used on the machine.

Without digressing into compiler versus interpreter theory, keep in mind that most early home computers used an interpreted form of BASIC (Beginner's All-purpose Symbolic Instruction Code), backed up by some assembly language. Compilers were largely left to the realm of mainframe and minicomputers; the rest of us had to hand-craft our assembly language code for maximum performance. This allowed games like *Elite* (BBC Micro) to achieve effects over and beyond what the engineers behind the hardware believed possible.

Now, let us again deviate slightly from the core theme of this book and look at just how hard it was to draw a simple line back in 1982. Imagine how a line is plotted on the screen, pixel by pixel. You mathematicians will know that a diagonal line can be drawn by taking the gradient and advancing one pixel in a given direction while simultaneously advancing proportionally along the other axis.

So, look at a simple command for drawing a line, such as:

```
Draw x1, y1, x2, y2;
```

This will result in many calculations, starting with trying to figure out the gradient, and then the most efficient way of plotting the line. Coupled with this, there is the possibility that the processor cannot handle floating-point math, so all the calculations need to be performed using integer mathematics. Clearly, there is more to this simple act of drawing a line than meets the eye.

Now imagine that you are drawing a square . . . or a circle . . . or triangle. How about filling a 3D shape made up of several hundred polygons, complete with shading? This is why hardware APIs and standards are so useful—they make developing graphics software for today's systems much more accessible than in the early days. This encourages game development for those who have the drive, talent, and suitable tools.

These days, of course, machines are faster, compilers are *much* more efficient, and fewer people use raw assembly language (or machine code) as a way to get that extra five percent of performance from the system—which is a pity, because that extra five percent might push a game from "marginally believable" to "really realistic." Still, there is something to be said for standardization, particularly in graphics, sound, and physics APIs and engines.

One step up from the pure black-and-white wireframe model is the shaded polygon. Historically, while most games were based on some kind of sprite system, part of the market was developing games that made use of shading the various sides of a wireframe model to produce a pseudo-3D image.

3D Art

This is where the original 2D wireframe concept becomes 3D. Three-dimensional graphics were a leap forward in rendering video games. Generally speaking, 3D can be viewed in three different ways, starting with pseudo-3D, in which 2D effects can be used to impart a 3D depth to the game. *SimCity* (Maxis) used subtle shading to convey the height of buildings in the game. (The game, itself, somehow managed to straddle the line between having a 2D, top-down view and an isometric game view.)

Next there is the constrained 3D environment, in which real 3D models are presented, detailed and shaded accordingly so that they have depth, breadth, and height. The player, though, is constrained in the amount of freedom they have in exploring the game universe. Good examples are the isometric game *Populous* or the original *SimCity2000*, in which the jump from the top-down view to a 45-degree angle was made.

Finally, there is the aptly named "true 3D," in which the player is free to move through all three axes in their exploration of the game universe, and all the models that depict adversaries, allies, and other game objects are also rendered as objects that can rotate through all three axes, as well. *Elite*, even in its original, unshaded black-and-white wireframe form is a true 3D game, since the player can fly with complete freedom of movement.

Pseudo-3D

One of the earliest attempts at pseudo-3D in the arcade game industry was the use of layered backgrounds, each of which moved at a different pace. In Figure 5.1, for example, we can see that there are three layers. There is, in white, the Foreground, upon which the player will drive their vehicle. Then there are two kinds of backgrounds—Middle and Far Distance. These scroll past at two different speeds; the Far Distance scrolls an order of magnitude slower than the Middle Distance. The Foreground will scroll at a speed that is as fast as possible while retaining the player's control, and the scroll speeds of the other two layers will be set accordingly with respect to this Foreground focus speed.

Interestingly, the reader should also note that the amount of variation of the line that represents the landscape being scrolled also changes depending on whether the line represents something in the Foreground, Middle Distance, or Far Distance. Landscapes closer to the player can be more varied, but the farther away objects are,

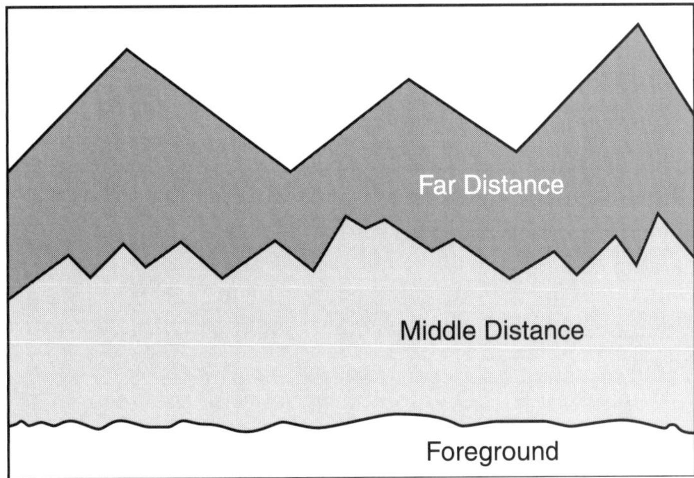

FIGURE 5.1 Layered backgrounds.

the less detail will be visible; hence, less variation can be used. However, the degree of each variation can become more pronounced, from the gentle, undulating hills of the Middle Distance to the mountain ranges of the Far Distance.

Objects can also be rendered in pseudo-3D simply by adding some shadows to them and allowing parts of their sides to be displayed. It is important to note that isometric views can be considered to fall into either the pseudo- or constrained 3D category by virtue of the fact that they model 3D shapes, but the techniques used to display them can also be achieved with 2D sprites.

Note that isometric, 2D tiled game universes have a specific consideration—what to do when two objects overlap. When designing the sprites, we should treat the entire viewable play area as a series of square cells that are sheared on one side by 45 to 60 degrees, making them trapezoids rather than traditional "chessboard" squares used in a 2D, top-down sprite model. In this sheared configuration, the screen dimensions change slightly, because in order to retain some semblance of realism, space has to be left "above" the grid so that it doesn't look as if the camera is pointing right at it, which would give the player a feeling of claustrophobia. In the worst case, between one-quarter and one-third of the available screen real estate can be lost due to this refinement.

Constrained 3D

Taking the classic isometric view one stage further, we can enable the full screen to be used if we tip the angle of the tiles such that (if required) an entire object can be viewed from the top to the bottom and on both sides. On the other hand, we cannot allow the player to alter the camera angle, because this would reveal the fact that we are still using 2D sprites instead of real 3D models.

Another aspect of a not-true 3D engine is the lack of particle physics and other details that are only possible if we can use real models. If real models are not an option, then explosions, for example, will lack the detail expected in real life. The two approaches, can, however, be combined.

The tilted camera and shaded models are still used in some games today. The advantage with such an approach is that we can offer the player depth of vision without needing to tackle the complex mathematics that real 3D needs to take into account.

When we offer 3D graphics, we increase the freedom of movement that the player is allowed. In 2D and constrained 3D environments, it is accepted that the player's motion will be limited, and we can even predict which planes he will move in. In 3D, however, we need to be constantly aware that the player can move in any axis, giving them the potential to go anywhere. So, we cannot predict their positioning or the planes in which they will move. This being the case, we need to calculate every aspect of the player's in-game persona or vehicle, and how it relates to all of the other game objects.

This increases three complexities—the design, the development, and the resulting platform. We need a more-complex design to build in contingencies that true 3D requires, we need to make sure that we have the tools and knowledge to create a 3D environment, and we need to be sure that the target platform is up to the job.

Isometric, constrained 3D still looks good when done properly and is less of a technical headache than true 3D. However, there are instances when only true 3D will do.

True 3D

When going beyond using 2D elements to give a 3D look and feel, we need to introduce the concept of models that can be rotated in any direction, viewed at any angle, and react in a way that is in keeping with their "solid" appearance. This is not restricted to the game objects, either. Everything, from the scenery to the weapons, needs to follow the 3D-model philosophy.

Games such as *Tomb Raider*, and the *Quake* and *DOOM* series, and even *SimCity 4* are all examples of true 3D engines. *SimCity 4,* however, still adheres to an isometric, restricted-camera 3D view because of the complexity of the graphics; allowing the player full freedom of movement is prohibitively expensive in processing power. *SimCity 4* is still one of the most supremely detailed games, as is the

Sims. The attention to detail is astonishing. This detail is made possible by the true 3D engine behind it that models everything, including little ant-like inhabitants, as models. There is a particle physics engine in the design too, which makes for convincing firework displays, explosions, and even realistic fires.

Luckily, there is a way out for most game designers that allows effective 3D model rendering without the need to model detail right down to the particle level. It is the key to producing games such as *DOOM*, *Quake*, and other first-person shooters, and even space battle games, such as the *Elite* series, among others; and it is something that is well-supported by tools and libraries, and will translate effectively to all platforms that support the handling of images.

The technique employed is to create a set of polygons and layer bitmapped graphics onto the visible faces, stretching and compressing a single example of each bitmap so that the polygonal models become *textured*. Those bitmaps are known as *textures*, and can be produced from very simple images that can be distorted, speckled (granulated), or transformed so that they look like any surface, from rough to smooth, without having to actually model each specific particle that makes up the surface.

To add even more realism to the mix, we can also position virtual lights around the immediate game universe, which use the well-understood, particle physics concept of light traveling in straight lines, to apply a network of shadows to the textures.

Of course, doing this in real time is processor intensive, so it has to be used sparingly. Luckily, there are some techniques for producing an acceptable effect without actually modeling the light sources in real time, and for less processor overhead.

Since this book deals with design and not implementation, all that the reader needs to be aware of is that models can have a high or low number of polygons, which enables the system to render them in varying levels of realism. The more polygons a model has (its "polycount"), the more realistic it will be in terms of shape, and the resolution of its texture will also contribute to the eventual level of detail that can be displayed.

One final point to note is that the core technology behind polygonal modeling with textured surfaces has been given a boost recently by a very important advance made by a German studio, CryTek, for their game *Cry Freedom*. In the game, models are created with a special tool, which the studio is making available to the general public (at a price). This tool enables the designer to create a model with a high number of polygons, and then a mesh is applied that effectively creates a map of the high-polygon model, complete with textures, and transforms the model into a low-polycount version. The low-polycount version, by itself, would be quite unrealistic if it were displayed in the game, so the mesh is used to transform the low-polycount version into a high-polycount version, which has a much higher level of realism.

This also reduces the processing overhead of the game when actually trying to manipulate the model during the play session, since the machine only needs to worry about the lower number of polygons that are present in the model. It is only when the model needs to be displayed that the mesh is applied—thus, the bulk of the realistic rendering is farmed out to the graphics engine.

The whole process is simply more efficient, which frees up capacity in the core game for other duties. The balance is also slightly different, with the graphics engine doing the actual rendering, and the game engine manipulating a low-poly version of the model to be manipulated. Rendering the low polycount model in conjunction with the mesh is what produces the realistic on-screen result.

Sadly, these techniques will not necessarily be applicable to the handheld market, which still use a system of sprites and memory mapped to individual game objects. The immensely popular Nintendo GameBoy series of machines all use sprite and sprite-like technology, from the black-and-white LCD original unit through to more-recent models like the GameBoy Advance.

However, modern graphical subsystems used in high-end consoles like the big three from Microsoft, Sony, and Nintendo all have graphics engines that can cope with images, particles, and all manners of seemingly semi-magical transformation functions.

Of course, game programmers, mathematicians, and engineers can explain fluently what the transformation functions do; that would be for a more technical volume. In essence, there are plenty of mathematical techniques that can be applied to calculate the way the graphics should look after an event has taken place, but they seem magical to the uninitiated.

Shading and Tiling

A technique that is common to both 3D and 2D game design is the use of textured tiles that can be layered to produce surfaces that look like they're covered with a material, while only needing to store one small sample of the texture in the game resource memory. Furthermore, the needed set of textures can be reduced by simply maintaining "common variants" of textures and rendering them differently during the play session, depending on what they are supposed to represent.

Thus, there could be a set of "rocky" textures used for sand, gravel, and even asphalt, simply by storing a monochrome texture and coloring the result during the play session. Shading the tiles in this way is a variant on bump-mapping (see the section on True 3D).

A recent trend toward using textures that are "pure" uses the concept of "cel-shading." The term comes from the animated movie and cartoon industry—particularly the world of Japanese anime, made famous by the "manga" (Japanese for "comics") adult cartoons. In anime, graphics are represented by pure colors that are lit in such a way as to cast shadows; there is no texture to the models.

The effect is that of a cartoon and not realism; however, the end result is guided as much by the style of characters as it is by the nature of the modeling technique being used. Generally, the models are rendered in bright primary colors, or monochrome with splashes of color. Gravel, for example, is a pure gray, with no real substance or rough texture.

The smooth look of cel-shaded games has won both critical acclaim as well as substantial disdain by fans of ultra-realistic graphics. The player will either love or hate the result, a fact that should not escape the video game designer.

Art Formats

Finally, we need just to touch on the various ways that images can be encoded and used either as tiles, textures, or even as shaders. A shader is a special kind of texture that is designed to be used in conjunction with another texture to increase the resolution, and hence provide an additional layer of realism to the end result.

Generally speaking, images can be encoded as pure bitmaps, or compressed in some way using either a lossy or lossless algorithm. The reason for the compression will become apparent as we look at bitmaps;—it boils down to a question of size.

A monochrome bitmap 16-pixels wide and 16-pixels deep requires storing a one or a zero for each pixel. Hence, a total of 16 × 16 values need to be stored. Assuming one byte per pixel, this yields a result of 256 bytes. This may not sound like much, but it doesn't scale very well; textures offering a high resolution may be up to 128 × 128 pixels in dimension, which would need 16,384 bytes of storage—a significant amount, especially if it needs to be applied many times in a scene.

Getting around this requires that we step briefly into the realm of development and realize that a byte is expressed as a series of bits. Each bit can either be on ("1") or off ("0"). Consequently, since we know that there are 8 bits in a byte, we immediately see that there can be a reduction if each bit is set according to the pixel value; we only need to define a monochrome image in this case.

Hence, 100 × 100 becomes 13 × 13 (100 / 8 = 12.5), with half a byte unused due to the fact that 8 does not divide perfectly into 100. This reduces the storage from 10,000 bytes to a mere 169 bytes. Furthermore, the storage requirement of a 500 × 500-pixel texture is reduced from 250,000 bytes to 3,969 bytes (63 × 63). We call this format "1bpp," or 1 bit per pixel.

What happens when we need to display colors? Each pixel now has to be represented by a mixture of Red, Green, and Blue (RGB) intensities. An RGB image can be stored as 8bpp, 16bpp, or 24bpp. The difference between the formats hinges on the way that the three values for the red, green, and blue intensities are combined to produce a single color. Without going into details that are beyond the scope of this book, the more bits per pixel we can afford, the higher the color depth of the image, which can be described as hundreds, thousands, or millions of colors.

Millions of colors require 24bpp; a 100 × 100-pixel image needs 30,000 bytes of storage space, and 750,000 bytes are required for a 500 × 500 image. It is effectively the same as having a red, green, and blue image layered together to produce the final result. Each of these "color planes" is rendered using a full byte (8 bits) per pixel.

Naturally, there is a way out. We can use palettes. A palette is a list of colors used in the image, and it can contain a varying number of elements (representing red, green, or blue intensities), depending on the amount of storage assigned to each palette element. If 8 bits are used, we have 256 possible entries; 16 bits allow 32,000, and 24 bits allow millions. The advantage is that only the colors needed in the image are actually represented in the list, and each pixel can be rendered simply as an index into that list.

Incidentally, 24-bit color is sometimes called "true color," since it is also possible to represent each pixel as a combination of varying intensities of red, green, and blue, the three color planes. This allows us to represent any one of the colors that the human eye can perceive.

Luckily, there are various levels of compression that we can apply, some of which effectively lose data in expansion (lossy) and others that do not (lossless). There are many different formats capable of different levels of compression, and with different color depths. Some common ones are GIF (255 colors maximum), JPEG (up to 24-bit color), and a variant format, PNG (Portable Network Graphics).

Bearing all this in mind, the designer is equipped to make decisions regarding the type and format of graphics that will be used in the game, and also ensure that the platform restrictions are respected. The first step is to create some "dummy" or "mock-up" packages of artwork and sound that can accompany the game design to flesh it out further.

Concept Art and Sound

Concept artwork is important in video game design for two reasons. First, it adds dimension to the design, which proves that the designer has thought it through far enough that the work required to turn the concept into a real game will be purely implementation. Second, like writing down the game ideas, it forces the designer to think about how the idea and genre are going to mesh together.

Creating Concept Artwork

Many game designers cannot draw or even create reasonably realistic textured models. It helps that there are a number of great freeware (and shareware) packages on the market that can aid the creation process. Some enable the designer to make models that can be imported into the game proper at a later date, which will enable the *real* graphics department to get to work that much quicker and without trying to guess what the designer wants from a collection of rough sketches and vague descriptions.

Unless the designer's best friend happens to be an animator or artist, he will have to contract out the concept artwork. Existing pre-design sketches might be appropriate at first, but when the design matures, it will be necessary to try and convey professionalism, and create proper storyboards—even animated sequences.

The artist might be tempted to create something that is, in itself, a work of art; but it is important, if he has never worked in the industry before, to try and persuade him to only create something that can be implemented. The reason is that, as a video game designer, you might want to re-use some of the artwork in the game itself as a way to reduce the end product's time to market. It pays to ask the artist, up front, how this will affect his fees; he might require a royalty payment for his work and/or the game's licensing to use it. This problem won't exist if the artist becomes part of the eventual team that creates the end product, which will only be the case if it is to be an independent release. Game studios will want to use their own people.

Creating Concept-Spoken Audio

As was previously mentioned, it pays to avoid using friends, family members, or random people off the street for in-game spoken audio. It might at the time seem like a cost-effective use of money—after all, it will be cheap . . . and so will be the result. Of course, the chances that the designer has actors in his circle of friends and family is fairly slim, so there's few ways around this point—use real actors.

While friends might have great in-person voices, just try taping them (and yourself for an uninspiring experience) and playing it back. It will probably take many false starts before you actually get audio that is sufficient. Actors might be expensive, but you will get usable audio much more quickly.

This is as true for the game design as it is for the game proper. After all, if the design has reached the point that a "show-reel" is needed to help to sell the project to a publishing house or development studio, then investing a little more than just time in the project is worthwhile.

Creating Concept Music

When it comes to music, there are three approaches. Either the designer is also a musician, or he has a friend who is a musician, or he can acquire music from the many public-domain sources that exist on the Internet. This last option is a great way to get used to creating music, by downloading pieces that fit the moods for the game, seeing how they are put together, and trying to replicate them.

The average video game designer is likely to be quite creative, and so this kind of "borrowing" and re-use is probably going to be second nature. However, be careful when using music that has been created by someone else; there might be legal issues. Always ask first.

There are plenty of formats to choose from, but for editing, something akin to the MODule file format is recommended. It is worthwhile to look at how a piece of MODule music is put together from the ground up, in a descriptive way.

The basic idea behind a MODule is that it uses samples of real instruments, played at different notes, volumes, and tempos to create a piece of music. This is where the download, analyze, and recreate technique comes into its own. Each piece of music is broken down into tracks so that two or more instruments can be played at the same time, and looking at how each one is created, using an appropriate editor, is a great way to get started.

The designer can load the music into a MOD editor (known as a Tracker) to see exactly which samples are cued at given time increments, as well as their pitch, length, and volume. Using the samples and the original musical score as a template, we can use the Tracker to experiment with a new piece of music until it matches the mood of the game.

The final step is to export the MOD file to another format, such as MP3, which can be used in conjunction with a piece of code that can decode and play the music. These are available in the public domain. There are also many public-domain sample packs available for would-be musicians, which cater to a variety of different musical styles and instruments.

The Show-Reel

The resulting concept art, sound, and music should comprise the show-reel. As in the movie industry, the goal is to show off the concept at its best, with as much work as is necessary to try and convey what the finished product will be like. Even if there is no actual programming completed to speak of, a show-reel can always be put together that contains small animations, pieces of artwork with some background music, and, ideally, a voiceover that introduces the viewer to the game.

Of course, show-reels can be interactive. This need not be any more substantial than a mock-up of the user interface in a suitable, prototyped environment. Even an HTML interface can be used, which will give the designer an opportunity to show off the artwork and sound, and the show-reel can also do double duty as a Web site.

Summary

The game universe and the interaction of the player with that universe have graphics and sound as their backbones. In the design phase, there are decisions that need to be made, and these decisions will affect the eventual product. The reverse is also true.

The job of the video game designer is to decide how the vision will eventually be implemented, and while this task has to be abstracted as much as possible, it pays to be aware of the eventual platform and delivery medium when designing sound, music, and graphics. If a game engine has already been chosen, the designer must know what is and isn't possible with that engine.

Some graphics will look wonderful in the concept stage, but do not easily translate to a sprite-based platform. Or, the title sound track to the game might be so complex that the eight tracks provided by the portable gaming system will not be able to cope with it.

Being aware of how the game will be implemented is part of the way in which the video game designer takes a great idea and makes it into a great game. It will also sell the concept to the publisher or studio, or whoever is putting up the money to develop the end product.

References

[EDGE01] *EDGE* magazine, No. 115, October 2002, p. 67.
[Jacques01] Richard Jacques in *EDGE* magazine. No. 115, October 2002, p. 71.
[Saltzman01] Marc Saltzman, *Game Design: Secrets of the Sages.* BradyGames, 2000, p. 263.

6 Object-Oriented Game Design

In This Chapter

- OO Primer
- Relationships
- Object Model

It is impossible to write a book on game design without at least being aware of the principles that drive the software engineers and programmers who are responsible for turning the design into a product. Without some appreciation for the methods and techniques that are used to implement software, it will be difficult to organize the design in such a way that makes it easy for the programmers to deliver a video game that meets with the designer's expectations. Also, the end product will be higher in quality if the same principles are used in the design phase as in the development. Following techniques such as Object-Oriented (OO) Design will force the designer to plan in a methodical way.

Although this sounds suspiciously like software engineering, some of the finer points of Object Orientation and software engineering will be set aside in our effort to introduce these techniques to the game designer. Whole books have been devoted to the subject for those who want to take their studies further (see the Appendix).

It is true that the video game designer will also have to be part software designer—he will need to have an appreciation of the basic principles. It never hurts to be able to insert the odd piece of code; it shows a deeper understanding of what makes a video game and helps the designer to think carefully about the design and its possible pitfalls.

OO PRIMER

Game players, without realizing it, already have a fairly good idea of the key elements behind Object Orientation. When we come straight from the real world to the programming world, there are no preconceptions to contend with—which is an advantage. This book introduces Object-Oriented Design without trying to break through the barriers set up by classic programming paradigms—and offers an apology to traditional programmers.

OBJECTS AND PROPERTIES

In essence, Object-Oriented Design is a way of mapping the real world onto a collection of items—objects—that can be modeled by a computer. If there is a bucket in the game universe, then somewhere in the depths of the game machine's memory there will be a bucket object. For each virtual object that the player encounters, there will be a corresponding object coded in memory, also.

Each object, such as the bucket, will have a set of properties associated with it. The bucket might be pink or of a certain capacity, and represented by depth, circumference, and skew (tapered angles). It might have a handle and be empty or full of another object, such as water.

The water represents an object on its own. Or, to more-accurately implement the real world, the water would be a collection of objects—water molecules. A single water molecule object consists of two parts hydrogen and one part oxygen (H_2O). These could also be created as objects with certain properties and added to the growing collection of objects in the game universe.

All of this is fine if we are only modeling a bucket. If, however, this approach is taken for each object in the game universe, then we will never get around to actually designing the gameplay. We'll be stuck on that first, perfectly modeled and realistic game object—what an achievement.

The message is clear. The designer has to know where to draw the line. Fortunately, there are some tricks that can be used for modeling objects as accurately as possible while keeping within the scope of the game. There is also the related problem of storage space. Computers are wonderful and fantastic machines, but there remain, however, some aspects in which they are very limited—and storage space is one of them.

It is not a full hard drive that worries game designers, but the temporary space (RAM) needed to store all of the game-object information. This averages 512MB in the PC world and is less for consoles. Consoles have less, too; but can do more with it, since they don't have to worry about the operating system, drivers, and so forth that the average PC has to content with.

Now, 512MB might seem like a lot of memory, but it really is not. Think of it as 512 million letters. Then imagine that our pink bucket is full of water. How many molecules of water are there likely to be in it, let alone atoms? And then there is the bucket, itself—possibly made of wood, possibly aluminum. Either way, there are molecules in the wood or aluminum. We will quickly run out of space, even if only the chemical symbol for each of the molecules is stored—512MB really is not that much memory storage space.

So, before sitting down with the programming or scripting team (even if it is a team of one person), it is important to think about the objects that will be needed. The objects can be broken down into two sets: concrete objects that will represent the various things that the player will be able to interact with, attack, take, use, or just look at; and abstract objects that do not necessarily have a visual aspect. An abstract object might be the player, himself (such as in first-person shooters), that will have properties such as wealth or health (which might be represented by an object that is part of the graphical user interface).

Some objects will necessarily be built from other objects (compound objects), but the designer has to decide which these are. For example, a racing game will include vehicles, such as automobiles or planes. Each vehicle can be modeled as a single object, unless they can be altered over the course of the game by a crash, a lost wheel or wing, or a malfunctioning engine. In this case, each piece of the vehicle will need a life of its own and require an object in its own right.

A useful side-effect of using compound objects is that each can be built from similar objects that have their own unique properties. An automobile, for example, is a compound object that can be used as a container for other automobile parts. A mix of parts with different properties will make automobiles with different external characteristics. Red and blue automobiles will share many of the same objects, but each will have different color properties that will give the automobile its distinctive red or blue features.

We define these objects once and then define a set of properties with ranges. Let us illustrate this with a much easier example. The well-known game *Tetris* is possibly one of the easiest to visualize (with the possible exception of *Pong*, which has its own mathematical complications). Each falling object in *Tetris* is comprised of a number of blocks. Each block can be one of several colors—red, green, blue, and yellow. Therefore, we can define a *Tetris* block as follows:

```
Object
       Block
Properties
    Color : { Red, Green, Blue, Yellow }
```

When we need a block, we can *instantiate* an *instance* of *type* `Block` and assign it a color, such as `Red`. In this way, we only need to store a global definition of `Block` that can be used as a generic template. The `Block` objects can be combined to create a compound "shape."

There are many ways to do this, one of which is to add some properties to `Block` that set the location of the `Block` object from a nominal reference point. In addition, since these `Block` objects fall toward the bottom of the playing area, they need another property to represent this, which we shall call `Velocity`. To make the "shape" fall, we set the `Velocity` of each `Block` to a value, say "1." When it reaches its resting point, we can give all the `Block` sub-objects a velocity of "0"; the shape is no longer moving.

Our final definition for `Block` might look something like this:

```
Object
       Block
Properties
    Color : { Red, Green, Blue, Yellow }
    Horizontal Position : { 0–4 }
    Vertical Position : { 0–4 }
    Velocity : { 0–10 }
```

We also need to define a `Shape` object, which is a collection of `Block` objects:

```
Object
       Shape
Properties
    Horizontal Position : { 0–Play Area Width }
    Vertical Position : { 0–Play Area Height }
Contains
    4 x Block
```

These objects are sufficient to store abstract information about the game universe, but are restricted to this function. Before they can be useful, we need to do other things to them. The first is to set their properties so that when we create a `Block` object, we can choose a color and initial location for it. Then we need some way to tell the object to move, display itself, or remove itself from machine memory when no longer needed.

Methods

The way in which we communicate with objects is by using *methods* that affect the data stored within the object, retrieve data from the object, or tell the object that it needs to communicate with one or more objects that are related to it by function. For example, a "Block" object will need to tell a "Display" object to paint a designated place with a set of pixels that represent the "Block"—assuming, of course, that the "Display" object has been told how to do this.

Traditional OO designs require that only the object knows its own properties. Among computer scientists, this is known as *data encapsulation*. Strict encapsulation means that from outside the object, it is impossible to know what data it holds. This is like meeting someone for the first time. There are things that should be obvious from simple observation, such as their gender, height, hair color, and other physical attributes.

Then again, there are other things make up a person—such as their name, profession, or intellectual capacity—things that cannot be known unless we ask them. (Of course, there might be visual clues, such as a policeman's uniform with a name tag.) Only then will we be able to work with this data; for example, we might need to address mail with their professional title.

In the real world, we ask the person for his name; but in programming-speak, we invoke the `Name` function, which returns a representation of the person's name. This may seem convoluted, but some actions that we need to perform on objects have no parallel in the real world.

Before we look at one of the most powerful manipulators of these object templates, we should introduce this technology's programming terms. There is a difference between the design terminology and programmer terminology. In design terms, we talk about properties and methods of objects, but the programming terms that describe them differ from language to language. In C++, one of the most common programming languages, generic objects are known as *classes*.

Each *class* has a *private* part and a *public* area. The `private` statement is typically used to encapsulate the data that describes the object, while `public` is used for the methods that access this data (ask the object to perform certain tasks). These methods are called *functions* in C++ parlance. So, to implement the previously described simple block object in C++, we use code like this:

```
class Block
{
private:
    Color cColor; // Assumes data type Color defined
    int nX, nY, nV;        // Vert./Horiz. Position & Velocity
public:
    Block ( Color cColor ); // Make a block of this color
    ~Block (); // We no longer need the block
    Color WhatColor (); // Tell the caller our color
}
```

This simple definition allows us to obtain the color of the block by calling (invoking) the `WhatColor` function (method). The returned value is the color. This could be used by all manners of other objects that need to know the color of the block.

In this way, the internal representation of the block and how it can change over time is of no interest to us, but we can obtain state changes from the block. In the case of the block's color, this might not be terribly complex or useful, but when it comes to changing velocity, this method might comprise some complex mathematics that adjust the velocity depending on the block's interaction with other parts of the game universe.

All of this has touched dangerously close to programming, which this book has tried to avoid as much as possible. It is, however, necessary to at least introduce some aspects of programming, since the scripting language behind many game engines is based on C/C++ syntax. Coupled with the fact that these objects are also Object Oriented in nature, this means that we need to understand how programming is related to design, and how design is related to the real world. What links them is programming language.

INHERITANCE

Now that we have an idea of how the game universe is populated, we see that objects will share certain properties and methods. Here is where one of those previously mentioned tricks appears: We can isolate the traits of our objects and use them to create a "super-object" that is more generic than the objects themselves. This is called *inheritance.*

The word "inheritance" in software design circles means the same as it does in genetics. Some classes inherit their attributes from classes that are similar in nature and add their own specific attributes to the class, which further personalizes the class. For example, a dog has four legs and a tail, as does a cat, horse, cow, or sheep. They are all quadrupeds. All have a tail, but these animals differ in terms of ear shape, muzzle length, teeth type, neck length, an so on. However, they *all* have ears, muzzles, teeth, and necks—which is the important point. A cat is a member of the set "quadruped," so it inherits from the base class quadruped and adds certain aspects, overrides (alters) some, and does not use others. However, what inherits from the "cat" class? That depends on how the cat-inclusive world is broken down. "Kitten" might inherit from "cat," for example, but "flea" probably would not.

We might not put cows and horses in the same set, although they are both quadrupeds; or all animals might comprise the same set, regardless of how they are related. The design trick is to decide what attributes these objects have that relate them to each other and to the project, and to capitalize on these connections.

Subclassing

Inheritance operates at the class level, and some software engineers prefer to think of Object Orientation and inheritance as an implementation solution to design problems. In standard application development, this is probably a wise level of abstraction, but in real-time systems, where we over-compensate the design in order to make the result extremely resilient, every interaction must be looked at in advance.

Besides, we can realize some reasonable cost savings by simply reusing pieces of the design where appropriate. Subclassing enables us to do this. It combines inheritance with the standard object-oriented approach to data abstraction.

In order to do this, we need to know what granularity we are going to develop the design at. At this stage, we might not want to go into any more depth than is strictly necessary, because the game universe can be described in a few well-chosen objects, as discussed in Chapter 3, "Video Game Design in Practice." Then again, we might require subclassing to organize more-complex designs.

There will likely be some collecting together at the abstract level. In other words, some classes will be natural superclasses (parent classes) that will not usually share attributes. The subclasses (children classes) will derive their cores from the parent and then be in a position to be refined by the addition of new attributes or methods.

The only caveat is that there might be a situation in which we decide that the subclass has become too customized, and that it has a right to exist as a superclass on its own. At that point, we should re-examine our level of abstraction—our superclass definition—and how it affects other objects in the game.

For example, the Windows operating system (and most operating systems that rely on a graphical user interface) is a network of subclassing opportunities. Every graphical display is a window that is based on a superclass that defines the basic behavioral template. We can then create different classes of displays—edit boxes, dialog windows, list boxes, and so on—each of which has basic attributes that define the item being instantiated a display type in the Windows system. Each of these classes can then be *subclassed* to provide user-defined behavior on top of the inherited, customized attributes and behavior.

So, we might have a list box that is subclassed to provide additional display attributes such as a check mark next to a selected item. Or, we might have an edit box that only accepts numbers, or letters, or that automatically converts URLs to hyperlinks that can be clicked by the user. All these behaviors extend the class that they are derived from.

So, we can design an application (perhaps a game) that redefines a Windows "edit" function, such as "add rich-text editing" to a window that the user can type in, or set text attributes to bold or italics. Now, we might decide that we have created something that is so completely different from the original Windows editor, that it might be useful as that starting point for our own word processor. It would then become a class of its own, ready to be inherited from. We cannot, however, redesign the Windows operating system so that the granularity is changed. But if we design without relying on existing Windows classes, then the option to adjust granularity might exist.

Multiple Inheritance

Sometimes a class can borrow definitions from two superclasses. Some designers shy away from cases in which a single class can inherit from two parent classes, as if it indicates some flaw in the initial design or game universe view. In a sense, they are quite right.

The abstraction of a game universe is slightly more pronounced than in other application design areas. This means that in some cases, we can make design decisions that run slightly counterintuitively. When a class has multiple base classes, there is the risk that some of the methods clash or have the same name, and this confuses the design. Therefore, it pays to minimize the use of multiple inheritance as much as possible.

Relationships

All the objects in the system will be related through interactions to each other. They will have complex relationships that affect each other and the game universe. We have seen how to break down the game universe into objects, and how they are described within that system, their external and internal properties, and how those properties can be altered.

The relationships between objects are mainly governed by their ability to communicate. This may be as simple as feeding the output of one object to the input of another. In more-complex situations, the properties of certain objects can be used as input for other objects, allowing them to interact directly.

There is a problem when designing computer systems—and like it or not, a video game is simply a computer system. This problem is often ignored by designers who see it as part of the implementation and leave it for the programmers to worry about, rather than treat it as a design issue. This problem called *intangible nature* of software, which means it has no form, cannot be viewed (except in an abstract way), cannot be touched, and success can only be measured by effect.

The objects that make up the software system suffer from the same problem. They cannot actually interact directly, because they have no substance. Their interaction is therefore limited by the way in which the design provides channels between objects, enabling them to communicate. When we refer to objects in this sense, we are not just talking about chairs, tables, bricks, or plants, but also player-controlled characters.

As a simple example, consider the game *Tetris*. Colored blocks drop from the top of the screen, and the task of the player is to arrange them as they fall to create single-color lines of blocks. The lines disappear when complete, a value is added to the player's score, and there is then room for more blocks. If we were to build a *Tetris* machine in the real world and drop blocks in at the top, they would stop when they reached the bottom. Physics dictates the hard floor stops their descent as much as gravity dictates that they fall.

In the software equivalent, the objects cannot fall back on their physical presence to provide this automatic behavior. We have to provide a mechanism that bridges the intangible nature of the software objects with the way that we want them to interact on the screen, mimicking the way that they would in the physical world.

We need to provide a way in which the objects can relate to each other, so that they know how each one behaves. This should lead to their interaction, but it requires some knowledge of the internal data, communicated indirectly.

Object-Oriented Design requires (or at least encourages) that as much internal data as possible is hidden from objects. They have access to their own states, but not the states of other objects. This contrasts with reality, because for animate objects (those with an awareness of their surroundings), there are some states that can be perceived, such as the appearance of an object. The animate object can also affect such states, even if the recipient is, itself, animate.

Inanimate objects (which will form the bulk of the game object universe) have neither awareness of the states of the objects surrounding them nor, in most cases, an awareness of their own states. On the other hand, their states can, without their awareness, be affected by other objects in the game universe.

So, the entire OO paradigm is based on designing a model of the universe in a way that it becomes an abstraction. This makes the universe easier to encode as a computer program, which is the eventual job of the programmer—so it is a good model to use. It has one further advantage—objects cannot become corrupted without the express knowledge of the programmer.

Messaging

As we have seen, the eventual game is broken down into pieces, all of which need to have some way to communicate. The best way to do this is with some form of underlying messaging system. This is especially true of video games that will contain a large number of heterogeneous objects, all of which have a part to play—but which also need to influence other objects.

The messaging system will establish a central point of reference for all game code. That is, it might be a kind of message "loop" in which the system is either dealing with the transfer of a message from one object to another, is triggering other events, or is idle. This borrows from the theory behind most modern operating systems. In the Microsoft Windows environment, for example, the user is never in control. They are simply interacting with Windows (the entity that is really in control). The video game is no different. The player feels in control, but nothing could be farther from the truth.

The messaging system is primarily designed to allow the player to interact with the system. Pressing a button generates a message, which is passed to a handler, which looks around at the objects in the universe and decides what action to take. Among these could be the decision to generate another message, which would be passed to another object.

When designing the messaging system, it helps to at least have an idea of what the different kinds of messages are that the video game needs to handle. At the very least, there will be system and control messages.

Consider the control mechanism in place for a simple shooting game. The player is represented by a spacecraft that inhabits an area at the base of the screen. The joystick controls the movement of this spacecraft object. The Fire button releases a missile or a stream of missiles. A system message must relate to the player's action (moving the joystick and pressing the Fire button), which needs to be harvested from the input device and translated into a message that is sent to the spacecraft object in a way that it understands what to do. The first is a *system* message, the second a *control* message.

The difference between the two is that the first message has no discernable effect. The player only sees the effect of the translation of the system message into a control message—the spacecraft moves from one position to another, and a stream of missiles erupts when the Fire button is pressed.

If this is all that the game needs to do, then a simple two-message system will be enough. Then again, we need to know what happens when the missiles leave the screen. Another system message needs to be generated (possibly by the missile, itself), which causes that object to be destroyed and the spacecraft informed that another missile can be fired. This type of message is called the *communication* message. It allows objects to not only communicate, but to receive feedback on previous events—which is the crux of the entire system.

STATES

The last relationship topic that we need to discuss involves thinking about what happens to the game objects when they receive messages. Generally speaking, a message invokes a change of state in the object, possibly via an action.

Thinking in terms of states enables us to ensure that a vital part of the design has not been missed; each property of each object should have a set of possible states. Even those properties that will be used merely as counters can be associated with a state change. It has a starting state with a given value, receives the command to add a designated value to itself, and moves to another state in which its new value is greater than the starting value.

It is important to understand the principle behind states, state changes, and messaging. They need to be linked in order to be able to create a succinct and complete object model. States are described with state tables, and each row looks something like the one shown in Table 6.1.

TABLE 6.1 The State Machine

Starting State	Message	Action	Ending State

"Message" is some form of input, and "Action" is something that is performed that affects the object, or which causes an effect on another object via an outgoing message. Of course, there could be a combination of these, and the designer needs to decide how to tackle cases in which the state change needs to simultaneously cause a property to be modified inside the object, as well as cause a change in another object. In such cases, additional state table rows can be used to manage multiple actions—such as when a value changes, a message is generated and sent to the system or another object.

Once all the states that the property (or object) can be in are known, we can work out what messages are needed to alter the states, and whether other objects need to be notified about the state changes. We can then build a list of messages that apply to this object and add them to a list of all messages that the system manages.

Finite State Machine

The previous section described a loose definition of what is called a Finite State Machine (FSM). Each FSM is an entity that can be in only one state and can move between states only if certain conditions arise.

Table 6.1 is one representation of an FSM. However, it can be easy to miss state transitions, so a better approach is to graph the FSM in a model that shows the states as nodes and the transitions as lines between those nodes (see Figure 6.1).

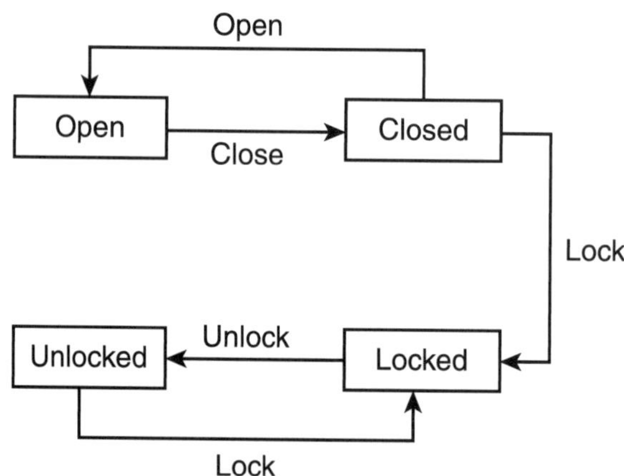

FIGURE 6.1 FSM model.

FSMs and FSM modeling are valid techniques in software engineering for real-time systems. These are the hardest kinds of systems to design, and video games fall into that category of software.

We also want to be as precise as possible about the timing of the FSM state transitions, which is important. In flight systems, for example, the incorrect timing of a state transition can result in the aircraft crashing; virtual aircraft are no different.

On the other hand, it is unlikely that something terrible will happen if a word processor fails to get the timing right when moving between states. It can usually correct the issue at a later stage.

So, FSMs are a good way to define and design the interactions between objects, and the relationships between states in a video game system. They also help the designer to visualize his view of the game universe. This will be vital in the smooth transition from idea to game, as will be the embodiment of the actors who will be using the FSMs—the Object Models.

Object Model

The principle goal of all this clever design methodology is to produce, as part of the design of the game, a complete breakdown of all the objects in the system (game) and discover how they relate to each other. This sounds like more of a chore than it really is. Some people even find it to be an exhilarating and rewarding exercise. Others will insist that it is all superfluous, and that we've taken the responsibilities of the designer too far. If the designer is creating a *Pac-Man* clone, then this is probably true. On the other hand, if the game is so simple that it seems a waste of time to create a list of all the objects, then making that list should not take too long, should it?

Either way, creating an Object Model will cement the designer's ideas while simultaneously revealing potential design flaws and problems before any money is injected into the project—a safeguard that is highly recommended. This point is not a trivial one. The cost of finding errors in the design phase is almost zero; but at later stage, if the game code has to be picked apart, byte by byte, to remove an error, the programmer's bill will be horrendous—and all the direct result of not having prepared an Object Model.

Imagery

Take a piece of paper. Draw a large oval, and write in it the name of every object type that will be in the game—not the individual instances of objects, but just the type. A simple, vertically scrolling shoot-em-up will have the player, the enemies, and the bosses, not to mention bullets and missiles, and probably some form of power-ups.

Take some more paper, and write the types of objects on separate sheets. You should now have a collection of papers that are blank, except for the title, which is a type of game object. The other sheet of paper with the oval contains the video game domain.

Now, write the types of object that have nothing to do with the video game environment, itself, *outside* the oval on the first piece of paper—things like the score, the control mechanism, and so forth. These are objects that control external influences.

Next we need to create state tables for the each object's properties and a list of messages that the system needs to support these states. By the time this phase is complete, all that remains is to define messages that need to be exchanged between the external objects and the internal objects.

So, it is time for more paper—this time, one for each object that is outside the video game (oval) proper. Each of these needs to be examined in terms of the objects that are within the video game proper, and messages listed for the various relationships that exist between these objects. They also need to have state tables created for their properties, especially since these state changes will be caused by objects within the oval.

To cross-check that the state tables are correct, FSM diagrams, such as the one in Figure 6.1, can be created. Actually, we can create the FSM diagrams first and then work back to the state tables to get a list of all the various state transitions. However, it helps if we have a list of the states first to ensure that all the states are covered.

All of this will be much easier with some kind of diagramming tool, and plenty can be found on the SourceForge Web site (see the Appendix). Choose one that you feel comfortable with, because it will take some time to get the transitions right.

Objects

Up until now, we have only looked at object types or classes. We also need to consider specific instances of the types—the objects themselves. A chess game, for example, only contains a single type of object—but has many pieces. Each piece is a specific implementation of the object type, which has properties such as color (black or white) and its own rules of movement.

These are static properties. They are set when the piece is created and never change. There are other properties, such as the position of the piece on the chess board, which may change with time, as well as a piece's removal from the board at a given moment in time when they are "taken" by an opposing piece.

Other games, such as *Space Invader* clones, might have three types of object—the spacecraft that depicts the player, the enemy spacecraft, and missiles. Each of these will have some form of graphic associated with it, a position, and relative strength. Missiles do damage, different types will do different amounts of damage, and each will have an effect on the object that they hit.

Missiles can travel in a variety of directions. The original *Space Invaders* game allowed for missiles that were fired by the player toward the advancing enemy spacecraft, or dropped as bombs by the enemy.

There are other objects, too, such as power-ups and buildings that represent barricades against the onslaught of enemy firepower. These additional object types can be added later, since we have created an open-ended object model.

Of course, within our specific video game domain, each object might appear once or many times, in identical or slightly different guises. The designer has to know when to stop decomposing the object model. Too much, and it will become over-complicated; too little, and some objects will likely be forgotten.

Practice will make the task easier. A good way to develop a sense for a comfortable level of detail is to take a well-known game like *Space Invaders* and try to create its object model, and the various state tables for the objects. Your goal is to achieve a complete description of the video game without having to define each and every instance of objects that will be created during the play session.

SUMMARY

Object-Oriented techniques create a "guide" that is supposed to enhance the programming team's understanding and make their task easier. It is not the end goal of the design, nor will it suffice on its own. It is just a way of breaking down the idea into manageable chunks that can be thought of as work units. If you need to farm out the game's creation to a team, the pieces can be created independently, and the system should still work flawlessly.

The programmers should not need to know how the game objects are implemented in order to use them. This is the principle behind having a robust messaging system. Each object just needs to be plugged into it.

Of course, this chapter did start to touch on implementation, which a book about design should try and avoid. But if the video game designer can try to understand the programmer's methodology and design in that light, then life will be easier for everyone. You will also avoid costly mistakes further down the line.

A continued study of Object-Oriented design methodologies will reveal that, while this chapter provides a good introduction and starting point, OO principles reach far deeper than those presented here. There are also some great modeling techniques that allow very detailed models to be created—so detailed, in fact, that the code almost writes itself.

7 Game Mechanics

In This Chapter

- Game Rules
- Game Physics
- Game AI

This chapter is about the rules of the game universe—rules that apply to the player, the limits within which he can affect the game environment and the objects in it, and rules that dictate the behavior of the objects and universe toward the player. The mechanics of the game dictate the unique feel of the game and will determine the exact style, genre, and pace of the game, itself.

The mechanics are key to the eventual success of the game. It is quite possible to have a state-of-the-art graphics engine, perfect sound, and a wonderfully rich plethora of game objects, all communicating within an underlying messaging network, and still have lousy game mechanics.

Game mechanics are partly based on predictability. Gamers like certain aspects of the game to be predictable, and more importantly, repeatable. What works the first time in a given game situation should work in all subsequent play sessions. This enables the player to adopt a specific technique that should bring them success every time; in effect, he gets better at manipulating his character within the confines imposed by the rule system of the game universe.

This does not necessarily mean that the rules should be so rigid that the player can succeed every time he plays the game. It is still a good idea to introduce a certain level of chaos into the mix and give the player new challenges—otherwise, the game will become boring and have a very short play life (of course, this depends largely on the audience and platform).

A coin-op video game, for example, needs a game universe where success always seems to be just out of reach. If the player believes he will succeed "next time," he will come back. Just as important, the player should not be in a position to win every time until he has achieved a level of play that surpasses the expectation of the video game designer. If the game is too "easy," then the play session will be so extended that the machine will not make repeat-play money for the owner, thereby defeating the prime purpose of the game—to make money. Subsequently, the game may not achieve the market penetration that a good design deserves.

By a similar token, a game that is destined for the home entertainment market needs to remain on the player's list of favorite pastimes in order to bring the designer success. This means that each play session has to be enjoyable and have few shortcuts to success; and again, draw the player in so that he feels that ultimate success (completing the game) is always just out of reach.

On the other hand, the PC market has an escape route via the Internet, through which it will be possible to update the game on a frequent basis and add new challenges, provided the player has access to suitable hardware. This route to game longevity also exists for certain Internet-capable consoles, too, but if the game is to be multi-platform, then care needs to be taken to include players whose systems do not provide connectivity to the Internet.

In essence, game mechanics are all about balance and providing new challenges. The player might not succeed at the first time, but not because the game breaks its own rules. This applies equally across all genres and styles. The rules that bind the player must also bind the nonplayer characters. Otherwise, the designer will be accused of cheating the player out of the full gaming experience.

This applies equally to making the game too difficult. For example, it is quite easy to give the enemies a "sixth sense," since the program controlling the video game is aware of everything within the game universe, anyway. If the player hides behind a door, waiting to crash through unexpectedly, it is easy for the game to place a guard behind the door, ready to pounce on the player when he crashes through, blissfully unaware of the threat. This kind of "stacked-deck" approach will not win the designer any fans. On the other hand, if the game intervenes in such a way that the consequences of the player's actions are toned down, we are also cheating the player out of a full gaming experience:

> "The level of CPU adjustment is absurd. Crash horrifically, and you can actually see rival drivers slowing down on the overhead map." [EDGE01]

This comment was made in the review of a racing game. The gist of the article was that no matter what car the player chose or how well he drove it, only the last lap of any race counted, since the rival drivers were artificially slowed by the game design so that the player could catch up. This is an example of over-compensating by the game design; it wrecks the balance of the gameplay and does not give the player enough motivation to improve.

If we assume that the AI is at fault, then the workaround that leads to artificial slowdown is a badly implemented "trick." In the author's opinion, it would have been a far better game design to properly balance the AI so that it made mistakes, rather than slow down other drivers. This may have been the original plan, but the workaround was put in place due to time constraints.

GAME RULES

First, we need to define a set of rules that apply to the way in which the player travels through the game and provides him with a way of measuring, against previous experiences, his overall success, position, and current status. Although this sounds a little like video game college-speak, it is, of course, just a fancy way of referring to the player's "score."

Video games are all about scoring. In the earliest games, the rules for scoring were very simple. Eat a dot, get a point. Shoot an enemy, get a point. Get a thousand points and be gifted with an extra life. Lose all your lives and the game ends. These are all rules. They are predictable and generally based on the binary decisions of the game world.

The first step toward today's sophisticated video games was the invention of gradual damage. Take a hit, lose some life force, and when it runs out, lose a life—or even the game. You could recharge your life force by scoring points or advancing to the next level, perhaps by successfully completing a mission.

A slightly more sophisticated mechanism was introduced with the invention of the classic FPS, in particular *Half-Life*, where recharging power required locating a specific machine that you plug your suit into, and it soaks up power until either full or the machine's supply runs out. A similar mechanism exists for the player's health, which is recharged from medical kits.

Often, the locations of these machines/kits indicate a specific path through the level or mission. This means several things. First, if the player has only received slight damage from the enemy in getting to a specific point, he can get a quick health recharge that will help them through the rest of the mission. Second, if the player sees a few health packs or ammo caches in an otherwise empty room, he should be on his guard, because there will undoubtedly be a price associated with collecting these supplies. Finally (and this is tied to the other two), it means that the mission/level designer has to place these objects to correctly steer the player's direction, as well as make sure the player is rewarded for accepting the risky route. This is the crux of mission design.

Missions have always played a large part in gaming. Ever since *Space Invaders*, in which the mission was to destroy waves of nasty aliens before they destroyed the player, designers had to come up with ever-more inventive ways for players to progress through a game while improving their score.

This eventually leads to concepts such as the *Pac-Man* perfect score (eat all the dots on every level, as well as all the ghosts for each of the four Power Pills per level, *plus* all the fruit bonuses). Similar challenges exist for many other mission-based games. Can the player get through the level and collect all the hidden items in record time without sustaining damage?

Even driving games have the notion of a perfect lap, in which the car is undamaged at the end of it. This changes the game rules and balance slightly in a way that a mere goal-based mission cannot—unless, of course, it is combined with some kind of level mechanism.

With the invention of levels, the player now has two ways in which he can measure success and compare it with others' successes (and decide for himself whether he chooses to boast about it or hide it). We shall cover the construction of levels and missions, and how they can be combined; but right now, it is worth noting the distinction between the two.

Levels or Missions?

A level has a set goal, an end point that can take many forms. Over the years, video game designers have played with a variety of constructs. Two remain—the concept of an exit from the level (dungeon, tunnel, building) and the destruction of the level's "boss." These methods have been used separately or in tandem, and even determined by the context of the current play session, although rarely dynamically.

A mission tends not to have a set end point, but a vague goal. It is possible to say when the mission is complete, since the game rules dictate that there is a set collection of events that should have taken place, such as objects collected or destroyed. However, the goal's completion is different from a level's, since there may be no final battle or discrete exit. Several levels can make up a mission, and each level can require the defeat of a boss—each boss in theme with the current mission.

There might be sea creatures to destroy in an underwater level, and the mission might require recovering objects that are only available once all the levels have been completed.

The more missions the player completes, the more access is granted to future levels, missions, vehicles, and even weapons. It is the completion of the missions that is important—the levels (or episodes) exist just to help steer the player through the difficulties of the particular challenge. The real prize is the bonus awarded when the mission is completed.

This is known as "unlocking." It has been used with great success in extending the shelf life of games—in particular, the racing genre. After all, once all of the tracks have been completed, there is very little left to do in the game, so the designers allow players who finish with consistently high scores to have access to special features or vehicles. These features are unlocked based on performance.

When discussing gaming, "level" can have two meanings. We used the term "level" here to define a part of a mission. However, historically there was a different meaning for "level"—"episode." For example, each level in *DOOM* is called an episode, rather than a level or mission.

The other meaning that can be attached to the term "level" is the difficulty setting. An "easy" setting will have fewer monsters and perhaps low-power weapons, while a "hard" level (like the *DOOM* Nightmare mode) will be almost impossible to complete. Other games have similar mechanisms. *Pac-Man* speeds up, *Singstar* asks for more musical accuracy, *Dance Dance Revolution* puts the player through some impossibly difficult foot moves, and rally games contain rivals that get increasingly faster.

In RPGs, characters have levels and missions become quests. Our original terminology fits with this genre—for example, mages level-up upon completing a quest that involves some kind of spell-casting solution.

Within the game design, there will be a natural balance of all three definitions of "level" that fits the designer's requirements. There is no hard and fast rule, nor even a rule of thumb. However, consistency within the game design document is absolutely critical.

If the game has varying difficulty settings, then we can opt for a more personalized representation, such as "Amateur" and "Professional" modes, rather than calling them "Level 1" and "Level 2." If a game is episodic, we might choose that as the general mode and retain "level" to describe the difficulty setting.

Missions, however, usually mean one thing only: a complete story (or at least part of it) with a set of objectives. And, the player needs a way to gauge how far into the mission they are, how much he has completed, and how successful he has been thus far, overall.

Game Rules in Detail

The set of rules that govern the measurement of player success should be kept apart from rules that govern the way in which objects interact. In Chapter 6, we saw how the entire video game universe can be broken down into objects, each of which have behavior, properties, and the ability to communicate with other objects and the rest of the game universe.

Rules are specific to the unfolding of the play session as it relates to the viewpoint of the player. They form part of the game mechanics, because there is a sought balance in fine-tuning their interactions, as we shall see later on.

The game rules that we are concentrating on now are far more abstract. They are the guiding philosophy behind the game that is being designed and need to be in the designer's mind from the project's start—and probably drive the entire design machine.

An example will make this much clearer. In the game *SimCity*, the idea is to build up a city from a blank piece of real estate by placing three types of building zones on a map: residential, commercial, and industrial. Each of these zones will need power (utilities), and road and rail systems—and the demand for resources/infrastructure fluctuates depending on the business/population growth. Building costs money, as does providing power and roads, and money is raised through taxation—just like in real life.

And just like in real life, if you have no residents, then you have no tax revenue. If the residents have no jobs, they will be unable to pay tax. Furthermore, if there are no residents, then there will be no need for commercial zones, since there is no one to go shopping, watch football games, or buy vehicles. Also, without residents, there will be no industry because there is no workforce.

The objects in *SimCity* are represented by tiles that are roads, zones, or some other form of infrastructure, like a football stadium. Rules govern whether or not they are inhabited, based on the tile type and surrounding tiles. Residential zones placed next to industrial zones make them less attractive to new residents, commercial zones need to be between residential and industrial zones, and so forth—all in order to promote the healthy growth of the city.

These discrete rules apply to individual objects. The behavior of the entire game universe, which represents the unfolding city, depends on how the tiles react to each other. Those rules that govern this interaction can be used to balance the game so that it is predictable and enjoyable, but also at the right difficulty level.

The game strategy, however, has less to do with the objects, themselves, than it does with their placement; the game rules that cover wide areas of tiles is far more important than whether an isolated residential tile in a sea of commercial ones becomes inhabited. The rules govern the player's popularity, which influences the number of new residents, and the city budget must be balanced (taxation versus spending) so that growth continues smoothly—and this is the core of the *SimCity* design philosophy.

This "smooth growth" is important because roads that are under-funded and impossible to drive on lead to congestion elsewhere, which in turn leads to the population's discontent and defection—and less tax revenue. The game even warns the player when discontent is so high that threats have been made against the administration, and unless a suitable (and expensive) police force is in place, the player risks being toppled from power.

This brief summary of a few of the game rules that drive *SimCity* illustrate how a complex and sometimes quite difficult game can evolve from the interaction of simply stated concepts. We will not cover some of the game's subtler rules that govern more-abstract areas, such as when to build an airport; after all, this book is not a strategy guide. Our goal is to examine and digest how successful designers have approached the problem of game rules.

DRAWING THE THREADS TOGETHER

In essence, the game rules tie together the whole package. One key phrase should be able to sum up the overall goal of the game. For simple shoot-em-ups, this key phrase could be "destroy all enemies." The rules that stem from this phrase include: how often enemies should fire at the player, how many have to be destroyed before power-ups become available, and what events will enable passage from one level to another.

This touches on the system object (see Chapter 6). Say, for example, the game rules state that a certain type of enemy fires once every 10 seconds when within a designated distance from the player. Knowing when to fire is based on an object-specific rule and a system trigger. Thus, the different parts of the game system are coupled by these abstract game rules.

Being able to define the rules and how they relate to the game objects in order to provide the best possible balance is difficult. It is often a good idea to begin with a simple design and some simple rules, and try to achieve a good balance for them before adding more object types with their specific rules.

In a sense, it is the proverbial "chicken and egg" situation. On the one hand, we can see our game universe as a set of interrelated objects (Chapter 6) that, when put together in close communication, make up a network of events that create a game. On the other hand, we need to make some game rules that restrict the way that the objects can interact, or make those restrictions part of the object model.

These ideas need not be contradictory. All we are saying is that the object model details what is possible for each part of the game universe and the entities in it, while the game rules govern what is allowed under the terms of the game design. The designer needs to decide what is a game rule and what is behavior for each piece of the universe.

Let us look at a shoot-em-up, for example. We might have classes in the design to represent an alien, the player's craft, and some basic weaponry. Each one has attributes that tell the system how their capabilities are measured, and what options the instantiated object has.

Aliens can be described in terms of their velocity, current position, damage, weapons, and so on. The player can have a craft that is defined in similar terms, while the weapon objects might include attributes that indicate how much damage they inflict; assume that we have three kinds of weapons—lasers, mines, and bombs.

Then, we have the movement of the aliens, which is part of their behavior. This movement information needs to be made part of the object model. If it will be a game rule, then it does not belong there, but the mechanics that allow us to instruct the aliens must be.

Now, we can either build some kind of intelligence into the alien class behavior and feed them simple instructions based on the game rules, or we can dictate everything to them up front. The "game-rule" approach might state that when a quarter of the alien population is destroyed, the speed of the remaining aliens speeds up by five percent.

In the "object model" approach, we would need to store values for alien speed and behavioral triggers, and call triggers more rapidly to simulate faster movement. In both cases, the system object has to be in a position to try and manage this behavioral change. Finally, a game rule will state that on completion of each level, any aliens of the same type that are reconstituted in the new level have a higher firing rate than before. Here, we can set a property in the alien class definition that governs the alien's firing rate, or we can trigger each and every shot.

The point is, there must be a balance between game rules that prompt behavioral change (and take the responsibility for that behavior away from the object) and the ability to allow certain game rules to evolve from the behavior of well-defined objects (and "bend" the game rules).

To alter the game rules in a fully distributed system, behavioral models and state engines in the design must be changed. In this case, the system object's game rules revolve only around difficulty ramping (speed), and resource depletion (the number of objects).

In the end, the exact definition of the game rule and the object's behavior will change from game to game. Some games have complicated rules and simple object models (like chess), while other games have simple rules and highly evolved object models (like simulations).

Two aspects of the game rules will need to be abstracted into class descriptions: physics and intelligence. Physics dictates how objects interact in the game universe. If physics does not exist, then it is probably a non-action game that has its own static set of design possibilities. Intelligence dictates how the actions are triggered.

The remainder of this chapter looks at how game physics and intelligence fit into the general set of game mechanics. Bear in mind that the rules, physics, and intelligence are all intimately related, as are the game mechanics with the object model.

GAME PHYSICS

Some games put a lot of emphasis on reality—that is, a realistic game universe that respects at least some of the laws of physics as we know them. To emphasize this a bit, let's look at what it means to create a video game as an interactive multimedia experience.

As in the movie industry, the majority of video games try to persuade the player to suspend disbelief when a scenario is unfolding. This can only be done if the player is able to identify with the basic rules of the physical environment. This means that as game designers, we cannot disregard all of the rules of physics; but we can bend those rules that add new aspects to the game.

Consider films like *Star Wars* or, more recently, *The Matrix*. They present alternate realities that have their basis in our day-to-day experiences and, therefore, enable us to believe in them, even though we know that they are not real.

The spacecraft in *Star Wars* are classic examples of an alternate reality. In this universe, everyone can own a space vehicle and travel from planet to planet—for example, Han Solo and his Millennium Falcon. The atmosphere is generally lighthearted with little emphasis on scientific details—*Star Trek*, it isn't. In contrast, the *Star Trek* universe is more reality-based, with the Enterprise as an expensive and powerful interstellar exploration craft that makes a greater effort to adhere to established (or at least envisioned) scientific principles—for example, power via dilithium crystals.

The ships fly through space and respect most of the rules that terrestrial physics impose on us, with a few notable exceptions. There is the sound of crafts whistling past, and weapon fire is accompanied by blasts of sound—none of which bears any resemblance to reality. Any physics student will tell you that in space, where there is no atmosphere to carry sound waves, battles would take place in complete silence.

Both *Star Wars* and *Star Trek* share one thing in common. Despite the many cinematic liberties taken with the irrefutable laws of real-world physics, enough rules are respected that we can connect with the reality presented by the movie and accept the rest on faith. We have suspended disbelief.

This also applies to games; we expect the environment to be presented and react in a certain way. If the craft is in space, we expect it to move with a different set of parameters than a land-based vehicle. We expect flying vehicles to give us a different perspective than submarines or race cars.

We also expect weaponry to react in a certain way—at least the common ones, like guns. If they do, then we are quite happy to allow the game to occasionally take liberties in the form of a patently impossible weapon. *Wipeout: Fusion* is a good example.

So, here we are, flying around a track at impossible speeds or hovering above the ground. Given the shape of the machine and the engines being used, it all looks quite plausible, even though we know that such machines do not exist. They fly well, are nicely balanced, and feel familiar and in line with the physics of the known universe. We can pick up weapons, from missiles to plasma cannons, and they react as we expect—with a loud "boom." The missiles are perhaps a bit more intelligent than we might imagine, but this is accepted because it feels in line with the rest of the game universe.

But, suppose we pick up a weapon that causes a local quake—in other words, it vibrates the game universe. There are two things wrong with this. First, if we are hovering or flying through the air, would our vehicle actually be affected much by a quake? Second, the weapon follows the track around as it shakes, and a quake would surely spread out in a circle from the point of agitation. Even so, if we have accepted everything else thus far, despite being a weapon that violates physics as we understand it, we accept it because belief is not such a big jump. Game designers can take many liberties with physics, setting games on different planets or in different times, but there is one area that seems to be protected more than most: particle physics.

Particle Physics

This subject sounds more complex than it really is. Particle physics only means that the very basic laws of physics relating to individual particles have to be respected. For example, things cannot (without good reason or explanation) fall upward. If something explodes, its particles are thrown outward and disappear into the distance; they do not pop and turn into a puff of smoke, unless that is what the player has been conditioned to expect.

Take a game like *Sonic*, in which a hedgehog spends his time running around a game universe that uses particle physics, gravity, and the fact that hedgehogs roll to present a video game that we can happily adapt to. If, in the game, the hedgehog rolled down a hill at a constant speed, the player would find this unrealistic. We are comfortable with certain aspects of our real-life universe, like gravity, and the fact that ball-shaped things roll according to the rules of gravity cannot be rewritten in a video game. Immersion depends on the player not being surprised by "contrary" physics as they play the game. The moment that particle physics and the rules that govern it are abused to the extent that the gamer is not longer immersed, his chances of coming back are reduced.

Part of it is fairness and the way we expect the game universe to react; our only reference is real-life experience. On the other hand, we do not see many *Super Mario 64* players complaining about the fact that he can turn around mid-air, something only cats seem to be able to pull off. Apparently, for *Super Mario 64,* directional change during a jump is an acceptable and nice addition to the false reality of the video game.

Despite being easy to grasp in concept, particle physics is a horrifically difficult thing to actually implement, so the budding game designer has to decide whether or not the game will benefit from the addition of strict particle modeling. Given that we have just categorically stated that particle physics is one aspect of universe modeling that cannot be deviated from, this might sound a little odd. After all, if we need it, we need it. But, we do not have to model every single particle in order to get the behavior right. Some particle physics engines actually simulate things like explosions and deformations by modeling them at the particle level (or perhaps just above it) to add realism.

Physics engines are increasingly common as machines become more powerful. The designer now has the option to create game universes in which surfaces can be deformed and flying wreckage can be accurately modeled and depicted.

For a high-profile console game, this is fine. For a low-budget PC game, this might not be such a reachable reality. We can take some short cuts, though, and suggest the presence of particle physics without modeling each particle separately.

For handheld games, a simple explosion sprite is probably going to be the limit of what the design can contain. The trick is to use the game rules to express an accurate, underlying physics engine. Get that right before adding any special effect physics.

These rules will manifest themselves through the movement of the objects within the game universe and the way in which these movements change, depending on each other. Even if we do not design a complex representation, at least the movement's basic physics must be right; but we can take liberties, as long as it is in keeping with the character of the game and/or genre.

MOVEMENT

One aspect of video game design that the designer has some degree of control over is the movement attributes of the player-controlled character. From *Lara Croft* to

Sonic and the various characters in *Street Fighter II,* indeed the whole fighting genre, there is a more-liberal interpretation of the laws governing movement.

The designer has to decide between smooth-slide or a jerky run-and-jump movements, and this will depend on the game style. Weapon recoil is one aspect that is most-acceptably ignored—how else can *Unreal Tournament 2003* players fire such enormous cannons without being thrown back against the nearest tree? Some effects, such as recoil, can turn a fun game into a nightmare simulation, and are largely ignored in order to allow liquid gameplay. This is not restricted to game objects, either. Kicking and punching, or simply running around and jumping, can also be ignored if they detract from the player's enjoyment of the game.

There is one rule that can only be broken with good reason: The opponent must not have better options than the player. This aspect of fair play needs to be respected. Racing games are particularly vulnerable here; balance can be easily broken if the opponent's vehicle is better (or worse) performance-wise than the player's—or (more troubling) if the opponent's skill level appears to change, depending on the performance of the player.

There is a fine line between simulation and believability, which needs to be respected at all times. There is nothing worse than climbing into a rally car, and finding that it handles like a Formula-1 vehicle on-road and a tank off-road. This breaks the illusion enough to reduce the game's enjoyment factor by half. The failure to correctly balance vehicle movement is a real problem in multiple-vehicle games, such as many of the pseudo-military games on the market. The physics engine and movement models used seem to be obscure at times, as if the designers did not have the time or inclination to model them correctly. Sometimes the vehicle-handling is modeled to appeal to the mass market, which means that hardcore gamers get bored with the experience before they really experience the deeper aspects of the game. (Of course, we can cater the vehicle-handling to advanced players, but this only makes sense in pure driving games.)

Movement can also be dynamically adjusted to meet the requirements of the player. We can allow the game to intervene and change the movement profile of a vehicle—such as autopilot, automatic braking, or over- or understeer correction—depending on whether or not the player needs this kind of help. By a similar token, adjustments made to the underlying structure or components of a vehicle might alter its movement profile.

Similarly, fatigue will affect the movement profiles of players in team sport simulations. Being shot will affect the way that soldiers move, and energy boosts might temporarily speed up movement (like *Sonic* and his special go-faster power-up boots). All of these can be applied to either the player or the opponents.

It is up to the designer whether or not to apply the same movement-altering measures to both the opposition and the player's own in-game persona. Obviously, fatigue and being shot affect all entities. Then again, this is only true if we compare similar entities; soccer players are reasonably equal to each other, but some monsters can sustain more hits than the average player entity.

So, the designer has some scope when enhancing the game mechanics of movement profiles, hopefully without making the game unplayable in the process. Ultimately, play-testing is the only way to check that the feel is right, and in the design phase, this will be difficult.

When the movement rules in the game mechanics are designed, we can afford to be slightly vague in certain circumstances. However, if the movement algorithm is part of the underlying game description, then it must be detailed in the design—in other words, the movement is what makes the game unique.

TIME

Finally, one of the least-abused aspects of video game design (until recently) has been modeling for the passage of time. The movie *The Matrix* is credited with the invention of bullet time, which was put to good use in video games, such as in *Max Payne*. During bullet-time moments, the pace is slowed so that the enemies explode upon impact in a surreal, cinematic way. In fighting scenes, this intentional slowdown enables additional powers for the entities that use it correctly, and the end result is often spectacular. (Of course, they are also given the ability to move at increased speeds to avoid bullets.)

In *The Matrix,* this is merely a nice special effect. In a game, the player can choose to move into bullet time in order to destroy as many enemies as possible in as short a space of time as is allowed.

Then again, more-recent games like *Blinx: The Time Sweeper* offer precise control over the passage of time, including stop, rewind, and slow play. This effectively enables the player to be in two places at the same time—which is a necessity, given the nature of some of the game's puzzles. Unfortunately, this tactic seems to have been abused; many critics have declared that the mechanism is, at best, artificial. We should be clear on this point: If time passage is "bent" in a way that allows the player's control, it needs to be done in a less-prescribed way than is seen in games such as *Blinx,* and allow the player to feel that their influence extends past simple video recorder–style time manipulation.

Remember that a video game is a real-time system. In other words, time is discrete. Things happen within discrete units of time, which is important to the underlying game. Clever time manipulation that is contrary to reality is, granted, creative, but other mechanisms exist that are equally necessary.

Sports simulations, for example, often speed up time so that a game takes a few minutes, rather than most of the afternoon. This can be done in one of two ways—in a real-time gaming simulation, the clock is sped up; but in a simulation that does not involve following a match in real time, the actual game is sped up. The result is that the player has no chance to play if he has to interact with the game in real time (because 45 minutes are compressed into 45 seconds), but at least he gets the same level of play for each match—albeit at high-speed.

Naturally, we can also offer the player the option to watch or participate in real time. Where possible, this should be allowed. It is a very easy thing to design in, and there is no point in denying a real-time experience to those players who wish it.

Game AI

The mechanisms behind implementing artificial intelligence will be covered in Chapter 12. Here we will only look at the kind of AI that the game should exhibit, depending on the game's genre and style. When people discuss the AI of a game, it is usually about the way in which various enemies react to the player—whether they dive behind barrels to escape an onslaught of gunfire, climb up ladders to evade, or just sit there while the player pounds them with laser fire. Everyone will have an opinion as to whether the AI was done well or badly.

For games that rely purely on the puzzle aspect of gameplay, or which have no "enemies" to speak of (just two humans against each other or themselves, as in some athletics simulations), the AI is limited to the connection between the player and the game. This intelligence is encapsulated in the way that the vehicle, object, or player-controlled character reacts to the control mechanism.

This might not seem obvious—after all, the player presses "left" and the car goes "left," right? In fact, the game's control systems need to be a little more sophisticated.

What Is Game AI For?

The answer to this question could take us into many different corridors of video game culture. Since this book tries to help designers get a handle on how to define their games, it makes sense to try and the answer the title question in a ready-to-use format.

Unfortunately, this is difficult. Our preconceptions have conditioned us to think of AI in the terms of smart robots and mastermind chess pieces. Of course, chess-playing software needs to use AI to outsmart the player, but this is often not enough—just ask Kasparov how many times he has beaten chess computers (including Deep Blue)—but AI helps.

In many games, AI is present as a way for the computer to compete with the players—*Othello* (otherwise known as *Reversi*) is an example, as is *Connect Four.* These are both games in which mere rule-following is not enough; there are multiple choices, each of which can have a dramatic effect on the outcome of the game.

Deciding which choice is the best course of action, is, of course, one aspect of AI. And in this respect, the AI always wants to win—or at least the game designer wants the AI to win every time, and designs with that in mind. However, sometimes we need to let the player win (or suffer the alienation of our audience). Then, somewhat paradoxically, there is another use for AI: to let the player lose.

So, game AI exists to enable better gameplay, to let the player feel that the game is, itself, a competitor, and to increase immersion in the game universe by providing a more natural feel to that world. Simply put, the player wants to have fun while being challenged.

AI can help adapt the game to the player, beat the player, let the player win, and model the environment so that everything hangs together properly, making the player feel at one with the game—while also providing a way for the opponents to behave in an intelligent way. It all helps make a better game. As soon as AI fails to do that, it becomes more hindrance than help and can be removed. Unfortunately, we often cannot know if the AI serves its purpose until we see it in action.

Control Systems

Video games have often been described as the most sophisticated simulations that modern computers are capable of. Some of the best video game techniques were first used for military applications, and there is a lot of cross-pollination between scientific and entertainment applications for producing graphics that border on reality. Great examples of how control systems use intelligence are in the racing and flying genres, where the game mechanics are a mixture of player intervention and intelligent reaction to the environment. This is often known as the "handling model" and can make or break a game. In fact, the difficulty of a game (as well as its realism) is determined by the level of intelligence designed into the control systems.

Games that are governed by realistic physics and implemented using an intelligent control system tend to be more difficult to play than earlier games with simpler control systems. On the other hand, implementing a "flexible" intelligent control system is useful when presenting a level of reality to the player that they can cope with. That is, if the designer wants the game to be enjoyable to a wide variety of players—casual and hardcore, experienced and inexperienced, or even an audience that spans different generations—then the levels of simulation must vary accordingly.

Take a Formula-1 game for example. The "Easy" setting could be a fully automatic gearbox with automatically corrected skidding and no fishtailing. This makes the simulation less realistic, but the game will be much easier. The car will not over-steer, and the rear end will not spill out if the player attacks a curve too fast. At the other end of the spectrum is the "Professional" setting with a manual gearbox, sensitive handling, and less-forgiving steering and damage model, coupled with differing amounts of traction, depending on tire type, fuel level, and road conditions.

The intelligence behind the control system will enable the logic to be fuzzy—that is, not based on binary decisions (we will deal with this in Chapter 12). In essence, *Space Invaders* used a control system that was based entirely on "yes" or "no" decisions. The player moved the joystick left, and the spacecraft moved to the left.

Over the years, arcade games have become more sophisticated, and shoot-em-ups now use control systems based on "degree of action"—not only what direction the player moves the joystick, but also how long he holds it there.

We can even have an adaptable control system, and if it is flexible enough, the same system can be used for different vehicles by simply tweaking it a little. The transition between aircraft and ground-based vehicles might be too tricky for this approach, but there is no reason why a ground-to-sea-based vehicle control model could not be designed.

Single Versus Multiplayer

In a single-player environment, any adversaries need to be endowed with a certain level of intelligence that can range from simple preprogrammed patterns of movement to full-scale adaptive behavior with some basic variations. One such variation is the "hunt-and-seek," where an enemy moves with hostility toward the player, impeding the player's progress through the game. Usually, this is applied with a pattern-based movement algorithm, such that individual enemies either break away from the pattern and attack the player head on or move into another pattern that is triggered by the enemy's vicinity.

This kind of trigger-based AI is called "knee-jerk AI," because response is only based on things that the player does—just like a leg's reflex "jerk" when the doctor hits the right nerve on the knee with his little rubber hammer. There is nothing that the enemies can do about it; they are reacting in an entirely involuntary, prescribed, and predictable way. When the enemies reach a prescribed "firing zone," then they fire. This kind of AI is fairly easy for the player to beat, once the pattern is discerned.

A step up from this is to allow some form of adaptive behavior—that is, a choice between patterns that can be used if conditions indicate that the player has managed to guess what the enemies will do in specific situations. Adaptive behavior is better, but not as good as allowing the enemy objects, themselves, to decide which pattern to apply . . . except when it comes to movement. AI can never allow the enemies complete free choice in their movement. Some games have tried in the past to apply unrestrictive AI, and let the opponents do whatever they want, but it generally leads to situations in which they do things that are not very clever at all.

The reason is that it is often very difficult to predict what the output of an AI implementation will be, given a set of inputs. No two players will play in the same way, and the opponents might also move in subtly different ways based on behavior that has been allowed to emerge as a result of input from the player and other objects within the game universe, as well as themselves.

The gaming experience begins as a small seed. The results can be unpredictable, which is the point of the AI, but this unpredictability can also be its undoing. Therefore, it is better to design behavior patterns in a way that is fairly certain to fit the game's context, whatever actions are chosen. At worst, we will have a vaguely intelligent reaction to variations in the environment, and at best, we will have a perfect response.

Of course, we can also look at the single-player system as a multiplayer game, with scripts replacing the intelligence exhibited by real human players. This is the approach taken by *UT2003*, in which the single-player game relies on bot-script opponents. A bot script is a simple way to implement the movement patterns of an almost-intelligent entity.

Actually embedding player-based AI in a game is difficult, and using scripts (rather than hard-coded routines) makes the whole design, including the AI parts, much more accessible to team members other than the programmers. This is important, since extensive testing of the AI will be necessary, and programmers are probably one of your most expensive team resources. By removing dependency on the programmers for the game AI, the designer opens the door for play testers and level designers, enabling their access to the behavior of the various in-game opponents. They can then verify that the AI is working correctly and alter the bot's behavior as seems fit to better reflect real multiplayer gaming. This will also mean that the players can create their own bots, which will allow them to create dumb ones for practice purposes and even trade them with other players, adding a new dimension to the game.

Emergent AI

The definitions of emergent AI and emergent behavior differ, depending on your point of view. Emergent AI can be seen as the result of a single entity gaining experience over time and adapting their AI processes to suit. Emergent behavior, on the other hand, can be seen as the combination of many different AI processes that adapt to each other within a single entity.

For the sake of our discussion on video game design, that entity could be a crowd or a single in-game object. Either way, the set of rules that make up the AI system can be adapted over time, and then recombined in a variety of situations.

We will look more closely at this in Chapter 12, which covers the actual design of AI in video games. In implementation terms, the AI topic is a book in itself. In terms of an entire video game project, it is only a part of the whole. Therefore, we are quite safe in vaguely describing AI as emergent in the design document.

However, we still have to allow for it in the game design. We cannot leave it entirely to the implementation stage for two reasons. First, doing so would mean that whoever reads the design document will not be able to ascertain what AI was being used for in the game. Since the design document is intended for potential stakeholders who are going to invest resources to help get the game developed, they need to know that the designer has his finger on the pulse of AI.

Second, something might have been left out of the design document that is needed for the AI, and which might cause other changes to be required. As was mentioned in Chapter 3, fixing errors in the design is cheap compared to finding and repairing them once development has begun.

As designers, it is also quite tempting to pay lip service to emergent AI, because it sounds good and is different from what the competition is using. This is the perfect way to make sure that the result contains no more than a whiff of any AI, whatsoever. Game journalists will be impressed, and the investors might be fooled, but somewhere along the line, the emergent AI will fail to . . . emerge.

Education is, of course, the key. Know what kind of AI is possible, as well as what kind of AI needs to be included that will form a vital part for your game design, rather than just be window dressing.

Pure AI and A-Life

Part of the education process is in knowing when AI becomes A-Life. Are you scratching your head at this point? Then let us just clarify. AI is artificial intelligence in broad terms, which allows the entity to decide, based on in-game information, what to do next. As we have seen, this information can come from the player's in-game persona, control systems, the opposition, or even the environment. Artificial life (A-Life in video games), again in broad terms, simulates the behavior of life-like entities within the game universe. There is a fairly gray area that overlaps the two in video game design and development.

For the record, when this book refers to AI, we mean the application of game rules that cause the system to behave in an intelligent fashion. This includes trying to outsmart the player, deciding what to do next, finding paths between two points, and so on.

A-Life, as it is used here, means the discrete behavior exhibited by individuals or collections of individuals in attaining a specific goal. That goal could be managed by the AI—player versus in-game opposition—or it could be an aesthetic goal intended to make the game universe more immersive. Let us look at two examples to illustrate the difference between AI and A-Life.

If an entity works out a path from *A* to *B* that takes it into contact with the player at some point, and has worked out where the player will be in *x* units of time, then that is an illustration of quite advanced AI. AI is involved in calculating the possible paths, choosing one, and then extrapolating the position of the player's units, based on the game rules.

Once the entity has encountered the player's units and applied their AI algorithm, which determines that they should attack based on their status at that time, then A-Life algorithms take over to simulate the battle. If the game allows us to zoom into the battlefield, we might see many AI-controlled warriors fighting in related, but different ways, and exhibiting life-like behavior.

Another aesthetic example of A-Life is very simple—the flocks of birds in *WRC II Extreme*. Your first thought might be that this is a seriously decadent use of PlayStation 2 resources. These birds probably did not even figure in the design document, but their presence is so real and so unexpected—and so familiar, it enhances the game experience.

As part of the general game mechanics, this attention to detail can often be the difference between a good game and a great game. *WRC II* is fun, but the addition of mad spectators and flying birds makes it more so. Wherever A-Life is used, it makes an impact.

AI, on the other hand, must be used correctly to be effective. There are so many examples of bad AI in video games that it is surprising when a game gets the AI right. Chances are, the AI was designed into these successes from the start, rather than the developers having had a vague notion along the way that the monsters should be "clever."

SUMMARY

This chapter has been full of ideas about how to organize the game mechanics in such a way that the experience is a pleasant one for the player. Each of the techniques discussed covers some aspect of simulation, which is, in effect, what a video game is—a simulation that is dependent on the game's genre and style.

It is tempting to throw some rules into the mix and see what kind of behavior will evolve, which is the long way around. It is fun and will yield a better game, but the designer should always try to create an entirely predictable system first; use a set of rules that complement each other and predict whether it will be fun before trying to go down the evolution path.

There are many aspects of game mechanics that are overlooked during the design phase, since the temptation exists to leave it to the programmers; let them come up with some neat rules to "accessorize" the core idea and artwork. This will not necessarily lead to an enjoyable game. It is much better to design in the game mechanics—including AI and control systems. These two issues are frequently ignored during the design phase, but they should be addressed early on in the design so that they can be refined with respect to the rest of the system.

REFERENCES

[EDGE01] Review Section, *EDGE* magazine, No. 121, March 2003.

8 Mods, Scripts, and Development

In This Chapter

- Modding Explained
- Scripting and Modding
- Developing in Perspective

When creating a video game design, there are several ways the final product can be put together. Most video game designers immediately think about hiring a programmer if they are not capable of handling the programming, themselves. Then they worry about hiring artists, sound technicians, creating or buying a game engine, and finally, implementing the design. Before long, your initial, great project can look like it will take years—and the initial idea will suddenly look quite flimsy. Even in early stages of the design process, when it is necessary to produce a demonstration version in order to drum up support or cash, designers may be tempted to hire some talent.

It may not be necessary to embark on a development project just to prove that an idea is a good one. In fact, it is quite possible to create an entire game without actually writing a line of code. There are several stages that we can work through in order to create the final product:

- Modding—taking an existing product and modifying it to fit our idea;
- Scripting—taking an underlying game engine, such as *Quake,* and adding new behavior; and
- Developing—building the idea into a complete product.

Any one of these phases might yield a respectable first game. In fact, as we shall see, there are some products that have been derived from modifications and scripts, and even some complete games based on somebody else's technology.

We have to sound a note of caution at this point. Never, *ever*, take somebody else's game, derive a commercial product from it, and attempt to pass it off, or remove any restrictions that the original develop and publisher put in place. It is one thing to modify a game and distribute the modification within the terms of the copyright imposed by the owner of the game's intellectual property, but it's quite another to claim it's your own. The trick is to find a ready-made game, and use the built-in editors and tools to create your own derived version. Of course, most likely, gamers wishing to play your game must already own the original game that it is based on.

The original publishers like providing access to their game engine and letting players loose on its inner workings. They actively encourage it; not only does it help the budding game designer by saving him an awful lot of time, but it sells copies of his game. Just think how many copies of *Half-Life* were sold on the back of the *Counter-Strike* mod.

The proposed game must have an exposed scripting interface, which is used to attach actions to objects within the game environment—for example, *Quake* (as well as other id Software titles), which also has widespread appeal and support. This gives the avid designer the ability to create their own objects and in-game actions for those objects. Modding is likely to become more widespread, especially since many games are now being offered as freeware, such as *Halo 3*, before the final versions are released.

Again, though, there is a huge legal difference between taking a game that has some of its workings exposed and creating a mod based on it, and reverse engineering a product. Reverse engineering is a breach of the copyright that governs the intellectual property that is the game. The message is clear; buy the game from a shop, and only consider modding it if such is explicitly allowed within the licensing of the game.

Some developers have also released source code for their creations—id Software for one—and these also have licensing restrictions that may or may not permit you to build your own video game around them. Again, if it is not explicitly mentioned, then assume it isn't covered or allowed. In any case, seek professional legal representation, or you may find yourself in court.

That said, modding and tinkering with commercial games is a great way to learn about video game design in general. It's just that the result of doing so is not likely be something that can be commercially exploited.

There are many different software packages that allow the designer to create an entirely original game based on a simple scripting language. These also often include a user-friendly interface to attach scripts (actions) to objects. They also allow the designer to import assets such as artwork and sound, and otherwise manipulate the game universe. We call these *game creation kits,* and we will be looking at them in more detail.

Thus far, the designer has been in charge of creating the embodiment of his idea. However, it is likely that at some point, development will require some programming. Help is at hand, though; there are libraries available that lift much of the complex graphics and sound work off of the developer's shoulders. This chapter will discuss all the available options so that the designer can choose which technology to use in order to create a demonstration version or the final game—or just try out some of the theories that video games rely on.

Modding Explained

"Modding" has probably been a part of gaming culture since the first days of home computing. Initially, it was made possible by the fact that home computers provided an open platform (more or less) for gamers to alter code in memory. In the early days, modding was used by gamers to alter the way in which the game was played, or change the constraints placed on the player by the game's designers—often to the point that hackers devised ways of getting around some of the consequences of the game. These "cheats" included the assigning of infinite lives or unlimited energy. Many gaming magazines picked up on this practice, and readers tried to outdo each other at providing ever-more exotic and useful cheats—often mere weeks after the game was released. Strangely enough, no one has ever devised a cheat to directly alter the score of a game in order to achieve acclaim. Apparently, this must be part of the gaming subculture mentality—cheating is permissible, but only up to a point.

This is not to say that cheats for score-altering don't exist, because they do. It's just that they belong in a category in which they are the means to an end. By altering the score, one can unlock special features or obtain in-game advantages. It's unlikely that a gamer would change his score for the sole purpose of pointing to it and claiming that he did it all on his own.

These modifications require the computer code to be loaded into memory and then altered; and a video game, like any other program, has to be executed in order to be played. When it is "run," the computer loads the game into memory and then executes the code. This has not changed since the 1960s. Computers have always loaded programs from external media into memory before running them. This left a loophole for gamers, who could modify the program after it was loaded into memory and before the machine ran it.

However, this approach only worked because it was possible to perform the load and run as two separate operations. In fact, the complexity of games with respect to the platform often meant that they were loaded as separate files, leaving plenty of opportunity to interrupt the process and interfere with the recently loaded code.

These days we have hard drives. The hard drive takes the place of memory and stores the program (or video game) until the gamer wishes to play the game. Therefore, if a gamer wants to apply a cheat, he must modify the code stored on the hard drive.

In addition to being stored on the hard drive, the code is also executed directly. Today's operating systems load and execute the code in a single step. This is as much a consequence of our faster use of local hard drives, as it is the design of the operating systems, themselves . . . which illustrates the point; it is both easier and harder to create cheats for games these days. Cheating is easier, because there is more-sophisticated technology available; but cheating is harder, because the game creators have kept up with these technological advances.

Changing the actual computer code in order to make the game easier to play is a primitive form of modding—although usually, our focus is to make the game better. There have been numerous examples throughout the history of video games in which gamers took a game and altered it to improve certain aspects that they thought needed some attention.

One of the most famous was the *Elite Plus* modification. A programmer took the original *Elite* game, reverse-engineered it entirely, added a host of new functions, rebuilt the game, and made the new *Elite Plus* available as freeware. The legal ramifications of doing something like this are clear—it is punishable by law. In 1981, *Castle Wolfenstein*, one of the original first-person shooters, was modded to produce *Castle Smurfenstein,* a cosmetic adjustment to the game. Other mods followed: from adding *Simpsons* voices and graphics to *DOOM*, to (just after the start of the second Gulf war) completely redesigning the graphics and gameplay of *Battlefield 1942*.

Some of the early mods were created by third-party tools that read the game data and enabled changes by the *gamer*—often without the commercial developer's/publisher's consent. Eventually, in the 1990s and 2000s, game developers saw the benefit in offering the gaming fraternity the ability to modify their games. They began to supply the tools used to create the games, levels, and logic, along with the games themselves.

Games that can be taken by gamers and modified in this way will sell more units. They may well build followings where the game is purchased for the sole purpose of playing the mods that appear for download following release. On the one hand, publishers are protected by the copyright laws that prevent anyone trying from to pass off a game, but on the other hand, they benefit from allowing a certain level of modding to take place.

Enabling modding is a by-product of the way that modern games are designed and built. Most games revolve around an *engine* that handles the processor-intensive tasks, such as graphics, sound, and math. The engine also handles complex tasks, such as rendering the relationships between in-game artifacts. These are often stored in a separate file that holds the sounds, models, and graphics—collectively known as *assets*—as well as the descriptions of how they interact and where they are placed in the game universe. This file is known as a "level file." Different level files produce different environments; the complexity can range from simple spatial descriptions (a true game level) to completely scripted, interactive environments with their own assets, rules, and mechanisms

Taking this approach makes it easier to create the game in the first place. Level design, art and sound assets, and scripted AI can be dropped into the mix without recompiling in some cases. Games are not generally designed to be modded, but their modular design does make it easier to add this if the publisher chooses to do so.

Built into the engine is a processor that can read and execute *scripts*. Scripts are the pieces of code that control how the universe unfolds and the way that objects react and interact. There are several reasons why games use engines. The first is that many are licensed engines that are available on the general market, which the developer can purchase and use in their products. This greatly reduces their development time and costs.

For example, games have been built using the Unreal Engine, which was the underpinning technology for the game of the same name. Others have been built on CryEngine, by Crytek, which was used for the groundbreaking title *Far Cry*. A pattern emerges here: Hit games often spawn great engines, which in turn spawn new hit games. To keep the actual implementation within reach, and to relieve the developer from having to cut and splice source code to create his game, the engine programmers can opt to leave the scripting of events and objects open, usually by employing a special scripting language. The Torque game engine, used for games such as *Tribes 2*, uses this technique and is available for about $100 per programmer seat.

Using commercially available engines such as Torque (which is now supported for platforms such as Xbox 360/XNA) gives the developer the benefit of a plug-in engine without the legal ramifications of modding. It is almost as easy as modding, is well supported, and gives ample possibility to try before you buy.

Another advantage to building games this way is that it allows a degree of flexibility. For example, pieces can be changed that do not seem to fit the feel of the game, without needing to resort to the source code. This enables a game designer to transform the mod's look from that of the original game to something new.

Script-based engines also mean that modifications can be carried out by non-programmers, which is a good idea, since it leaves the door open for designers to get their hands dirty; they can alter their games to more-completely match their initial visions. So, designers who are willing to put a little effort into understanding the mod kit for a specific game can sculpt their own game universe for very little outlay in time and cost. In addition, when development of the game does actually begin, letting designers write scripts will pay off in a better game. After all, if they can play around with the internals and make the game under development fit their vision, there is no need to try to convey that vision to a programmer.

The script and play-test approach mentioned earlier might take some additional resources to set up but will pay off in the final product. As the game development progresses, so the design will evolve and change, and if specific gameplay features (such as AI) can be rendered accessible through a script interface, then the game can evolve with the design much more quickly.

Using an engine that allows scripting also provides a design outlet for the level designers, which can offer entry into the video game industry (more on level design, later). In the same way that a popular mod can become a game in its own right, game levels can make their creators famous. When these novel levels—which typically consist of new sounds, graphics, and models—are combined with the open scripting provided by a good engine, entire new games can be created. There is a caveat: These games usually cannot be sold because of their resemblance to the original game, which is protected by copyright under international law.

Opening the game engine's scripting interface to gamers is usually an easy decision for game publishers. One of the most famous is the *Quake CTF* mod, which is a game in itself. Two teams try to kill off the other side in order to capture their flag. Capture the Flag is a game that is played by children all over the world (without the killing part, of course), and the *CTF* mod was so popular that it has since been made an integral part of *Quake*.

Other success stories include *Team Fortress,* another *Quake* mod, which was acquired by Valve, who made it a commercial success. Valve seemed to make a practice of acquiring entire mods; they also purchased *Counter-Strike*.

The reasonably well-received *Gunman Chronicles* started out as a mod, but was eventually released commercially. It seems that this practice doesn't work out too well; mods that are offered as freeware, with the hope that gamers will buy more-complete versions, do not pay commercially.

Thievery, a game that was inspired by *Thief* (Looking Glass), is based on the *Unreal Tournament* engine and offers a multiplayer *Thief*-style game for fans who want a true multiplayer mode. Finally, there is the previously mentioned *Desert Combat*, a mod of *Battlefield 1942*, which is based on the second Gulf war, with a few artistic licenses taken—the opponents have better weaponry, tactics, and organization than the real-life opposition exhibited during that Gulf conflict.

Mods often find their way onto the covers of magazines, too. Feature articles on popular game extensions compel readers to buy, and also get the mod creators some good exposure. *Quake III*, for example, was considered by many to be a lackluster game, but a great platform for creating new mods. It is possible that gamers bought it for just that reason; promised adaptations coupled with new games modded from the original were enough to power sales, whereas a less-complete platform might have failed.

In short, we can create a game from a game, based on tools that are offered by the original developer, often for free. The new game may or may not look like the original, and we can even sell the result in many cases. Modding is accessible to designers, programmers, gamers, and artists—who were among the first to take advantage of this ability to create new assets for in-game characters.

ARTWORK AND AUDIO

Some of the most configurable parts of the game engine are the graphics and sounds, which can be imported and replace the ones already in use. For example, look at the *Simpsons* patch for *DOOM* (precursor to *Quake*), and before that, the *Castle Smurfenstein* mod. In both cases, the mod replaced the artwork and audio supplied with the game with new artwork, which turned the game characters into popular TV show icons.

Eventually, these simple adaptations were refined; engine developers realized that the game would have a longer shelf life if players could customize it to their heart's content. Thus, *skinning* was born, and it applies to all kinds of software, not just video games.

Team games (or mods for games like *Quake*) provide skinning as a way to clothe players from the same team so that they can be discerned from the opposition, like with football jerseys or baseball shirts. This is a useful addition, but it can theoretically allow players to modify more than just their clothing.

A soccer simulation game was released that allows the player to scan in a photograph and attach it to the face of a player on the team. The age is fast approaching in which we can star in movies, be sports heroes, and become involved in all manners of experiences without ever leaving our armchairs—all thanks to video game technology.

A specific game might even embrace skinning as a way to increase the inclusion of specific gaming groups, be they aligned along gender or ethnic boundaries. It might not be too much of a leap to say that female gamers would be more willing to play a game if they could swap some of the stereotypical male-oriented elements for something more appropriate to them.

So, modding can be as simple as changing graphics or sound, or as complex as adding new models for vehicles, characters, or weapons, along with some scripts to make sure that they work as planned. We can even go one step further and alter the nature of the game to create an entirely new one, as the authors of the *Quake CTF* mod have done.

If you own games based on the *DOOM* or *Quake* engine and would like to play around with the under-the-hood level structure, there are great reference materials available on the Internet. To understand them, it is useful to become acquainted with the format of the WAD file.

While not all game engines use the WAD file in its original format, the theory behind it is important and deserves discussion. The principles behind the WAD file have been used in many engines as a way to keep all the level information—maps, sounds, and artwork—together.

Settling down for an afternoon of modding the latest PC version of *Quake* is quite a big task, so we are going to discuss well-understood and supported (if a little dated) technologies. It will be easier to start with these and then ease into designing a mod that is on the cutting edge of game technology.

As far as graphics are concerned, there is another caveat when working with the latest games—they can contain thousands of polygons just to model, for example, a head. Tools that create these models are not only expensive (thousands of dollars in some cases), they are also very complex. On the less-expensive end, tools like Gmax offer a noncommercial, high-quality toolkit, but these only export to certain licensed games. This may or may not matter, but the same problem exists—they require a lot of time-consuming work and expertise. So, for beginners who are cutting their teeth on game design, it will be easier to stick with the earlier-generation technology.

WAD Files

The WAD file format was developed by id Software for describing the various elements that made up the levels of their hit game, *DOOM*. It is a structured file—that is, it contains a set of folders, each of which contains a collection of artifacts that make up the level. There are folders for the actual level design—the walls and floors that make up the area in which the player can travel. There is information pertaining to the placement of objects, weapons, enemies, and health packs.

Within the WAD hierarchy there are also folders for storing textures that are used to cover the sides of exposed 3D objects. In conjunction with special codes that denote the purpose of objects, these textures also indicate what the object is for.

In recent years, scripts have also been added to the folder structure so that it becomes possible to define an entire game concept as a WAD file, not just aspects of the player characters. Even the behavior of enemies can be encoded to a certain extent within the WAD file, itself.

To access WAD files, special tools are required. The most popular is the Quake Army Knife (QuArK). This freeware utility can be used to edit a variety of WAD files, but offers little support for actually building a level. Fortunately, the makers of modern games provide tools that can be used to edit the unpacked elements of WAD files.

Note that creating a WAD file is a multiple-phase operation. First, a tool such as QuArK or Wally is used to unpack the WAD file, and save it on the hard drive as a series of folders. Next, various graphics and logic tools, such as Q3Radient, are used to edit the level file, and the sound and graphics elements of the level. Finally, the entire structure is repackaged as a WAD file for use in the game. The intrepid game designer also needs to have a full version of the target game present for testing purposes.

Beyond WAD Files

The WAD file was created in the 1990s. It is showing its age a bit now, and does not offer enough scope for intrepid gamers turned developers, or designers showing off their skills at creating original intellectual property. WAD files were good for:

- Level designers,
- Multiplayer level designers, and
- Artists.

What was needed was access to the game rules so the designer could change them. Each in-game entity needed a WAD description that was translated to the game engine, and this description would reflect the needs of the designer. Since these were needed for the actual game, anyway, developers eventually left them as editable text files. Sometimes they would even make little instructional text files for would-be modders.

This approach gets painfully close to programming. At the very least, it can be considered scripting (which we'll get to soon). What is important to note is that WADs help the designer prove his game before thousands of dollars are spent on promotion (and potentially thousands in development dollars), and this help exists for anyone with a few spare hours and some patience. Exactly how much time and patience is required depends on which game the designer chooses to mod.

Choosing a Modding Platform

For an aspiring game designer getting his feet wet in the industry, modding is a low-impact testing ground for great ideas—a way to see if the idea will fly, and whether or not it is meaty enough to base a game on. But note that a mod can rarely transcend the platform (original game) on which it was based—that is, a mod of a first-person shooter will likely remain a first-person shooter; there's no easy way to make it something else—for example, a racing game.

We will deal with this shortly, but for now, let us look at modding as a concept and try to put together a few pointers. How do we choose an appropriate place to start? As of 2007, there are (generally) two kinds of games that have opened themselves up to modding:

- First-person shooters—for example, *Half-Life*, *Quake*, *Far Cry*, and *Crysis*
- Storyline genre games, such as *Deus Ex*

These two genres offer more than just in-game level editors, and range from the latest *Stuntman* series to games like *Lemmings* and *Worms*. Level design is a skill (but not one that we deal with here).

The designer's first choice is in the tools available for these two genres, and the limitation is in the quality of the tools. Some developers merely package up their existing toolset and merge it with the game distribution. The most notorious of these was the *Thief* toolkit (Looking Glass), which offered very little help to prospective modders. The tools were fairly powerful and almost impossible for a novice to use.

At the other end of the scale, Crytek added some fantastic tools to *Far Cry*, which allowed the modder to create breathtaking islands, rivers, forests, and so on within seconds. This also illustrates another aspect of the toolkit; the mod tools should be more than just editors. Otherwise, it will take a very long time to create something that even faintly resembles the initial idea. Editing models, placement, and so on is a time-consuming task.

All of this will be helped by a solid, mod game community. Try to find out ahead of time what kind of forums, mod-related walkthroughs, tools, and tutorials are available before settling on a game platform. Otherwise, you might find yourself on your own.

Finally, note that modding is more or less restricted to the PC platform. If the mod is to get any serious attention, it should be either completely original or based on an already popular game.

With these pointers in mind, the game designer should be well on his way to prototyping his ideas. But, what happens if more flexibility is needed—if the genres covered by modding and third-party tools simply do not enable us to create the prototype we would like? At this point, we need to consider taking a step up. In terms of technology, time, resources, and skills, scripting sits uneasily between modding and programming, but is a perfect playground for technically minded game designers.

Scripting and Modding

One step beyond simple modding is to license a game engine or acquire one for free, which can explicitly script a whole new game. This would allow us to leverage the power of the engine, while also adding on new functionality that the original developers might not have thought of. Suddenly, our creation is no longer a mod; it begins to look like an original piece of intellectual property.

Think about this for a moment. The difference between modding *Quake* and creating a game from scratch, based on the *Quake* engine, is fairly slim. On the one (modding) hand, we add some new levels, assets, and events to the familiar *Quake* universe—on the other (scripting) hand, we throw away everything except the engine and start over.

One thing that is required is quite a lot of programming knowledge. This is because scripting is usually rooted in languages such as C++ or Visual Basic. So, to go beyond modding, we need to start thinking a bit more like programmers.

However, if we are going to do *that*, then we might as well look at ways to create a game that does not rely on an existing package. Granted, an avid gamer-programmer can put together a reworked, sunken-ship version of *DOOM 3* for fun—but, we want to create a commercial game. There are plenty of tools that are accessible, require very little actual programming, and can be used to prototype or even create a full game. In short, as long as we can find an engine that matches our genre, we can create a game.

GAME-CREATION KITS

This is where the game-creation kit comes in. These range from simple point-and-click applications that allow the designer to import graphics, and assign actions and behaviors to objects, to full-fledged development environments. As game designers, we would like to achieve our goal without having to understand a programming language, but there are many other things to consider.

Game Maker (GM), for example, is free to use, and the games can be sold without paying a royalty to the developer. It does, however, have a limitation—several of them, in fact. The first is that it cannot create full-3D games, and creating isometric games like *SimCity*, although possible, is quite difficult. GM is geared toward platform games—maze games or any side-on or top-down scroller. It does this kind of game very well. The designer is presented with a palette of different icons that can be used to build the behavior of an object, and play-testing can be done inside the editor. For more advanced users, the scripts can be edited. An easy-to-understand script language is supported.

Another great (though commercial) tool for creating games is The Games Factory (TGF). It is slightly more powerful and easier to use than Game Maker, but the user must pay a fee to distribute stand-alone games that do not require the TGF software to run. So, while it is great for making prototypes or demos that can be shown to prospective publishers, the designer will have to make a decision, at some point, whether to purchase the software license or re-develop the entire game using another method.

If the game will be based on 3D technology, then there are specific tools to support full-3D environments, such as Reality Factory by Rapidgames. Billed as a "no-programming" tool, Reality Factory is an enhanced extension to the Genesis 3D engine. The two are closely related and can be used together to make prototypes of video games.

They are easy enough to use, but due to the nature of 3D game creation, expect them to be more difficult to work with than 2D tools. This equates to a greater learning curve, as well as a larger investment of time for level creation and editing. To anyone who has already added levels to games like *Quake,* using the free tools available on the Internet, working with these toolkits will probably be second nature. For those who have never attempted level-creation, it will be tricky at first and require time to become proficient with the tools.

Both Genesis and Reality Factory base their design and development on a series of entities that can be manipulated, given sounds and graphics, and events. The nonstatic parts of the engines—for example, moving and shooting—are prewritten. This means that only FPS games can easily be created with these tools. Anything else is going to have to squeeze into a predetermined world view.

In 2004, the creators of DarkBASIC (The Game Creators) published a tool called FPS Creator, which was specifically aimed at that genre. This is probably as close as one can get to a real piece of middleware or development pipeline that can be used to create original games.

There is a full list of "no-programming" or "low-programming" game-creation toolkits in the Appendix. Some will be of more value to the designer than others, and kits exist specifically for text-based adventure games, RPGs, 3D FPSs, platform games, and most other subgenres. Conspicuously, a whole genre is missing—that of simulation games, such as racing or sports simulations. This is due to the fact that their game mechanics vary more from one game to another, than other genres.

A step up from these kits are those based on a scripting language that resembles Visual Basic—for example, Dark Basic (which is not free, but is a quite affordable package). Its object-oriented approach uses Basic to attach methods to objects inside the game universe. Dark Basic does not offer the power of Torque, but its use of Basic means that it is easier to become proficient within a short time. The more complex the engine, the more the need for a language that is closer to traditional programming scripts. Traditional programming tends to be stricter and less verbose, making it easier and faster to turn scripts into machine-executable code.

Licensed Game Engines

A game engine is merely a piece of software that handles much of the difficult, behind-the-scenes work needed to run the game. Strictly speaking, Genesis is an engine, the tools that support it make it a game-creation toolkit. Typically, game engines are extremely expensive to license. After all, the programmers have put a lot of effort into creating a robust, strong engine to provide an in-depth gaming experience.

By extremely expensive, we mean tens or even hundreds of thousands of dollars, which will be out of reach for most first-time game developers—not to mention the fact that studios such as Crytek are often wary of licensing their engines to inexperienced game developers and have a rather extensive application process. The upside of this, as well as the high price tag, is that the end result is guaranteed to be a framework capable of delivering the dream of the designer.

However, success relies on many different facets coming together to produce an outstanding game. The design has to be up to scratch and deliver a unique idea, or at least a unique take on an existing idea—for example, the *CTF* mod for the *Quake* engine. The balance has to be perfect, play-tested, and above all, the models used to display the game universe, as well as the sound effects and music, all have to add realism to the mixture.

If all of these demands can be satisfied, and there is a coherent Design Document (see Chapter 3) of the final product—perhaps backed up with a limited demo, video rendition, or at least storyboard, concept artwork, and sounds—then there is a chance that a publisher can be persuaded to part with enough money to begin developing the game. On the other hand, if budgetary constraints are in force (as they surely will be for most projects), then there are plenty of other options. Some are listed in the Appendix, and all bear further research.

There is a marked difference in budgets, however. Money will always be a factor in deciding the development environment. An independently funded game creation project will usually have less money to be constrained by than the fifth in a successful series backed by a big publisher.

Smaller projects with smaller budgets might need to set their sights on more modest toolkits, and first games usually fall into this category. The tools have to be fit for use, but they also have to be financially accessible.

One of the key contenders is the Torque game engine. The brains behind Torque produced the outstanding game *Tribes 2,* which is a first-person shooter. Torque is not freeware, but neither is it exorbitantly expensive; it costs $100 per programmer seat. So a team of 10 programmers (quite a few for a first project) will therefore only cost $1,000, as opposed to the $100,000 asking price for a typical, high-power game engine such as Quake III.

(In both cases, it bears mentioning that the employees still have to be paid and the office space rented. These are costs that cannot be avoided, and depending on the project size, the game engine license may or may not be the largest outlay.)

All kinds of games can be created with Torque. It is not restricted to FPS development; some puzzle and vehicular games have been developed using the engine. Bending the engine to other genres is a bit more difficult, but is by no means impossible.

Using the engine is easy, since it is based on an open design that exposes much of the engine via a scripting interface. This makes it easy to implement games, especially for programmers who have already worked on similar projects.

Support via the Garage Games Web site (http://www.garagegames.com) is excellent. Its extensive community is a gold mine of information shared among intrepid game programmers. There are some great tutorials for free download and even some books being written that will help Torque SDK license owners to get the most out of it.

Garage Games also provides a delivery channel for completed games via their Web site. This leads to instant exposure as well as a very real revenue stream. All in all, for the beginning game designer who wants to have a chance at implementing their own game, Torque is the best option—but only if the designer is willing to spend time learning how it is put together, and is willing to invest in the tools and books required to create games.

Again, most of these tools are aimed at the PC platform. This is due to a number of factors, not least of which are issues relating to quality control and the high price of developer kits, coupled with often complex and difficult-to-understand platform topographies. But once more, *Torque* is something a bit special. Microsoft has been enthusiastically making game development accessible (through the XNA platform tools) and delivery of games easy (through Xbox Live Arcade), so Torque X provides console-development opportunities to PC-based, independent developers. To take advantage of this, though, we have to shift up another gear—from design to development—and probably acquire some new skills. True development is out of the scope of this design book, but it doesn't hurt to know what is available so dreams can be correctly prototyped and developers are not asked for the impossible.

Developing in Perspective

With all this support for game engines and simplified game creation kits, it would seem that real development only complicates the issue. Of course, this is true if we are creating a game that is already backed by standard tools and code bases. There are some genres, however, such as racing and some sports simulations, that cannot be developed using a standard engine or only substantial modifications to the underlying source code. Also, there are some platforms that really do required best-in-class tools to help us manage the development effort. This comes in the form of middleware, which bridges the gap between the platform (console, PC, handheld) and the developer.

Of course, everything has its cost, and it is best to enter the game-making business well-informed. The rest of this section takes the budding designer through the terms and technologies that he will encounter when the time finally comes to create a game from the ground up.

Source Code

Some of the games created by id Software, such as *Wolfenstein3D* and *Quake,* have had their source code placed into the public domain. This means that video game studios might be free to take the source code, pick it apart, rewrite pieces of it, and compile the whole project back together as a completely new game.

Again, however, we need to stress that the license under which the code is released should be subjected to legal scrutiny before any work is carried out. The code was released to be learned from, in the main, and licensing and copyright laws must still be respected at all times.

The fact that these games are no longer considered to be at the cutting edge of video gaming technology is one of the reasons why there appears to have been little capitalization on this stunning display of generosity. On the other hand, we can learn much from reading the source code.

If the designer wishes to base the game on an entirely new engine, custom-built for their project, there are a few aspects to be aware of before writing it into the project plan. This is not to say that once the decision has been made, it cannot be reversed, but the Design Document will reflect the designer's wish to create an entirely new product, and that risk will factor into the equation.

If the designer is angling for finance, and the plan indicates that the product will be developed from the ground up by a team of programmers, there is a certain "unknown" that the investors take on. Due to the nature of computer software, it may be difficult to obtain financing unless that "unknown" is removed by licensing an existing, tried-and-true engine. For example, the development cost is predicted to exceed $100,000, but an engine that satisfies *most* of the designer's requirements can be acquired for $10,000. A choice must be made. Are the additional features that make this game unique worth the additional 900% in development costs? Or can a reasonably accurate version of the game design be created for one-tenth as much?

The next step in the evaluation might be to refuse financing on the grounds that the 10% that remains is simply not worth the investment, and that the total bill, which is 10 times greater, is not worth the risk. This highlights, once again, the adverse nature of the video game development industry. On the other hand, if we are talking about a really cutting-edge idea that pushes the art forward in a memorable way—the way that *Super Mario*, *Pac-Man*, or even *DOOM* did—then chances are that financing will be easy to come by; and furthermore, it will be easy to entice programmers on board who will be happy to do the work for a share of the profits.

This last point is very important. Programmers are a strange crew; most people cannot keep up with a programmer's train of thought—and some are slightly out of touch with reality. These are people who will happily spend hours writing code, just for the sake of producing something "cool." They may be eccentric, but they are not mad. They do know the value of a fledgling project, and if they find it interesting, they will probably trade their time for a share of eventual profits. Remember, id Software started out as a team of two, as did the Bitmap Brothers studio, creators of the *Micro Machines* racing game for a variety of platforms, which was sold under the Codemasters label.

It is difficult to know whether a design requires a unique piece of programming, and as a general rule of thumb, the answer will be "no" for a first project. This results from a very simple piece of risk analysis. Nikolai Josuttis, software engineer and author of several tomes about programming, once commented that risk analysis in software engineering projects starts with an attempt to minimize the number of "firsts."

If this is the first time that a game project is attempted—with new hardware, a new team, an original idea that has never been tried before, and new source code—then the risk is at a maximum. Compare this with a tried-and-tested idea on hardware that is familiar to a programming team, and who all know each other, and is based on public-domain source code; the risk will be at a minimum.

So, a first-time game design should try to remove some of the risks—not all of them, but enough to provide a minimum-risk starting point for the "dream project" in mind, and we can always build up from there. Game design is not a one-shot proposition. The designer must be in it for the long haul, and as such, once it has been established that the full project cannot be achieved using existing engines (for one reason or another), then perhaps a series of short-term projects will help reduce the number of firsts, rather than implementing the long-term goal of a full design.

Many projects start out as smaller, more-achievable targets and turn into larger projects in time. This might be as simple as preparing a new technique that is designed for the full game, but ahead of time. Or it might mean creating tools for building the end project. The designer can even begin with a limited demo version that uses existing technology to prove the game mechanics, and leave the more-advanced areas for later.

Imagine creating a game like *SimCity* from the ground up. In order to get the balance right, the designer decides to ignore the graphical front end at first and builds a simple text-only demo. The demo ignores things like zone placement and roads, and concentrates on verifying a correct balance of zones to utilities before weighing the results according to proximity—for example, people hate living next to power plants, but they like having a road to get to work on.

We have already looked at how the game universe should be broken down into objects, but if the designer arrives at the point where he needs to choose between a game-development kit or building the project entirely from scratch, then the research needs to be taken one step further.

Source Code Components

Video game software (for any platform) can be broken down into a number of components, each of which fulfils a specific task:

- Sound (effects and music)
- On-screen graphics (the action area)
- User-interface graphics
- Person-machine interface (keyboard, joysticks, controllers)
- Core game logic
- Scripting (where applicable)
- Artificial intelligence (where applicable)

These components will at some point have to be integrated with the design's object model (see Chapter 6). Using existing source code will remove much of the work while leaving the same level of flexibility, albeit with a result that is probably not at the cutting edge of technology. A licensed engine will produce a game that is closer to competitive products in terms of technology, but will probably also be more restrictive—only the most expensive engines allow the license holder access to the core source code, with the exception of the Torque engine.

In the realm of game-creation kits, all the responsibility for handling graphics, sound, and the person-machine interface (and possibly the GUI, as well) is closed up in a little black box to which we have access, but cannot change. This provides a level of robustness that is a great boon for the novice, but it also means that we have to provide the models and graphical elements in the format prescribed by the underlying engine, and have no power to change the way they are shown on the screen.

Finally, when it comes to modding and scripting, we have only rudimentary control over the in-game objects, and probably none over the core game logic or user interface. Extending the logic might be possible, but a shooting game will remain a shooting game.

This should give the designer cause to sit back and wonder exactly which options he is going to implement in the game design. The reason for covering the options here, and not at the end of this book, is that they need to be fresh in our minds when we discuss the remaining six chapters, which are geared toward the practical side of the design. For now, let us take a small breather and look at a few items that will take some of the pressure off the programmers.

Libraries and Middleware

Fortunately, there is a halfway between full development and buying an expensive game engine license. Many game studios, such as Crytek, license portions of their source code base for use in rival game products. For Crytek, it is a novel way of specifying and displaying in-game 3D models in a way that the processing power required is lessened somewhat by rendering a texture map over a low-polygon model.

The cost will probably be less than buying a license to use the Unreal Engine. On the other hand, the underlying technology probably means that acquiring a CryEngine 2 license will be as much about proving oneself as a studio as the money needed to acquire it. In addition, companies like Qubesoft produce entire products that can be used, in some cases royalty-free, to develop games; but these products only provide the means, and not much more. They differ from game-creation kits in that the components are provided to perform the various tasks required, but without any prescribed uses. They are, in effect, tools that need to be given data in order to make them do something useful.

They can also lack "glue," the gaming logic code, that will bind them together to make a cohesive whole. For example, one library is capable of displaying high-quality 3D models, but the work of actually obtaining the model data, arranging it in a way that can be displayed, and pre-processing it so that it can be fed to the display library is left to the programmer.

There are many free libraries available on the Internet. Visit one of the open-source repositories, such as http://www.SourceForge.net, and do a quick search. It will probably return a number of prewritten components that could be of use. One such set of libraries is the Allegro graphics library, which is a very capable open-source gaming library.

As usual with open-source software, care must be taken with the licensing, since most licenses require that the source code for the entire project be made open source. However, there are two kinds of open-source licenses. The first is the GPL (GNU Public License) and its derivatives. This license states that the code can be used only if the full source code to the derived work (your game) is made available for a specific time period following release of the work. It also states that the source code does not have to accompany the retail version, but that it should be made available upon request.

The other license type is slightly less restrictive and is known as the LGPL (Lesser GPL, and sometimes Library GPL). This allows the derived work to remain as object code only, if it is, itself, a library. Otherwise, it should be distributed with fully open-source code. This route is a bit of a minefield, and when choosing to use an open-source, licensed component, there is always the problem that its economy might prove to be misguided.

One thing that open-source components do provide is a complete and often fascinating look at how to manipulate game code. There is nothing to prevent the programmer from using the same techniques in his own, freshly written code. It would be nice, though, if new LPGLs that improve upon established techniques were made available to the entire community, and thereby advance video game technology.

DDKs

Manufacturers also offer Device Development Kits (DDKs), usually at a price, which contain source code, libraries, and an emulator to help budding developers. Nintendo is famed for its quality-centric attitude toward developing for platforms such as the GameBoy and GameCube. In fact, they require that the Nintendo development kits be licensed by any studio that wishes to create software for their platforms. As usual, there are ways around this, usually in the form of "unofficial" kits that at least allow the designer/programmer to play with the various techniques before applying for the official license, which is worthwhile, since these licenses are not cheap. In addition, there is always an extended and expensive testing period that platform manufacturers mandate before the games can carry the manufacturer's label. In the PC world, DDKs are useful for developing libraries for new graphics, sound, or input devices. Similarly, SDKs (Software Development Kits) are specifically geared toward providing a layer of transparency to the underlying hardware, such as graphics and sound cards.

Games destined for the PC platform are based around an open technology that has traditionally had fairly good industry support. It can often be easier to obtain a DDK for a particular piece of hardware from the operating system manufacturer than from the hardware vendor.

These two seem to be the bane of all video game developers, partly because technology moves so fast and is constantly being revised, but mainly because nobody has time to write games, follow the pace of change, and take full advantage of new options as they become available for each game.

One such development kit is the DirectX library from Microsoft. DirectX provides interfaces for all kinds of graphical wizardry, as well as ample support for gaming input devices and sound cards. The DirectX library appears to be the SDK of choice for game developers who do not wish to create their own version.

This is backed up by the fact that many PC games come with a version of DirectX that has to be installed before the game will run. There is opposition in the form of the OpenGL library, which performs many similar functions that are either better or worse, depending on who you talk to.

Middleware

From 2006 to 2007, there has been an expansion of middleware into the game development arena, not to mention an integration of middleware, development tools, and frameworks into the true pipeline development of games in a way that is seamless for the designer, artist, and developer. One example of this is the CodeWarrior Radix Studio by Freescale. Another is the Q environment by Qube. The middleware concept provides a set of services that are broken down into collections of plug-ins. This means that the middleware, itself, becomes a framework for all the individual pieces. Some of these pieces might not even "belong" to the middleware vendor. They could be bits brought in from third parties and made to work within the framework. Usually, they will be interfaced with a standard piece of code provided by the vendor.

For example, Biographics AI.implant provides behavioral modeling, and is so specialized that it is unlikely to be part of an actual framework. Instead, it is middleware that can communicate very specific services. Also in this category are 3D sound packages like GameCODA (Sensaural), which provided a cross-platform solution that also stands apart from the framework.

It is important to remember that the addition of middleware to a framework can extend it, providing functionality that other solutions might not. It is essentially an alternative to just using an engine—although the engine, itself, might also form part of that framework.

Middleware, like a game engine, is there to help ease the task burden on the programmer, thus freeing him to do other things. If the middleware takes too long to integrate and provides more of a challenge than a solution, then perhaps it is not the right choice.

Finally, middleware can help when porting to other platforms, if that is the end goal of the designer. Most games are developed for a specific platform, but middleware can enable games to be developed for multiple platforms.

Platform Notes

In the end, the route that the designer decides on will depend on the target platform. Developing for the PC, for example, leaves the designer with many different options, all of which are valid for most projects. Console developers, on the other hand, will find that their lives are made somewhat simpler by the fact that this platform tends to be less open. That is, consoles are specialized for the technology required to play video games and, therefore, require special support, special media, and even a special kind of compiler.

The most expensive, and probably the best option is Metrowerks CodeWarrior, which is a compiler that can be used as a cross-platform development tool for most target platforms. Most platform manufacturers prefer that their license holders use it and will probably even insist that a copy is purchased from them as part of the (official) development kit.

On the other hand, there is a substantial advantage in writing video games for consoles. Much of the complex graphical algorithms for effects have been written for the developer and execute in special hardware, which is much faster than executing in the game logic, itself. So, the cost of obtaining an official development kit balances the benefits derived by the team's not having to deal with the headaches related to platform-specific code.

A simple example is the GameBoy (the original, black-and-white version), where the underlying graphical unit is the sprite. The machine itself has some logic for manipulating sprites built in; the programmer does not have to create his own solution for drawing, pixel by pixel, a sprite on the screen.

On the other hand, for games that are not sprite based but instead based around line art, it becomes more difficult. The programmer has to then write line art code that manipulates the underlying sprite mechanism. It is this kind of sideways logical thinking that makes programmers so special.

The development process itself is both lengthy and requires substantial resources in terms of programming staff, support staff, and management. We simplify the process here so as not to digress outside the realm of the other parts of the game creation project.

Suffice to say that the Design Document is the input to the development process, but it will need to be translated into something that can form the basis for development. Each little clause in the Design Document will have to be translated into a technical solution.

Along the way, there will be feedback from the programmers and technical staff that will cause the design to change. There will be time constraints that will lead to compromises, and it will be the collective task to try to ensure that these are as elegant as possible.

SUMMARY

This chapter has been all about making a design choice that, only after much reflection, will dictate whether the game will be built based on mods or scripts. The designer also has to decide what phases the game design needs to pass through before full development is achieved. Along the way, the designer might decide that the project is too ambitious for a full-blown attempt to be made right away, and that it should be broken down into a number of smaller, easier projects in order to become familiar with the process, team, platform, and target market.

This approach is quite acceptable, even if it is not the first video game project that the designer has attempted. In fact, it might even bring financial gains that can be put toward developing the final project, and alleviate the need to find a publisher to advance funds on the basis of the project plan, alone.

At the very least, you now have a good idea of what the various pitfalls are in creating a game and what benefits the various approaches have. They can produce a large part of the game, themselves, and off-the-shelf products can be used to create demos that will prove the concept.

Modding is a great way to learn about video game design and to play with various concepts. You will most likely never build your own game this way, however, unless you strip away everything that the original game contained. At that point, you are essentially scripting an engine.

The result will be something that you cannot legally call your own. Gamers have to have the original game installed to play your mod, and everything that facilitates your game is owned under copyright by someone else. Even if the concept and gameplay is original, the final product is derived, and the only way to avoid lawsuits might be to license a game engine directly.

So, the first real entry point into video game development will be by leveraging an engine that has been licensed for the explicit use of creating an original piece of intellectual property. There are many game engines available, and you will be fairly sure of finding one that fits most mainstream games.

For the really original ideas, full development will be necessary. There may be some help along the way in the form of tools and development kits, but the game itself will need to be created from scratch. The upside is that you can, within reason, build exactly the game environment that you had in mind. The downside is that it might take longer and be more costly, and it is quite daunting for a first project.

Keep this chapter in mind when reading the rest of the book, since it will all be relevant to what lies ahead. Indeed, some of the choices made in the remaining parts of the design might even preclude certain approaches. In order to ascertain this, the designer needs to know what the implications of each approach will be—which is what this chapter has attempted to emphasis, albeit in a non-technical manner.

9 User Interface Design

In This Chapter

- The Physical User Interface
- The Graphical User Interface
- The Game Universe Interface
- The Logical Interface

Video games provide feedback to the user via the principle graphics and sound, as seen in Chapter 5, but the user interface dictates how the player will interact with the game and also provides vital information to the player. This information is usually in the form of status information—perhaps a map to help the player navigate a particular level or general status information on ammunition, health, money, or other measures of the player's success. This might be immediate or long-term information.

Put another way, the main screen graphics and sound effects tell the player what is happening at a given moment in time, whereas the user-interface graphics tell the player what his actions have been over the long term (or on a more permanent basis), as well as what might happen in the future.

If this was all there was to it, then the user interface would only rate a subnote in our chapter on graphics, music, and sound effects. However, the user interface is much more. It is a conduit for giving and getting information to and from the player, respectively. We can break the user interface down into three key elements:

- Graphical
- Logical
- Physical

As previously noted, the graphic user interface presents status reports on the player's long-term achievements. The physical user interface controls the game's actions in response to the player's input. The logical part of the user interface links the various pieces of the game together—that is, it links the physical and graphical interfaces to the game, as well as linking the player to the game universe.

Mixing these three types of interface together gives the game its character. Done well, they work together to make a more-immersive experience. Done badly, they can make the game nearly impossible to play. The user interface is important—as important as the main graphics, and even as important as the main game idea, itself.

The Physical User Interface

All gaming systems have a method to control the action. Without it, they are useless for gaming and most other purposes. From the simple GameBoy controls (directional keypad, two buttons) to the hybrid, mobile telephone keypad-turned-controller of a cell phone, controllers serve as the primary communication tools between the system and user. And on the PC, the keyboard-mouse combination plays a large part in the player's perception of the gaming device.

Some consoles, such as the Xbox, have been criticized for the way their controllers are designed for players. They are apparently too heavy for some people, too complicated for others, and have even been replaced with more-elaborate controllers, such as *Tekki* (*Steel Battalion* in Europe) for the Xbox, which was released with a $200 game-specific control unit with twin joysticks and plenty of ancillary buttons.

Then there are the various peripherals that bridge the gap between player and game—for example, the twin microphones necessary to play the PS2 *Singstar* series, the optional guitars for *Guitar Hero*, and the various dance mats, Web cams, and other miscellaneous peripherals that are required for more-active gaming.

The trick is to either decide early on what kind of controllers the game will require, and pick a platform that supports them, or be prepared to make some tough design calls when you realize that there are not enough buttons to support the game's needs. This cuts both ways; overly simple controls can also ruin a game.

Designers who aim at the multi-platform market have their work cut out for them, if only because a game will need to be substantially reworked to take advantage of more-advanced controllers or stripped down due to bare-bones controller support. The logical and graphical user interfaces can help with this to a certain extent, as we shall see later on.

It would be a pity to have to choose a platform based on the controller alone, and so the last word before we delve into the wonderful world of controller design is: "Remain flexible." The game design needs to accommodate the controller, and not the other way around.

> "The fighting is an abomination. Ever wondered why nobody maps main attack controls onto the DualShock2 shoulder buttons? . . . Play *Primal.*" [EDGE01]

This might have been the game's only available option at the time. Unfortunately for the studio, it just didn't work.

You, as a designer, should play many games of different styles to get a feel for all the different controllers that exist and how they are mapped to gaming environments. Then, figure out what the developer did right and wrong, or read reviews from different sources and try to gauge what is the best controller for the game design.

CONTROLLERS

There are as many controllers as there are platforms. They are all modeled around some very tried-and-tested hardware concepts. The differences are usually in the layouts. A little bit of controller history is probably in order here, since the options available have not changed greatly over the years.

The classic control devices were the analog joystick, paddle, and fire button. The early games had one joystick and one button. Move and fire. It is important to note that the joysticks were analog because of its control fluidity. Unlike a switch that is either on or off, an analog joystick reports *degrees* of movement to the machine, which can then work out "how much" the joystick is pointed up and left, for example, and translate this into an appropriate movement on the screen.

The first modern gaming consoles to hit the scene (16-bit monsters like the Sega Genesis and Super Nintendo Entertainment System) replaced the traditional joystick with a four-way digital controller pad. It had a little cross that could be tilted in several directions, but fed no information back to the system other than strict "clicking" movements. This meant that, while a player could be afforded eight degrees of freedom (see Figure 9.1), there was no way to move in a direction that was more left than up, say. It was left and up in exactly the same quantity—or left . . . or up . . . in the same way that a fire button was either depressed or not depressed.

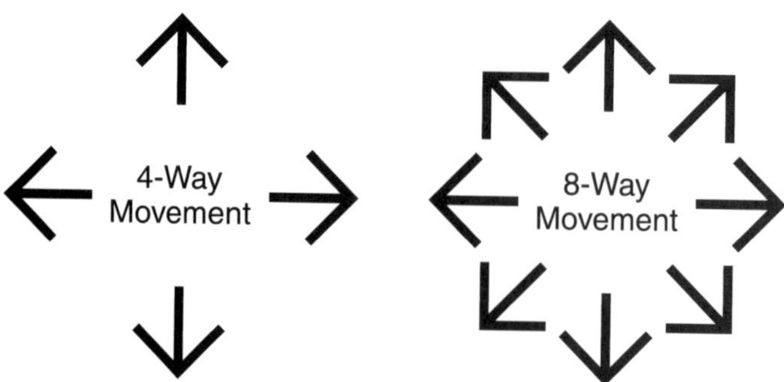

FIGURE 9.1 Four- and eight-way freedom of movement.

Incidentally, handheld gaming devices, such as the GameBoy, also have restrictive digital joysticks, as does the GameBoy Advance. On the other hand, console manufacturers, such as Microsoft, have tended to supply analog controllers in additional to digital ones, which can be used to control aspects of the game like camera angles, or serve as throttles. Fortunately, many games that do not need elaborate controllers offer analog directional control as an option, and people can choose their preference.

Essentially, the difference between analog and digital is user-facing. A digital directional pad (D-pad) consists of eight-way movement in discrete presses. The length of time that the button is held dictates the "extent" of the press.

However, an analog control stick on a PS2 controller (for example) allows a sweep across the directional range. Put another way, if the user moves the stick a little bit, then the resulting extent of the movement is small. A big movement toward one extreme produces a similarly big movement within the game environment.

Likewise, there are degrees of movement within the eight-way model that are more sensitive than with a D-pad. The result can take some getting used to, but is actually, in the main, quite effective. The switch from press and hold to the analog equivalent is like everything else in video gaming—a question of personal taste.

Recent innovations in controller technology include shoulder buttons, which increase the average number of controller pad buttons to between 6 and 10. This may seem like a lot of buttons, but the complexity of modern games, made possible by the underlying hardware, can make them necessary.

In 2006, Nintendo and Sony entered a new era of controller theory with their movement-activated controllers. The Nintendo Wii and Sony PS3 both offer controllers (wands) that can be waved around in order to guide action. For the Wii, it seems to be an integral part of the software as well as the hardware—games that make use of the controller wand abound. Sony, on the other hand, seems to have added it to the PS3 as an afterthought; the wand is not emphasized as a central feature in games launched on the market.

Thus far, we have looked only at controllers that enable the player to tell the machine what actions he wishes to perform. There are other innovations that allow the machine to tell the player what is going on, too. To date, the only one of note seems to be a vibrating controller. How successful these new inventions will be in the gaming industry, only time will tell.

Finally, there is always the option of building custom controllers for games. We have already mentioned the over-the-top peripheral that ships with *Tekki* (*Steel Battalion* in Europe) for the Xbox.

Other controllers include sets of pads that are placed on the floor and danced on in time to the beat of *Dance Dance Revolution (Dancing Stage Euromix)*, originally for the Sony PSOne and first released as an arcade game cabinet. Of course, the designer is limited by the machine's capability; there is no use in producing a peripheral with 50 buttons if the machine will not accept 50 signals.

Finally, there are various skateboards, steering wheels, cameras, microphones, bongo drums, guitars, and even game show buttons—all of which promise to offer extra dimensions to games. They are either optional (you can play *Guitar Hero* without the guitar controller) or necessary to the game (*Singstar* needs the microphones, which pushes its price up).

Consoles might seem restrictive at first, but this is as much a blessing as it is a curse. Standardization is to be welcomed, despite the heavy price of endless rounds of quality assurance. In the PC world, things are not quite as straightforward; especially in the area of controllers, the stakes are higher.

Keyboards and Mapping

PC game design is blessed with one of the most versatile of all gaming systems. Not only is there a 102-button keyboard and mouse, but there are also ports for plugging in joysticks, USB peripherals, and even serial devices. Most PCs also come with the ability to easily upgrade hardware via spare card slots (PCI) in the rear of the unit, To cap it all off, the machine can be programmed to accept signals that are digital or analog, and in an almost infinite number of combinations.

A short walk through the aisles of the technomarket, specifically the PC joystick section, will reveal the multitude of various devices available—feedback steering wheels, joysticks with absurd levels of built-in technology (such as auto-fire), even full airplane simulation kits complete with throttle, steering column, and pedals. It will not be long before the PC screen will only be used for graphics, and games will need specialized peripherals. Consoles have this issue too, but they are somewhat protected by their higher cost, making developers and studios more adverse to risk.

The point is, if a game is complex enough that 10 buttons and two analog joysticks are *not* enough to control it, then the PC offers more than enough options. Herein lies a problem, however. Each game developer is going to assign a set of keys, perhaps in conjunction with other devices, that will differ from other developers'. Hence, there is a need to allow the player to "map" the controls onto their keyboard in the way that feels most natural—or even map all games on the PC to use the same keyboard controls. In fact, this already happens, and is the hallmark of a well-though-out concept. The designer provides the player with an easy way to map their controls, which not only makes gameplay easier, but also reduces a barrier to actually getting into the game.

With the proliferation of PCs in homes all over the world, there is another great reason to use a mappable keyboard interface. Keyboards have different layouts in different countries—for example, the Q key moves, depending on the country's keyboard layout. A poorly written game might map controls onto a keyboard layout that makes them difficult or impossible to access. With no way to change the mapping, the game will become unplayable, and it will be abandoned by your fan base.

There is another small disadvantage to the PC platform; no two are ever exactly the same. One player might have twin joysticks, another might have a mouse with a scroll button. The designer needs to make sure that he is not cutting any players out of the market by requiring nonstandard peripherals for the game.

The Graphical User Interface

Not a lot of game design books have paid much attention to the Graphical User Interface (GUI). This is probably because it is one of the less-interesting aspects of game design. As Marc Saltzman writes:

> "A bad user interface (UI) in a game can be its own demise, regardless of how good the content is . . . if the game itself isn't good, the UI certainly can't save it. Nonetheless, it's one of the most significant areas of game design that's often overlooked." [Saltzman00]

Saltzman sets out several areas of the user interface, ranging from the *shell interface*, which is largely associated with everything that the player can do to set up their gaming experience, to the *in-game interface*, which can be seen during gameplay and should coincide with the internal state of the game, as well as with the control interface.

The in-game interface is worthy of further explanation. As game designers it pays to remember the special relationship between the hand and the eyes. Sports people, especially, know the importance of hand-eye coordination in playing golf, tennis, squash, cricket, football, and so forth. There is a long list of sports in which it is important to match your vision with hands/feet and events in the athletic world. The same importance needs to be placed on connecting the player to the virtual world—with weapons, cars, virtual hands and feet, and other objects in the game universe.

Some controllers are a little too realistic. For example, the Wii wireless controller picks up actual movement and translates it into in-game actions. Hack-and-slash games like *Manhunt* become a very real and personal experience—and probably too lifelike for most gamers.

Long-range combat games that use projectile weapons are slightly less reliant on the relationship between the control and user interfaces. Vance Cook of Sierra Sports is quoted here in a conversation with Marc Saltzman for *Game Design: Secrets of the Sages:*

> "You must make your customers feel connected to the game. The control devices must become an extension of themselves, and with time become intuitive. Anything you do to remind them they're playing a game will detract from the enjoyment of the experience." [Cook01]

He is speaking in the context of the pure interface (see Chapter 1), perhaps not with the depth that it deserves, but certainly enough to illustrate how the mouse and keyboard are used as an interface between the player and the game. In this case, however, we can also extend the theory to cover the *effect* of the various actions that the player makes in the "real world" as depicted by the GUI.

A golf swing, for example, will be monitored by the player via the GUI, though no golf games to date have been immersive enough to be able to play shots without a GUI to represent the amount of spin, for example. Possibly the PS3 and Wii wireless controllers might come up with a good solution. Time will tell.

There are always cases where the player needs another way to see the effect that he is having on the game universe and/or the game universe is having on him (such as hidden enemies). This is known as the Heads-Up Display (HUD), which traditionally shows the status of the player character and helps to cement the relationship between the physical and virtual interfaces.

SETTING UP THE GAME

The avid game player will know what to expect in terms of on-screen interfaces, depending on the genre. For designers, this translates to the importance of delivering on those expectations. For example, a car-racing genre can be (loosely) broken down into three parts: the circuit, the car, and the race itself, each of which can be modified depending on the mode of play—traditionally "arcade" or "championship."

In the "arcade" mode, epitomized by games such as *Daytona*, the circuit choices need only be "easy," "medium," or "hard." Car customization can be limited to automatic or manual transmission, and the race will lead to either a win (continue) or lose (stop).

While gaming consoles have the advantage that they are standardized, PCs do not have this trait, which means that there must be some way for the player to customize the graphical richness of the gaming experience so that his machine is used to its fullest advantage. This might mean that some gamers will need to tone down the graphics somewhat, because they do not possess the best hardware.

Likewise the sound and in-game music needs to be able to be adjustable to the player's taste or the capabilities of the target machine. This applies equally to dedicated gaming systems (consoles and handhelds); the gamer simply might not *want* to listen to your carefully crafted in-game music. Furthermore, they might prefer to listen to their own music while playing. On PCs, this is easy to offer, since they have CD-ROM drives and can load the music onto the machine ahead of time. Consoles with hard drives might offer this in the future—that is, load music to the hard drive so you can listen to it as you play.

Options should be presented in a simple hierarchical manner so that the player can easily find a specific function that he wishes to tweak. If descriptive icons need to be used so that the option interface matches the main game, then help text or button labels can be added.

An important point is that the language and pictures should reflect the general look and feel of the game, so that even though the player is aware that they are adjusting the technical aspects, it is not immediately obvious from the user interface that it is not actually part of the game.

The technical options should not be hidden from the user. It is quite proper to offer the possibility for the user to adjust the screen position and size from within a medieval role playing game, even if there is a technology mismatch. However, the presentation of options should not break the suspension of reality while conveying accurately what it is the player is able to tweak.

In the previous example, we might refer to the width of the "scroll," as this would be the in-game equivalent to the screen. Similarly, the language should fit the genre—"Can you see the scroll, my liege?"—such that the game's personality is stamped on the setup as well as through the play session.

The Game Interface

Although the main screen is where all the action takes place, its periphery can contain all kinds of information that the player needs in order to know how they are progressing through the game. Over the long term, this information can also tell the player's state, the state of the environment, and what the future might bring.

Much of the interface replaces senses that are "missing" or restricted by the gaming hardware. For example, our sense of smell is missing, and the senses of hearing and touch are severely limited in the virtual world.

The HUD

The traditional mechanism for displaying game status information is the head-up display, a term borrowed from military and other real-life information displays. As in these real-life situations, the idea is to present as much information as possible with as little distraction as possible to the viewer.

Various kinds of information can be shown in the HUD, which can be either semi-transparent (allowing the underlying display to show through) or completely opaque, as in an automobile dashboard. There are reasons for choosing between the two approaches, such as the amount of screen real estate available, which in turn is governed by the screen resolution and monitor size.

In the PC world, this can be quite important, since some monitors cannot support high resolutions—1024 × 768, for example. The relationship between the resolution and available screen real estate is quite simple. Lower-resolution screens (640 × 480) will look constricted if a large portion of the display is used by the HUD.

Consoles do not suffer from this problem, since televisions all operate at the same resolution, but playing on smaller screens will mean that any text used is respectively smaller. This can make games with a high proportion of textual information difficult to play on anything smaller than a 21-inch television screen.

The Apple Macintosh has a further complication. Unlike the PC, Mac screens work on the principle of "real" screen real estate; that is, a larger screen automatically increases the available desktop, and the pixel size remains the same, meaning that bigger screens have more space available. This is in contrast to the PC, which simply increases the pixel size for larger monitors and leaves the resolution choice to the user.

Other devices, such as handheld consoles, have their platform-specific constraints—smaller screens, smaller resolutions, and different pixel lighting. All of these issues mean challenges that lead to porting and design headaches for the GUI designer. Text, for example, should not be used in HUDs implemented on such small screens.

If there are any rules, then they are vague ones—more like guiding principles to follow. First, the amount of space that can be used by the HUD will depend largely on its opacity. The more of the game screen that can be seen through the HUD, the larger it can be, since it will interfere less with the action screen.

Second, HUDs can be positioned more or less wherever the designer wishes, so long as the principle elements are at the edges of the screen. The center of the screen should only have the bare minimum of information required to illustrate the actual on-screen action.

Finally, multipart HUDs that expand as required and provide contextual information to the player detract less from the gameplay than ever-present status indicators. Examples include games like *SimCity 4*. Other contextually sensitive HUDs appear in games that involve multiple vehicles, such as *Halo*. These actually change depending on what vehicle is being used at the time.

As an example of how *not* to implement a context-sensitive HUD, consider climbing into a vehicle, and having the dashboard take up most of the remainder of the screen, rather than having the in-game HUD adapt to the vehicle. This approach should be used only if there is no other HUD to speak of in the game proper. Screen shots from *Tekki* (*Steel Battalion* in Europe) seem to indicate that this has been the approach taken. The action part of the screen seems very small (roughly one-quarter of the screen, in the center) compared to the virtual dashboard. This leaves us wondering if there were some restrictions in the Xbox graphics engine, which lead to the decision to render as much of the screen with static graphics as possible. The entire effect is claustrophobic.

Using Colors, Dials, and Bars

At the risk of excluding the color-blind, note that colors in video games, and especially in the GUI, have specific meanings. Red is almost always bad. Green and yellow are universally accepted to be nonthreatening colors. Blue is rarely used, except in a kind of light-blue haze that provides a neutral background to place indicators on. Silver (light gray) is almost always used when a metal-effect, virtual dashboard is needed.

One of the most common HUD elements is the energy bar. The bar level goes down when hit and up when recharged. In addition, the bar's color can communicate additional status information—for example, a low bar level that has turned red means the player is dangerously close to death.

As an aside, colors that are ingrained in the human psyche have meanings that are expected by the player. Red, universally a color that represents danger (or, in certain circumstances, love and passion), is one such example. The player will attach a heightened level of excitement (positive or negative) to certain colors, like red, so we need to respect these built-in responses and not try to circumvent them.

Therefore, the player rarely has to look at the actual level, since the color gives immediate information. The lower the bar, the more the color will change from green to yellow, and just before destruction (the final 25%), it will turn to red. Below 10%, and it will start flashing urgently. If this is what gamers in a particular genre expect, then this is what the design should give them. Again, playing games in a variety of genres will give the designer a good idea of how the interface elements should look. Their arrangement will largely depend on the game design itself.

Dials can also be used. Remember that right is high, and left is low. This is a Western standard that is nearly universal. Still, it will be little help to the gamer if an empty energy tank is indicated by the needle edging from five o'clock to seven o'clock, rather than the other way around. Going against the player's expectations in UI design is one of those mistakes that will spell disaster for a game's success.

Dials and bars can also be combined to produce curved bars that follow the color logic of energy bars and the circular motion of dials. Alternatives include "segments" of glowing green (or blue) arranged around a circular icon that represents an aspect of the player's gaming universe. A collection of gauges, bars, and dials can be seen in Figure 9.2, including a segmented gauge.

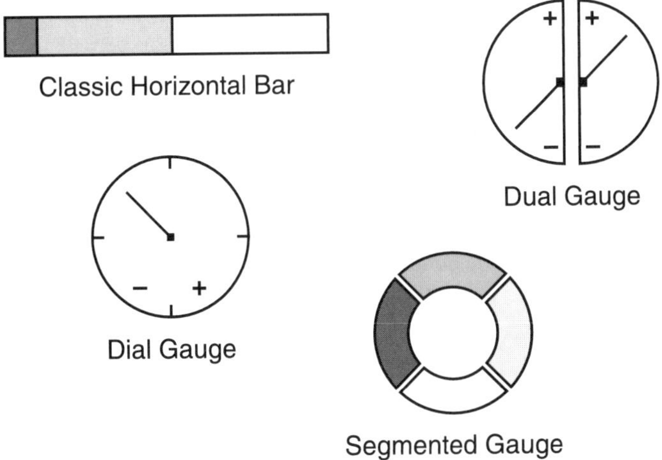

FIGURE 9.2 Gauges, Bars, and Dials.

Ammunition levels are often represented by vertical bars that indicate the number of bullets in a clip or the charge level of sophisticated energy weapons. Horizontal rows of bullets have also been used to great effect, but there may be a tendency, when dealing with finite quantities, to neglect what happens when the player is so good that they acquire more ammunition than the designers bargained for.

For example, *Asteroids* machines had a mechanism for displaying the quantity of remaining lives in a play session, which used miniature spacecraft pictures. One little spacecraft was equal to one life, and players gained additional lives by reaching a certain number of points, among other goals. On the other hand, lives were lost by collisions with asteroids or other spacecraft, or by being shot out of the sky. The designers neglected to think about what would happen if the players *never* lost lives. They did not put in a limit on the number of lives that a player could accumulate during the play session. This did not matter under normal circumstances, but if the player became very adept at building up lives, at a certain point the machine would begin to slow down. The reason was that the machine was taking longer and longer to draw the many little spaceships (lives), which hindered its getting back to actually managing the other aspects of the game. The play session continued, but as the players got more lives, the machine slowed down.

The designers were at a loss to figure out why this was happening, because the little spaceships were being drawn off-screen, such was the vast quantity of lives that had been amassed. Eventually the situation was rectified, and only the very best players ever managed to amass enough lives for this quirk to make a difference. It is, however, a good illustration of the way that the game mechanics, interface, and in-game logic work together. The designer needs to remember that the interface is as much a part of the game as the rest of the design, and it uses resources in the same way.

Radars and Proximity Detectors

Other aspects of the GUI control the ability to see beyond the immediate game universe in some way. *Elite* had a radar, as did *Starship Command*, and more recently, *Delta Force: Black Hawk Down*, as well as various racing games, such as the *Colin McRae* rally series. In various genres—shooting versus racing, in this case—radars serve very different purposes.

Shooting games, for example, involve knowing where the opponent is so that they can be avoided, and the addition of radar might at first seem like cheating. In a racing game, radar shows the player just how far behind, or ahead of the race leader he is. This approach makes sense, as does being able to detect spacecraft from a distance; that is, it makes no real difference to the outcome of the engagement.

Being able to detect an enemy hiding around a corner might seem a bit trite, especially with radar that can tell friends from foes. This is where the proximity detector comes in. These can inform the player that there is another entity within the vicinity, but they do not tell the player who or exactly where the entity is.

Reality dictates that proximity detectors merely replace some of the senses that cannot be reproduced on current video gaming systems. That is, they provide additional information that would otherwise be available to the player if this was a real-life situation. Therefore, being able to determine the nature of the threat before it is seen would dangerously stretch reality (see Chapter 7, "Game Mechanics").

Games such as *Elite* implement a radar system that indicates, on a two-dimensional screen, the distance of any surrounding spacecraft, along with their sizes. This remarkable depth of information is conveyed in a variety of ways. Color coding reflects the sizes of crafts, and varying tail lengths on the ship icons indicate how much above or below the player the craft is. The position information uses a top-down oval, which can show whether crafts are in front, behind, or to either side of the player, as well as the distance.

The key to choosing which method to employ is rooted in the overall technological level of the game, coupled with the desired level of realism. A well-balanced combat system can be destroyed if the player does not have to work to establish where the opposition is.

As far as displaying the information goes, sometimes it makes sense to make an overlay of the player's immediate vicinity, such as in buildings or tracks. These are definitely GUI components that will require space, and as such fall into the semi-transparent solution. For most games, a sound approach is to ensure that at least some of the underlying play area can be seen through the radar display.

Innovative Monitoring

We have mentioned that proximity detectors and radars use clever GUI components to enhance the interface and replace some of the senses that the player does not have in the virtual world. In *Soldier of Fortune II: Double Helix*, this is taken one step further; hearing is replaced with a sound monitor. This serves two purposes. It tells the player how much noise his is making, as well the general noise level in the surrounding area.

Power monitoring is another one of those unusual GUI elements that seems to break the rules. Golf simulations usually measure shot power with a gauge that runs counterclockwise, despite our previous logic that says gauges should always have a clockwise bias. There are various ways to display shot powers or build-ups of weapon power (such as the colored crystals in *Blinx*), all of which should reflect the game genre.

Dialog Boxes and Textual Information

A dialog box can communicate information to the player or allow them to enter information pertaining to the game. Generally speaking, dialog boxes break the flow of a game, and so are unsuitable in many cases. They also have a different look and feel than the average video game interface, and are often tied to the underlying interface unless steps are taken to change this.

In general, dialog boxes are good for holding static information, such as notes on what the current mission entails. *Soldier of Fortune 2: Double Helix* uses them in this way, but styles them to match the general look and feel of the game. If the target game is an RPG, for example, then perhaps a notebook-style dialog box can be used to store information about the contents of the player's backpack.

The other aspect of dialog boxes involves getting information from the player. There are areas for entering text, pressing buttons, and setting radio buttons and check boxes, which makes them useful for adjusting the settings of a particular play session.

There are two main guidelines to follow when designing dialog boxes for games. The first is to only use them for setting up the game or to convey information to the player that cannot be conveyed in a dynamic, interactive way. The second is to respect the look and feel of the game's universe, and if this is not possible, exclude dialog boxes during the play session, altogether; though they can be used during the pre-play session, because the player has not yet been immersed into the game universe. Anything that breaks the player's suspension of disbelief will detract from the success of the game—in the same way that split screens that contain commercials will detract from the enjoyment of a movie.

Of course, badly designed video games will remain badly designed, while movies can be "remastered" with errors fixed in subsequent releases. However, the memory of a bad experience will still linger to the point that, when the moment arrives at which the film erred, the viewer will still tense up and look for the mistakes—again distracting from enjoyment. Video game mistakes have the same effect; they just cost more to correct, if they can be corrected at all, and the end user (the player) will be infuriated to the point that the game, the studio, and even the publisher become unattractive.

THE GAME UNIVERSE INTERFACE

So far we have looked at direct UI—ways of providing the player with the chance to interact with the game and ways for the game to give the player information that relates to their immediate situation. The game universe also needs a way to present itself for the user. Now, this is really only relevant for 3D games, since other games have very simple mechanisms for displaying the game universe.

The first of the following two sections deals with an aspect of game design that is often badly conceived and implemented—the camera through which the player views the game universe. Scrolling shooters, platform games, and fighting simulations do not have problems with displaying the game universe, since the camera is fixed either to the side or above the player. Even isometric games have a fixed camera. You may be able to change the view (as in *SimCity*), but you cannot swing around and freely explore the game universe. The camera is fixed at a 45-degree angle.

Following the camera section is a look at how maps can be implemented in games. This is another technique that can be done badly, and one that is often found in 3D and 2D games.

Cameras

The camera is the player's eye. In 3D game universe implementations, there are many places that the camera can be. These include positions such as over-the-shoulder, as in *Tomb Raider*, or behind the eyes of the player character, as in *DOOM*-like first-person shooters. Both of these games use a fixed camera system, which implies that the viewpoint is always the same. The camera is a bit more mobile in *Tomb Raider*, because it needs to switch sides when the character performs a roll, and it has to compensate for jumping. The *viewpoint* remains the same, however.

First-person shooters were pioneers in cinematic cut-scene gaming, starting with *Quake,* in which the camera detaches itself from the player in the closing stages of levels, when bosses meet their grisly ends. More recently, *Severance: Blade of Darkness* employs a similar technique, a swing around a courtyard, which is used in conjunction with some fairly majestic music. Despite being a movie-inspired special effect, the scene reveals the next challenge to the player. The swing around the courtyard (the player hovers above) tells us how many bosses are parading around. Otherwise, the player would have to get up on a wall and look down at them—at which point, of course, he would be seen.

Some games employ a floating camera, which is where the trouble often starts. It is very easy to find a problem with the camera in every truly free 3D perspective game. Allowing the camera to find its own vantage point will always mean that there are people for whom it is in the wrong place.

Badly behaved cameras seem to appear in almost every issue of *EDGE* magazine. Look over the bulletin boards dedicated to any action game that has a free camera, and you will see that gamers tend to agree: It is an aspect that is frequently badly implemented.

Some designers attempt to get around the complexities of camera AI by allowing the player to move the camera using either a joystick or keyboard arrows. They seem to forget that the player has enough to do without fiddling with a camera angle, blinded, while the enemy is pelting them with artillery.

Cameras are to be treated with care. Even fixed ones are not immune to gross misconduct. Every *Quake* player has probably noted that under certain circumstances, it is possible to see through walls by running very close to them at full tilt—and it happens at quite inopportune moments of gameplay, but is not predictable enough to use as a "cheat."

Semi-fixed cameras, like those used in *Tomb Raider* and *Red Faction,* also suffer from difficulties, because the player cannot move the camera, himself. These cameras usually inhabit a space that is behind and slightly above, and points at an odd angle. What happens is that the player performs an action that the designer was not expecting, which results in the camera accidentally being placed inside a wall. For a technical explanation of how this is possible, the designer should be aware of the nature of video game programming. The programmer cannot check to see if every part of the immediate game universe (arms, legs, cameras) is separated from the inanimate surroundings—such as walls, floors, ceilings, and so on. Instead, he checks to see if certain points on certain planes are likely to be on one side or the other of the plane before allowing the movement to happen. Then the scene is redrawn. If, as can happen, the camera is caught on the wrong side of a surface when it is redrawn, it gets caught inside the plane. Granted, this should never happen, and play-testing should ensure that it doesn't for the most-popular paths through a level. There is always one player, however, who tries something different, and the fragility of the underlying gaming system risks being revealed.

We have picked on a handful of games, perhaps unfairly. They were just the lucky few. Even the superlative *Super Mario Sunshine* has a camera that refuses to behave from time to time, and the highly acclaimed *Indiana Jones and the Emperor's Tomb* is plagued with camera problems during fighting scenes.

3D Spatial Sound

The floating camera allows for more freedom of vision than a fixed one, but the real clues to the nature of the surrounding universe come with the use of surround sound. Not every gamer has access to true 3D sound, which requires five speakers set up to direct specific sounds, so care has to be taken when using it. On the other hand, simulated 3D sound, which uses a mixture of stereo (two speakers), Doppler effects (for distance), and logical audio and visual combinations, can be very effective. The trick is to make up for the fact that the player's usual, near-180-degree field of vision is restricted to less than 90 degrees, depending on a number of factors (see Figure 9.3). Instead, off-camera audio cues are given.

Note that these representations simply approach reality and are by no means scientifically proven. This book is not a scientific journal. The general principal is that if something moves out of the player's field of vision, then it should still be detectable by the sound that it makes—be it past 160 degrees (regular vision), 90 degrees (movie vision), or 60 degrees (regular TV) with respect to the player's point of view.

In other words, the heavy grunting heard to your left when playing *DOOM III* is probably a good indication that there is a creature about to attack you from that direction. The distance to the threat can be indicated by a number of aural facets;

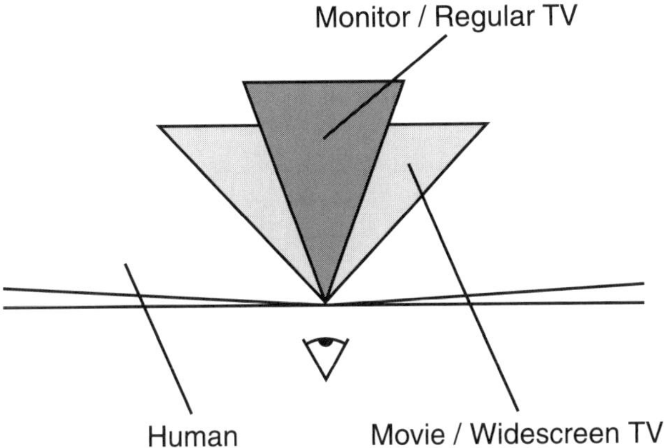

FIGURE 9.3 Fields of vision.

it could be quiet or loud if the player is outdoors, or it could echo down the length of a corridor.

Sounds that come from behind the player are a little more difficult to project without true surround sound, but this can be achieved easily in racing games where there are alternative cameras (rear-view and side mirrors). These can be combined with the sound to produce the Doppler effect of vehicles that approach from behind and overtake the player.

Similarly, a quieter than normal sound directly in front of the player, combined with common sense that dictates that if nothing can be seen in front, then it must logically be behind, has to suffice. As with free-floating cameras, the designer needs to be very careful with directed sound effects, because they can ruin the game if implemented poorly.

AUTO-TARGETING

Yet another aspect that often suffers a lot of criticism is the use of automatic targeting of enemies. In essence, it is often maligned as something that detracts from the gameplay because it diminishes the amount of control that the player has over the game. Usually it is to be avoided completely, unless the game interface is so complex that it becomes a requirement.

Using auto-targeting with a standard weapon in a first-person shooter or scrolling shooter, where the player only has to point and shoot anyway, would only require that the player press the fire button at the appropriate moment to be guaranteed a hit on the target. Traditionally, the auto-target feature is used for limited-quantity weapons, such as heat-seeking missiles.

Of course, there is always an element of automatic targeting and range-finding associated with weapons that have a projectile or energy beam. The reason is that most games involving gunplay have only one control, be they space fliers or dungeon busters. Auto-targeting changes both the direction of travel and direction of firing; put the crosshairs on the enemy, fire, and you will probably hit it.

There are those games that lean toward reality by jigging the crosshairs to simulate the effect of real-life gun sights while the player is in motion. This adds a level of sophistication to the aiming and firing mechanisms, but the end result is still the same. The trick is to ensure that the player either does not notice that the firing is guided, doesn't care, or is grateful for the help. As soon as combat becomes trivial, much of the balance of the game is destroyed.

Some melee games, such as those involving swordplay, also rely to a certain extent on clever targeting techniques that feel entirely natural. One such title, *Severance: Blade of Darkness*, uses the feature to enable the player to "lock onto" a target before attacking. This releases the controls to the player for choice of attack, rather than wasting the directional controls on placing the shot.

Fighting games, like *Street Fighter II* or *Mortal Kombat,* also ensure that if the player is heading in the right direction and performs the manual dexterity required to deliver a blow with the correct timing, they do not have to worry about directing the attacking limb down to the point of contact. Part of this is a restriction in the control interface, part is to allow for spectacular combinations and special moves.

Other games, such as *The Getaway,* employ automatic targeting on the most dangerous enemy in the immediate vicinity. Considering the fact that the viewpoint is constantly changing from vehicle to street level, as the player climbs in and out of cars, this is a case where the feature is a welcome addition.

Maps

In the same way that radar affects game balance, maps also have a high impact on the playability and longevity of a game. Racing games almost always provide a graphical map of the course, however rudimentary, on the screen during the race. Rally games in which there is a co-pilot also call out the twists and turns just before they happen, which reflects the real-life experience of driving a rally car.

Maps are a necessity in driving games, because they show where the player is in relation to the rest of the field and also give advance warning of the track's layout. This information is immediately accessible to the player—as opposed to real life, where drivers spend hundreds of hours driving around a course before actually racing it. The map ensures that a player can sit down and race a new course as if they had been around it before. The map on the screen replaces the map in the head of the experienced professional driver.

On the other hand, providing the player with an extensive map that shows the layout of a *DOOM* level would remove much of the exploration challenge of the game—a bad thing. Of course, players of the *DOOM* series will remember that there is a map, but only the places that have been visited by the player are shown.

We shall call these two map styles "static" and "revealing." The static map is given to the player gratis, while the revealing map has to be earned. There is also a third kind of map that is provided to the player when a certain object is obtained—be it an actual map or an electronic version that is loaded into memory. These tend to be static in nature. A further twist in the mapping technique can require the player to obtain the needed map by purchasing it or by defeating an enemy that is carrying it.

Either way, maps provide a way for the player to navigate without having to worry about remembering all the places that have been visited, which is a must for the casual gaming market. Hardcore gamers have had these mapping devices implanted in their brains at birth; it is part of what makes them naturally good at playing video games.

The provision of a map in the UI and the importance of it within the game are therefore very genre-specific. The use of maps also tends to mimic reality. There are no maps in *Colin McRae* rally games; instead, there is a co-driver to tell you what's over the next horizon. This mimics the real-world universe.

Skinning

One of the recent trends in GUI design reflects the natural desire of players to personalize their games. Microsoft understood this and gave their user base a desktop with icons labeled "My Documents" and "My Computer." Skinning takes this a step further and, with a technique that Microsoft has also used, allows users to assign their own graphics to icons.

Providing a changeable user interface is one thing, but in-game skinning has taken off in a big way when applied to team games. Online gaming has evolved to the point where teams of people are meeting in cyberspace to run around a virtual maze and shoot at each other in high-tech paintball simulations.

One of the principles behind *Unreal Tournament*, skinning has been extended to individual players (although other online first-person shooters also offer similar functionality). Ranging from a simple team color approach to more-sophisticated renderings of custom player graphics, this is an interesting social twist to gaming. We now have clans of gamers, all sporting the same logos on their player character's attire, fighting it out in cyberspace (and possibly with real-life garment versions hanging in their closets). An extension of this would be, in the future, the marketing of attire in the virtual world, much the same way as in the real world. How long will it be before there is a virtual Formula 1 Grand Prix, complete with sponsored cars and players, earning regular income from their virtual success?

Skinning, which ranges from simple console customization to changing the player's appearance, is here to stay. In a recent magazine, a new kind of soccer game was showcased in which players could send their photos to the game's manufacturer and have their likeness grafted onto virtual soccer players—the ultimate skinning, and made possible because photorealistic gaming has truly come into its own over the past few years.

The Logical Interface

As an extension of the regular game interface, many genres also allow for sequences of commands to be carried out via an accumulation of other commands, through specific programming, or by proxy. We will delve into this later; for now, suffice to say that there are two kinds of macros that can be considered: internal and built.

The first is hardwired into the game and can be classified as an internal macro. Internal macros can manifest themselves to the player via the observed behavior of other game objects, including the player character. But, they cannot be altered by the player, unless cued by something that the player has done to affect the game universe.

The other macro type can be built up by the player either directly by a specific sequence of executed commands, or indirectly by performing actions through game objects, with the nature of the commands and the sequence dictated by the order of those actions. If this is too abstract, then rest assured; all will become clear as we progress through this section on UI design.

Combos

Combos fall into the category of internal macros that cannot be influenced by the player in any way. They are merely unleashed after certain in-game conditions have been met.

Most gamers will remember the term "combo" from *Street Fighter II*, which was possibly the first mainstream fighting game to use special move combinations to enable devastating damage on the opposition. Since then, the repertoire of fighting games have increased somewhat, as have the death-dealing moves, such as the *Mortal Kombat*-specific climax that saps the last life blood out of the opponent in one of various particularly gory and gruesome ways.

Of course there are more abstract examples, such as the eating of ghosts in *Pac-Man*. Each ghost eaten in sequence adds more points to the player's tally than the last. Sports games (usually fighting games) also have a scoring mechanism that relies on combinations of moves, which is less visually impressive, but adds another fun dimension to the game.

Almost any game genre can have combos in addition to those listed here. The trick is to spot where, in the rules that make up the game mechanics, there is an opportunity to create point bonuses or some form of superior power. This can be won in a short time span (as in *Street Fighter II*) or over a longer period, such as when training in a variety of different skills will reward the player with the ability to cast specific magical spells.

Object and Location Macros

While combos only relate to the player character, object and location macros relate to other entities within the game universe and the way that they can interact. For example, a macro might dictate that, when certain conditions are right, a collection of objects will be placed at a specific location.

In conjunction with player control, macros also serve as commands applied in a given set of circumstances, such as while holding or using an object. One of the simplest examples is in the text adventure genre, where the player enters commands via the keyboard. Usually these adventures revolve around exploration and collection of objects, some of which are "treasure," but others are function-specific.

One such game released in the 1980s required the player to possess a magical wand and a collection of treasure items, take them all to a specific location, kneel, and wave the wand. This is an example of a combination of object and location macros. Inside the game engine, the triggers for the game's completion depend on objects being present in a specific place, and the player holding a specific object and performing a specific action.

Spells are also forms of object macros, since they usually require that the player have a specific set of skills in combination with magical objects. Casting a spell is especially relevant here, because it effects a result in one move that would otherwise require many moves to achieve, if at all.

Even car racing games can have macros—especially if the player is required to amass funds to make his vehicle better in some way. Certain parts purchased for the car will interact with other parts, making the car a more competitive vehicle than before.

User-Defined Macros

The easiest form of a user-defined macro is the simple keyboard-binding system, which allows the player to retain a similar set of keys across a number of different games. This can be extended to mapping other user-input devices, especially in situations where the platform controller has less versatility than is required by the video game—for example, when a game is being ported from a platform with a keyboard to one without.

User-defined macros allow players to customize the mechanics of their gaming experience in the same way that skinning allows them to customize the visual aspect. For example, a series of commands, moves, or actions could be assigned to a specific key and executed in succession.

Scripting is a more-complex example of user-defined macros, which are applied to nonplayer characters rather than the player character, himself. The amount of control that the game designer offers to the player will be determined by the genre. The macro approach might only work if the game lends itself to this kind of extension being offered to all players. Scripting is usually reserved for advanced players and developers.

SUMMARY

This chapter dealt with techniques that video games use when providing ways in which the player can interact with the game machine. We looked at some examples of how other designers have approached the problem, as well as highlighted some of the problems associated with the different platforms that video games can be written for.

Each genre, and platform, will have different ways in which the interface affects the way the game is played, as well as how the player's information must be displayed. It is no good using *Star Trek*-style technology in *Mad Max and the Thunderdome.* For example, RPGs set in ancient times will not usually have an interface that looks modern.

There are always exceptions, as well as cases where the interface needs to adapt itself to the surrounding game universe—for example, a status display that alters and provides different information types and functions if, say, the player climbs into a vehicle.

Two aspects of the UI cannot be altered, ever. The first is the viewing ratio of the screen—TV, game monitor, or widescreen. If a game is created using widescreen technology as standard, then it will appear in "letterbox" format on a standard television. The designer needs to be aware that on a small screen, this may ruin the effect of the game; it will not have the same impact as it did when tested as the huge, widescreen plasma version.

The other aspect is the player's physical control over game. Controllers will have an important part to play in the design of the game—from the four-way controller that a GameBoy has to the multifunction, PC keyboard device. Once a console game is developed, however, the controller that was available at the time it was shipped is the one that will have to remain in use throughout the play session.

The visual interface can change, as can other aspects of the game, but the controller remains static. This leads us to the last point of the chapter—testing. All interface aspects have to be tested even more than other aspects, simply because the interface will make or break the game.

A bad interface will end the game's success. It is that important. The interface will also help to sell the game, even if the actual idea is not totally original. Dancing and Karaoke are, ultimately, not really all that original in terms of the actual idea, but the interfaces in *Dance Dance Revolution* and *SingStar* help to make them incredibly popular.

On the one hand, the dance mat, screen, and gameplay of *DDR* keep players coming back for more, and on the other, the onscreen scoring system helps *SingStar* players gauge their success and improve over time. If it were "just" dancing and "just" singing, it would cease to be entertaining. The interface is such a large part of game design that it is impossible to ignore.

REFERENCES

[Cook01] Vance Cook in a conversation with Marc Saltzman, *Game Design: Secrets of the Sages.* Macmillan Publishing, 2000, p. 252.

[EDGE01] Review Section. *EDGE* magazine, No. 121, March 2003, p. 92.

[Saltzman00] Marc Saltzman, *Game Design: Secrets of the Sages.* Macmillan Publishing, 2000, p. 249.

10 Level and Mission Design

In This Chapter

- Introduction to Level Design
- Designing Buildings
- Mission Design
- Integrating Levels and Missions
- Other Level and Mission Types

By now, we have looked at all of the basic elements of game development. We have looked at the idea, the design of the game, the *assets* (which include artwork and audio, as well as the planning that goes into initial development), and then the product. We have rounded it out with a graphical user interface that will allow the user to interact with the game.

What we do not have yet is structure. We do not have a game structure into which we can drop all of these wonderful ideas and assets. In part, the GUI will fit into this abstract structure, also; so far, we have only planned for how the game will present itself toward the player, not how the game will progress.

The game design, itself, should include clues to the general game structure. There are, however, details that need to be dealt with before the remainder of this book can be adequately applied.

Vehicles, terrain, weapons, and game AI all need to fall into the level and mission design that the game is based on. A good example is *Halo*, which has multiple vehicles that can be explored and exploited, but rigorous rules, such as the player only being able to carry two weapons at any one time. The combination of game mechanics and mission structure means that every move has to be carefully thought out.

Traditionally, when we think of *levels*, images of platform games or generic shoot-em-ups come to mind. Speak of *missions*, and guns, camouflaged soldiers, vehicles, and other military game–style scenarios spring up. A level, though, can simply be a group of game elements that present a challenge to the player in achieving the goal of either that particular level or the game, itself. These elements could be a cunning set of puzzles, reduced time allowance, or a challenging arrangement of game objects—or even, ideally, a combination of them.

The layout of a *Pac-Man* level is no different than the previous level, except that the ghosts are a little quicker or more intelligent. In *Space Invaders,* aliens shoot faster with each subsequent level, and *Quake* is based on puzzles, mazes, and the player's need for biosuits to dive into tanks of strange plasma. These are all levels, and level design is an art that is directly linked to the type of game that is being developed. Like all other facets of game design, there are "good" examples and "bad" examples.

Introduction to Level Design

So, what is a level, exactly? Once again, we turn our attention to a venerable tome on game development, *Game Design: Secrets of the Sages,* for an authoritative definition, which runs something like this:

> "Every game has one overall mission or goal. The game then is made up of many single levels. Every level in turn must also have one overall mission." [Willits01]

Readers of *Game Design: Secrets of the Sages* will remember, and fans of id Software games, such as *DOOM* and *Quake*, will agree with the following words:

> "And every map must have a reason why it exists." [Willits01]

Clearly, the book is geared to the FPS (First Person Shooter) community. It is worth remembering, when perusing other design books on the market, that other genres exist, but these days the emphasis is clearly on 3D, and the FPS seems to be the genre of the moment. Other game designs, even those that start out life as ladder-and-level-style games, are being bent toward the 3D FPS formula.

Take the excellent *Super Mario Sunshine*, produced for the GameCube by Nintendo and released in mid-2002. It is worth checking out the Nintendo of America site (http://www.nintendo.com). Search for *Super Mario Sunshine* and take a look at the (eye candy) screenshots. Even a "platform" game like *Super Mario* has been updated to reflect an FPS, over-the-shoulder 3D feel. This is partly due to the phenomenal increase in console processing power, but at least a small portion of the credit is due to studios like id Software, who almost created the genre; but perhaps the transition would have happened anyway.

More processing power lets us have better 3D representations, and that would not have been possible with the same finesse under previous generations of console. It's almost as if Nintendo waited for the hardware to catch up before producing *Sunshine*, not wanting to compromise the intellectual property by trying to squash the game onto inferior hardware. One thing is clear: The GameCube is certainly more than capable, whereas the N64 would have struggled.

The points in the quote [Willits01] have been applied to the FPS genre, which is not surprising considering Willits' position as lead level designer for *Quake II* and *Quake III: Arena*. They apply equally, also, to any game that has a level-oriented structure, even simulations and sports. Consider tennis games, for example. The more opponents that are dispatched, the harder they are to beat. Beat-em-ups, car-racing games, and even creations like *Dance Dance Revolution* all employ increased difficulty.

Tetris speeds up, as does *Breakout*. Arcade racing games, such as *Daytona*, apply ever-decreasing time limits to complete laps (or to achieve checkpoints). Fighting games use the player's remaining energy as a gauge of success when adapting the opponent's difficulty—so that the next victory seems to be only just out of reach.

Clearly, the word "level" can have many different meanings, depending on the game genre. So, some interesting philosophical questions arise—such as, "What constitutes a level in *SimCity*?" The definition of a level then becomes somewhat dependant on either the player's or the designer's point of view. In some badly thought out games, the developer *thought* there was a clear structure, only to find that when the game went to market, the players felt that the game was *too* structured and rigid. In the very worst cases, levels seem disconnected, because the designer has a different view of the game universe than the player and has failed to clearly communicate his ideas.

History is littered with examples. For example, the repetitive *Stuntman* levels require pixel-perfect accuracy. If the player fails to complete all the various stunts, he is required to start the entire level again, with a lengthy video cut-scene, to boot. The developers might have had *realism* in mind when they designed the game, but it appears to have simply translated to *frustrating*. Of course, it will appeal to some, but the game misses the mark when it comes to mass-market appeal.

Level Types

Due to the subjective nature of the *level* concept, we shall deal with it in two broad categories, which I call *goal oriented* and *scenario based*. In a goal-oriented level, a specific objective must be achieved. This could be as simple as defeating an opponent in a one-on-one fight, as in *Street Fighter II*, or finishing in the top position in a race—at which point the level becomes scenario based.

The single race is goal oriented, where the point of finishing first might be part of a larger scenario revolving around improving your vehicle, trying to win a championship, or some larger goal that transcends the intermediate goals. As we move through this section, the definitions will become clearer.

In fact, it is difficult to imagine a complex goal that doesn't become scenario based. These two broad categories do overlap in a gray area, such as in some games that, when many little goals are achieved, culminate in a final goal—and all laid out in scenario fashion. Most FPS games fall into this gray area. They tend to be less linear (allowing for multiple paths through each level) and have a clear goal; but the way is dangerous, and progress through the level is based on the game's central storyline. These levels then evolve into missions.

The best example of a goal-oriented, scenario-based level and mission structure is in *Soldier of Fortune II: Double Helix*. This game has come under fire for a variety of reasons, many linked to the haphazardly implemented random mission-generation extra, and some criticism directed at the general physics of the underlying game universe engine.

The random mission generation is not as revolutionary as it might seem, consisting only of a few ways in which some very standard scenarios can be tweaked. The mission structure of the main game, though, is excellent.

Each mission has a clear goal. The first requires that a game character is rescued from prison and smuggled out of enemy territory. This mission is part of the underlying storyline—thus, each mission contributes to the overall goal of winning the game. Each individual mission is broken down into levels, and each level has goals that are linked together in a scenario-based fashion. This contributes to the continuity of play and general immersion into the game universe.

At any given time, the player can press a key and review completed goals, current objectives, and those in progress. In some cases, tasks will be completed at different times; the game tends to become less linear as it progresses.

This is the hallmark of a good FPS—the transition from a purely goal-oriented level structure toward a multipath scenario structure that indoctrinates the player into the game universe gently, with clear tasks, before specifying broader tasks that can be achieved by performing a series of lesser tasks. More freedom is given to the player regarding the order in which these tasks must be completed.

So, goal-oriented levels can be viewed as distinct tasks that the player must achieve, with a clear definition of success—for example, kill all the marauding aliens, eat all the dots, or just stay alive long enough to reach the level's exit. Scenario-based levels, though, weave a thread of storyline in which the current level is just a phase, and the decisions made in completing the level will have repercussions on the overall storyline or affect other scenario-based levels. Generally speaking the key difference is that a goal-oriented level usually occupies a piece of game universe that does not change, whereas a scenario-based level might be played against a backdrop that is entirely different than the preceding level.

Games such as *SimCity* are entirely scenario-based, and the decisions that the player makes in trying to succeed at a given scenario carry forward to the next scenario. For example, building residential areas is great, because it brings in tax revenues. Once a certain level of population is reached, however, the player is required to provide services, such as water and power. Make a bad decision and you are faced with a double whammy—the people leave, tax income diminishes, and services break down due to lack of funding—which only encourages more people to leave town. Renovating real estate usually costs more than the original upkeep, and who knows, the people might come back if we wait long enough. It is a delicate balance, and not a challenge for the casual gamer.

This brings us to the next section: risks and rewards. Take a risk, reap the rewards; but take too much of a risk, and the rewards will not be worth the effort.

Risks and Rewards

Once we have decided on a format, we need to evaluate the extent to which the player will have to work in order to reap some kind of game-based reward. Good examples can be found in many games, especially in first-person shooters, where the balance of risk and reward plays a pivotal role in the success of the title. Get the game balance wrong, and the player's enjoyment suffers, sometimes to the extent of frustration. Take, for example, the ill-fated *Capcom vs SNK 2 EO*, which was ported to the GameCube. The control system was mapped to the twin GameCube analog sticks that control the character—a main error. The result was that one stick controlled *all* the special moves:

> "There is no skill or thrill in dragon punching your way out of a corner, no subtlety, nothing to learn, and no reward. There is no *difficulty*." [EDGE01]

In other words, there are not enough risks for the player to take; there is no challenge in making a well-timed, special move if all it takes is a simple flick of the joystick. The same applies to level design. There must be some balance of risk and reward, which means not swamping the player with the insurmountable or offering too many rewards, such as the opportunity to squander ammunition or health because more lies just around the corner. Of course, misleading the player is also strictly off-limits:

> "I once played a game where there was a tower in the middle of a courtyard with some monsters in it. It looked important and it was a centerpiece of that courtyard. I killed the two guys in the upper portion and navigated to the top. I was pretty disappointed when I finally reached the top and there was nothing there." [Willits02]

So, what makes a good FPS level? Tim Willits has some advice on level building:

> "It's a challenge that the player must face and overcome in order to continue with the game. A single-player level is a collection of these mini-missions tied closely around unique areas in some cohesive manner." [Willits03]

The challenge need not *just* be linked to an enemy or enemies. It could also be an obstacle that needs some kind of interaction or manipulation. *Quake*, for example, has several of these, which range from targets that can be shot at to paths to otherwise inaccessible areas, or buttons that, when pushed, electrocute monsters. These can also lead the player through the level—a kind of clue as to where the exit is.

We should also note Willits is talking about *single-player* levels. Multiplayer or massively multiplayer levels may not adhere to the same principles. Designing a level for a game based on Capture the Flag, for example, presents its own challenges.

It is often important when designing multiplayer levels, such as those for Capture the Flag games, to balance the level differently—after all, there are other human-controlled player characters running around, which is challenge enough for the team, so there is no need to add additional pitfalls. However, the structure of the level, itself, becomes much more important. There must be places for players to hide in wait for their adversaries; there must, of course, be the occasional health pack, just in case a player gets caught by an opponent. On the other hand, the difficulty needs to be balanced so that neither side has an unfair advantage over the other.

It is this balancing act that makes a game playable, and easy or hard. The risks have to balance the rewards, and the rewards have to be placed so that the player believes that he is justified in taking the reward because it was earned. If the rewards are too easy to achieve, then the risks become very "cheap." The player will feel cheated—but not as much as if there were no rewards to be had.

Some rewards always remain out of sight. How many people have actually completed *Space Invaders* or *Pac-Man?* People are more than likely to continue playing even without achieving the final goal. The reward might simply be to surpass the last score achieved or to acquire the kudos of the gaming community, such as gamers who wear the badge of the "perfect" score.

These are not complicated games that have simple game-based and non-game-based rewards. More-sophisticated games need rewards that are greater, since the risks are higher. There are other risks associated with long-term game playing, such as addiction and even physical damage that results from extended play. On the other hand, it is not good to create a game that can be played through from start to end on the first attempt, in under an hour.

Finally, there is the financial risk. Unlike gambling, arcade games do not reward the player with real-life cash for the financial risk that they take, even though the risk is much less. The only likely reward the player will receive is to have his name on the high-score roster, however temporarily—but the rule still applies: Balance is what will make the game successful or kill it entirely. It is time now to return to concrete aspects of game design, actually put the proverbial pen to paper, and work out the look and feel of some levels and missions that will make up the game.

Designing Buildings

Many games will take place inside a building of some sort. Maybe not all the action will take place in buildings, but most games will require them. Some buildings will not be visited, but will only serve as a backdrop to the game. Others will be needed as places for exploration, problem solving, or somewhere to store game objects.

The Designer's View

The first thing to do when using a building or enclosed space as a level is to draw out the floor plan on paper. Without this, the building will be very time-consuming to create. Drawing it out allows the designer to make all his mistakes on paper, where they are easy to correct.

Of course, the tools used to create the game must include some kind of application for designing levels (buildings). All commercial (and most freeware) tools do, and there are many available for games based on popular engines. For example, the QuArK creates level files for use with Quake, and the Q3Radiant tool can be downloaded and used to create the buildings that go into the QuArK level files.

This may all seem a little complicated; surely, for a simple game we can allow the programmers to hard-code level information? This is possible, of course. It is always better, however, to store the level file externally, read it into the game engine, and display it as and when needed. Even in a simple game such as *Space Invaders*, the layout of enemies, backdrop, and any power-ups should be contained in files that are separate from the game engine code.

Programmers might be scratching their heads at this point. Surely they are the ones who make all the coding decisions, right? While this may be true historically, there is a lot to be said for making sure that there is a mechanism whereby designers get to make design decisions, and not programmers.

Hence, using level files, or parameterized settings that can be understood and changed by nonprogrammers (designers, level designers, and so on) will prove to be an advantage. All games might well be unique, but they can be coded according to common principles, and, above all, any team able to reuse code across projects will have a natural advantage.

So, when designing the mechanism behind the game, we need to always make sure that there is some way for the level designers (who might also be the programmers in a small project) to import the level files and edit them. The simplest way to achieve this is to use a plain-text format and edit the files in a text editor. At the other end of the scale are multi-part, structured files, such as the WAD files used by id Software titles.

Of course, plain-text files can be altered by gamers, too, which may be permissible or not, depending on the intentions of the designer. On the other hand, it will not be long before the hardcore gamers (who are, themselves, programmers) figure out the format of a closed binary file and develop application software, like QuArK, Wally, and others. Either way, it will be a design decision that may, in the end, be a purely practical one based of the type of level that needs to be designed.

Platform games or other 2D variants, such as scrolling shoot-em-ups or fighting games, usually have a level design that is based on layers. There is a background, often a picture that is static, and a number of foreground layers that may or may not scroll, depending on the requirements of the game. If the illusion of speed is required, such as in the arcade game *Moon Buggy*, the designer can specify a static starscape with a slowly scrolling mountain range and a faster-moving uneven surface, which the player's vehicle or character moves along as they progress through the game. Games, such as *Castle Quest* or any of the 2D *Mario* series, use a similar technique.

This information can be stored as plain text or encoded binary, and each position on the game's internal map is populated with a code that represents a piece of the game universe. The file is essentially flat; a world that is 80 × 80 cells in size will require a sheet of virtual paper that is also 80 × 80 cells, with each cell occupied by a piece of game universe—be it a wall or an enemy's starting point.

Thinking in three dimensions makes the whole exercise trickier. Now we have to worry about the elevation and depth of these pieces, and levels can no longer be described in terms of a simple flat-text or binary level file. Each piece will have a specific set of properties that tell the game engine how it is oriented in the game universe, and how high, deep, and wide it is. Hence, the application needed to edit it will be much more complex. Bear this in mind when deciding between a 2D or 3D format for your game.

(A note: Here we are talking about level files. They are read in and interpreted by the game engine, and they give a way for the level, balance, and other parameters of the game to be altered without needing to change the source code [C/C++, and so on] that the game engine is actually implemented in.)

Themed, Enclosed, and Linear Maps

Whether the game is top-down 2D, side-on 2D, or full 3D, maps will generally fall into one of three categories, which I have chosen some descriptive names for, finding industry terms not to be precise enough. *Themed maps* have areas that follow the evolution of the story; *enclosed maps* provide an area in which the player can roam freely, but not escape; and *linear maps* are simply paths that start at one point, and the player can move forward through them but not retrace his steps.

(A side point. The industry term *linear* can also mean that there is only one logical path through a level [map]. The player can usually retrace his steps, up to a point. The problem is that there is a gray area between *linear* and *on-rails*. *On-rails* implies that the player has little or no directional control. *Linear* just means that the path is in a straight line—forward and backward—so I have chosen the term *linear map* to cover the gray area between the two.)

The enclosed map can also be broken down into two categories: arena and multipart. An arena, such as that used in the arcade game *Smash TV*, is simply an area of space, often fairly featureless, in which the battle is fought. Think of a boxing ring or football field. There are areas that have meanings, such as the ropes and the goal lines—but by and large, the only purpose of the arena is to provide an enclosed space for the action.

A multipart, enclosed map has specific areas that fulfill specific functions. Most commonly used in multiplayer death-match-style games such as *Quake III Arena*, they provide places to hide and store weapons, and some areas are intentionally difficult to reach. The principle is that none of the players have any kind of starting advantage, but they can use the environment to their advantage, if they wish.

A themed map is somewhat similar in that each of the areas that the player visits serves a useful purpose, but these tend to follow the storyline or enable the player to progress within the game. They may revisit the locations if need be, or not. *Max Payne*, for example, has a level structure that is partly themed and partly linear. There are places that simply tell a story, and which the player can never return to, but there are others that may be revisited at specific times—which brings us to the classic map style: linear.

A player is never expected to actually visit the same part of a linear map twice, and indeed, the game design may actively prohibit this by employing locked doors or simply transporting the player from one level to another. Scrolling games such as *R-Type* and many arcade games use this kind of approach.

There is one other interesting property of linear levels. They can be generated by the game engine on the fly—that is, there is no reason to actually create and store them, since the player will only see them once. They can be generated by the game engine, displayed, and then forgotten. Using a clever series of "pseudorandom" numbers, we can generate the same set of digits each time the sequence is required and make anything, from mountain ranges to twisting tunnels to fields to planet terrain.

Game designers who wish to exploit pseudorandom number generation should read the two books in the *Infinite Game Universe* series (Charles River Media), which deal with the mathematical and practical approaches to generating levels, among other fascinating topics.

Object Placement

The final area of level design that we need to discuss is the location of game objects. These can be anything from health packs to weapons and ammunition, or simply clues to what the player is supposed to be doing, either now or in the future. Placement also includes the starting position of the player, any enemies that are required to add spice to the game, and the end point or goal.

Objects fall into three categories: static, mobile, and constant. Static objects, once placed, do not move, but they can be consumed or transported by the player. Power-ups fall into this category. Mobile objects start off in one place but follow certain rules that enable them to move around. NPC enemies fall into this category.

Constant objects cannot be moved or are replenished when they are consumed. Water in the form of a lake or stream fulfills both these conditions, whereas a rock that the player cannot move is a static, constant object.

The way that the level designer places objects often has a direct impact on whether the level is considered to be well crafted or not. The designer also sets the difficulty level of the map at the same time. We have already covered the principles of basic level design, such as balancing risk and reward, but this is only part of the story.

As far as static objects are concerned, it is quite easy to play around with the map's balance until it is just right. Then, to make the map (or level) easier, the designer can simply add more rewards or diminish the risks. To make it harder, the rewards can be removed and some risks added, or if there is a time limit, simply reduce it.

Mobile objects are much trickier. The designer needs to be aware that if a monster is going to start moving around at a certain time in the play session, it has to be tracked until it is rendered immobile. Some adversaries might never be rendered immobile, and it is no use pretending that just because the player cannot see them, they have stopped moving. The game engine has to know where the mobile objects are, just in case the player re-encounters them.

Clearly, the designer's approach to tackling mobile objects is going to change, depending on the kind of map. Arenas are easily dealt with, but the processing overhead needed to track multiple moving objects may prove too much for the target platform. To complicate things, tracking a mobile object in an arena will mean that the entire map needs to be held in memory at once. These restrictions will all provide food for thought.

Linear maps are not quite as troublesome, since once the object wanders off of the map, we can more or less forget that it exists. After all, the player will not notice, because they will have moved on and be more concerned with what is coming up next. But it would be very unsettling to leave a monster in a cell behind a locked door, only to continue bumping into them as the monster's position is reset by the game engine every time a piece of the map is reloaded.

Mission Design

A level or map is a concrete game device. It has shape, form, and function. A mission is an overall guiding objective. A campaign is made up of many missions, and a mission is comprised of many levels. This is a loose description of how levels roll into missions, which roll into campaigns.

However, mission design is also about tying together the map, story, and game context, as well as balancing the whole game so that it is fun to play. A mission should have at least one goal; if it has more than five, then it is overloaded. The player will find himself unable to prioritize, or even remember, more than two or three mission objectives.

Location-Based Mission Design

When thinking about missions in the context of a story, it is easier to base each scenario on a location that the player must visit in order to succeed. Think in terms of a logical progression of events or locations, and trying to ensure that the player will not be penalized if they visit the locations in a different sequence than planned. The player needs to be steered toward a successful completion of the mission, but only penalized for doing it out of sequence if doing so could have been avoided.

This also means that the player should be able to complete the mission on his first attempt if he is adept. It is not good to present the player with an inappropriately difficult or impossible situation in the hope that he will simply avoid it the next time around. But, if clues are present, and the player chooses to ignore them, it is allowable to present him with a *seemingly* impossible mission. Some parts of games like *Double Helix* and *The Plan* use this design strategy, whereas games like *The Getaway* tend to have missions that seem randomly impossible, and which take long, frustrating hours to figure out.

Each location should provide a specific target, one piece of the solution to the overall mission. Steering the player around the various locations is a design skill in itself. There is an art to striking a balance between hand-holding and leading on, between giving out clues and forcing the player to follow a path that the designer has, in effect, presupposed.

Then again, the emphasis on paths for the player will depend on the game genre. An FPS in full 3D that emulates desert warfare will need to allow almost complete freedom of movement, while a 2D top-down scrolling shoot-em-up like *Ikaragua*, or *R-Type* will impose a path simply because the player's movements are limited. This is even more pronounced when a game penalizes the player for touching the screen's edges, and can be avoided simply by splitting the screen into two tunnels, which forces the player to make a choice.

This is not to say that 2D scrolling games project a claustrophobic feeling—far from it. Games such as *Sonic the Hedgehog*, any of the 2D *Mario* games, and the 2D *Metroid* series, to name a few, allow a freedom of movement that is often not surpassed even in full-3D games. They achieve this by virtue of deft mission design—platforms, ladders, and the player's ability to jump. They also use location-based missions. Take a game like *Metroid*, for example. Each location has a type and can be used for different things. The player should be able to spot very quickly what kind of location they have arrived at, so that he can immediately prepare for what might happen next.

In addition, a location's function should remain as true to its primary purpose as possible. If a room design has only been used for, say, computer access to information (denoted by keyboards and computer screens), it should only be used for hostile alien life forms if the player is given ample time to transition into fighting mode. The original function of the room was research, not combat.

An example of this is in *The Plan*, where, from the outset, the player knows that he has to first fight, then research, in the prison control room. The method imposed (stealth) gives the player ample transition time between killing and research, helped by the fact that the two modes are closer together than if it had been a violent brawl followed by the research.

The game design also helps; precise instructions are given at the time that leaves the player in no doubt as to the function of the room. Kill the guard, and take control of the prison door remote control function.

Games that have done this well include *Wolfenstein 3D*, although the dense population of AI soldiers in the rooms can at times be unsettling for the player. It is bad design to have guards that exhibit some kind of digital sixth sense, and who blast the player before he has had a chance to look around; this is simply irritating. On the other hand, the guards do have to be somewhat aware that the player has entered the room in order to avoid being sitting-duck targets.

This is often a balance of AI and object placement. If the AI dictates that guards can never be surprised and always behave like perfect soldiers, and can spot the player before the player can spot them, they should not hide behind doors and leave the player no chance to react. Even if that *is* fairly realistic, it will anger the player if it happens too often.

So, locations either fulfill specific functions that lead to the completion of missions, or they allow access to other locations that are needed in order to complete missions. The location could provide a hiding place for a boss creature that needs to be killed in order to complete part of the mission, or it could be a travel device, such as an elevator, which takes the player to another set of locations that are needed in order to complete the mission.

Object-Based Mission Design

The locations, themselves, do not usually offer enough flexibility to build an entire game around. Objects are also required. Like locations, objects either serve a direct purpose toward completing a mission, perhaps providing access to otherwise unreachable areas, like keys, or are indirectly useful in completing the mission—for example, weapons, power-ups, or health packs.

Objects can also provide visual clues that are useful to the player, such as messages written on pieces of paper, or actual clues to what the purpose of the current location is. Take, for example, the bowls of food in *Wolfenstein 3D*. More often than not, they indicate that some vicious dogs inhabit the room, dogs that need to be destroyed before they attack.

To some players, this attention to detail is just that—detail. But for some, these details are useful extensions to the game, which allow the player to infer the purpose of objects. Done successfully, the player may not even realize that the objects are visual clues.

The pinnacle of design achievement might be when the player stops looking for these clues. Although they are there, they have become part of the game immersion.

Of course, in some games, the objects are the goals of the mission. Collecting all of them actually constitutes completion. Puzzle pieces are a great example, since the completed puzzle can be anything from a master potion that saves the universe, to a cryptic clue that leads to the location of the mission's exit.

There is also a parallel with real life to consider. Almost anything in a game that can kill the player can kill the enemy. If we accept this basic premise, then we can, as game designers, actively place weapons around the game that will kill the player or the enemy, depending on circumstances.

The toxic waste barrels in *DOOM* are examples of this. I strongly suspect, although I've never tried, that contact with them would be fairly unpleasant for the player. Shoot them from a distance, however, and they will explode and destroy any life forms in their vicinity, alien or not.

A more subtle approach would be to force the player to use such artifacts, by making it the only way to remove the opposition. The traps kill the player but will also kill the enemy, leaving the player with the interesting and novel task of developing a strategy to bring the two together, while avoiding their own comeuppance.

Empirical Missions

The easiest kind of mission to create is based on the classic shoot-em-up school of game design. Think back to games such as *Space Invaders*, *Pac-Man*, or even *Sonic the Hedgehog*, in which completing each mission or level revolved around killing all the enemies, collecting items within a given time limit, or consuming objects in order to progress to another level.

Empirical mission goals are simple mechanisms to indicate progress to the player. They also provide a way for the player to check their current performance against past performance. For example, highest score or shortest time to completion (which appear on the high-score table) are mechanisms that increase the game's longevity and replay value by developing player competitiveness outside the game, itself.

As a game designer, it is always tempting to fall back on some kind of abstract scoring mechanism as the sole reward to the player. In other words, we can dress up the visual cues to make a sophisticated playing environment and then add all manners of intelligent life to it, just to represent the final outcome as a single, abstract number.

Defcon, for example, does just that. The game is immersive, tense, realistic, and at times almost telepathically clever, but the goals are still empirical—dispatch your enemies without getting everyone killed.

We can mix empirical design with other kinds of design. The empirical could reflect the amount of success the player has had in completing a given mission. First-person shooters usually offer statistics at the end of a mission, such as time taken, secret items found (or killed), ammunition expended, and so on.

INTEGRATING LEVELS AND MISSIONS

In *Quake*, the world was divided into "chapters," much as it was in predecessors *DOOM* and *Wolfenstein3D*. Each chapter contained a level, and each level was subdivided into specific contests—sublevels that revolved around specific puzzles. While these chapters cannot be considered missions *per se*, each "level" could, in fact, be considered a mission.

As was previously mentioned, a mission can be subdivided into challenges, and each challenge can be considered to be a level. Complete all the levels (challenges), and the mission is either completed or perhaps leads to another challenge that needs to be overcome in order to complete the game, itself—for example, a big boss level—a design mechanism that harkens back to earlier games.

LEVEL GROUPING

A set of related levels, grouped together, comprise a mission. In military terms, the mission might be to liberate a prisoner-of-war camp. For example, level one involves stomping through kilometers of undergrowth without being killed. In level two, we neutralize the outer perimeter (kill all the guards), while level three is stealthy search of the enemy camp to locate the prisoners—which just leaves level four: remove the guards and release prisoners; and level five: escape. Finally, the mission is complete, and the success of the mission is then graded by the number of POWs that made it back to home base without being killed in the process.

Each level satisfies a goal that has to be negotiated in order to succeed in the mission, and a game can have several missions that are either disparate or part of a wider campaign. Here, the term "campaign" can be used to group missions within a wider context in the same way that missions can be used to group levels according to the "big picture."

Of course, levels and missions do not always need to respect this parent-child relationship. This mechanism merely adds continuity to the game proper.

Most RPG, action, and strategy games will use strict grouping in accordance with the storyline to fill out the game universe. This gives the player some context in which he can place himself, the game objects, and NPCs, which helps to give the game realism.

Difficulty Ramping

The last level of a mission will typically be harder, longer, or more complex than the previous ones. The player needs a period of familiarization followed by mastery, and then on to success, which should remain just out of reach long enough to give the player his money's worth, but not so long that they lose interest and abandon the game as impossible.

This transformation from novice to expert needs to be reflected in the game mechanics. The enemies might become smarter, better equipped, or more alert as a reflection of their position in the game. They might become more numerous or faster. The player might find himself in increasingly difficult puzzles or in situations that require the help of NPCs.

All of the above constitute *difficulty ramping,* and this comes in two flavors. There is the natural difficulty progression that we discussed, which is based on the player's voyage through the game. Then there is the ability of the player to adjust the difficulty level, depending on his skill level. This requires that the player has, in effect, passed through the game once or twice and knows where the various pieces of the puzzle are. This equips him with an internal map of the path needed to take him from the start of the mission to the end. The next step up for the hardcore player is to do it all again, but with twice as many enemies.

However, clever game design can come into play at this point and ensure that not only are there twice as many enemies, but the path chosen by the player the first time is no longer possible. A more substantive, complex, and taxing path now needs to be taken. Dynamically altering the mission structure in this way is also a form of difficulty ramping. It adds a new dimension to the game, increases re-playability and shelf life, and will probably keep even the most hardcore gamer coming back for more.

A final note on difficulty: Games often use a mechanism known as "unlocking" to reward the player. Unlocking means that if the player manages to complete a specific task perfectly, then he will be rewarded with something else—another level, a better vehicle, or simply a new twist to the game—perks that are denied to less-skilled players.

Unlocking also keeps players coming back—in effect, encouraging them to achieve special prizes before they continue on to other missions and the game proper. This technique should be used with extreme caution, though. There is a fine line between luring the player back and alienating him completely.

Easter Eggs are a special kind of unlockable feature. In fact, they're usually not unlockable at all, but are only available through a special sequence of events or by performing certain tasks in certain places. Developers like to leave Easter Eggs lying around their games, and it bears some research on the Internet, whenever you have a spare moment.

Sports Games

Do sports games follow the same philosophies as the other games discussed thus far? In a sense, yes. If the completion of a soccer game is achieved by winning the trophy, then this constitutes a mission. Each soccer match that is played along the way could be considered a level. This may be stretching the analogy a tad, but even in soccer, as the game progresses, matches provide a way for the player to gauge his success, and the culmination of all the matches, the winning of the trophy, gives the game closure.

The various tricks of location, objects, and difficulty ramping still hold, as well. Admittedly, location may or may not be very important. This all depends on whether the team prefers to play on home territory or not, and how far they have to travel in order to play their next match.

Objects are probably best left to training devices. A successful athlete/team might be able to afford buying good training equipment by acquiring enough sponsors. This will, in turn, contribute to success in bringing home the coveted award.

So, all the same mechanisms are in place, but the context changes. It is this context that either gives the game appeal or, even though the design might be exquisite, makes the game unplayable.

Simulations

This genre is tricky when it comes to defining missions and levels, mainly because most simulations tend to be fairly open-ended. True simulation games, such as the legendary *Sim* or *Tycoon* series, are open-ended to the point that they have no real final goal. The player simply plays them (hopefully) forever.

Early *SimCity* games did have a concept of missions, scenarios in which the player would inherit a city design—along with its problems, such as fires, earthquakes, and congested traffic. The goal was to improve the situation without having the city disintegrate into chaos, and without the mayor (player) being unceremoniously ousted. In fact, simulation games can be thought of as a collection of little levels and scenarios. All the challenges that are presented are a direct consequence of the player's actions—and if things go wrong, he knows that he only has himself to blame.

Other Level and Mission Types

The majority of the examples in this chapter have specifically referred to action games, be they FPS, shoot-em-ups, scrolling adventure, or 2D fighting games. Not everyone will be building these kinds of games, or some may wish to create games that span different genres, so we will now take time out to look at other types of games, and how level and mission design can apply to them.

Puzzles

Puzzles present more to the player than just a challenge to be solved before proceeding to the next piece of map. This is only the FPS way of looking at the puzzle concept, and games that are based purely on solving puzzles, such as cult games like *Myst*, *Leisure Suit Larry*, and *Gabriel Knight*, adhere to principles that are stricter.

The simplest form of puzzle is the jigsaw. A game could at some point require the player to solve a sliding-square challenge or piece together a jigsaw, and this would constitute a puzzle—albeit lacking slightly in innovation. A step above this is to require the player to gather objects from the game universe in order to solve a puzzle—collecting the jigsaw pieces, for example, before arranging them.

There are puzzles that require interaction with nonplayer characters that can give the player information to help him solve problems posed by the game universe. The driving force behind being able to complete the puzzle is, ideally, something that requires in-game knowledge coupled with common sense, and perhaps the discovery of clues left by the designer, which are designed to either help or mislead the player.

Creating puzzles of the right difficulty level for the target audience, and which are relevant to the game universe and storyline, is quite a feat. Only certain people are actually gifted enough to do this with any flair. It is one of those aspects of game design that takes talent, like artwork, but which can be learned—up to a certain level of proficiency.

The trick is to imagine the start and end points of the level, quest, or mission, and look at how the player is expected to evolve as they travel from beginning to end. Then, place traps, puzzles, and other obstacles in the player's way, as if you, the designer, are testing the player's "mettle" as master of the (game) universe, and the sole judge of the player's worthiness to succeed.

Clearly, this is not always easy. It is essential to keeping the puzzles relevant to the genre and atmosphere of the game. The player needs to think like a priest in the

Middle Ages if that is what they are, and the puzzles must support this persona; he does not expect to be confronted by an electronic listening device fabricated by the CIA. On the other hand, a talking bird could be used to spy on the enemy and recount the conversation at a later date.

Messages returned to the player will also help in solving puzzles. If, for example, he needs to climb up onto a rooftop in order to retrieve a specific item, then the first attempt might result in a message indicating that he needs to get a ladder or rope. Consider the following (fictional) adventure game extract:

```
Player > LOOK
You see a high wall, with a scroll perched on top.
Player > GET SCROLL
You can't reach that.
Player > CLIMB WALL
It is too high.
Player > JUMP
It is too high. You would need a ladder.
```

The last message provides a clue. Now, all the player has to do is remember where he saw a ladder, go back and get it, return to the wall, and use the ladder to climb up and reach the scroll. Hopefully, the designer has not betrayed the player by having the scroll stolen by a magpie during his hunt for the ladder. Don't rule anything out when designing a cunning set of puzzle-oriented levels, but try not to betray the player's trust. It doesn't pay to anger your audience—for example, if a magpie did steal the scroll, leave another message clue to suggest where the bird has gone.

Some puzzles should also be solvable simply by brute force, rather like a criminal trying every three-digit combination to open a locked briefcase. The player might be encouraged to use more-lateral thinking and educated guesswork via a trial-and-error method, using memory or pen and paper.

Text Game Levels

Text-based adventure games, once the most popular genre for home computer gaming, seem to have been replaced by more adrenaline-filled action games. However, perhaps it is time for a comeback—especially with the increasing popularity of the Internet. In fact, the popularity of adventure games geared up when the Internet was invented.

The main points to remember about text-based adventure games is that they do not require the transmission or storage of large amounts of data. This means that the game universe can be much larger than in other genres; there are no graphics to store, there is limited sound, and the user interface can be described as minimal, at best—which made them perfect for early home computers and slow Internet connections.

Now that industry-level convergence is becoming a reality, with mobile communication devices approaching the sophistication of entry-level Internet-capable systems of the 1990s, the text adventure might just take over the future of gaming with its almost infinite game universes that are populated by multitudes of players—all controlled by central computers (servers). We just need to see the right games, mixtures of elements, and platforms.

One of the strongest points in favor of text games is that they are largely platform-independent. Mobile telephones, Internet-enabled PDAs, game consoles, and home computers are all capable of displaying and transmitting text. Not only does this mean that more people can be involved, but also that a person can play from anywhere in the world, provided that he takes their mobile, Internet, or text messaging device with him.

The verbosity of the game probably needs to adjust along with the platform, due to display restrictions, but by and large, there is very little modification of the actual game that needs to take place. The vast majority of the game universe takes place on the server, and consists of locations that the players can visit and explore. There are also objects to be taken from one place to another, rivals to attack or coerce, or friends to ask for information.

There is also an overshadowing "real-life" interaction that is bound to take place over and above the game itself, which is also made much more attractive since the advent of text-to-email mobile telephone services. Different languages (as extensions to the game universe) and even game variations can be worked into the concept, which leads to a very powerful paradigm for the future.

Designing a level for a text-based game hinges on the same basic principles as puzzle design, with some form of combat thrown in for good measure. All of this needs to be thought through when designing the game—especially considering that the player will be using an interface that either involves typing in commands or clicking relevant icons on the screen.

Story-Based Levels

Role-playing games, the pinnacle of adventure games, began as pen-and-paper style table-top games in which the players' imaginations created the gaming universe. Evolution of the genre yielded table-top figurines, maps, and tiles that could be cut out and placed onto a movable surface, and a whole visual aspect was added to the genre. With the advent of the computer, the RPG concept has been turned on its head, but two critical elements remain—imagination and story.

In the original RPGs, the dungeon master was in control. Now, computer-based RPGs use the game engine as DM. By and large, all that it needs to do is calculate the outcome of battles, display the area that the player finds himself in, and keep track of the player's moves at each juncture.

All of the other facets of text-based gaming and puzzle design hold true, with the addition of a solid backdrop that revolves around the story. We have previously noted that all games need some kind of story, if only to situate the game. This goes double for RPGs, where the story also sets the genre, tone, and quests for the player to follow, and relies as much on the players' imaginations to solve problems as it does on their reading the immediate environment.

GAMES WITHOUT LEVELS

Finally, there are genres that have no level structure. Usually in these cases, it is the player that sets the tone. Games such as *SimCity* have no traditional levels—the player does not suddenly achieve a higher status when he accrues a certain amount of money, experience, or realizes a goal. Rather, the evolution of the game as set by the player and the rules that govern the gaming system lead to an advance in the session's difficulty. *SimCity 4* serves as a good example and gives us a great backdrop for understanding how a game without discrete multiple levels works.

(Industry veterans will point out that a game with an environment that gets harder has levels. However, I have chosen to divide game design theory into Difficulty Ramping and Levels, rather than sticking with the regular terminology. Of course, a game can have both but usually needs one or the other.)

The player starts with $100,000 and zero population. There is no enemy, except greed, and the only reward is in seeing a thriving metropolis grow from empty real estate. With version four of this classic game, there are high-level graphics that change depending on the relative properties of the buildings that the player builds.

So, here is how it goes: According to the rules of *SimCity 4,* a village can exist without water. At a certain point, though, the village grows into a town, and the population reaches a certain size—and does require water. Therefore, the player sinks a well, and two things happen. First, the thirsty people stop complaining, which is good. On the other hand, the well has a monthly cost that is funded by taxation. The player has two options—increase taxes to compensate for the additional cost or build more housing and try to increase the population to raise more tax revenue.

Increasing the population and keeping them happy will mean that the player receives more income, but those additional people will require more water and other services, like roads. These also cost money, so the player faces a continual balancing act of income versus expense. The more the city expands, the more expensive it becomes; but since the goal is to create a metropolis, the player will always risk expansion over budgetary prudence.

In essence, the problems that the player faces are all self-created, but the game rules present the logical progression of the problems. This is part of the attraction of the game—that and the fact that it is essentially an open-ended experience.

The last genre that has non-level systems is that of sports simulations. Here, things are quite complex. First, soccer and football simulations are nonlevel in the same way as *SimCity*, but with subtle differences. It is the players' progression through the tournaments that dictate how much more adept their adversaries are.

Then there are games that use time limits as a method for increasing difficulty. There is no inherent level system in place, but unless the player constantly improves, they will not be able to beat the clock. Arcade racing games use this approach. The first time around, the player is allowed 60 seconds to complete a lap. If they manage to do so inside the time limit, then they are allowed slightly less the next time. Exactly how much less depends on how fast they managed to complete their first lap.

This would all be very easy if not for the other cars that also need to be beaten in order for the player to receive a top spot. Without that top spot, players will not advance to the next stage (track) of the game. Therefore, as in *SimCity,* they are enticed by their own drive for success to do increasingly better, but their improvement will inherently be their downfall.

Summary

Clearly, the designation of levels and missions is dependent on the game genre. Similarly, the fact that the game is divided into missions and levels by design does not necessarily mean that it is a military FPS or action game. "Level" and "mission" are just terms used to describe the way in which the game is organized.

Certain rules need to be respected—mainly that the game needs to increase in difficulty as the player progresses through it, and there should be some form of context into which the game can be placed. Of course, it is hard to imagine what kind of context could be dreamed up for a game like *Pac-Man*, but abstract games such as this do not necessarily need more context than that offered by the game, itself.

Game mechanics, therefore, have as much to do with level and mission design as the location or map in which the action takes place. The term "map" is often used interchangeably with "level," but they are really two different concepts. A map is a place in which a level can take place. The level is defined by a mixture of map and game mechanisms. A hard level can have an easy map, a somewhat challenging map, or a complex map. It all depends on the balance of game mechanics, objects, and map design.

REFERENCES

[EDGE01] *EDGE* magazine, Review Section. September 2002, p. 94.

[Willits01] Tim Willits, Interviewed by M. Saltzmannin *Game Design: Secrets of the Sages*. BradyGames, 2000, p. 112.

[Willits02] Tim Willits, Interviewed by M. Saltzmann in *Game Design: Secrets of the Sages*. BradyGames, 2000, p. 113–114.

[Willits03] Tim Willits, Interviewed by M. Saltzmann in *Game Design: Secrets of the Sages*. BradyGames, 2000, p. 113.

11 Using Vehicles and Objects

In This Chapter

- Vehicles
- Objects
- Nonplayer Characters

Many games rely on the use of vehicles and objects to help the player solve problems, attack enemies, and travel around the game universe. However, there are a few issues to bear in mind when designing a game based on objects and vehicles, as opposed to simply offering them within the context of a wider universe.

Several types of games use vehicles in a central role, ranging from regular racing games in which the player controls a vehicle as the principle task, to those where the player can either climb into a vehicle at will, such as in *Halo*. The player might not even be aware that he is in a vehicle, such as in arcade games like *Terminator 2* and *Alien*.

Terminator 2 and *Alien* are known as "on-rails" games. The player can travel forward or backward while shooting at targets, but cannot move in a third dimension. The vehicle in both games is entirely virtual—an artificial container for the player.

The vast majority of games also contain objects. An object, as defined here, is an item that offers substance to the game universe, a piece of the game universe that extends the power of the player in some way. Some objects are inanimate; that is, they display no outward behavior or movement. Others can be scripted, and might move around and perform tasks either to the benefit or detriment of the player. These are known as "nonplayer characters"—usually only when they carry outward characteristics that closely match those of the other characters in the game universe. There is a difference, say, between a gargoyle that starts out as a statue, and a statue that doesn't move except when it falls over when the player shoots it.

As we shall see in the Artificial Intelligence (AI) chapter, almost everything in a game engine is scripted one way or the other. NPCs usually have more AI than other objects and are controlled in part by scripts, with the underlying AI engine augmenting the basic step-by-step behavior to offer more of a challenge.

Vehicles

As we have noted, vehicles are used in video games as either secondary transport or a key feature of the game. Some vehicles are seen from the outside, and others are principally seen from the inside, such as in some racing games. These games also feature nonplayer characters in other vehicles that are comparable to the player's, and they usually offer external views in addition to the inside view, which is usually the default.

Sometimes the player's vehicle can be customized, depending on the game structure and balance. These customizations can take the form of spray paint and external add-ons, or fine-tuning and changing the actual mechanics of the vehicle.

Other games use vehicles simply as something to shoot at, such as in the arcade games *Afterburner* and *Space Harrier*. Others include vehicles that are merely implied; a *force* moves the player along, rather than an actual vehicle.

Vehicles and Viewpoints

However the vehicle will be used, there are many different viewpoints at the designer's disposal. Just as in any other game, the viewpoint depends largely on the genre and perspective of the game: top-down, isometric, through-the-windshield (TTW), behind-the-vehicle, 2D, or full 3D. The options are almost endless. The most common perspective used for racing games is through-the-windshield, a race-car version of the traditional first-person-shooter perspective. This only works, of course, with full-3D polygonal representations.

These games also usually come with the ability to alter the viewpoint. With the tap of a key, the player can choose views—from TTW, back to a 45-degree view behind the vehicle, or straight back to a larger angle, with the camera positioned high above and behind the vehicle. Some arcade racing games, such as *Daytona*, even allow a front-fender-view, which adds to the illusion of speed.

Other games use an isometric camera view that places the camera permanently at an angle slightly behind and to the side of the vehicle—usually an aircraft, as in the classic *Zaxxon*, which was the first-ever isometric arcade game. Some cross-country racing games also use this kind of perspective, and zoom out so that the entire track is in view. This is an advantage of the isometric perspective; it alleviates the need for a map of the track.

Finally, when it comes to 2D games, a top-down camera view is used, because a side-on view would make it impossible for the player to control the vehicle; and this relates purely to racing games, where the enemies are moving in the *same* direction as the player. Side-on scrolling shoot-em-ups could possibly be classified as using vehicular side-on 2D cameras. However, the player's craft is treated more as an actual character in these cases. The side-on scrolling shoot-em-up is a genre of its own—the player versus enemies that move in the *opposite* direction.

On Rails

Games that use a side-to-side or forward-to-backward perspective, in which the player character cannot be controlled in 3D, are often called "on rails." These games tend to have the player shoot in various directions, like in an FPS. With the advent of true-3D first-person shooters, this genre has become somewhat obsolete, except in the arcade or as a subgame element.

Arcade examples include all those that use some form of gun that can be pointed at the screen in order to shoot enemies, a genre which started with cabinet games such as *Terminator 2*. A pedal is used to either slow the advance of the action or move backward. A fixed gun, mounted on a swivel, was the weapon of choice in many cases.

Many gamers, including those who are also industry journalists, sneer at "on rails" games, often referring to them as "duck shoot" games. The lack of a third direction might detract from the difficulty of the game in some cases, but in most, the restricted movement also makes the on-screen action more intense.

In the end, the game designer need only take care that the game is balanced in such a way that the player does not feel short-changed. This includes simulating the ability to shoot accurately. Point-and-shoot is easy to implement with a pivot-mounted gun that can move as fast as the player can, but it is harder when the player is using a controller or joystick. The movement of an eight-way switch-based joystick tends to be too discrete to allow the freedom of movement that an analog swivel device offers. This is where the light gun comes in, of course, which allows the player to point and shoot wherever he likes. PC mice also allow freedom of movement—they are, after all, analog devices, too.

Newer consoles with wireless controllers that the player can wave around in space and see their gestures replicated in-game also add a dimension of freedom of movement; almost perfect for on-rails shooters.

It is worth mentioning that the reaction speed of a game in the on-rails environment is doubly important in most cases. This is because compensation for the lack of a third degree of movement is often the appearance of more enemies on the screen. This, in turn, necessitates that the player be more adept at shooting, and that the hardware be perfectly in tune with the game, itself. The player cannot be expected to hammer hundreds of enemies if the pointing device moves sluggishly. The most-adept players must be able to eliminate enemies faster than more appear.

Vehicle Interiors

So far we have only considered vehicles as objects within their surrounding game universe. We have not looked at the vehicles' interiors—that is, we have not discussed how the traditional aspects of vehicle interiors, such as the dashboard, can be modeled. This usually depends on the role the vehicle will play in the game.

For example, games in which the primary playing mode is as a classic FPS often simply render the vehicle interior as if it is room; the player climbs in, he sees the controls, the dashboard, and the windshield. (We have previously noted that this can also unsettle the player as he moves from an environment that allows virtually unrestricted movement to one that seems very enclosed.)

The designer must take into account the viewable area when considering the interior of the vehicle, which is a restriction. Of course, in real life, we get the same effect when climbing into a vehicle, except that our eyes allow much more visual information to be passed to our brain than a computer monitor can display.

Our field of vision is typically wider than a screen, and we also have some built-in mechanisms to restrict our area of concentration. So, although we can "see" the dashboard, mirror, and other in-vehicle artifacts, we're mainly looking through the windscreen, trying not to crash.

The real solution is to have monitors all around the player, each one designed to display a view from one of the many windows that the vehicle might have. Remember the movie *Lawnmower Man?* Some arcade machines can offer this, but it will probably never be seen in the home console market.

One of the key mechanisms used to get around this is the virtual dashboard, which floats on top of the screen in much the same way as the status information (see Chapter 9). This means that even if the viewpoint changes, the dashboard stays in place and shows the same range of information at all times. It is simply a way to display information about the vehicle without needing an accurately modeled dashboard.

The player may also not be the driver of the vehicle, which means that there is no need for the dashboard; but the interior still needs to be modeled correctly and take into account whether the vehicle is moving or not—unless, of course, there are no windows. In this case, simply jiggling the screen will sufficiently suggest that the vehicle is moving. Imagine, for example, that the player is in the cargo hold of a train with no windows and little visual evidence that the train is in motion.

VEHICLE PHYSICS

Like any other aspect of the game universe, the physics that dictate vehicle movement should be as realistic as possible. However, the game's genre and target audience will always dictate the level of realism that is required.

Casual gamers, for example, will not appreciate movement that is as realistic as driving a real vehicle; the problem is one of immersion. It is almost impossible for the player to release the subconscious awareness that he is not driving a real vehicle, but that he is simply controlling a computer that manipulates a game universe and creates the illusion of driving a vehicle.

By way of an anecdote, as a casual gamer, I found *World Rally Championship 2* to be fun and immersive. It was not physically as accurate, or as visually appealing as, for example, the *Colin McRae Rally* series. However, I didn't have the patience or time to master the additional realism as a casual gamer.

Part of the problem is lack of feedback. When people interact with the real world, they are aware of all kinds of sensations on many levels—the grip of the wheels on the road, the gentle sway of the vehicle cockpit, the vibrations and G-force during acceleration and cornering, and so on.

Arcade cabinets go a long way in feeding information back to the player, complete with steering wheels that send tactile sensations to the player. There are peripherals available that provide similar kinds of interactions, but designers should remember that not everyone will be able to afford wheels and pedal sets for gaming. The only way to ensure that the player has access to these peripherals is to provide them with the game, which might force the price beyond the reach of the mass market—case in point: *Tekki* (also known as *Steel Battalion*) and the $200 joystick.

If a game is based on a vehicle that needs accurate physics, the model used to develop the "feeling" should take into account the device being used to control it. A mouse just does not deliver the same control as a keyboard or steering wheel. Tuning the vehicle physics to the hardware and play-testing with a variety of devices will be key in achieving wide-ranging acceptance.

Therefore, wherever possible, the physics should be tunable by the player and encourage him to set up the vehicle (and thus, the game) in a way that feels natural. What it should *not* do is affect the playability—just the comfort level. As soon as a specific setup affects the difficulty, players will feel short-changed, and reviewers notice absolutely everything.

Some racing games offer clever mechanisms to help the player adjust to the physics of driving the car. For example, at least one Formula 1 game eases the player in gently by allowing him to turn on a number of "driving aids," such as automatic brakes, throttle control, and could have been augmented further to allow steering correction. *Formula 1 2001,* for example, gives the player many such driving aids, and more recent incarnations have gone as close to automatic steering as possible by providing a magical green racing line to follow. So long as all these are not activated in competition, it is familiarization and training rather than something that could be considered close to cheating.

All of these help the player compensate for the lack of real-world experience and in-game deficiencies. With practice, the player adapts to the "feel" of the car through visual, audio, and other feedback paths. When ready, he can begin to turn these driving aids off and get on with actually playing the game.

Our discussion here applies mainly to vehicles that have friction points—wings, wheels, or even ship hulls in a water-based game universe. Most spacecraft do not require the physics that account for friction, but they come with their own specific problems. In space, there is negligible gravity (which increases if the player approaches a planet) and no air to provide friction. Therefore, movement needs to reflect a floating feeling as the craft moves through space.

The designer needs to determine exactly how the movement is modeled. For example, in a 2D shooter, holding down a key can make the craft accelerate in a sideways direction, while in a 3D version, it might make the craft roll around on its central axis. The feeling is substantially different and will be entirely dependent on the designer's chosen viewpoint.

The freedom of movement offered will be the deciding factor in the model used for vehicle physics where a spacecraft is involved. It is not possible, for example, to apply traditional up-down-left-right movement in a spaceflight game that is fully 3D. Instead, because we are moving in three axes, these usually become pitch, yaw, and roll, with velocity dictating how tightly the craft can maneuver. It will simply seem wrong—unless, of course, the player is not actually flying the craft, in which case (as in *Tailgunner*) the game is classified as "on rails"; the player simply moves a crosshair around and shoots at enemies. In this case, up-down-left-right is appropriate as a control mechanism.

Likewise, it is difficult to get the camera right if 3D physics are applied to a game that is set in a 2D game universe. Imagine, for example, that the craft moves freely around its center of gravity, rolling, pitching, and yawing. This means that if an exterior view is chosen (which, for a 2D game is almost obligatory), the camera will have to be extremely well-tuned in order to follow the movements around without making the player irritated or even nauseous.

Games such as *Frontier (Elite II)* allow an exterior view to be chosen, which means that the player can see his craft from a vantage point that works well in level flight, but is untenable as soon as the player starts 3D space flight. The camera always seems to be just behind the craft, which is, of course, opaque.

Now, imagine what happens if the same technique is applied to a truly 2D game universe. The craft will be pin-wheeling around and pivoting in every possible direction, but the rest of the game will be moving in a straight line. This effect can be achieved, but it is very difficult, since the craft will be moving over the landscape at some speed and will never be pointing in the right direction. The situation in which this attempted is within the confines of an eight-way isometric scrolling game with a fixed camera.

OBJECTS

Most games will need objects. The main genres that use them extensively are RPGs and FPSs. RPGs traditionally used objects as ways to achieve specific tasks or perhaps as treasure, and FPSs traditionally used objects as weapons. These are their primary uses; the evolution of gaming has added other uses for objects, and there is substantial crossover between the way they are used in different genres.

Historically, ladders-and-levels games, such as *Mario* or *Castlequest*, have also used objects. Even *Pac-Man* uses expendable objects (fruit) that need to be collected in order to achieve a perfect score.

OBJECTS AND STORIES

We have seen how some of the best games rely on a strong storyline. Obviously, this does not necessarily apply to "abstract" games like *Pac-Man*, but with the sophistication of players and hardware always on the increase, such games seem to be falling farther from hard-core gamers' affections.

However, a good game is still a good game. And a good game design is still a good game design. Arguably, the bells and whistles, as we have previously pointed out throughout the book, will not save a poor game. On the other hand, a great game design can be successful with less accomplished or sophisticated techniques.

(Recently there have been many rereleases of older generation classics from the back catalogs of Sega, Namco, and so on. There is an appetite for these retro games that proves one point—there's money in good game design.)

Objects can be woven in with the storyline, and as with level design, each object needs to have a use. "Red herrings" will serve to annoy the player unless, of course, they are expected to be useless. Similarly, each object can have a storyline of its own, which will add to immersion into the game universe.

Often in RPGs, for example, several objects can be used in conjunction, or have special meanings or uses during the game, itself. The sequence of objects in a linear game can also build up a storyline, but this cannot be used in game universes that provide unrestricted navigation through the various parts, since there is no guarantee that the player will encounter them in the right order for the story to make sense.

Forcing the player to follow the whim of the designer will probably result in a rather frustrating game. We cannot expect the player to only visit rooms and collect objects in an order that seems logical in the design phase, and then revisit rooms later on to retrieve the objects in the correct sequence, with no other clue than the storyline. Even so, with a suitable level structure, it could feasibly be the basis for a successful game.

A recent (2003) game, *Clock Tower 3*, uses this technique. In the words of a reviewer writing for *EDGE* magazine:

> "Items need finding . . . and taking to distant places. Lazy design even within these familiar boundaries means that some events simply won't work at the 'wrong' time . . ." [EDGE01]

This quote highlights several aspects of object use within an evolving storyline. First, finding and transporting objects is a tried-and-tested formula, but it needs to be done in a way that, if the player is allowed to *locate* the objects at a certain moment, the game does not disallow their *use*. Otherwise, as in *Clock Tower 3,* the game rapidly deteriorates into a memory-challenge experience.

In this case, objects are used to either trigger events or as a response to other changes in the game universe, such as putting ashes on a fire in order to smother it. Unfortunately, though, even if the fire is blazing and the player has the ashes in hand, it cannot be smothered until the player has visited another, specific room—which brings us to the ins and outs of using scripted objects.

Scripted Objects

As we saw in the preceding section, objects can be associated with scripts. A script in this case is simply a list of actions that will result from player interaction with an object in a prescribed manner. The object's use should be apparent from the current situation within the game universe, as well as obvious from the type of object.

One example is *Severance: Blade of Darkness.* The player finds himself trapped in a courtyard where the exit is blocked by a stack of wooden crates. The only other exits are in places that the player has already been, and after a little exploration, it will dawn on him that the only way to progress is to find a path through the crates.

Experimentation will reveal that the player cannot jump over the crates or hack his way through them with his sword. Obviously some other, slightly more innovative solution is required. The answer (those with an aversion to spoilers need to look away now) is to get a flaming torch that is hanging on the wall, and throw it at the crates, which are then reduced to cinders.

This is an example of a scripted event that is attached to an object. The scripted object also has some other attributes. Run with the flaming torch and it will go out. Stand too close to the crates while they are burning, and the player will get burned, too. Throw it from too far away (blowing out en route), and it will fail to burn down the crates. The mix has to be just right, and the player will probably make a couple of mistakes along the way, which will require a restart.

There is a fine line in this case between level design (and game play balancing) and AI; commonly scripted events of this nature are placed in that category by default. However, my contention is that there is a separation between rule-based AI (see next chapter) and level design using scripted objects. The line between them is blurry, granted, but modern AI is usually more than just attaching a script to an object.

Previously, we noted that a skilled player should be able to complete the game in one run. In other words, they should not be punished unnecessarily. The "restart" rule is a good indicator that the game is balanced on the wrong side of the line that separates mass-market from hardcore titles. It is a fine line, but as a general rule (actually, a guiding principle), if a player needs to restart the game (or level) more than three times in order to complete a task, then that is one time too many.

Objects can also trigger events; a script is simply a conditionally executed series of triggers. This simply means that the object performs different actions depending on certain conditions being met or not met, as the case may be. A trigger is there to enable the object to always elicit the same reaction from another object—or conversely, have an action caused to it as a result of the proximity of another object.

Clearly, the organization of this network of object scripts is a design issue. Typically, there will be two or three classes of objects—static, scripted, and trigger objects.

Static objects are there to be collected or possibly dropped. They do not do anything. Scripted objects, as we have discussed, do different things depending on circumstances, while trigger objects always do the same thing, which may be tied to a specific object or location—a script with one action and one condition.

There is another kind of object that will cause things to happen to the player. Food, for example, might replenish energy; collecting crystals might increase the player's score. The scripts associated with these objects are called *reflexive* scripts, because the object causes an effect on the character employing them. This is distinct from a *projective* script, which causes an effect on another object or character.

Collectively, these are known as power ups, and their placement around a level is often vital, as we saw in the previous chapter. There are also other industry standard terms, but they do not often accurately reflect the abstract nature of game design except to those already in the profession, and even then they can be ambiguous.

So, the author has chosen terms that seem more logical, not to start a trend, but to be more accessible to those approaching the field from the outside—whether as a gamer, an enthusiast, or casual observer.

Object Inventories

In games where the entire session involves obtaining, transporting, and using objects, there will need to be some form of inventory system so that the player can effectively manage his possessions. On some online RPGs, players spend *upward* of 20 percent of their time managing their inventories.

Given that players are typically people who enjoy exploring and collecting, perhaps it is not surprising that an ineffective inventory design can cause a promising game to fail. Yet, in all the books that have been written about game design, inventory management systems get short mention. In the same way that music and sound sometimes seem to be tacked on as an afterthought, along with adaptive behavior and AI routines, inventory management never really seems to be part of the overall design document in all but a handful of games—which is a shame. A really good inventory management system can make a game much more enjoyable to play, as well as give players a feeling of *ownership* in having a well-stocked inventory of in-game objects. They will want to look at, manipulate, and show off their inventories.

Whether the designer decides to go all the way and allow for an interactive mapping system that reminds the player where each item in his inventory came from, or whether it will be left to the player to remember where items came from and what their uses are, there are several key areas in which the design will have an effect on both the experience and the implementation.

First useful hint: Pause on access. Even if the system uses on-screen icons as a form of user interface, the game should pause while the management system is being accessed. At the very least, the player should not be required to play at that time. This might seem obvious, but it has been forgotten in past game designs. Juggling inventory while your character is having limbs cut off is not a good in-game experience. Of course, there are also games like *Sudeki*, which slow down the action while the player accesses a translucent menu system. This at least gives the player a chance to organize his inventory while keeping an eye on the action; and since the action plays out in slow motion, he also has a decent chance of being able to rejoin it without much penalty.

Of course, protecting the player while he has his backpack open is a solution, but the balance has to be struck between making sure that he is not penalized and not offering an unfair advantage. The pendulum swings back if we disallow attacking while the backpack is open (counteracting the unfair advantage that we are protecting the player), but then this might be construed as penalizing the player unfairly.

There is a difficult balance to be struck.

Next, the system has to be in line with the platform. There is no point in creating a magnificent, elaborate inventory-management system that requires a collection of five keys for access if the game is targeted toward handheld consoles.

Clicking the up and down arrows, along with various combinations of fire and select buttons, just to open a virtual backpack, will quickly become very tedious and give rise to a bad playing experience—which brings us to the ordering system to be used. There are various options that fall into two camps: random access or sequential. Sequential systems can be LIFO (Last In, First Out, as with a sack) or FIFO (First In, First Out). The genre will dictate which system to use, as will the objects being stored.

There is always the possibility that the player will wish to reorder everything—for example, to put the weapons on top—and he should not be penalized for this. Random-access inventory management will solve this. In essence, this means that the game puts the most-useful items on top so that the player can quickly choose one, or at least allows the player to select items without having to go through the rigmarole of taking items out, stacking them nearby, and returning them to the inventory in a different order. On the other hand, this might be part of the game's style. Some games revolve around this exact kind of object-in-a-sack manipulation as a part of gameplay.

Somewhere between these two extremes is the idea of slotting the items. A number of slots can be defined, with each slot capable of holding a specific type of object. Therefore, the player has some slots dedicated to weapons, some for food, and a sack for everything else (treasure). There will need to be the inevitable discussion about how the slots are activated, especially on platforms where keys are limited to five or six buttons. This system does, however, enable fast access to items, removing the need to make sure that the weapons are on top. The player can grab the nearest one by selecting the appropriate slot.

If some form of intelligent system is to be put in place, then it can also offer clues to the player. For example, a spell-scroll icon placed above an axe icon would indicate that the axe was a magical weapon.

Of course, the player should never be penalized for a decision that he has not made himself. This is an important point that is sometimes forgotten. If the game decides to offer the player one option, when he really wanted another, the design should allow the player to rectify the decision before it becomes an issue.

Inventory display is another aspect entirely, and will largely depend on the platform choice. The smaller the screen resolution, the less likely it is that an icon system will be usable. The trick is to try and provide as much information as possible on screen and in session, with as little reliance as possible on the manual/in-game instructions that came with the game (virtual, multilayered, or otherwise).

Players will quickly get used to icons, no matter how strange they look at first, but they will tire of resorting to a paper manual or having to drill down through five levels of information on a tiny screen. The key is to combine an iconic class system with a descriptive in-game information system. The larger screen platforms allow for better looking icons and floating textual help for beginners.

Take, for example, a spell scroll that is designated with a simple, rolled-up paper icon. The color might indicate the type of spell that will be cast if the scroll is activated. On the handheld version, the player might be required to remember the scrolls that he has picked up, and the color will provide the clue to the scroll's spell. In this case, it will be necessary to try and minimize the possibility that the player holds two scrolls of the same class at once.

Counters can be used above the scroll icons to indicate that the player is holding multiple scrolls, but then they must be of exactly the same type—the handheld version not allowing as detailed an icon as console or PC versions of the game.

Of course, console or PC versions of the game can allow for a little picture to be added to the scroll, which can detail the spell to be cast. In this way, the icon system can be extended so that the player never has to refer to the detailed description of the object or resort to a printed manual.

There are two kinds of objects that are special and can be held outside of the inventory-management system if required—weapons and tools. These two classes of objects are special because there may not be time in the course of gameplay to pick them from a list of other objects, even if an intelligent system is in place that places them on the top of the pile. Also, these special objects might impede the player's movements in the game (usually due to their greater virtual weight or difficult handling), causing them to walk slower, as in *Severance: Blade of Darkness*. When the sword is held, the player moves much slower than if it is stowed in its scabbard. One click of the mouse and the sword is brought into play, unless the player is next to an object that can be picked up. The first time the player picks up an object rather than draws his sword as desired, he will be mildly disturbed, but will probably not do it again.

Weapons

This brings us to the use of weapons (or objects used as weapons) within the game universe. Some pieces of the game universe can have a dual purpose—from chairs and chalices to pieces of the environment. Objects that are to be used as weapons (either dual use or single use) are examples of projective scripted objects. That is, they cause an effect on third parties. Weapons should be quickly selectable from the primary control peripheral—keyboard, mouse, or controller.

They should also look like weapons, even if they are dual-use objects. For example, if a chalice can be used to drink from, throw at something, or used to club an enemy over the head with, then it should be accordingly well built. It should look strong. Swords should look sharp, and clubs should heft nicely in the hand of the player character, perhaps with some off-balance effect to reflect its rougher construction. Part of this illusion can be implied by visual clues that are not part of graphics directly associated with the object. That is, the player should list slightly when he picks up a heavy club, and it should look like effort is required to use it. In this way, the club will look and act like a useful weapon, making it a reflexive as well as projective scripted object. It causes an effect on the player as well as on third parties.

Weapons should, of course, be in line with the theme of the genre that the game is based on, except in cases where a cross-genre game is being created. It is also acceptable to produce mixed genre games, in the same way that it is possible to create mixed genre movies. *Mad Max*, *The Matrix: Reloaded*, and *Waterworld* are examples of movies that have many genre elements—high tech, low tech, and sci-fi.

On the other hand, there are few excuses for allowing the use of a laser weapon in a Middle-Ages role-playing game, but there is plenty of scope for a sword in a space drama. Weapons and genres seem to follow a cultural given: Low-technology weapons are acceptable in a futuristic game environment, but high-technology weapons have little or no place in historic environments. Skillful and careful consideration by the designer is needed if weapon assignment is to work properly.

Tools

A tool is an object that can be used to affect the game environment in such a way that it either enables the player to perform an action more efficiently than he could without the tool, or it helps the player perform a function that would be impossible without it. Hammers are great examples. A player can probably hammer a nail into a piece of wood using a rock or their fist (if it is balsa wood), or some other convenient object, such as a shoe. On the other hand, a hammer can accomplish the task much more efficiently.

Tools are scripted objects that cause an effect in the game universe, which can be described using a series of actions. They are usually trigger objects, because each tool has a specific purpose that needs to be obvious from the shape of the object.

Nonplayer Characters

Any character that cannot be controlled by the player is an NPC. Even some of the characters in online games fall into this category. The only difference is that the player is usually not allowed to kill another player—only NPCs.

The game controls NPCs. In the days of tabletop gaming and *Dungeons & Dragons*, NPCs were controlled by the dungeon master, who dictated how the NPCs would move within the game universe and react to the player. So, in the modern version, it is the game engine that serves as DM for the player.

Of course, there are also specific rules that govern player-NPC interactions, once the player has engaged one of them. These rules, along with the DM-style intelligence needed to move the NPCs around, needs to be encoded in the game engine to enable correct management of all the elements in the game universe that are not under the direct control of the player.

Behavior

The designer needs to establish how the various NPCs are going to react within their game universe, and this is called their "behavior." An NPC can be either a "helper" or a "hinderer." Helpers try to act in a way that furthers the player's advance through the game, whereas hinderers can be enemies that try to prevent the player's progression—or they can be passive entities that just seem to get in the way.

NPCs should follow all the same rules of consistency that the player is bound by. That is, they should not be able to manipulate the game universe in a way that the player cannot, without good reason. Good reasons include spell casting (if it is that kind of game) or the ability to cause greater damage with weapons (say, if the player has less-powerful weapons). They should not be able to abuse the general, core principles of the game universe, like the basic physics of the game engine, unless the player is able to do the same. Take, for example, *The Matrix*, in which this is a familiar concept.

Imagine that the player sees an NPC jump into the air and hover, defying gravity. The designer should have a mechanism in place to allow the player to do the same. Otherwise, the player might feel cheated.

Games are becoming increasingly less abstract. It did not matter in the early days of video games that the opponents had powers far in excess of the player character, because the game universe was abstract enough that it was simply accepted. The more concrete the game universe seems, the less accepting a player will be when NPCs appear to be superbeings that can always defeat him because they can move faster or exhibit some sort of sixth sense—even as the player's own character slows down. There is no worse feeling when playing a game than the slow realization that the machine is *cheating*.

Naturally, this goes both ways, such as cars that slow down when the player has a near-fatal crash, allowing him time to recover and catch up. Sometimes, this is a useful mechanism, but to some players, it will look as if they are being encouraged to cheat. For example, some soccer game NPCs let the player run rings around them, pretending to be dumber than they really should be. Anything that makes the game seem too easy will irritate the player.

Some players might at first be glad to find a game that they can actually complete, even when on the highest difficulty setting. But then what? The game goes on the shelf and is quickly forgotten, at best. At worst, the player wonders why he spent so much money on a game with so little appeal and challenge. Then they tell their friends, who tell *their* friends, and perhaps a reviewer or two, who will probably blacklist the game for being too easy. And that brings us to the concept of intelligent behavior that changes with respect to the player's success in the game universe.

Adaptive behavior is one of those industry buzzwords that game programmers like to throw around in the early stages of game design, but which gets swept under the carpet at the last minute when it becomes apparent that it is much quicker to just make sure that the behavior is always the same. Adaptive behavior enables NPCs to react to the player's unique style.

It is a concept that the designer needs to fully explore before exploiting it. The cars slowing down in the previous example is not adaptive behavior, nor is a soccer team that intentionally plays worse than the player. A fighting game in which the opponent leans heavily toward head shots, because the player seems unworried about blocking, *is* an example of adaptive behavior.

Games exist that use adaptive behavior to tailor NPC actions according to the player's own style, and generally do so in conjunction with some form of difficulty ramping. The theory is that the difficulty increases as the system adapts itself to the player's strategy.

Emergent behavior is another buzzword, and is used to refer to behavior that is based on giving a collection of rules to an NPC, and letting the resulting behavior emerge by itself. The best way to think of this is to consider a collection of weighted rules that link NPC actions with player and game universe actions. Each rule is evaluated with respect to their weighting, and the resulting action or set of actions will result in a change in circumstance. This change might then fire other weighted rules, which also cause actions that result in changes to the NPC's situation. The actions, all taken together, cause the NPC to exhibit specific behavior. Truly emergent behavior occurs when the game engine has the power to alter the rules or weighting of the rules so that the end behavior is modified.

Let us assume for a moment that a script offers three possibilities—attack, defend, and run away—and that the weights attached to these mean that most of the time, a given NPC will tend to defend itself rather than attack or run away.

Now, if the game engine is given a specific power to adjust these weights toward aggression when the player has been injured, the result will be, seemingly, emergent.

All the enemies will become braver and more aggressive the more the player is injured. This is a simple example; much more complex interactions can be built up.

The collective behavior of the NPC grouping will also be emergent. One great example is a collection of flying bird NPCs. Each one has a rule that governs the direction in which it moves, such that it tries to remain a certain distance from the birds around it, and travels in more or less the same direction and speed. This causes the bird NPCs to flock, and if slight random variations are brought into play, then they will always travel as a flock, but also move around within the flock. Each bird is simply following a set of weighted rules, the effect of which is to alter speed and direction slightly, depending on the output of those weighted rules.

A weighted rule, in this case, is simply a rule that, from a set of outcomes, chooses one according to an algorithm that tends toward a certain behavior. In the case of the flocking birds, we might have rules to follow, avoid, and move in a variety of directions. If we weight the rules such that, nine times out of ten, the bird will follow its peers, then tight flocking will result.

If we allow a variation to creep in such that we weight the rules toward avoidance behavior, then the flock will begin to split up, as birds repel each other. This weighting can happen over time to manipulate the flock formation.

Altering behavior in these ways in real time is quite processor-intensive. In other words, part of the reason that games do not seem to make as much use of these techniques as we might like is because the platforms cannot cope with the additional workload. In addition, the result can be unpredictable. When trying to temper the unpredictability of the behavior, we need to put down rules that limit the worst excesses of the emergent/adaptive behavior. This not only increases the processor burden further, but also begs the question as to why we bothered in the first place. The resulting behavior might be so limited that we would have been better off with basic, flexible rules. We will look at these two fascinating areas in more detail in Chapter 12.

Scripting

You will have realized by now that if behavior (emergent, adaptive, or simply predetermined) is to be implemented in a video game, then someone needs to program the machine to react in the way that the designer wishes. One of the critical tasks when designing NPC behavior is to define how the NPC will react to changes in environment.

There will also be different classes of behavior. For example, not all NPCs will exhibit the same behavior, and it is the responsibility of the designer to make sure that each type of NPC is modeled correctly in the design phase of the video game project—not to mention the fact that the balance of the game is going to be affected by the combined behaviors of all the various NPCs.

All of this means that not only do the actual NPC actions need to be isolated and properly encoded, but also the parameters within which they are applied. For example, we might want an NPC dog to run toward the player only when the player is detected within the same room. The behavior's trigger, which ensures that the dog runs toward the player, has to be set so that it is only activated when the player is a certain distance from the dog and without intervening obstacles that make the player undetectable, like walls.

This means that there are several items that need to be designed into the engine. First, the NPC has to be able to move. Next, it is necessary to indicate the direction in which the NPC has to move. Finally, triggers need to be set to ensure that the NPC is acting within the confines of the physical game universe.

In our example, this means that, since the player cannot see through walls, then the NPC dog cannot, either. If we use a basic proximity trigger, then the dog will attempt to move toward the player, based on the closeness of the player to the dog. This is not realistic, since if there is a wall between them, then the dog will probably not notice the player character.

As for the NPC dog, there are several triggers to consider. The dog will be able to see, hear, and smell the player. Each of the triggers needs to have a level associated with it to ensure that it is activated in the same way that a real-life dog would use these senses.

We have illustrated the concept with an NPC dog, but it applies to many aspects of game design, including reactions to objects, NPCs, and almost all aspects of the video game that rely on interactions inside the game universe. Of course, this could just be written into the game engine. However, doing so makes it very difficult to alter the trigger levels and other aspects of the behavior without diving into the source code. The changes must be made, and the entire game recompiled and sent back to a testing cycle, just to make sure that everything works as designed.

This route has many drawbacks. First, it takes a programmer to alter even the smallest piece of game code, and programmer time is expensive—money that is better spent on other aspects of the game. Second, it is globally time consuming to edit the engine, since each little change needs to be tested to ensure that it has not had an effect on some other part of the system. Then, there are all the little problems that stem from having the game behavior encoded in the source—from the maintainability of the engine to not being able to re-use the code in other projects.

Therefore, scripting is a much better solution. It is important that the engine design allows for scripted behavior in as many aspects of the game as possible, but mainly for NPC interaction. In many recent FPS games (*Unreal Tournament*, *Quake*, and *DOOM*) "bot" scripting plays a large part in the core game engines.

Take *Unreal Tournament 2003*, for example. It relies on a multiplayer gaming engine with full Internet capability, allowing players to log on and play against each other or as teams. The single-player version is identical to the multiplayer version, with one minor difference; opponents are scripted entities—robots that are more or less intelligent. The player can dive into the scripts and alter them in order to alter their behaviors, thus rendering the game more or less easy, depending on the skill of the player-programmer.

This enables the game engine to remain the same, whether the vendor wishes to ship a full-multiplayer variant or one that is essentially a single-player game. Naturally, the engine can be licensed for a fee, so that future video game developers can take advantage of this robust, highly flexible, fully scripted engine for their own games.

Summary

This chapter has presented a somewhat detailed overview of the use of vehicles and objects in video games, but it is by no means the last word on the subject. Experimentation with various techniques and further research will prove to be the best ways to ascertain which of the features are useful in the game that you (by now) have in mind.

Hopefully, you played games that use or abuse these techniques. Learn from these experiences. In the end, it is player's view of the game universe and everything in it that will affect the success of the game. Some rules can be flexible and some even broken, but it is only through play-testing that the designer can be sure that the correct balance has been struck.

It is also important that the advice on scripting versus programming be taken to heart. All but the simplest games will need to be balanced by adjusting various parameters—that is, fine tuned. This is especially true in the case of vehicle handling and the use of objects. The most efficient way to edit these parameters and the actions that they control is with a robust scripting interface.

Finally, playing the game is key to ascertaining whether the vehicle feels right, the objects act correctly, and so on. Although concept art will help you test the graphics before they make their way into the game itself, the design of the game should also be tested with respect to the target audience venue.

References

[EDGE01] *Clock Tower 3* review for *EDGE* magazine. No. 124, June 2003, p. 101.

12 Video Game AI Design

In This Chapter

- Genre-Based Video Game AI
- State-Driven AI
- Behavior-Driven AI
- AI and Evolution
- Communicating AI
- Beyond Event-Driven AI

Artificial Intelligence (AI) is often perceived, both by engineers and in the media, as a "sexy" computer technology application. From *2001: A Space Odyssey's* HAL to *Star War's* C3P0 and R2D2, the media and movie industry give AI a lot of hype, forever claiming that some day computers will rule the world. They must be disappointed, in a way. Science has not yet lived up to that promise.

On a more serious note, AI has the potential to enhance the world, and arguably one of the best testing grounds (or proving grounds) for AI might well turn out to be in video games. Subsequently, all video games contain AI to some extent; how else would they present the player with a challenge?

AI takes on a slightly different role in video games than in hard computer science, and is a vitally important, yet often neglected aspect of game design. This might be because, despite the obvious mass appeal of humanoid machines, within the game industry, AI is considered *tricky*—something that you need a brain the size of New York to fully understand, and also something that is *disposable* when the budget gets tight.

Let's get one thing straight: All games have rules that make it a game, and as such, many game designers and developers will claim that all games have AI. This is quite correct if the definition of AI is following rules set by the human game creators. Rules that are designed to mimic natural intelligence might work under similar circumstances.

The potential for AI is much more than that, though. Game developers understand AI to a level which is, for the most part, playing catch-up to the cutting edge, when one might expect it to be pushing the technology forward more than it currently seems to be.

Surprisingly, *EDGE* magazine has become accustomed to video game designers whose good intentions turn to mush as soon as they actually have to implement AI. *EDGE* is forever lamenting the AI in video games (as well as camera design), and freely admits that AI is an easy target for criticism.

In the course of research for this book, several sources managed to discuss game design and programming without ever touching on the science behind AI—at all . . . not once, even in passing . . . which might suggest that this is a trivial chapter, were it not for the fact that a game without *some* AI is rather like pizza without cheese. It will work, but the consumer will always feel like there is something missing.

These sources actually do discuss rule mechanisms, scripting, and other things that provide game AI, but they don't seem to expose enough of the science behind it to help people push it forward. Games need good AI, and designers need to understand that there is more to AI than just the rules that govern a game. This analogy brings us to another aspect of video game AI that needs to be understood. Like pizza toppings, there are those players for whom AI should be toned down. Casual gamers who play for a bit of fun after a long day at work do not have the same expectations as hardcore gamers who consider video games serious business.

Here is an important point: AI in computer science and the media is there to provide *intelligence* that is *artificial*—modeling and surpassing observed human intelligence, for example. Some scientists are *still* working to persuade computers to display rudimentary intelligence on the level of mice, with the assumption that it is easier to understand and mimic how a mouse's brain works than our own.

On the other hand, AI in video game design is there to make the game fun. It needs to enhance the experience for the player, and if it does not, then it has failed. Some players might *like* the fact that their opponents appear to be deaf. Others might find it strange if a trained soldier that is guarding a door does not notice that the player has just come tearing through it, guns blazing—that is, until the player points his gun *at* the soldier, to which the soldier fires once straight at the player's head and kills him. The player might find this a bit irritating.

So, AI in video game design walks a fine line between simulation and entertainment. Cross it in either direction, and the game risks ridicule, especially if *EDGE* magazine gets hold of it:

> "AI. Two little letters that most developers seem to treat with scorn . . . While they may make all the right noises during early demos of the game: 'Intelligent pathfinding,' they'll chirp; 'Group dynamics,' they'll enthuse; before finishing with the coup de grace, 'Emergent behaviour.' But mostly it's a smokescreen designed to impress naïve game journos." [EDGE01]

This was the impression of an *EDGE* journalist who had been to a meeting of game designers who were early in the design process. Of course, when they actually had to start development, AI was the first aspect to suffer; therefore, when the actual game was reviewed, the journalist had this to say:

> "The AI in . . . is typical of most FPSs. It's not terrible, but it's not great either . . . the developers are just happy to trot out the same kind of behaviour patterns we've seen a thousand times before . . . why don't we just coin a new term: 'Duck shoot AI.' Because that's what you're getting in everything from *Project IGI* to *Turok Evolution*." [EDGE02]

This might sound harsh, and it probably is, but the reviewer neglects to mention that there are people for whom "duck-shoot AI" is a blessing. Some people who don't have time to master games may never get past the first skirmish, and will abandon the game if it is too tough. A casual gamer will download the demo, and only purchase the game if it seems likely that he can complete it within a reasonable time. This is an aspect of video game design that should not be forgotten.

When the reviewer refers to behavior patterns, this touches on an interesting point. Some designers and programmers believe that AI in a game should stop with a basic, discrete, decision-making apparatus, which can be easily represented in the game as a finite-state machine, but is rather predictable.

It is that predictability that reviewer is criticizing, believing that it is easy to make the behavior less predictable and more lifelike—which it is. To do so is a challenge, though. We must ensure that the AI is consistent, provides depth of gameplay, does not hog resources, *and* be delivered on time and within budget. That is the hard part.

One last piece of wisdom from *EDGE* before we get on with this chapter:

> "The AI is particularly retarded. Adversaries will walk into their own grenades, run around in circles, and climb up and down ladders like demented steeplejacks." [EDGE03]

Even the most casual gamer will probably find this kind of behavior lamentable. Consequently, "dumbing down" the AI to the point that it is not so much artificially intelligent as artificially stupid is probably not a good idea, either. Yes, it is indeed a fine line between entertainment and realism.

This chapter will concentrate on two main themes of video game AI. It is a subject fraught with buzzwords and scientific terminology, which we shall try to keep to a minimum. The two themes can be described as *linear AI* and *behavioral AI*. To keep it simple, linear AI refers to the "clever" aspects of a game, while behavioral AI refers to the reaction of entities to particular situations.

Using human behavior as a model enables us to think in terms of analogies, which is always helpful when trying to come to grips with new terminology. So, an example of linear AI is the (cliché) human male that refuses to read instructions and instinctively knows how to put a shelf together. In video game parlance, this is akin to an entity knowing how to use an object that they have never before encountered, and without being told.

The behavioral aspect creeps in when the human male, confronted with 17 bolts left over and the realization that maybe the instructions should have been followed, makes a decision as to what to do next. Depending on his personality, he might give in and read the instructions, hide the bolts, or wait and see if the shelves fall over.

A similar theory can be applied to behavioral AI in video game design. When a specific object has been acquired, the entity might choose to use it in a variety of ways, depending on the situation. The difference between the two situations is that while one can be designed into the game so that every possibility is accounted for, the behavioral aspect should emerge from a set of basic rules. Here again, it might seem a fine line of distinction, but they can be modeled in two very different ways.

Genre-Based Video Game AI

Depending on the genre of video game being designed, there are different techniques that can be used while still respecting the fundamental rules of hardcore versus casual gamer. Chess games, for example, use a very different kind of AI model than fast-paced, first-person shooters. Still, even a chess game needs to cater to both types of gamers.

Then again, there are aspects that relate to the precise nature of the gamer's character within the game. Two-dimensional vertical shooters such as *Space Invaders* only require that there is an emergent pattern, due to the restrictive nature of the game universe, while full-3D map-based games such as *Unreal Tournament* need to take into account that both the player and the adversaries have much more freedom of movement.

Simulations, such as rally driving and individual sports (track and field events), have other distinct requirements placed on the AI, which need to reflect the fact that the player is controlling an athlete whose body reacts in a different way than his own, and therefore, the model needs to enable the player to do things in the game that he is unable to do in real life. AI is still required, but it is the AI of the game engine, or level. It must react to the environment and extend the controller so that the player can persuade his in-game persona to react in a realistic way, as opposed to controlling adversaries.

By a similar token, simulations in which other, similarly endowed, machine-controlled, entities share the universe with the player (such as Formula 1 racing games) need to be able to exhibit AI that reflects the desire to win at all costs. Such games have additional constraints, since they are based on a nondestructive premise that respects certain rules, and these rules cannot be ignored without risking dire consequences. They are inherently different from games in which the adversaries exist to inhibit the progress of the player through the game by use of force, alone.

Finally, there are team sports and pseudo-sports simulations that need to exhibit intelligence of an entirely different nature, often to the point of being able to almost second-guess the player. For example, the player should not be allowed to pass the ball to an empty space in a football simulation. There are a number of mechanisms (made famous by the *John Madden* series of football games by EA Sports) that use plays to enable a certain amount of predictability to be built in, but which also allow the player freedom to change his plans mid-play, depending on the actions of the simulated opposition.

In between all of these are games of the genre made famous by the *SimCity* series (Maxis)—simulated cities, individuals, environments, and even animals. Each game has specific pieces of both behavioral and linear AI built into the code. Modeling complex environments such as zoos, theme parks, planets, and cities come with additional AI burdens.

This may be a good time to try and categorize some of the aspects of artificial intelligence. We will be using super-categories of the previous two (linear and behavioral). In other words, we are about to embark on a quick tour of some of the ways in which the AI can be dissected and designed into the game; each piece will require some linear and behavioral AI techniques, or even a unique technique of its own. All of this will be discussed in terms of the relevant genre and will give us a foundation to discuss how AI problems can be solved to create a believable, but fun, game universe for the player.

Environment AI

Each game environment (in open games like *Grand Theft Auto*), or each level (or track, pitch, and so on for games based around these environments), contains objects that interact as well as other elements that may be modeled as objects, but which manifest themselves purely as effects. Anything that makes up the environment in which the game is played and that have an effect on the way in which the game is played can be classified as environment AI.

This is the most vague and gray area of AI that we will discuss. Simulating a real or perceived reality and using rules that can be applied in many situations can be classified as either AI or simply game mechanics. However, the ability of the game to take information out of context and apply it in a different situation requires something more than simple adherence to the strict rules of game mechanics.

Imagine, for example, a cloud. It is a collection of water particles that have specific relationships that can be modeled using simple game mechanics within the known rules of physics. The machine must know that the precipitation from these clouds will change depending on temperature variations—that is, as rain, snow, sleet, or hail—and this lies between game mechanics and AI.

Taking the water-based cloud out of context and using it to produce a storm of rain-like particles on a distant planet with a methane atmosphere, or modeling a cloud of flies to look like a cloud of snow under the correct conditions, reflects superior AI. One is linear and the other is behavioral, in this case dynamic AI.

Entity AI

The player will share the game universe with a variety of other entities. They might be other players in a multiplayer gaming environment, or they might be computer-generated and AI-controlled. Either way, the entities have capabilities that are similar or different to the player, depending on how they are modeled. Like in *UT2003*, they might even be modeled on players to the extent that they share the same weapons and have the same desire to get the biggest, most powerful gun available.

In a game, anything that controls the way in which these entities react to their immediate game universe relies on AI; this might include the player, or being observed by or hidden from the player. The reaction of entities to each other, the player, and the game universe can also be described in terms of linear or behavioral AI.

The simplest form of linear AI that controls entity movement can be seen in *Pac-Man*, where the ghosts follow a discrete, set pattern. They "guard" their corners and move in a way that is reliable and predictable. They are obviously adhering to a set of rules (or even a set of commands) that tell them how to move, and would do so indefinitely if it were not for the behavioral side to their virtual personalities.

This behavioral side comes into play when the ghosts "become bored." From the player's point of view, entities' behavior patterns change after a while, and they begin to close in on the character being controlled by them.

This mode of behavior is only dynamic up to a point. Once the ghosts have locked on to the player's character, it is quite simple to draw them on, so that they follow the player around the screen in a line. On the other hand, they will only do this for a while and eventually revert to their "guarding" state. In between, a proficient player can tease the ghosts into a corner, grab a power pill, and eat them all for maximum bonus points. In addition, the ghosts have a third mode of movement that involves their slightly absurd flight from the player if a power pill has been consumed, and thus avoid being eaten. This is an example of entity AI that spans several techniques, from simple linear "follow the instructions" AI to more-complex "react to the player and environment"-style behavioral AI.

There are also games that can be modeled using entity AI that is not immediately apparent—for example, chess. Entity AI can be used for decisions regarding which piece to move, based entirely on the prospective outcome for that piece. The piece with the highest possibility of avoiding capture or aiding in a winning formation is the one that will be moved.

Chess can also be considered in terms of linear versus behavioral AI. In fact, it is quite possible to stick to simple linear AI, which does not need to adapt, only recalculate the linear portion each time a move is required. This is entirely different from the way in which humans play chess; they usually have a plan (strategy) that can be adapted, depending on the opposition's moves.

Simple chess computers use an uncomplicated reactive approach—their performance depends on the player's performance. They always start the game in the same way, simply because the evaluation process that determines the piece with the highest "score" never changes, and unless the player moves one of his pieces in a way that affects the outcome, the computer will continue to play in exactly the same way as before. It is entirely predictable, up to a point.

Before we move on, it is worth mentioning that the reason a "dumb" chess algorithm can consistently beat a novice human player is that the computer is capable of simulating possible scenarios to a much greater depth of play than a human. The computer can, in effect, play out hundreds of variations of the game and choose the one that offers the best outcome. The computer can simulate its own moves plus those of the opponent in the same time that it takes the human to make a move that is part instinct, part plan, and part calculation. By the same token, two identical, computer-simulated machines playing each other will inevitably result in a draw, but a human with a good playing strategy will always beat a computer that follows strict calculation.

Object AI

This slightly strange topic requires devolving some of the responsibility of the entity AI to the objects that they are likely to encounter. In a game universe that is effectively devoid of sight, it becomes difficult for entities to observe objects and see the way in which they work. Most humans, when confronted with a picture of a weapon, will fairly quickly figure out how they are supposed to work, even if they lack the technical or practical know-how.

Weapons designers, whether they be for real-life applications, films, or video games, also go to great pains to visually indicate that an object *is* a weapon—unless, of course, the intended user wants to engage in some kind of subterfuge, in which case only close (and often fatal) inspection and experimentation will reveal the true purpose of the object. In either case, AI-controlled entities lack the visual cues that humans use to figure out what an object is designed for. Thus, it is necessary for the object to tell the entity what its purpose is. This is an example of linear object AI. A weapon, for example, might indicate to an AI-controlled entity that it has certain capabilities, a certain weight, and can be used in certain situations. The evaluation of all this information lets the entity decide whether the object is desirable as a weapon. This process is similar to the one used in *Unreal Tournament* robot player scripts.

Player AI

Surely, the player is, after all, *supposed* to be the most intelligent entity in the game. On the other hand, the player is controlling a character that is merely his extension into the game world. It is not possible to control every aspect of that character, such as with a sensor-impregnated suit that can sense the player's movements, except in very limited game environments, such as a top-down 2D vertical scroller in which the craft can move left, right, up, down, or fire.

More-complex games need a certain amount of linear AI, such as if the character is multi-limbed and needs AI just to keep from falling over. Of course, the entities are modeled in such a way as to make this impossible. But it is also a fact that on occasion, the object will need to react in a way that extends beyond the player's current ability to control it.

For example, in *Severance: Blade of Darkness*, sword fighting features prominently. It is a PC game marketed by CodeMasters (U.K.) that challenges the player to simultaneously control a sword and walk around without getting slashed by his opponent. The directional keys are used by the player to determine the style of attack or defense to be used in conjunction with his weapon of choice, so any responsibility for moving the player character's legs is assumed by the AI.

Of course, the AI will probably be accused of favoritism toward the simulated enemies if it under-performs. Players will claim that the AI moved them in the wrong direction just so the opponents could do them in. With the reputation of the game at stake, this kind of accusation has to be avoided at all costs. If that means favoring the player from time to time, then so be it.

The fact remains that the player expects his character's AI to react in the same way that he would in a given situation—or at least react in a way that is sensible and predictable. This is what player AI is all about and is nearly always linear, so that the player can learn what the rules are and adapt their playing style accordingly.

PUTTING IT ALL TOGETHER

We have seen the *what,* and now it is time to consider the *how.* Keep in mind that each of the techniques we are about to discuss can be used in a variety of situations. The key is to establish the various theories that define how a specific form of AI is to be applied, and not to worry about the actual implementation.

There are some techniques that will have to be toned down when it comes to developing the game itself, but at least the design should accurately reflect the theories available. There are also ways to implement certain techniques that rely on other, more-technical forms of AI, which will not be covered here. Here we are concerned with determining what kinds of behavior the game is expected to exhibit, not how the developer is going to actually engineer that behavior.

STATE-DRIVEN AI

Computer scientists are fond of referring to FSMs when discussing rudimentary artificial intelligence. The finite state machine is a cornerstone of state-driven AI, so is worth looking at in a little more detail. We'll be working with the *Pac-Man* ghost, since it is a piece of game design history that most people can relate to.

In the "Entity AI" section of this chapter, we saw that the *Pac-Man* ghost can have one of three modes of movement. There is the "guard" mode, in which the entity wanders around its corner of the maze, following a set pattern; there is a "hunter" mode, in which it tries to back the player into a corner; and there is a "stealth" mode, which is used to evade the player. Each of these modes can be referred to as a *state.* The ghost is free to cycle between these states, depending on the specific states of the environment, itself, and the player. Assuming that these are the only states that the ghost can be in at any one time, it is representing an FSM.

The ghost has a finite number of states and moves between them like a machine following instructions.

What the ghost does to fulfill each of these states relies on other AI techniques (which we will come to soon), and there may even be other FSM implementations nested within the master FSM. However, for now we will only deal with this key FSM. We can draw a diagram to represent the "Master FSM" (see Figure 12.1), which will clarify how the ghost gets from one state to another.

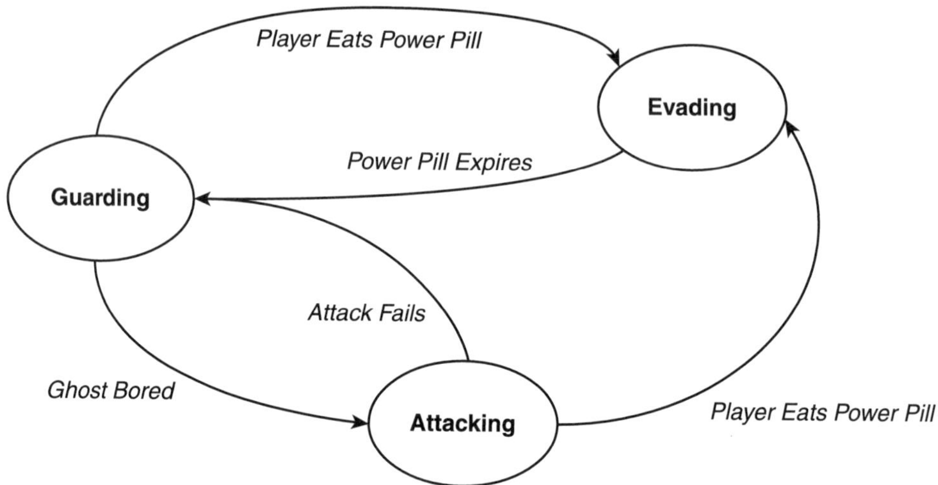

FIGURE 12.1 The ghost Master FSM.

This diagram, while useful, is only part of the process. The next stage involves creating a table (Table 12.1) that details the start, event, and output states that drive the FSM. It is a translation of the diagram into something that is closer to the actual implementation. In fact, the diagram phase could feasibly be avoided entirely; simply hand the table to the developer and tell him to get on with it. Here, however, we are concerned with the design—and more important, communicating that design to others. Some of these team members might not be developers, so they should be given both the diagram and table versions.

The accepted "technical term" for Table 12.1 is the "State Transition Matrix." From it, we can see that a ghost can go through the following stages:

Guarding ➔ Attacking ➔ Evading ➔ Guarding

We can also see that there is no path from Evading to Attacking, without passing through Guarding first. This makes sense, because if the player has eaten a

TABLE 12.1 Ghost Master FSM Transition Matrix

Start State (Current State)	Event	End State (New State)
Guarding	Player Eats Power Pill	Evading
Evading	Power Pill Expires	Guarding
Guarding	Ghost Bored	Attacking
Attacking	Attack Fails	Guarding
Attacking	Player Eats Power Pill	Evading

power pill, it is useless to move into the Attacking state, since it will end in the ghost being vanquished.

The final element is to know what the starting state is for a ghost that has just been created. We can choose from any of the three states, but the logical one is the Guarding state. Moving from one state to another requires only that we know how to react to a given event and also what state the ghost is in at any one time.

FSM Networks

When a ghost moves from one state to another, it is also an event that can be fed into the FSM that relates to another entity within the game universe. This other entity could even be another ghost; in this case we could add another branch from Guarding to Attacking, to reflect a "mass attack" in which all the ghosts suddenly turn on the player.

These kinds of FSM relationships and their associated events are called FSM Networks, and it is important to separate those events that are part of a specific FSM belonging to a group of entities, as well as the controlling FSM that acts as a trigger. Therefore, we need to build diagrams to display nested collections of FSMs that communicate with each other.

Behavior-Driven AI

State-driven AI is a very logical. The state is either happening or it is not. One or zero, on or off—the choices are *binary*. We can build up a reasonably complex pattern of behavior using these binary decisions, but at the end of the day, it is only useful in restricted environments. *Pac-Man* may be a lot of things, but it is not an example of complex AI. On the other hand, each of the ghosts has a state in which they need to behave in a vaguely intelligent way and use modeled behavior that does not result in binary decision-making to control their movements around the maze.

A ghost, wandering around the maze in Guard mode, knows where it is in relation to the player and the other ghosts, but has no knowledge of the maze layout. All it has is its FSM to follow. If that was all, the ghost would probably never get past the Guard state. The first binary decision in our FSM relates to "Ghost bored" (Figure 12.1). How is that measured? Clearly not by an FSM modeling degrees of boredom.

The chances are that it is a timer of some sort. Maybe the ghost has to follow a set pattern and wander around a corner of the maze five times before deciding to hunt down the player. Having evaluated (using a nonbinary technique) that it is "bored" (an aspect of behavior), the ghost makes the binary decision to move into the Attack state.

Now, modeling an attacking ghost probably seems like an easy proposition. After all, the ghost just needs to know where the player is and then go get him. So, the distance is measured between the ghost and the player, a decision is made about where to go next in the maze. Since the ghost does not have a built-in map of the maze, there is no way of knowing (beyond measuring our environmental changes, and distance to player and other ghosts) whether or not the choice was a correct one.

All of these could be represented by a series of FSMs, but it is much more entertaining to use behavioral modeling with a touch of random variation to keep the player on his toes. Maybe the ghost will speed up, as well, depending on how close it is to the player's little yellow *Pac-Man* character. Depending on the level of aggression (a facet of ghost behavior) the ghost will relentlessly pursue the player until it is either bored, the player is vanquished, or the player eats a Power Pill.

This last event would lead to the Evading state, which reflects human emotion of fear. "The player has eaten the Power Pill, and now he's coming after me . . . or is he?" Here again, we need to dispense with the FSM approach in favor of being able to measure the ghost's fear and translate it into evasive behavior that fits the ghost's situation.

The ghost's basic movement is also an example of behavior; it cannot be modeled by an FSM because there are states that require data on the distance covered, or the number of turns taken at a specific juncture in order to decide whether to turn left, right, or go straight.

Emergent Behavior

In the introduction to this chapter, an *EDGE* magazine game review lamented the AI. One of the buzzwords that gets thrown around in developer/journalist circles is *emergent*—or, in AI terms specifically, *emergent behavior.* The *EDGE* journalist had decided that it was part of a sophisticated smokescreen.

First, we should probably try and attach some meaning to the phrase, since despite what *EDGE* might think, giving substance to behavior-driven AI is a valid approach. Since these subjects are always better understood with an example, we will use one here.

Imagine a virtual ant that is controlled by an FSM. The ant inhabits a universe in which there are three kinds of objects; ants, food, and empty space (the absence of ants or food). The ant is equipped with sensors that tell it what is directly in its path, and an FSM controls the ant's response to finding objects in its path. Based on a set of rules, the ant will be able to move forward, or turn to its left or right; these rules are encoded in the Movement FSM.

The ant also has an internal state modeling its behavior, which enables it to gauge how far to apply the Movement FSM that controls its reactions to the immediate universe. Hence, the ant is controlled by linear AI, which dictates the level of response, and behavioral AI, which embodies the extent to which the Master FSM is to be respected when choosing one of a set of FSMs that can be applied.

Therefore, if the ant is hungry and food is directly in front of it, and the Master FSM reports that the ant should move toward food, the ant can apply the relevant rules for feeding. When the ant is sated, another FSM (perhaps the Exploring FSM) can be applied.

The Exploring FSM might react to other ants in a given way, such as telling our ant to move toward another ant and engage it in a battle. Suppose that, applying the Battle FSM, the ant finds itself damaged, the Self-Preservation FSM is selected by the Master FSM, and the ant attempts to flee.

If the two ants are identically modeled, they will dance around each other until one is vanquished. Some variance needs to be built in to enable one ant to exhibit different behavior. The idea behind emergent behavior is that the ant can control, to a certain extent, its own responses to the surrounding universe, based on experience. Moreover, emergent behavior considers what occurs in a group of like entities that are all capable of re-programming themselves, based on their individual experiences. If we introduce the concepts of "friend" and "foe" into our virtual ant universe, different behaviors will emerge—perhaps distinct "tribes" of virtual ants will be observed if the simulation is left to itself for long enough.

Even reproduction can be added to the mix. Different behavioral patterns can be merged to create new breeds of virtual ants that might be more or less successful than the two "parents." These offspring will either live long enough to breed or die so quickly that they never have a chance of producing inferior virtual offspring of their own.

So, emergent behavior is based on the experiences of the entities within the game universe, coupled with their actions and reactions in a group. It is a definition that is very difficult to nail down accurately without drifting into the realms of science and science fiction. This is perhaps why video game designers are quick to use the phrase "emergent behavior," but when it comes to actual implementation, they fail. The question is, "Why isn't emergent behavior carried into the implementation of the game?" The answer is that there is some misunderstanding of how much emergent behavior can bring to a game and exactly what the science behind the phrase means.

Bringing emergent behavior to a video game need not be a complex, resource-intensive bag of tricks. For example, chess games that can adapt their strategy to the moves of the player, self-reprogramming robots fighting in an arena, or groups of entities that respect a simple set of rules (birds flocking) all exhibit emergent behavior that can enrich the player's experience.

Fuzzy Logic

One of the cornerstones of behavioral AI is the ability to compare weighted decisions—the inherent "cost" of performing an action against the benefit of a likely outcome. The FSM, as already noted, relies on a series of true or false comparisons. An event is a discrete value that either occurs (in which case we can apply a rule) or does not occur (in which case we might find another rule to apply). This is strict logic, the foundation of computer decision-making.

The alternative, *fuzzy* logic, relates to the extent an action should be performed. An FSM network can result in many different possible outcomes, especially if the Master FSM incorporates the ability to trigger events simultaneously, or very close together.

Of these outcomes, additional events can be applied to an extent that is based on a "fuzzy" analysis of the expected result. This may all sound very theoretical and vague, but it is important that the budding game designer is aware that mathematical techniques can be applied that result in not only choosing or performing an action, but also specifying how "hard" to apply the result of that action.

So, fuzzy logic incorporates the vagueness of inputs to arrive at a definite output:

> "FL provides a simple way to arrive at a definite conclusion based upon vague, ambiguous, imprecise, noisy, or missing input information."
> Seattle Robotics Society Web site [SEATTLE01]

In video game design, it is also helpful to be able to act upon that conclusion in a fuzzy way, incorporating the extent to which the action should be performed. This will also feed into other fuzzy decision-making processes.

Humans do it all the time, especially those who drive road vehicles. The vehicle might be in a state Accelerating, and the FSM dictates that when Accelerating, if there is a vehicle in front that we are approaching at some defined speed, then we should Brake. The extent to which we should Brake is dictated by fuzzy logic, which determines that if we are approaching the front vehicle at a rate described as "slow" then we need only need to Brake lightly.

On the other hand, if we are moving toward the vehicle in front at a rate described as "fast," we need to Brake harder. If, by braking harder, we still touch the vehicle in front and cause an accident, then we know that next time, we need to modify our behavior so that we Brake sooner or harder still, and the emergent behavior increases our skill as a driver. On the other hand, we might choose to perform another action at the last minute, such as "Swerve," to avoid the accident, and decide that this is a good behavioral pattern to follow—the possible emergent behavior: decidedly aggressive driving, with little reduction in speed, but a lot of maneuvering at high speeds, instead.

(Level design also produces emergent behavior. Consider a race track with a series of hard left-right-left bends in quick succession; if the AI controlling the cars has them slow down to allow the player to catch up—some games do use this mechanism—then there is a point at which they may form a traffic queue going into the zigzag. The game developer has not programmed a traffic jam, but it emerges, nonetheless.)

Emergent behavior is not a new idea. The driving concept has been around since classical times, and in video game terms is a consequence of the addition of the effects of all the input behaviors, rules, and interaction with a potentially unknown force—the player.

This additive effect produces behavior that has not been explicitly defined within an FSM but which takes shape as the various FSMs that make up the AI behind the game each have an effect on the emergent behavior. More to the point, it might not be possible to determine why the behavior has taken place. This is called *strong emergence*, where the individual causes cannot be determined from the net effect.

AI and Evolution

Throughout this chapter, AI has been discussed as if the rules, once laid out, do not change. Of course, in the real world, this is seldom the case. Intelligence can grow with experience, with the rules governing behavior changing accordingly. And the same is true with video games; the level of growth depends somewhat on the platform that the game is destined for and the storage options available.

It is difficult to enable the machine to take advantage of past experiences if those experiences are lost when the play session ends or the machine is switched off. Of course, a certain amount of evolution can be built into the play session itself, but this will always be more of a knee-jerk AI response to the player's actions than real evolution.

For example, there are some games that have a difficulty level that is linked to the player's success within the scope of the current play session—such as in sports simulations, be it soccer, tennis, or football. The winning margin is used by the machine to gauge the skill of the player; subsequent games will feature an opposition that plays a better (or worse) game than the previous one.

This is artificial to say the least, and it's an example of *prescribed AI*. The AI does not evolve; but the way in which the AI is used and the levels of mistakes that it makes differ, depending on whether the last game was played by an expert or a beginner. Once the player figures out that this is happening, it becomes second nature to try for only a one-point win.

This sort of behavior causes the designers, when tweaking the game, to consider both the speed at which the players scored the winning point as well as the number of points that they won by, and link them to the difficulty of the opponent. This pushes the players to try and score later on in the game, in the hope of tricking the machine into believing that they are less skilled than they really are. Now the players try to get as much out of the session as possible, without increasing the difficulty level excessively. This is as good as it gets without external storage.

Add a hard drive, memory card, or other device, and new possibilities open up. Historical data can be analyzed in order to gauge the true skill of the player. But AI analysis can go deeper. The machine can also look at the performance of its own AI-controlled entities under certain circumstances and begin to learn what tactics will outwit the player. The machine will *evolve*.

Coupled with emergent behavior, evolution provides an additional aspect to the game that can lead to true innovation. How far this will take the current crop of video game designers is left to the imagination. Our purpose here is to sow seeds of information in the hope that they germinate into something more powerful than what this book, itself, has to offer.

Emergent behavior and digital evolution are not necessarily new ideas, as noted above, but they can offer real avenues for exploration that have not yet been fully exploited. Games such as *Black&White* and the *Creatures* series take a really serious view on evolution and AI that communicates into a great video game, but the techniques are equally applicable in other genres.

COMMUNICATING AI

Underpinning an AI implementation is some form of communication structure. We have discussed events and how the results of those events are fed to other entities' FSMs and FSM networks; but we have not addressed how the developer will approach the problem of communication between entities. The answer is to design a robust AI *engine* that will facilitate the decision-making processes and information flow through the system.

In Chapter 6, we encountered messaging in the context of object interactions—feeding information between objects. Now, rather than simply feeding messages around, combining the AI engine with the communications system allows the designer to build a robust framework for the AI. Because this framework requires information from all of the objects, its design is dual-use. In fact, Steve Rabin, writing in *Game Programming Gems,* (Rabin01) notes that the three most important problems that the AI engine solves "automagically" are:

- Communication
- Behavioral modeling
- Event recording

Behavior modeling and event recording deal with providing a modeling system for the behavior of the objects, and their interactions with the system and other objects. Event recording addresses the storing of what each object has "thought" and the resulting actions, which is useful for error trapping.

MESSAGING SYSTEMS

The decision to design a communications system must be made early. Will it have poll-based or event-driven architecture? Simple games with very few objects can be built on the premise that an object can "poke" its environment to find out what is happening in the immediate vicinity. This is called polling. It is one way to provide passive communication between objects. In fact, it is not really communication at all, but is just a way for the objects to make decisions based on observations of their environment. It is quite easy to implement, since we only need to provide a way for the objects to interconnect, as we saw in Chapter 6.

However, polling becomes impractical when there are many objects in the system, since each one will need to be aware of all the others around it in order to know what effect they have had on each of these other objects, as well as the effect that each of these objects has had on it. In other words, polling is only practical with very few objects. Otherwise, the objects become pro-active, which is expensive in terms of processing time and complex in terms of design.

The alternative involves designing a messaging system based on events. Each object that causes an event will pass a message to the central AI engine, with details of that event. The central AI engine will decide which objects in the system need to have this message passed on to them. By passing the message through a central point of reference, they can be trapped and logged as necessary, and the whole system becomes easier to envisage and design.

The generic design of a robust messaging system requires a message definition and a router as a bare minimum. The router will accept input from all aspects of the game universe, but the designer will decide whether or not the AI communication system is distinct from the player-machine interface. In cases where the interface is provided for, we could have an object that represents, for example, a joystick. A message needs to have four basic elements:

1. Destination: Who the message is for.
2. Source: Who the message is from.
3. Event: What the message represents.
4. Parameters: Any optional data.

There are two ways to implement the routing system. The first is to assume that all objects will be able to determine what other objects inhabit their sphere of influence, and will be able to send them messages—for example, a missile landing in an area that is populated by tanks. Using the simplest routing method, the missile needs to generate a "hit" message for each of the tanks, as well as optional data indicating how hard each tank has been hit, possibly as a function of the distance between the missile and the tank. This places all the intelligence inside the missile, and the data cannot easily be re-used elsewhere.

The alternative is to place the intelligence inside the message router. By doing this, the router will receive a single message from the missile stating where it hit and how hard. The router will then need to *spawn* a series of other messages throughout the system, one for each of the tanks that are affected, in an intelligent manner.

This approach places the intelligence in a central location where it can be re-used. For example, we could add a bomb or even a bullet object that could use the same message, but with different parameters, and it would be treated in a slightly different way by the router. It saves a lot of duplicate code and makes the general design of the system easier to envisage, since it more closely matches the real world.

Beyond Event-Driven AI

Until now, the AI covered in this chapter has been event-driven. All of the previous examples have been related to an entity moving between various states—alive, moving, shooting, dead, looking, hiding—all are behavioral, in-game entity states.

Objects have similar states, and it is up to the state machine (FSM) to manage the transition between states, in response to events. Once in a state, of course, the object or entity can also emit messages through the system that indicate its current state. Transitioning between states then becomes a simple matter of sending the right message to the right object/entity to get the state machine to react. Is there an advancing enemy? The system sends the appropriate visual cue message to the entity, and it changes state.

The drawbacks are obvious. Each state is finite; the object/entity is either in it or it is not. Fuzzy FSMs might allow partial state changes or weighted selections between possible states, or even a newly connected, random state to be selected in order to make the behavior more natural. In the end, though, the AI is still state-driven. However, behind those states, we have the ability to implement another layer of AI, so that not only is the object or entity in a given state, but it is also able to do something unique in that state.

State-driven architectures are fine for behavioral models, but not as great for things like problem solving, prediction, pattern recognition, or path finding. So, a different approach is needed if we want the behavior to be both reasonably natural *and* capable in adapting to situations that go outside of the FSM architecture.

We can mimic trial-and-error behavior reinforcement with an FSM architecture. Put in simple terms, we can force the system to choose wisely based on experience by reviewing the outcome of a particular set of choices in a fuzzy FSM, and the likelihood of the same sequence occurring again is downgraded.

To do that, we must both store and recall the sequence. In design terms, this is not so straightforward, unless we have some better AI mechanisms. And there is another poor aspect of the FSM system: It cannot easily be used for prediction.

We do need the system to be able to predict. More-complex game designs, such as *Populous* or *Civilization*, require learning and prediction, because the opponents are controlled in an intelligent fashion. The more they can learn from mistakes made in the game—their own, their opponent's, and the player's—the better they will be able to react to actions by the opposition, each other, and the player.

FSM networks do not bring us this level of sophistication. They might play a part in the design, but they need to be leveraged hand in hand with other approaches that can store, recall, rebuild, and predict patterns. Fortunately, there are some very good design patterns that can be borrowed that enable us to implement these routines. They handle, among other things:

- Learning and recall of behavioral patterns.
- Prediction and move analysis.
- Path finding and weighted decision-making.

All of these use two specific techniques—neurons and neural networks. These are reasonably advanced concepts; from the design point of view, we can only scratch the surface. Before attempting to deploy any of these techniques in a video game, it would be a good idea to make sure the development team understands them fully. Otherwise, as we noted in at the beginning of this chapter, resources will be wasted, and the entire AI part of the project might be shelved.

Along with the terms adaptive/emergent behavior and group dynamics, networks rank high in the list of "buzzword" phrases that are likely to attract funding; but designing the AI around them and deploying them in a video game might be an entirely different matter. This is partly because the techniques rely on emergence to work, and they operate at different levels throughout the AI system. On the one hand, emergence is poorly understood, and on the other hand, both developers and designers presume that neural networks can in some way just be bolted on to the AI and used.

In fact, a lot of thought needs to go into choosing the level at which we will deploy the neural networks throughout the system. To do that, we need to understand what the purpose and capabilities of a neural network are. First, however, let us introduce the neuron.

NEURONS

A neuron is a single decision-making component in a biological neural network. It is reasonably sophisticated, being able to filter, select, and evaluate information that it receives through connections known as synapses, before passing information on.

We are going to simplify the biological model somewhat and consider how we can model this useful biological decision-making mechanism artificially. Since we are creating a model of a neuron, we shall call it a *node*. The first thing to consider when creating our nodes is what kind of input information they will take—usually very simple—just a signal value, usually binary, either 1 or 0, or in some cases a +1 or –1 value.

The first qualification is that the nodes can take multiple inputs. There are no hard and fast limits on the number of inputs that each one can accept, however a node should only produce a single output.

That output is a signal based on the weighted sum of the input data, coupled with its own internal latency. In other words, a node attaches different levels of importance to each incoming signal, adds up the weighted values, and then compares *that* result with a threshold value. Figure 12.2 shows the general schematic for a neuron, the basis for our nodes.

The power of our node is that we can train a single node to always reply with a positive response to a given set of weighted inputs. If we want to change the configuration so that the node replies more strongly to one of the inputs, we just adjust the weight of that input so that its value is given more importance in the equation.

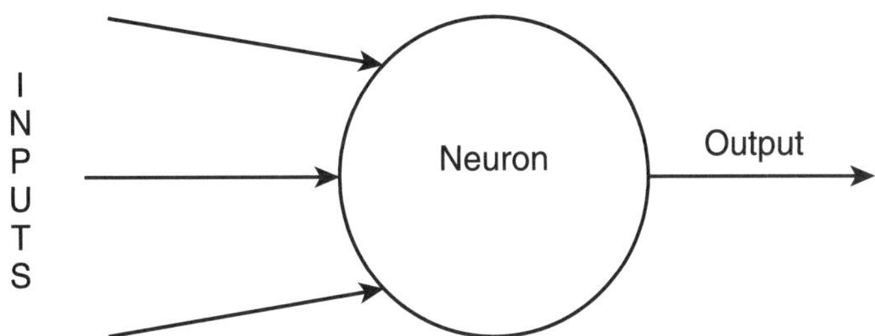

FIGURE 12.2 A neuron schematic.

This is like training an FSM. Imagine that there is a node at each decision point, whose weight is based on historical success or failure rates. We would like to use the node to decide what state we move into in the next time slice.

In this simple way, we can enhance our FSM decision-making apparatus, enabling it to respond in a given way, based on experience. Good decisions can be strengthened, and the FSM is trained accordingly. The FSM can also be put into a new situation in which the input values have never been used, and we can be fairly sure that the FSM will react appropriately. Now, imagine that a node has, as inputs, different results of different possible FSM networks. Suddenly, another layer of decision-making has been built up that allows for even more sophistication.

The FSM networks provide us with state-change information that can be evaluated together in order to trigger actions. This result may be fed into other FSMs or FSM networks. We can also feed information back to the nodes to indicate whether the choice was acceptable.

We can *train* the network to react in a given way in a given situation, and then apply the result to a new situation. The more training we give it, the better the output response will be in new situations. This is like having a simple neural network. The collective power of the nodes is greater than each, alone. The addition of nodes to FSMs and FSM networks moves the behavior from finite (or pre-scripted) to emergent. Suddenly, we can train related behaviors so that the network is capable of making informed decisions from a set of data, even if it is incomplete. What is more interesting, we can do this within a play session; the network of behaviors adapt as a direct result of gameplay.

The key is to allow the behavioral FSMs to affect each other at both the input and output levels. With these connections to the various behavioral states that we define, coupled with external inputs from in-game sensors—position, ammunition, health, range, energy, and so on—we can create emergent behavior.

This emergent behavior provides deeper gameplay. With only a few key concepts, we have moved into the upper stratosphere of game design. This is perhaps too advanced and on the edge of available resources for an FPS, but for a strategy or simulation game, emergent behavior is invaluable.

A true neural network operates almost in the same way, but allows for a few more useful, low-resource tricks. But before we throw all of our game design weight into FSM networks and nodes, let us take a look at the neural network proper.

Single-Layer Neural Networks

To recap, if we interconnect nodes along with inputs, we can create a sophisticated decision-making system. The preceding discussion put that in terms of FSMs and FSM networks, but this is only one way to use them. Another way is to make a simple row of neurons, couple all their inputs together, and read the outputs, as shown in Figure 12.3, which is a schematic of a biological neural network.

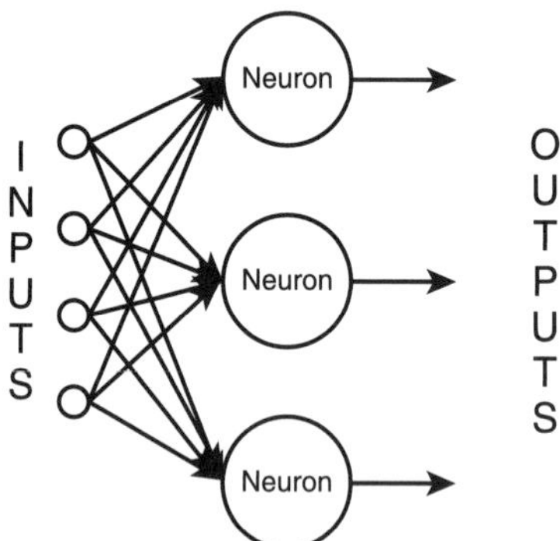

FIGURE 12.3 A single-layer neural network.

As before, all we need to do is adjust the weights on each node's input with respect to the desired output, and we can train the network to produce *multiple* responses from a set of inputs. This seems abstract, but it is really very simple. We know what the input sensors are telling us (this is the input pattern), and we know how we want the output pattern to be. In Figure 12.3, we have 4 inputs and 3 outputs, but these could equally well have been 35 and 2, respectively. What is important is that we have as many nodes as we have outputs, and that we have some way of measuring those outputs against something we know.

Let us pretend that we have two nodes that are designed to tell us the difference between two patterns—pattern A and pattern B—and that the inputs represent a kind of eye, broken up into cells. Each cell is connected to an input and is either on (1) or off (0).

We want one neuron to fire for pattern A and the other for pattern B. So, we set the weights attached to the inputs for each node to a random starting point between 0 and 1, each (that's 35 inputs for each node, so 35 weights for each one).

Then, the cells that represent the pattern components are connected to *both* node X and node Y at the same time, through the inputs. We show the network a pattern, and based on the sum of the weights attached to these input signals, one node, the other, or both of the nodes may produce a positive result (akin to the neuron firing).

We then measure the output signal from each node and check it against the pattern identifier. For example, if we want pattern A to yield a 1 on output X, we compare the actual output with 1. We also compare the output Y to 0, since we do not want it to fire.

Next, we use the difference between actual and desired results to adjust the weights on node X's inputs slightly, so that we raise the signal importance from the cells that have produced a signal. At the same time, we could lower the weights slightly for those that do not produce a signal, although at this stage it is optional.

After having done that for node X, the next step is to do the same for node Y, which should be producing a "0" signal.

We then feed the difference back through the weights so that each weight with an incoming signal is increased in importance, but with respect to –1 rather than the +1 value we used for node X.

The reason we use –1 for node Y, and not 0 is because multiplying by 0 would yield 0, rather than a true adjustment. Since we want to train the network to positively produce an output of 0, we need to use –1 as the multiplication factor.

Finally, we test again, and keep testing until we get the result that we are looking for. Each time, we present either of the two patterns and adjust the weights with respect to the node that we want to fire. At a certain point in time, the actual result will be close enough to the desired result that we can stop. At this point we introduce pattern C. Pattern C looks a little like pattern A, but is not quite the same. If we measure the results of this on the outputs from node X and Y, we will probably find that there is a better than 50% chance that the pattern is pattern A. This behavior allows us to approximate situations and generate a reasonable response.

In game design, we replace the pattern of cells with the parts of the game universe that we are able to measure. Rather than simply using the network for visual pattern recognition, we feed it actual game data. This becomes the *context*, and the outputs from the nodes become the reaction to that context in terms of in-game settings or actions. In a game session, these reactions can be the preferred behavior or just training data used to create a pattern-recognition system.

This is quite a leap. We have moved from some abstract pattern recognition to actually creating something that has in-game meaning. The best way to approach this from the design point of view is to think of it as a kind of contextual training system.

If the output signals are to be the preferred behavior—that is, we have matched the contextual patterns to output actions or settings—we can train the network during play-testing to arrive at that point. We only need to play-test the system properly.

On the other hand, we could treat those outputs as part of the training data. In this case, we can attempt to reinforce the behavior during automatic (unsupervised) training if we know the cause and effect. The upside of this is that we no longer need to spend as much time playing the game to train the networks. They will train themselves through many simulated game sessions. This needs to be part of the design, however, as the implementation needs to allow it. It is not complicated, just something that we need to make sure is taken care of.

Finally, in the play session, itself, the same theory can be used to train the system to recognize player actions as a consequence of the *context* and use that information in a predictive fashion. That is, we train the network to outwit the player by seeing how the player reacts in a given situation.

Of course, this requires that we create a mapping *from* the context *to* the player, or even in-game entity actions. Therefore, it again needs to be addressed as part of the design. These actions could be triggered FSMs that model discrete or fuzzy behavior, or they could be something else entirely based on the AI model. This approach taken one step further is called "associative memory," which uses a whole array of nodes to reconstruct patterns from lossy input—that is, input where something has been removed.

Associative Memory

The general reinforcement that we have seen so far is similar to what is called a "Hopfield network." This is a special kind of auto-associative neural network. In other words, it can teach itself. An array of nodes is used, whose inputs are fed by their outputs, as well as a starting configuration. The outputs are also used as a signal that can be read to feed the inputs.

When we provide a pattern to the inputs over and over again, the network learns the configuration. Each node learns what it must do to reconstruct the pattern that has been established. If we then give it a partial pattern, it can reconstruct the pattern in its entirety, tending toward stability.

So, we keep running the network until the outputs stop changing significantly. At this point, the pattern should have stabilized, and if there was enough input data, the pattern should be the same as, or very close to, the original.

This is self-associative memory and is useful in video game design, because it allows us to insert AI that is more or less able to be trained in very complex input patterns. In other words, if we have a number of these simple memories, we can recall and *reconstruct* things from parameter settings to behavioral modes. In addition, we can split the input pattern into a collection of parameters and results. So, some of the pattern would be parameters, and some would be results. This context might represent a state of affairs that is desirable—one that we might want to bring about again.

The parameters are the cause and the results are the effect. For example, if we assume that we are playing *SimCity*, and we know that certain monies spent on improvements will yield an increase in income from a rise in population, then we can set up the cause and effect in a Hopfield network.

If we only have half of the parameters and half of the results in another play session, we can find out what parameters need to be set to achieve those results—or, conversely, what results will likely occur from given parameters. This might not sound powerful, but taken one step further, a similar mapping of cause and effect can be used in a strategy game. The situation might arise in which we want half of one set of results and half of another.

So, we set the results, run the network, and pull off the outputs that are to be parameters—the parameters we need to set. And, if there are any deviations from our desired results, they can be read from the output of the nodes that are attached to the effect.

To leverage this requires that we create the array of inputs correctly. Consequently, it must be addressed as part of the design of the game from the outset. Understanding how it works is only the first step. The next step is to consider the patterns separately—that is, cause and effect as two layers of nodes. This is where the technical terms begin. Plainly put, we would like a layer of input nodes connected via weights to a layer of output nodes.

When an input pattern and an output pattern are presented, the algorithm sets the weights as the product of a comparison between the two signals. We simply multiply one by the other, and use that as the weight—re-based on a –1 or +1 value (binary), as before.

If we do this *just once*, then the network can be set to a state where, given a partial pattern on one of the inputs, such as a set of parameters or results, the network can stabilize on an appropriate set of patterns. It will oscillate between the two patterns, and missing information will be added until both patterns have stabilized.

Of course, although the system will try to *attract* a specific configuration, there is no guarantee that it will be the correct pair of patterns. As mentioned, that is largely a product of the amount of input data the network has to work with.

It is the responsibility of the game designer to make sure that when this happens, the result is not the kind of irritating behavior noted at the beginning of this chapter. AI is notorious for misbehaving. Correct management, however, can make designing AI easier.

The kind of responsibility attached to AI can make designers shelve some good ideas quite early on, but it is worth persevering. You should now be reasonably well prepared to know what would be asked of the developers in order to translate the design into reality. And if this isn't complex enough, there are also multilayer networks that can add more sophistication to the basic reinforcement and associative decision-making/associative memory paradigm. This will be our last foray into theory before looking at a more concrete example that uses guided decision-making as a basis.

Multilayer Neural Networks

A multilayer network consists of input, hidden, and output layers. In a single-layer neural network, we can just connect the nodes to themselves or each other, whereas a multilayer network requires that we cross-connect outputs to inputs of other nodes, as shown in Figure 12.4.

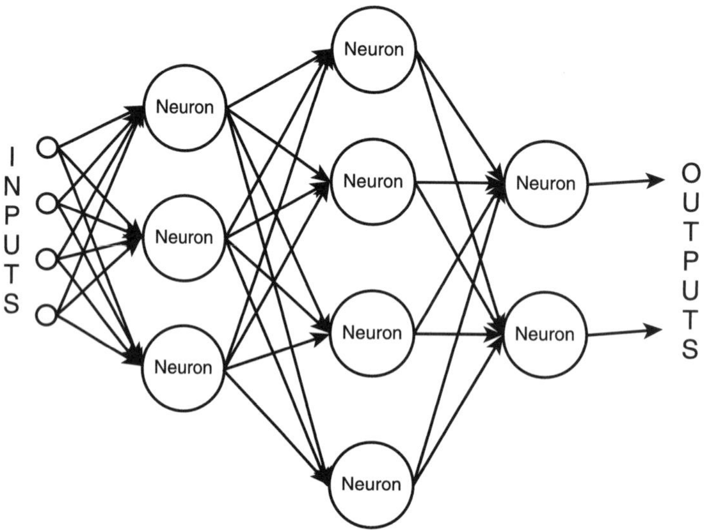

FIGURE 12.4 A multilayer neural network.

Notice that the nodes are connected together by weighted inputs and fire outputs. Each node has an internal function that limits the result of the weighed sum of its inputs, as before. This time, however, we have additional layers of nodes in which the *inputs* are the *outputs* of every other node in the preceding layer.

Yes, this is complex, and the behavior is strictly emergent—that is, sometimes it is not possible to derive the output from the input. This is also very hard to deploy in video games; we need to be careful that the result does not descend into chaos.

In addition, we have to consider that each network will take a lot of memory and processing resources. This makes them slightly more difficult to sell as part of a design. They sound impressive, they work well, but they can hog resources. On the other hand, they can be used to help train other networks in the design and development phases, and only fully trained, single-layer versions need be deployed in the actual game.

These kinds of networks tend to be quite good at predicting and recognizing, as well as helping reasoning systems to achieve a final result in new situations, based on previous input and output patterns. Training them might take a while, but they are very adaptive, given the right design.

There are a couple of crucial points here: deciding what inputs we want to map to what outputs (and they can be different in number) as well as how many nodes we want in the hidden layer. All of these need to be fed into the design and can only be answered by looking at the amount of input and output data we have in the game.

Training is done through back-propagation. In other words, we feed the error levels (actual versus desired results) back through the network and adjust the weights on each node's input. Again, this is like traditional feedback.

When a multilayer network is trained, inputs are put on one side, and the output of the entire network is tested. The next step is to feed the offset of actual versus desired signal strengths back through each layer until the weights have been adjusted appropriately. The exact formulas for doing this are beyond the scope of this book. This is, after all, a design guide and not a computer science manual. The designer can satisfy himself that his implementation is possible by talking to a developer.

In video game designs, using a multilayer neural network means that if there is a set of inputs (behavior) and a set of outputs (parameters or context), the network can be trained to reproduce one from the other. This means that we can present the network with the result and have it give us the likely cause, or we can present it with the cause and have it predict the result.

Coupled with FSMs to guide the discrete behavior, we can build up some realistic behavioral patterns from either being directly instructed (trained) or by watching the player. It is the combination of the network with other pieces of AI logic that will more likely produce the final result, rather than the network itself. After all, our brains just instruct. We have biological FSMs built in to our reasoning systems, along with all kinds of distributed behavior, such as muscle memory, which provide the actual response to those instructions. If we choose to leverage this kind of network in the design, complexity will be added, but so will a depth of gameplay that will provide a higher quality experience for the player.

By way of adding some more examples to the abstract discussion, Pavlovian responses are an example of biological FSMs. Pavlov conducted experiments whereby he would ring a bell and feed his dogs. Each time he did so, he was training their biological neural networks to respond in a certain way to the sound of the bell. They would salivate in anticipation of a meal.

After a time, he noted that, when he rang the bell, that was sufficient to spark the salivation by itself. Even without food, the dogs' neural networks produced the same result.

Guided Decision-Making

It is now time to look at AI that is a bit more practical. Guided decision-making, also known as expert systems, is a way to leverage all of the techniques we have looked at so far and write them into the design paradigm of one example.

Guided decision-making is based on asking a series of questions, and the system tries to figure out an answer by sequentially narrowing down the options. This is much like the game 20 questions; each answer narrows down the possibilities, and the trick is to know what *question* to ask next.

This is where the neural network can help. It eliminates fruitless questions, based on previous answers. For example, if the answer to the question "Is it green?" is "Yes," the network will thereafter not ask dumb questions, such as "Is it yellow?" The combination of paring down the network and reinforcement helps to create a sophisticated decision-making engine.

In addition, reinforcement can be used to create a system of weights that do not require a neural network, but are made up of chains of nodes. In this way, some of the decision chains that might make up a primitive animal's own expert system can be emulated.

Each node has inputs and outputs, and the selection of an output is based on a weighted decision. It is like having a multilayer neural network, but with many little subnetworks. Each one responds to a layer of inputs with a layer of possible outputs, from which we choose the noisiest—or the most likely correct choice.

This approach can become a bit more clever if the result is then fed into a node or network, along with the answers to other questions. The network then figures out which question to ask next. If the wrong question is asked—that is, the reply is "No"—then this data is fed back into the network, making it self- or auto-associative. By itself, this is effective, but it can be quite hard to design and implement, so some exploration is needed in order to make the best use of the theories.

Easier systems do exist, which explore all of the problems in search of the correct answer. These often require building a tree of all possible solutions and then paring down to the most likely sequence of events. The problem is that in a game like 20 questions, the tree is always growing—unlike like in chess, where there are always a finite number of possible moves/combinations from a given point.

However, we can use A-B pruning and backtracking to reduce the workload. These two techniques go slightly beyond the immediate scope of this book, but again, it is useful to know that they are available when designing game AI.

A-B pruning removes less-effective branches of the decision tree by using a special formula. This formula is outside of the design realm, but we need to know that it exists in order to communicate our expectations to the programmer. The second technique, backtracking, allows us to reverse a simulated decision and choose another one, while marking the old decision as bad. Most programming techniques that are designed to make use of a problem-space search implement backtracking as a way to roll back a decision.

Guided decision-making by itself is good, but it can be restrictive in the same way that an FSM is. A whole network of known options can be created, but as soon as something occurs that we are not prepared for, then it becomes harder to choose an appropriate response. To make the decision network more open, weighted options and some form of emergent gameplay should allow the system to make mistakes—but also learn from them. This is where the sum of all the theories in this chapter, put into practice, begins to pay dividends.

SUMMARY

The video game's complexity will govern how concerned the designer is over the systems that underpin its required AI. Simple shoot-em-ups do not require much intelligence, and state machines might even over-complicate simple fire-and-forget systems, such as in classic games like *Space Invaders* or *Centipede.*

However, it pays to think about the underlying communication system, even for simple games, because if the designer ever wants to take the game from single- to multiplayer, it helps to have a good messaging system as the backbone. Human players are largely unpredictable; they respect rules, but in a "fuzzy" way. The result is that without a robust messaging system, we would have to try and second-guess what the players are likely to do, and plan for every eventuality.

Combining fuzzy control methods with state machines and a good message routing system will enable the game to be extended easily, as well as ensure that the introduction of multiple human players will not cause the system to become unstable. For those designers specifically gearing their product toward a multiplayer market, the choice should by now be made.

As with other aspects of video game design discussed throughout this book, AI systems have to be applied with a certain amount of restraint. The enemies need to be clever, but not so clever that they detract from the enjoyment of the game. The closer the game steps toward simulation, the less enjoyable it might become.

One last word—no cheating. It is tempting to use tricks to simulate intelligence by allowing the game-controlling AI to have knowledge of the system that it should not have. For example, instead of designing a system in which the enemies exhibit cautious intelligence, the designer might be tempted to cut corners and allow them to see through walls, instead. But gamers aren't stupid. The player will eventually figure out where these shortcuts are, and will not be impressed. In fact, it will probably tarnish the reputations of the studio and the publisher. AI is also one of the most difficult areas to get right in video game design. In general, light AI is better than an AI that makes mistakes, cheats, or is badly implemented. A dumb game is better than a flawed game.

REFERENCES

[EDGE01] *EDGE* magazine. Future Publishing, November 2002, p. 34.

[EDGE02] *EDGE* magazine. Future Publishing, November 2002, p. 34.

[EDGE03] *EDGE* magazine. Future Publishing, October 2002, p. 94.

[Rabin01] *Game Programming Gems*, Edited by Mark DeLoura, Charles River Media, 2000, p. 221.

[SEATTLE01] Seattle Robotics Society Web site, http://www.seattlerobotics.org/encoder/mar98/fuz/fl_part1.html#WHAT%20IS%20FUZZY%20LOGIC?

13 The Official Design Document

In This Chapter

- Target Audience
- Content
- The Waiting Game

The game is designed. There is a demonstration version, albeit a shadow of the original vision, and we even have a Design Document (probably based on someone else's template). This document makes for wonderful planning and coordination, but it will never sell the game. This is the job of the Official Design Document. It will sell the game idea to prospective financial backers, and encourage future team members to share the vision and get involved. The document needs to be concise, well written, and get the principle idea across early on in order to grab the reader's attention and keep him interested.

The Official Design Document will showcase the design talent and capture the imagination, while remaining realistic in terms of what can be achieved. It will also be used as a template to build the game on, so the document had better be well thought out and workable.

You might have to make some changes when looking for funding; the first stab at the design is likely to be over-ambitious. In fact, many games never make it past an advanced demonstration version, simply because the Design Document called for something that was impractical, given the resources available.

Even for independent developers who are not actively seeking direct funding, a publisher will likely be involved to assist in marketing—getting the game into the hands of gamers. Some of the more recent advances in distribution help, such as the *Steam* channel by Valve and Xbox Live Arcade by Microsoft, but they still come with a cost. Finding that perfect team, investor, and/or distribution match will start with the Official Design Document.

Target Audience

According to Mitzi McGilvray (Electronic Arts), the Design Document is aimed at production, marketing, and programming staff. She states that:

> ". . . it should contain a way for production and marketing to understand and plan for what the game is intended to be, and a blueprint for programmers to create the code for the game . . ." [McGilvray01]

The first part is obvious, but her second point is less applicable to the focus of this book. In Chapter 3, we discussed the Design Document and its relevance to those actually making the game. The Official Design Document has to convey the content of the more technical Design Document proposed in previous chapters, in a way that is accessible by everyone.

Always remember that the best way to ensure that nobody will see your masterpiece is to send it as an unsolicited email attachment with a subject line that reads, "To the Attention of the Head Producer." In addition to being presumptuous and ill-mannered, and assuming that it isn't immediately relegated to the Deleted Items or Spam Heaven folder, your email will have to contend with a mountain of other submissions by game industry hopefuls.

Game publishers are very busy people. Even if you contacted them and they expressed an interest in your game's genre, they will not have time to read the entire Official Design Document, just to get a good idea of what the game is about. Instead, furnish them with a package that is negotiable—not an all-or-nothing proposition. For example, the cover sheet could contain a sample of what might be on the back of the finished product's box, complete with mock-up screenshots and a list of the key properties of the game. There also needs to be a reduced, consumer-friendly version of the game's central theme. Later on, we'll come back to the exact way in which this should be written.

The overview needs to convince the reader to read further. The first person to see the package might be a decision-maker in the publishing company, so it is important that it shines.

The next thing that your audience will be interested in is a CD. These days, it is much easier and cheaper to put a presentation on CD than to submit hard copy for reading. Therefore, an autoplay CD is recommended. It could start with a menu screen that lists the contents of the CD. Any movie demos that have been made should be first on the list (the attention grabbers). But remember, busy people do not have time to fiddle around through a multilayered menu system. They just want to press the Enter key, so keep the menu simple.

The final thing to remember about your target audience (the decision-makers) is that they love eye candy. Any technical analysis of the Design Document will probably be left to other members of their staff. They are marketing people (perhaps with a technical streak), and their prime interest is in finding games that will *sell,* technically excellent or not.

(One of the absolute best ways to get yourself into a position to actually hand your Design *to* someone is to know that person—or know someone who does. So, many budding game designers will get a foot in the door through association; make some friends in the industry, and you may well find yourself in a favorable position!)

Choosing Your Market

Choose your publisher wisely. Do not send a first-person shooter design to a company that is known only for producing sports titles, and it is unlikely that a company that usually publishes first-person shooters will be interested in a driving game. Each publisher knows their niche market(s) and the best products for it; this is common to all industries. They know their market so well that they are guaranteed a certain amount of success simply on reputation alone and the product's presentation on the shelf.

There are exceptions. EA has become known for sports titles, but it is surprising what their catalog offers from time to time. Publishers tend to follow the market, and they have become very good at latching on to trends within the gaming market.

This means that designers also have to take the market into account. Publishers will be more likely to be interested in a title that:

- Uses existing technology,
- Leverages trends in recently popular game niches, or
- Presents an original angle.

They are less likely to take on a new platform or a game idea that has never been tried, even if its premise seems safe and traditional. This is especially true of proposals from first-time designers.

That first project should minimize risk—which we have mentioned before and will mention again . . . and again. The risk of non-implementation should be low. The risk that the market will ignore the title should be low. Above all, the risk that the game never sees the light of day should be low. A first-time designer/developer is a high enough risk. The Official Design Document should not compound that risk by trying to carve out a new market. It is fine to have an original idea and premise, but an established market should come first.

Team Versus Designer

Publishers like teams and are much less accommodating to individual designers or programmers hacking away at their games in their bedrooms. If a polished demo can be put together, then that individual may have a much better chance, but the hard, cold facts are that there are many games waiting to be written, all at least as good as yours, and some far better. Publishers have the pick of the bunch.

A solid team can help to provide some assurances that the lone designer might not; it spreads the risk and helps provide balance. Each team member will have an area of specialty, and many people can be a little wary of teams of one person trying to do everything themselves.

Therefore, a single game designer will need at some point to build a team. If this is done before the idea goes to the publisher, then he needs to have the commitment of the team so that this can conveyed to the publisher.

On the other hand, if the designer specifies that a team will be required in the Official Design Document, then this lets the publisher know that the designer lives in the "real world" and is not just another "bedroom coder." Be aware, though, that building a team might take longer than the publisher will like. The publisher might suggest working with a studio that they have a good relationship with. Some publishers (usually the huge ones, like Sega) affiliate themselves with video game studios or have their own in-house teams. Therefore, they will have no problem finding talent—if the game is good enough. Development will probably be cheaper, as well; and publishers are very aware of this.

So, there is a strategy to choosing a publisher, and since the package has to be polished, do not expect to simply flood the top 100 publishers in the industry and come up with a taker. In this industry, well-applied marketing outperforms a brute-force approach, and it is far cheaper.

Structure

The best way to deliver the Official Design Document is with a paper version plus a CD, which should (in a perfect world) contain some artwork, real game code (such as a prototype built with a free tool), and some other assets, such as some audio tracks or full-motion video clips. If you can put the whole lot in one of those nice, glossy cardboard portfolios, then that's even better.

Professionalism is the watchword. The structure has to be right, the delivery has to be right, and the supporting material has to be credible. The more advanced the prototype (or interactive design) is, the greater the chance that a publisher/investor will pick up the project.

In addition, having something concrete to look at is a good way to motivate the programmers. Even if the end result is self-published shareware delivered via the Internet, the further we can push the dream in the Official Design Document, the greater our chances of making something great.

So, put together something that the team can be proud of, and put it in their hands. That way, you have a reminder and reference point when the project's direction seems too hard or lost.

Content

Each section of the Official Design Document package has to be carefully documented so that it is easy to read while conveying the designer's passion for the project. We will now take a look at exactly how the paper documentation should be written in order to retain the reader's full attention and help him to believe that the project is not only possible, but also sellable.

The Overview

The purpose of the Overview is to grab the publisher's attention, so it is worth getting a good artist to create mock-up screens, and possibly even hire a professional copywriter to reduce the game's plot and central theme to a polished piece of prose.

Some of the research you can do is to take a look at the retail boxes in your local video game store. Try to figure out what aspects of a game's box makes you want to buy the game or not. Active language, for example, is key to writing marketing copy that jumps out and grabs the reader.

Active language in this case includes verbs that instill a sense of action—of doing something—rather than a description of what can be done. For example:

"The Terrain tool can be used to create mountains."	Passive
"Create mountains with the Terrain tool."	Active

Generally speaking, a passive phrase describes, while an active phrase causes the reader to envisage actually doing. A list of active verbs (in the past tense) can be found at the University of Texas Career Services Center (http://www.utexas.edu/ssw/dccs/handouts.html) and is a great starting point for anyone creating active language phrases.

A good place to start is to use the tagline from the game Design Document as a subtitle. This example is taken from the back of the *SimCity 4* box:

"Build and run
your own city."

The formatting and font sizes are intentional. They draw the reader's eyes toward the key words in the tagline "Build," "run," "your," "city." Gamers are attracted to active verbs, such as build and run, as well as the promise that they can personalize the game and actually own part of it. Finally, the goal of the game (the "city") is also in a slightly larger font. Compare this with the following:

"Build and run your own city."

Other subtitles from the back of this particular box:

"PLAY GOD"
"PLAY MAYOR"
"PLAY WITH YOUR SIMS"

Note the emphasis on the word play, coupled with the three major elements of the game. Each of the phrases is followed by a bulleted list of features and a screenshot. The layout is also important. Figure 13.1 is a sample box back, based on the *SimCity 4* box layout.

The box is designed simply enough to appeal to all ages. On the other hand, a strictly adult title, such as *Soldier of Fortune 2: Double Helix*, might have an altogether busier design, as shown in Figure 13.2.

In this type of box design, there are many text boxes to read, each of which sings the praises of the game's advanced features. The graphics should be photorealistic, instead of screenshots. This implies the cinematic nature of the game, something that adult gamers appreciate more than children do.

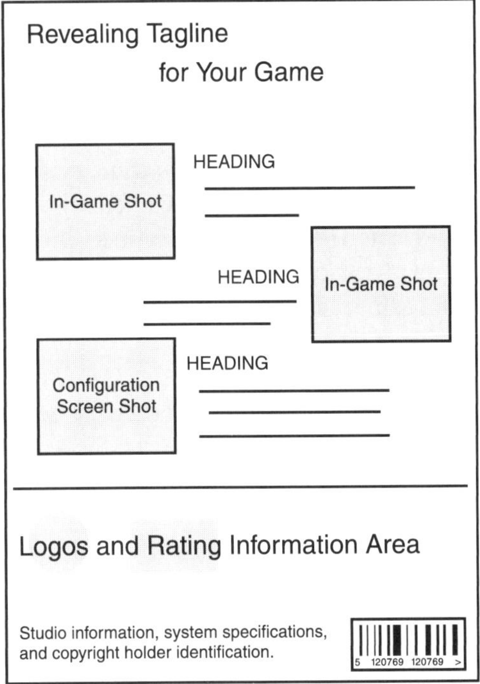

FIGURE 13.1 Sample of simple back-of-box layout.

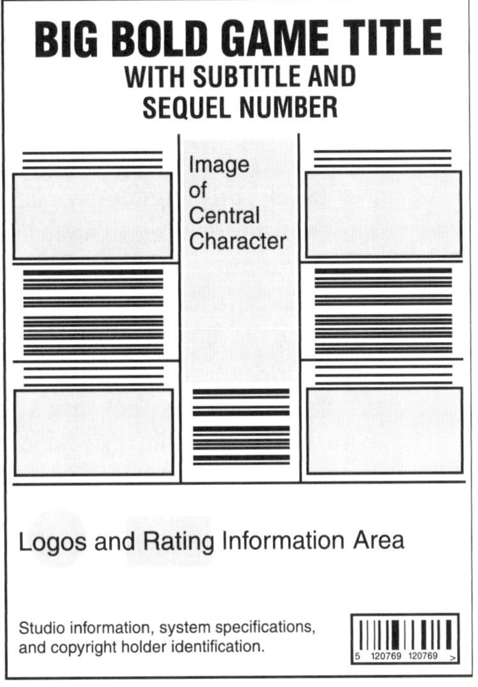

FIGURE 13.2 Sample of complex back-of-box layout.

When making a Summary Sheet, the equivalent to a back-of-box layout, there is no need to isolate the lower area for the logo, rating, and price information. The sheet will look like the top two-thirds of the examples in Figures 13.1 and 13.2. When putting the text in, try to emphasize features that will make the game stand out from the competition. Here are some examples from recent games:

- "Actually control the flow of time."—*Blinx: Timesweeper*
- "Random Mission Generator!"—*SOFII: Double Helix*
- "Swap your cities with friends…"—*SimCity 4*

Be careful with using these kinds of phrases, however. You will need to back them up with suitable examples from the game design, itself. Never try to pull a fast one on publishers; they have seen it all before, and are especially wary of a first-time game designer.

Story

The next sheet to include should cover the main storyline—the game's plot. In some cases this may seem unnecessary. Simple games do not, at first glance, seem to require much of a plot; but simple games are also less likely to attract the attention of a publisher, so it is best to try to have a sheet that explains the game's context.

Ideally, this should be broken down into three parts: prehistory, current history, and the future (the end game). The prehistory section sets the game in a specific time that is relevant to both the real world and the play-session game environment. In this way, the reader can link his own reality to the game, suspend that reality, and enter the game universe.

So, we will end up with sections with labels such as Game Set-Up, Game Play & Objectives, Overview, and so on. These are terms that publishers feel at home with, but then need to get the sense of immersion as well as the sense that the writer of the Design Document knows what he is talking about. After all, it's as much for him as it is for you.

Though this might sound a bit like a psychology lecture, it is important to realize that video games are increasingly compared to the movie industry and similarly require the player to enter a game universe that does not necessarily parallel his familiar, real world. The reader has to be gently eased into these new surroundings, and a little bit of prose is valuable in setting up a segue into your game universe.

One memorable example was the game *Elite,* which shipped with a book called *The Dark Wheel.* The book used a story to provide an overview of the game universe, and the game included a *Space Traders Flight Training Manual,* which instructed the player on how the game was to be played.

The Dark Wheel situates the player in the game universe. The player has been left a spacecraft and some money by an uncle as a deathbed gift. The first page of the manual could have been lifted directly from the Design Document's story page:

> "Welcome aboard this Cobra Mk III trading and combat craft. The ship has been supplied to you by Faulcon deLacy Spaceways, by arrangement with the Galactic Co-operative of Worlds whose Space and Interstellar Pilot's Exams you have just successfully completed."

After reading this, the player has been neatly transported to a universe whose rules, politics, and even spacecraft manufacturers are quite clear. It paints a picture of interstellar travel, introduces the two main facets of the game (trading and combat), and hints at the player's achievements (Space and Interstellar Pilot's Exams) before actually entering the game proper.

Similarly, this snippet from the *SOFII: Double Helix* manual is also a good example of narrative that is designed to give some historic context that the reader can use to situate himself in the gaming environment:

> "After a long and distinguished career in the Army's Special Forces, you're now in business for yourself, taking most of your contracts from a secret organization known as The Shop. Together with your old friend Sam Gladstone and your partner, Madeline Taylor, you combat terrorism around the globe." [Activision02]

Following the short history, the current situation is explained to the player so that he can locate his missions within this new context. Reality has been temporarily suspended in favor of the game universe, and the player can now explore the task at hand:

> "Your mission: root out the terrorist organization, uncover their secret plans, put a stop to their operation and bring their leader to justice." [Ibid.]

There obviously needs to be a little more than just this phrase in the middle of the story page, but its purpose is to state the player's predicament in a way that engages him. The nature of storytelling can be described as: Take the hero, put him in a tree, throw stones at him, and get him out again.

The prehistory part of the story document puts the hero into the tree, and explains who the hero is and what the tree looks like. The current history section defines the stones that will be thrown at the hero. In the case of *SOFII,* it is a terrorist organization; in *Elite,* it is survival, and the struggle to accumulate money and weapons without being shot out of the sky.

The final part of the story page deals with how the hero will be rescued from the tree and crowned king of the game universe. In *Elite*, this takes the form of an invitation by the powers that be to engage in several missions, once the player has reached Elite status in the game universe. Many games are open-ended in this respect (leaving their plots amiable to sequels), but the final part of the story sheet must spell out the features of the game that will either help the player complete the game or highlight features that will keep the player coming back for more, even though there is no concrete goal (replayability).

For those worrying about how this will look to a developer or publisher, it is important to convey a sense that the designer knows what must go into the game. However, if he loses interest due to the weight of reading that he is being forced to do, then your chances of success with him will be slim.

So, try to condense the whole gaming experience into a single paragraph, and have a good demo to hand out if at all possible. These improve the chances, and the Official Design Document will back you up. Anything that you can do to *show* progress, rather than just claiming it, will help your case.

Characters and Entities

Once the story has been set out, certain facets will need explaining. These fall into two categories: the characters behind the plot, and the various entities (places and objects) that will be encountered along the way.

Provide a bit of history for each of the characters, define friends and foes, and give some general descriptions of the tools that the player can use to complete the game, as well as rough descriptions of the settings that the player will find himself in. Again, this should be brief—for example, an excerpt from an imaginary user's guide and certainly no more than one or two pages long. An active voice can be waived in favor of descriptive sentences that pull the reader into the atmosphere of the game. Some specifics can be left out in order to create an air of mystery, but there should be no unanswered questions.

As a rule, first describe the player character in full, then the role of any helpers (there should be no more than two or three) and a description of the opposition. Bear in mind that humans have a short-term memory capacity that can only handle four to seven items at any one time, and it is important that the reader does not have to backtrack when reading the descriptions of characters/objects—otherwise, the spell is broken.

Level Descriptions and Game Mechanics

The reader is now situated in the game universe. We have explained what is expected of the player, the background of his character, and some details about game objects and locations—so it is time to talk about the specific mechanics of the game. It is important to describe as many unique aspects of the game as possible within a single page of text.

There will not be enough space to cover every aspect of the game; that is reserved for the Design Document, which is a detailed description of the entire game. In this part of the Official Design Document, we are trying to spotlight the features that make our game so special.

Recently, Sony released *The Getaway* for PS2. Its storyline involves stealing cars, driving them to different locations, and killing crooked cops. This description does the game a slight injustice, since the gameplay is a bit more complex; the lead character's son is kidnapped by a local crime boss, and players have the ability to play the parts of two characters by completing sets of missions.

While this had already been done by various games, such as *Grand Theft Auto* and *Driver,* an aspect of *The Getaway* makes the game unique; it takes place in a reasonably accurate rendition of London, U.K. From a marketing point of view, this provides the intrigue that a publisher will find hard to resist.

In addition, there is the promise of cinematic elements, such as camera angles that make the gameplay more like an interactive movie than a video game. Sadly though, according to *EDGE* magazine, the overall effect was less than perfect:

> "[The camera] twists in directions which might well be cinematic, but which aren't necessarily conducive to seeing who's shooting you in the chest." [EDGE03]

. . . Which just goes to show, game features that might look really impressive in the Design Document do not necessarily translate well to the gaming universe. On the other hand, there always needs to be something that will set your game apart from the crowd. *The Getaway* has a realistic street map of London, *Wolfenstein3D* had the ability to play through the eyes of the lead character, *SimCity* was unique in its accurate simulation of a city's growth—and your game also needs a "hook."

PLANNING

Games take a long time to produce, and publishers tend to think in terms of years, which may seem a little frustrating to a game designer. It pays to provide some realistic planning documentation to support your project, however. *The Getaway* took about two and a half years to produce from its first proposal to the polished product. Using existing technology for the game will help reduce the time needed for production, but it pays to overestimate slightly.

(The quicker a game can get to market, and the cheaper the whole exercise is, the better—from the point of view of the publisher, at least. While there are plenty of studios taking more than a year to develop a game, from start to finish, publishers ideally prefer to think in terms of under a year from the start of *their involvement.*)

Clearly, planning will comprise the amount of work that has been done in order to produce the fruits of Design Document. If a demo version has been created, then the publisher can assume that the mechanics and some of the assets are already in place, which will help.

There are no rules to estimating the time it will take to develop the game. The designer must rely on his best judgment and sixth sense. Contacting the artists, for example, will prove an advantage, because they can offer their opinions on how long it will take to provide the game's artwork, and this can be used as a yardstick for estimating the actual amount of work that will be required.

But, and it's a big but, the publisher will hold you to it. When the money is gone, the money is gone, so be very sure of the estimates before even approaching the publisher. It's all well and good to have a yardstick to measure by, but never make the mistake of thinking that a publisher looks much beyond the cost of its investment.

By a similar token, programmers and sound engineers can be asked for their estimations. As the game designer, and by researching the production histories of similar games, it should be reasonably easy to forecast how long it might take to create some workable designs for the user interface and game mechanics.

Then there is the integration of the game engine code, the scripting required for game object behavior, and the merging in of all the art and sound effects—not to mention phases for testing, balancing, bug location and removal, more testing, and production of box artwork, user guides, and a final field testing. Some of these tasks can be performed in parallel, others need to be done one step at a time, while still others can be attended to while team members wait on artwork, missing object scripts, and other inevitable delays. Again, it pays to overestimate, but there are no clear rules.

The producer will probably have a different opinion on production schedules, but if you provide some carefully considered information, it shows that you have at least put some serious thought into realistic planning for the product based on your experience (limited though that might be). This will greatly impress the publisher.

By the way, the producer, as we shall see later on, is the one who is responsible for making sure that the game gets made within budget, time, and to the correct level of quality. He will probably be assigned after the project has been cleared to proceed.

Milestones should be established, as was done with the Design Document in Chapter 3. Again, it proves that the designer has thought about the phases that need to take place, how they will be arranged, and what the dependencies are. It proves to the publisher that the designer is a "professional."

The Team

We have already stated that publishers are more amicable to team-oriented projects than lone game developers. Even if a team is not already in place, a part of the Official Design Document should at least lay out expected workforce sizes. Check the credit list for a game such as *SimCity 4* and you will find that the larger the publisher/studio is, the longer the staff roster will be.

Generally, try to describe a team that handles the main tasks of production—level design, programming, artwork, sound, production, and quality assurance. Also, this is a good time to point out some of the more technical aspects of the game, such as any needed special graphics programming that will be platform-dependent.

Finally, it is a good idea to anticipate any specialized engineers that might be needed in order to satisfy the requirements of a specific platform. This includes special controllers, networking, storage media, or other peripherals. One recent game was designed to work with both consoles as well as handhelds. Clearly, this required some level of specific engineering to bring the product to market. If these kinds of issues are not well understood and spelled out, they will be singled out by the investor/publisher, who will be very unwilling to fund research into "fuzzy" design areas. So, outlining a team with the right people to help with more-specialized areas of the game will be part of putting together a winning proposal.

The Storyboard

The final element of the package might or might not be included, depending on whether you furnish a CD that has directly rendered game sequences or a full-motion video mock-up. A storyboard shows some key sequences from the game—either from the introduction, or perhaps the opening sequences of a play session. The storyboard really needs to be created by a professional cartoon artist or gifted amateur.

The purpose of the storyboard is to supplement the concept artwork and show how the characters will behave in the game, such as specific animation sequences that illustrate their personalities. Anyone who has played *Sonic the Hedgehog* will recognize the storyboard possibilities that the natural cartoon aspect of this game offers. Even games like *Street Fighter II* can be rendered as a storyboard. It provides a great opportunity to use the visual medium of cartoon sequences to convey some aspects of the game that might otherwise require pages of text to accurately explain.

The Waiting Game

It is imperative to have some form of follow-up when submitting the package to a publisher. Keep a spreadsheet of the dates that you sent off packages, whom each was sent to, and who ended up with them. Most publishers fail to acknowledge receipt of proposals—accepted it as a fact of life. It will be difficult to know exactly where you stand when struggling to be heard through the traditional background noise that this industry has to put up with.

Following up ensures that the publisher digs out your proposal from the pile of submissions that have been accumulating over the past three or four weeks. Start with an email or two, and note where the replies come from. This will clue you as to whom to call in the next phase.

Telephone contact is great, because it puts the person on the spot, and you can quickly determine if the answer is likely to be "yes," "no," or "we're too busy right now." Do not push too hard or become a pest, as this will likely lead to rejection. Do appear persuasive and proactive; and don't forget to keep evident the passion for your project. Try to offer something more; suggest a meeting if that is feasible, but retain a professional distance. You do not want to appear either annoyed or desperate—even though you might well be.

If you are lucky enough to score a meeting, prepare a slick presentation, have your projected costs ready, and turn up on time reasonably groomed and full of adrenaline. It might not be necessary to wear a suit, depending on the publisher. Many work in jeans and T-shirts, which doesn't mean that they don't expect suits and ties on formal business meetings. An inside contact will be useful in gauging the culture of the publisher's office, or ask around on their Web site. If the publisher has a forum, for example, you might be able to discern the level of formality that the marketing department will expect.

The key is this: Be professional and persistent. Only dress down if your inner professional instinct seems to tell you that this would be appropriate. The first time, always wear business professional attire. A few meetings down the road, and other attire might be acceptable, depending on what others are wearing. If in doubt, remain in business-like clothing.

Persistence pays off; as long as it is delivered with that same professionalism. If you give up, you will never know if the idea was any good. If you think that you are pushing too hard, then perhaps space out the insistent contact a little; after all, it is usually about being in the right place at the right time and having the right idea for the publisher's current portfolio.

Summary

As a final note—remain positive. If you get knocked down, then get up. If you are rejected, then find a new door to knock on. You might run around until you feel like giving up, but don't give up. It is that kind of industry. Sometimes it is hard to keep sight of the goal—to get your game created and on the shelves. You may need to change your expectations over time, so that some progress is made.

For example, if every publisher on your top 10 list has rejected you, then perhaps it is time to create a working demonstration for the gaming community, free of charge. By doing this, you prove to publishers that you can at least complete a project, and hopefully that the game is good enough to attract gamers. Along with the game, give the community an easy way to provide feedback on your game, such as an email address, through a gaming Web site with forums, or simply via postcards. Take the gamers' comments seriously, and try to incorporate them into the Design Document and eventually into a re-release of the demo.

Listening to criticism from gamers, publishers, and even your friends, is easy. Taking it to heart is often painful, especially if their ideas are at odds with your own. Quite often, it is simply a mislaid path between the Design Document and the designer's vision. Even negative feedback provides a great source of information that can be worked into the design.

It is always a good idea to get some kind of peer review. If there is still no one willing to pick up the project, then it's time for alternative means—which brings us to the next chapter, where we look at how to find the money to do the whole thing yourself, without the help of a publisher.

REFERENCES

[Acornsoft84] *Elite, Space Traders Flight Training Manual.* Acornsoft, Ltd., 1984, p. 5.

[Activision02] *SOFII: Double Helix* manual. Activision, 2002, p. 3.

[EDGE03] *EDGE* magazine. January 2003, No. 119, p. 84.

[McGilvray01] Mitzi McGilvray, Interviewed for *Game Design: Secrets of the Sages.* BradyGames, 2000, p. 23.

14 Funding for Your Video Game

In This Chapter

- The Role of the Studio
- Intellectual Property
- Distribution
- Banks and Angel Investors

By now, you should have a good idea of how to turn a video game vision into reality, as well as a working design, possibly even with a demo of the game and advertising copy ready to be distributed on the cover of your favorite gaming magazine. It is time to make this all happen. However, one thing is missing: money. Even if your team is pulled together from the Internet and a great demo is in hand, and until now your only expense has been in time—this does not make a product. It may work for smaller projects and demos of larger ones, but to make a high-class game, the team will have to quit their day jobs and be ready to dedicate a couple of years of their lives to the project.

Unless they are independently wealthy, team members will need to be paid. There will be tools and equipment to buy, as well as marketing expenses, publication and production costs, royalties on third-party music and graphics, and licensing fees for the game engine.

Then there are the usual money sources—ranging from banks to angel investors (businesspeople giving a little back to those with a vision)—who can be approached to help produce video games. Unless you have a truly great idea, video game background, and ideally some projects under your belt, it will be hard to persuade them to take the risk.

They can be approached but will respond much more favorably if the proposition is a commercial one. Very small, bedroom coder style, video game developers will be unlikely to score funding here, and commercial video games have alternatives that follow a more traditional publishing path.

Commercial video games are produced by studios and marketed by publishers. This is the way it works and always has (except for the shareware revolution). So the way to go is to find a publisher that is willing to put money into your game and a studio that is willing to invest the time to create it.

Sometimes, finding the publisher is enough, because they can most often suggest a suitable studio. In Chapter 13, we discussed the Official Design Document and the importance of listing team members, which will prove to the publisher that you have seriously considered how the game will be created and who will be involved.

The Role of the Studio

Video game studios create games. They often have their own ideas, sometimes they build games based on licenses, but mostly they are a group of artists, programmers, and game designers who live, breathe, eat, and sleep video games—which makes them very valuable when you want an opinion on your game design. After all, if the studio does not believe in your vision, it is not going to want to make the game; and you already have one strike against you—you're an outsider to the studio, so the studio's enthusiasm for your project will be slim.

One important point that the designer should remember is that the studio also needs to fund the game's development. If you do not offer to pay the studio up front (and chances are that you will not have sufficient funds), then the studio will need to take money from its own bank account in *anticipation* of substantial returns when the game sells. So, they are taking a chance, and there are a number of ways in which you can persuade them to take that chance.

The best way takes time, but a good idea will wait. It is widely accepted in the industry that the best way to get your game idea published is to get an entry-level position at a game studio and work your way up for two to three years. Then, spring your idea on the management team, after you have a reputation. Of course, this way you effectively lose control of the product, but it will at least get published.

And, you need to get hired in the first place, which presents its own set of problems: Do you have a skill that a studio can use?

Most readers do have such a skill, from programming to game design to entry-level production jobs; someone once told me that tools programming was a good way to get in and a good way to get spotted. This makes sense, but the end answer will depend on the individual: Find a skill that will get you hired, and make sure that you get noticed.

Unless you are working your way up through the production side, any game ideas you have will not be under your control once the company takes possession of them. They will very likely be handed to a producer to turn into a product; the only way to be sure to avoid this is to try and *be* that producer.

Of course, any exposure to the game industry is good exposure, and one last point bears some discussion. As a good all-rounder, a budding video game designer may well find that he can do much of the groundwork in his spare time as he works in the industry, thus putting himself in a position to reduce the risk that the publisher or studio is exposed to.

As a lone designer/developer, working to your own timetable, you may just create something that the management finds easy to take forward and will make you part of the team (if not actually in charge of the project). This is a long shot, perhaps not the longest, but it can be done.

It is harder to pull together a team and start a studio with the sole purpose of making this one video game. It can be done, but it will require money.

Which brings us to the hardest way to publish a game. Banks will finance companies that are likely to make money and pay back their loans. So, if you really must set up a studio to make the game, then at least start by putting together a programming house (or art production company) and move "into" video game development gradually. A bank will be more likely to put money into a venture that already has a client list and is producing a low-risk product. The lower the risk is, the better. If you set up an art-production company, you will be producing art for studios or other third-party clients who will be taking the risk, themselves. As long as they pay your invoices, the bank will be happy. It may sound harsh and unforgiving, but business is business.

Assuming that you plan to go it alone and create the game as an independent studio, then there will come a time when the game has to be distributed to prospective gamers. Between the vision concept and the final product there is the studio that will do all of the work; but the studio will not actually market or distribute your game.

So, the developer (studio) will create the game, possibly having first pitched it to a publisher. The publisher invests its time and money in marketing, as well as paying the costs of the studio to develop the game and create a product from it. This product might be a game in a box (the traditional method) or a pay-to-play or download (through a channel such as Xbox Live Arcade or Valve's Steam).

Level Designers

All games will have structure. If the game's genre encompasses a repetitive-rule system and multiple circumstances in which those rules are applied, as in most shoot-em-ups and first-person shooters, then cunning level design will be the cornerstone of your game.

If games such as *Quake* or *DOOM* had bad level design, despite the eye candy and fluid gameplay, they would not be engaging. More than half of the appeal of these games is in the problem solving and exploration aspects.

A good level designer is part programmer, part artist, and part gamer. He needs to be able to suggest or even create artwork, while also knowing how the game is put together so that he can instruct the programmers. If the system embraces an open, scripted architecture, then the designer can make script changes, himself.

If there are any nonplussed programmers out there who disagree that level designers should be part programmer, think of it this way. They need to interface with code, be it scripts or source code, and it helps them to be able to at least think like a programmer when they do it. Programmers' jobs are safe—they cannot be replaced by level designers who claim to know programming. Programming is a skill honed by doing one thing and one thing only—programming.

Programmers

The programmers actually make it happen. They work out the best way to get the art assets onto the screen, implement the logic to make them interact, and provide a suitable interface to the game for the level designers. They might also have opinions about how the game should look. Listen to the programmers' opinions, because they come backed with the experience of having tried similar things before. The kind of expertise that they have based on their knowledge of the platform also makes them quite expensive. Most of the cash that the bank, investor, individual, or studio will pour into the project will find its way into the pockets of the programming team as wages.

Programmers are not, however, designers or artists. Their input is technical; when they have an opinion about how the game should look, it is based on that background—not artistic, but practical. This is why they should be listened to; it is up to them to make abstract design into reality.

By a similar token, there will probably be more programmers involved in a game than level designers or artists, and they are also usually not independent contractors, but permanent members of the team. In the game industry, there are many independent sound engineers and artists that offer their services to studios as freelancers, but few programmers do so; the intimacy of the relationship with the game and its studio tends to run deeper.

Artists

Without art, the game's visual impact will be minimal. Creative art is not always required, but when it is, it is always best to get a professional artist—one that cannot only draw and create textures, but who can also apply their ideas to models that can be manipulated by the programmers.

Games can get by with little artwork. Take a game like *Defcon*, for example. Here, the art is basic but very powerful, given the kind of game that *Defcon* is and the storyline behind it. It doesn't need any more art, in the same way that many other games, from shooters to racing games, definitely need as much as they can get their hands on.

Bigger games need more artists. Games that attempt to mimic the real world need more artists. Take the studio Climax (Brighton, U.K.), who is currently involved in creating the next-generation *MotoGP* racing game. The level of detail that the artists put into the game involved taking thousands of photos of real tracks and measuring everything accurately, right down to the heights of tire walls.

This kind of detail is expensive. Find a bunch of creative types, give them laptops, digital cameras, and rented motorbikes, as well as paying the track owners to let you wander around for a week or so, and the bills will mount up. Travel, technology, and licensing all have their costs. Plus, you have to pay the artists for their time, which includes repeat visits when, for example, they realize that a track width is missing.

Of course, imaginary game universes cost less in terms of real-world site visits and research; almost all the work can be done within the studio. Do not forget, however, that there will also be other costs, such as the technology required to create models that move accurately and, above all, an investment in *time*. Art takes time to get right, more so than the programming in many cases.

So, while you might think that it is cheaper to create an environment from pure imagination, having nothing to base it on will make it hard to get right. There will be more trial and error involved than just copying detail from a photo. This makes it as expensive, if not more so, to produce than deriving the environment from real-world examples.

Sound Engineers

So, visual impact requires artists, and audio impact requires sound engineers. The sound and music of a game conveys as much information as the graphics (although you can't play a game with the graphics turned off). One of the most common mistakes made in video game creation is to underestimate the importance of sound.

Sound engineers, those people with the big fluffy microphones who wander around recording things, are also professionals. Sound—music as well as natural sounds—can help to make up for other senses, like spatial awareness (3D surround sound), and it helps to convey and instill emotion very powerfully. There will be platform limitations, but it never hurts to start out with good quality source audio, even if the quality will need to be reduced for the final platform.

Many game designers assume that sound engineering is something that can, like artwork, be done by amateurs. This is a big mistake.

Another common mistake is to assume that if voices are needed for the game, then you can just ask one of the team members to speak into a microphone and use that in the game. Professionals, both actors and sound engineers, make up part of the studio, and they have associated costs in line with other industry professionals.

However, a good sound engineer can often get good results from amateurs, which will save having to employ professionals. On the other hand, even a professional actor will need to be recorded by a professional sound engineer to get the right effect. Just because they are actors does not necessarily mean that they instinctively know how to give you the audio that you need. Again, it's a mix.

Music is another game aspect that is neglected when funds run short. This can be due to insufficient budgeting when the designer thinks about the musical landscape that will accompany the game. Real instruments are often better than electronic ones for big backing soundtracks, and (like professional artwork) will take time and cost money. The cost of a full orchestra is usually out of reach for all but the largest studios. Professional musicians are another example of contract (as opposed to salaried) team members.

All of this makes the musical score more expensive than might have been foreseen. Even if real instruments cannot be used due to lack of funds, then musicians should still be budgeted in; they will often be able to closely mimic real instruments by electronic means. They also often come with their own equipment, meaning that the studio doesn't need to buy these tools.

Of course, the capability of the platform will dictate the result. If the target platform is a handheld LCD game that can only produce limited sound, then real instruments will not be needed. Similarly, electronic instruments have their place in producing music and effects that fit certain genres, where other types of sound would not be appropriate.

The key is in finding the right source quality and type to fit the game under development. A movie-style soundtrack might prove expensive to do well, and if the platform cannot make the most of it, then it may be money spent that could have been put to better use elsewhere.

Management

You thought you were in charge, right? Wrong. Game producers are very special people with wide-ranging talents. They have to be able to communicate with programmers, artists, designers, and musicians, as well as with the person(s) responsible for the initial design.

Producers are the final place that the buck stops. They have no one to pass it to, and as such are part administrator, part human resource manager, and part project manager, and they hold the responsibility to meet the deadlines imposed. Success or failure of the project often hinges on their ability to balance everything just right; they have the most stressful and tenuous job of all in many studios.

Managing a game from conception through to distribution is a challenge that only an experienced manager is prepared for. Such experience comes with a hefty price tag, but studios take on this financial burden in order to make a game a success. If you plan to go it alone, using a variety of professionals to handle the tasks of producing the game, and you wish to manage the whole project, then be aware that this is false economy, unless you have prior experience in multimedia project management.

Intellectual Property

We have touched on the use of Intellectual Property (IP) in several sections of this book. Whenever the designer borrows from someone else's work, be it licensing a character or an entire movie script, they are making use of IP that has been established, often at great cost, as a brand with a specific public image.

Using someone else's work without that person's written permission is against copyright law; some parodies (*James Pond*, for example) get away with it, but lifting recognizable characters, situations, backdrops, music, artwork, names, places, or anything else will likely lead to lengthy legal battles. The copyright owner (rightly) has more protection now than ever before, and if you even need to ask yourself whether it would be appropriate to use something, the answer is probably no.

IP needs to be purchased, though it can at times be used in exchange for royalty payments. Acquiring IP rights is usually an expensive business. The price tag associated with it is dependent on the original creators—costs that have usually been predetermined.

Before we have a quick rundown of IP laws and terminology, remember to always seek independent legal advice. We only touch on the basics here, and I am not a lawyer by trade. Having said that, only an expression of an idea can be copyrighted, not the idea itself. Genres cannot be protected, but instances of them *are*.

Licensing IP requires an upfront fee, for which you derive the right to use the IP; this is the same idea as the license that you buy for software. In addition, use of IP may require the payment of royalties (like a 10 percent cut of sales) on the proceeds generated by the product that contains the IP, often in perpetuity.

IP is about protecting the hard work of artists (both literary and media), inventors, and programmers. There are many games that have "borrowed" the rule-set made famous by the Dungeons & Dragons tabletop game, but this can be a dangerous area to enter (without a good lawyer at your side). One of these games, *D20*, has been released into the public domain, which means that people are free to incorporate its rules and calculation methods into their own games. However, they are not allowed to associate these new games with Wizards of the Coast (publishers of the video game *Dungeons & Dragons*), the series name, or the system itself. Wizards of the Coast holds the *copyright* to this material, as well as the company's identifiable image. They are assets of the company that created them; it is their IP, and they do not want other people to profit from their success (especially if it turns out to be a public relations disaster).

Which brings us to a final point about IP. Good IP can lead to game sales that might otherwise have slipped into obscurity. There is essentially no such thing as bad IP. If a movie, book, table-top game, or television show is popular, that means that it has its fans, and each of those fans is a potential customer. Investing in IP is simply a matter of balancing the possible returns against the costs associated with cashing in on its popularity (or for tools, its utility); in other words, is it worth it?

Sponsorship and In-Game Advertising

Some games might not make money solely from their retail price. In other words, some games might be priced reasonably to cover the cost of distribution and perhaps offset some of the creation cost, but there is no profit margin to speak of. Still, profits are realized, as we shall see.

The payment chain is quite simple. The gamer pays the retailer. The retailer pays the distributor (maybe through a wholesaler). The wholesaler has previously bought the products from the publisher. The publisher (who has funded the production of the game, one way or another) then has a number of options.

Ideally, the developer has already been paid by the publisher. If not (and in many cases, even if they have), the developer will be due some royalties. Those royalties are, in effect, the profit-making component of the game. What happens, though, when there is no money left to pay royalties? The cost of the development has been covered. The studio has been paid, but the royalties do not usually amount to enough to sustain the studio going forward. If there isn't another game in the works, then alternative revenue must be sought.

Alternative Revenue Streams

An increasing number of games are becoming sponsored. Big-name manufacturers of everything from soft drinks to sporting goods are eager to offer substantial sums of money to feature their brands. For them, it is a good way to reach their customer base.

This symbiotic arrangement can help make the game designer's dream into reality. No longer does the designer have to rely on a publisher or investor. A small, medium, or even large brand-name company might offer funding in return for in-game placement.

A studio might not get investment from a single sponsor to produce a so-called AAA title, but it might be able to find enough funding to help create a title. This could range from the brand paying part of the development cost, bringing in money through a publisher, or a combination of revenue streams helping offset the cost of a Web-based game.

(In 2007, Google filed several patents for in-game advertising, which seems to support the perceived value that is placed on this revenue stream.) The sponsor's level of interest in the game will depend on how much of a role their brand name plays. Games created around a brand in its entirety, such as *S.C.A.R* and Alfa Romeo, will be highly monitored by the brand owner. This is natural, because when it comes to the paying public, the sponsor's reputation is on the line.

Sponsorship, however, is only one part of the equation. Advertising is the other part—selling advertising space in a game in order to either help fund the actual development or to provide a steady flow of revenue once the game has been released. These options have been much enhanced by in-game advertising middleware and services, software that will help the game developer integrate advertising into his game.

Of course, this idea really comes into its own when dealing with the Internet, through which we can dynamically keep the advertising fresh. Of course, this only works with a game that is continually evolving or is designed to have a long shelf life. Once gamers stop playing, the advertisers will want to stop paying.

For example, a virtual soccer game, like a real one, can have advertising in it. A console soccer game with no connection to the Internet, though, suffers from a problem when deploying advertising. The advertising is likely to be static. Once integrated into the game, it cannot be changed. There is no way to update the advertisement. So, players will see the same old ads, over and over again. This lack of freshness will diminish the interest shown by advertisers.

The next step up is to deploy an Internet-connected game machine with temporary storage (hard drive). This could be a PC or a console. Now the advertiser has the option to update his message, thus keeping it fresh. This is where the middleware comes in.

Google, for example, has filed patents for specific advertising algorithms [EDGE02] that detect the game running, update the advertising data with fresh content based on a variety of different inputs, and display the result in proprietary "billboards." Although the technology is in its infancy, it already looks quite impressive. And, there is no need for the developer to get involved in the update process, once the middleware is installed.

From a design perspective, be aware that this middleware is vital for leveraging in-game advertising as part of the revenue model. If we want to get paid, we need to offer a solution, but we do not want to have our programmers tied up with this kind of development. So, we deploy middleware to do it for us.

There will be a cost associated with *that,* also, but if we can negotiate a royalty-based fee, where a first set percentage of the income is handed back to the middleware developer, then this might be the best approach. Otherwise, middleware becomes part of the cost of making the game and has to be recouped through the revenue.

However, our game still has a limited shelf life. As soon as a better one comes along, the advertisers change their approaches in the real world, or the players just get bored, the revenue will dry up. That is also part of the equation. Where this is less of a problem is in massively multiplayer online games, in which the game environment is constantly being updated. Usually reserved for PC gamers, these games offer unique in-game sponsorship and advertising opportunities. Their fans are loyal and number in the millions, but it is quite hard to establish a new game in the market. It takes time to build up such a large fan base.

Also, text-based Web games are now starting to look into these kinds of revenue streams. There is an online soccer game that allows players to sell advertising space (for virtual in-game money) on their pitch billboards. They can choose from ads by real-world advertisers, which are displayed along with, for example, game results or commentaries on virtual games. This is a very clever and innovative mix of the real and virtual, and it also makes money for the developer.

Distribution

Assume for a moment that your game is complete. Congratulations. Or, assume that it is in the process of being created, and there is a demo version that runs smoothly, has a collection of levels or missions, and minimal bugs. Maybe a studio is building it, and things are looking fairly good; the artwork is coming along, and there are some full-motion videos to look at. Again, congratulations.

Before patting yourself on the back, though, have you considered that you are possibly the only person who knows about the game? Word of mouth is a powerful thing, and you can usually rely on the studio staff to publicize the game for you, but only in a very limited way. After all, you are making video game history. It is time to consider how to get the word.

PUBLISHERS

The role of the publisher is very simple. Make copies of the game, put it in a box with some documentation, and place it in the hands of the consumer. Hopefully, your game will pass the point of sale and gamers will hand over their hard-earned money for your virtual experience. Pick up any boxed game, and you will likely see two logos on the box—the studio and the publisher. From the consumers' point of view, that may be all we see—a game in a box. Remember, though, that the box has come at a high price. It is the publisher that takes the calculated risk to have the game developed and hopes to reap the rewards. Games succeed and games fail, and it is largely the publishers, at the end of the day, who benefit or suffer.

After all, it's their marketing, duplication, and distribution costs, as well as the money they hand over to the developer.

Josh Resnick of Pandemic Studios notes that someone:

> ". . . would be absolutely crazy to do it all on their own." [Resnick01]

As long as the team is in place, or a studio is impressed enough to be interested in creating your game, publishers can be approached. Face it, you're going to be asking for a very large amount of money (perhaps spread over a time span of up to three years) before any kind of return will be forthcoming, so it is important that the information in your Official Design Document is 100 percent accurate. This includes knowing the costs of all the production components. Nothing should be overlooked. Even though they might have a good idea of how much development will cost, publishers need to be told, because it proves that the designer has thought out the project in great detail.

So, ideally, the publisher will pay for development but also take control of the project, right down to the hiring and firing levels. The good news is that a lot of the financial pressures will be taken off of the designer's shoulders. The alternative is to do it all by yourself, including creating the distribution media and shipping the product to distributors. The designer has to trade off one route against the other; each has its advantages and sacrifices.

SHAREWARE

The Internet has turned the publishing paradigm topsy-turvy in recent years. Id Software released their first game as a shareware title; their distribution medium was the Internet. *Wolfenstein3D* could be downloaded for free—at least the first few levels—and this "taste" encouraged gamers to order the full, registered game directly from id Software.

Their next release, *DOOM,* followed a similar marketing strategy, but *DOOM* was also offered in a "limited" version at a discount price in game outlets. Now it seems that all game publishers offer a limited or demo version of their games for download, with the full version available retail.

This means that designers who have at least a decent demo version up and running have a new way to get their game into the hands of consumers worldwide, and there is another aspect of shareware paradigm that will come as a breath of fresh air. Gamers have come to accept that downloaded shareware will not have all of the "goodies" that come with the larger, retail version. In other words, they are looking for solid gameplay, and not necessarily the "eye candy" graphics and sounds. If they are pleased, they will be back with the cash for the full version. (In most cases, the larger, full version is impractical to download anyway, and must be ordered via "snail mail.")

The secret is to have solid game mechanics and a good marketing plan. An absolutely critical part of shareware publishing is to get the game into the hands of Web surfers. A Web site will help, as will press releases, reviews, and industry magazine features.

There is one limitation: the platform. Shareware titles are more or less restricted to the PC and Apple markets. The steep cost of development kits and the requirement that the game be downloadable means that it is almost impossible to create shareware for consoles or handheld gaming systems. On the other hand, with the recent trend toward mobile gaming and devices that have built-in Internet connectivity, such as cell phones, this will become less of an issue. In addition, many handheld devices now have Java compatibility, as well. The boundaries of shareware publishing are being pushed forward every time a new platform is released. Upcoming devices to keep an eye on include the N-Gage from mobile phone manufacturer Nokia.

So what does this all mean? At best, some shareware games take in annual revenues of about $100,000, which sounds like enough to make it worthwhile, especially if half of these proceeds can be channeled to non-shareware titles or saved as an investment toward the designer's dream title.

Trade Shows

Video games exist in an industry that is still very much in its infancy, and as such there are many trade shows where new developments are discussed and products are showcased. The biggest is probably the Electronics Entertainment Expo (E3), which generally focuses on the top end of the market. Others, such as the Independent Games Festival (part of the Game Developers Conference), are targeted at up-and-coming designers.

There are also shows for specific trades within the industry, such as SIGGRAPH for artists and animators, and Milia, the International Content Market for Interactive Media. These are all of particular interest because they provide the most fertile grounds for networking in the industry. Exhibitors from all manners of electronic entertainment companies and investors (both business and individuals) attend, and there have been many success stories over the years from events such as the Game Village at Milia. Designers present their creations to people who come with the express purpose of taking a chance on an "indie" with a dream.

Banks and Angel Investors

Banks and "angels" are traditional sources of funding for any industry, and with some perseverance, it is possible to persuade them to help fund your project. Before approaching either, it is important to demonstrate your knowledge of the industry, and be prepared to explain more your project than if you were talking to a publisher.

These investors will look mostly at the business side of the proposition and be less enthralled by any technological excellence. A games publisher will instinctively know what a good idea looks like and whether it will sell, and will be able to estimate the worth of the idea. But those outside of the industry (who probably are not gamers) are often leery of products that are not within the traditional investment markets.

Banks

Be prepared for a frosty reception, and also be prepared to put some collateral on the line, such as your house or car. If your project goes down the drain (heaven forbid), banks need a way to recoup their investment, and liquid assets are used as collateral—which usually makes banks unsuitable for first-time projects.

On the other hand, banks like to fund businesses that represent a going concern. A video game project is seen as a one-shot investment and a one-shot product, while a video game studio has longevity. A company that performs a business function, such as printing, CD replication, or even an independent recording studio, presents the bank with not only a traditional investment that they can relate to, but also a longer-term business relationship.

It is hard enough to produce a game design, but it might be beyond most designers to also come up with a business plan that both stands on its own merit and attracts enough money to fund the game. Try offering some kind of service to the gaming community and fish for ideas. You can never tell what you'll come up with, perhaps even an idea that will be useful in producing the game.

Then again, a bank might just provide the start-up capital. If you can pitch the concept to a game-savvy banker, this will help. Try choosing a bank that has "start your own business" brochures in the lobby. Visit as many as possible. Pick up and *read* the literature, and make yourself as knowledgeable about business as you are about video games. Approach fund-raising like you approach the rest of your project—with passion. It is a means to an end.

There might also be some government money available to help you set up the studio. This is great, because a bank will accept grant money as collateral as quickly as your own assets, and it goes a long way toward proving that you have thought long and carefully about the business proposition. You might not even need to mention video games. Just try not to get too caught up in the business end, to the point where your great game idea is permanently shelved. That would be a shame.

ANGELS

Angel investors are hard to come by. Essentially, these are people (companies) who have money to invest for a high rate of return. They are usually venture capitalists with independent sources of income, who that tend to fund high-technology projects.

As with banks, getting an angel on board is easier when working with an industry product that they understand. Unlike banks, there is a greater chance that they will be at least acquainted with the video-game/electronics-entertainment industry, and will be much more interested in research on the aspects that they do not understand.

Angels also differ from banks in that they are more willing to take a risk—but they demand a higher return. Banks just want the loan repaid at a moderate rate of interest. Investors, though, are primarily interested in reaping a good profit, and want to do so quickly. The longer-term the risk, the higher are the expected returns.

Finding an angel to take on your project is a tricky proposition. A quick search of the Internet will yield some places where you can post your project description and wait for investors to pick up on it. A word of warning: As always when posting information on the Internet, remember that it is for all practical purposes in the public domain. Simply slapping a copyright notice on it is often a meaningless exercise. Ideas can still be stolen, and fighting for your rights means hiring lawyers . . . and spending a lot more money.

Of course even potential investors and publishers could steal your idea, refuse you funding, and make the game anyway. Though the industry is generally trustworthy, this has happened in the past and will probably happen again. The first stage in seeking protection is to get a lawyer to draw up a Non-Disclosure Agreement (NDA) for both parties to sign.

An NDA essentially forbids the investor/publisher from using or repeating any of the disclosed material without the permission of its owner, and it is dated. Another elegantly simple idea comes from the pages of *Secrets of the Sages*. Take a copy of the Official Design Document, and mark it "cc:" carbon copy to a trusted third party, such as a friend or relative (thus putting the publisher on notice that the document is protected). Seal it in an envelope and mail the copy to the third party by registered post. Tell the third party not to open it. That way, if there is conflict later on, you will be able to prove when the document originated (by the postmark) and solidify your ownership, in addition to having the third party as a credible witness.

A good place to find investors willing to embark on a three-year development cycle is the Milia show. They might even have booths that you can visit to pitch your idea. But don't get carried away; careless talk could cost you your project. Try to convey enthusiasm above all else. Essentially, just having a great idea is not enough. Often, mediocre ideas become games simply because the designer's enthusiasm shines through.

SUMMARY

Yes, parts of this chapter are a bit of a downer, but there is also some sunlight within these pages. The fact remains, though, that funding a (possibly) $1 million project is more difficult than thinking up the game idea, especially if you have no previous experience in the industry and no track record for potential investors to consider.

Therefore, your first project should be simple and easily completed. It may or may not bring in money. What is important is that the game works, is visible, and people can actually play it, have some fun, and spread the word. This makes the next project easier, since you will have been through the problems associated with creating a video game. The next time, you will know better ways to approach it.

Your project will probably make money, which can be used to fund a future project—and this is the real goal of the exercise. It might take a few projects (maybe three) before publishers begin to have faith in you and your team, but it is the best way to achieve your dreams. *SimCity* was pitched to eight different publishers before Maxis picked up on it, so be prepared to stick with it over the long haul.

Then there is the option of getting a job and working your way up through the industry until you are in a position where your voice will be heard, and then pitching the idea from the inside. This will take some time—maybe three years for a talented game designer, perhaps longer for an artist or programmer. Along the way, expect inconvenient hours, low pay, and possibly having to relocate to where the work is.

None of these options are for the faint-hearted, but stick with it. If you do, you will prove that you have the talent and dedication to make video games.

References

[Resnick01] Josh Resnick in an interview for *Game Design: Secrets of the Sages*. BradyGames, 2000, p. 342.

[EDGE02] Newswire, *EDGE* magazine, Issue 182, December 2007, p. 17.

Appendix

Tools, Magazines, and Web Sites

This Appendix lists some of the best tools available for creating video games as well as assets that can help you build a polished product. They are provided to illustrate the technologies that can be employed for production, as well as when putting together the Official Design Document package destined for the publisher. There is also a list of industry magazines that monitor game releases and publish reviews. These magazines, as well as their accompanying Web sites, are worth reading on a regular basis. Finally, there is a list of the best Web sites where you can explore all aspects of game design and related industries.

Freeware and Shareware Tools

One of the great things about the games industry is that it attracts a lot of attention from amateurs and enthusiasts. These people then put together information, tools, utilities, and even game creation kits that they then make available to other enthusiasts, often for free.

Please remember, however, that just because something is free doesn't give you the right to claim it for your own, resell it, or, in some cases, resell anything created by it. So, check the license conditions before use.

By a similar token, shareware is not freeware. If you continue to use it beyond the trial period that the author sets out in the license, you must pay for it. After all, if someone did the same to you, you would (rightfully) be irritated.

That said, there are some real gems here, and some great opportunities to hone both design and rudimentary development skills (scripting, usually), and experimentation is often the best teacher.

Modding/Scripting Tools

Most retail FPS games these days come with built-in tools for creating additional mods and scripts, such as for *Quake*, *DOOM*, and *Unreal*. Modding is primarily for PC games; most console games cannot offer similar functionality due to the closed nature of the platform.

A cursory search of the Internet for key words such as "WAD" or "QUake ARmy Knife" will return home pages for these excellent tools and in turn lead the reader to other sites that offer similar tools. These lists are always changing, so bookmark them for future reference.

Prototyping and Game Production Tools

A list of systems that can be used to build games can be found at the following Web sites:

- **http://www.dosgames.com/g_gcs.php:** The game-creation tools found here can only be used to create DOS-based games, but they work well under most flavors of Windows. The user should make sure that they have checked the "Run in Compatibility Mode" option in the Properties section for the application to avoid any conflicts.
- **http://www.cs.uu.nl/people/markov/gmaker/download.html:** Game Maker is an excellent free tool that can be used to create 2D and isometric games. It is one of the most well-supported freeware tools around.
- **http://gamedev.sourceforge.net:** For creating scrolling games, the GameDev project is an open-source engine that allows sophisticated scripting and animated tiles. It has its own built-in graphics editor.
- **http://www.cognitial.com/interax/index.htm:** Cognitial Software markets a kit known as InterAx that provides a holder application into which you can drop photographs, artwork, or audio files. It is perfect for creating interactive storyboards or high-powered presentations, but is a bit lightweight for creating full games, unless they are fairly simple. The price tag is worth it, simply for the sheer ease of use.
- **http://www.datawaregames.com/html/qc.htm:** For 2D RPG creation, there is Quest Creator from Dataware Games. Both a free, downloadable version and a retail version exist. The software enables the creation of games for distribution.

Commercial Tools

- **http://www.GarageGames.com:** The Torque game engine was used to create the game *Tribes 2*, and the programming team behind the engine decided to create a distribution network for independent game creators, called Garage Games. Their flagship product, Torque, is available for a one-time purchase price per programmer, and is downloadable through the Garage Games Web site.
- **http://www.QubeSoft.com:** Qube Software has released a series of products that can be used to create games for PC (free) and console platforms (per-game, per-platform license).

MAGAZINE PUBLISHERS

- ***EDGE* Magazine:** As evidenced by the numerous references to this magazine in this book, the reason that *EDGE* is so important is that it strips out the hype and presents an objective view of the games industry. These honest reviews are coupled with timely articles on the state of video game design. It might not be to everyone's taste, though; their editorial approach is often tongue-in-cheek, and sometimes downright superior.
- **Future Publishing, http://www.futurenet.co.uk:** Home of *EDGE* and many other multiformat review magazines, examples can be perused at their Web site.
- ***Game Developer Magazine:*** This is the only magazine in the industry devoted to the development of video games, and it excels.

WEB SITES

The following is a collection of sites that any video game designer should visit before writing the Design Document or even attempting to design a game. Although it might seem like a waste of time to continually download game demos and videos, doing so is vital to keeping abreast of the state of the art.

VIDEO GAME SITES

- **http://www.GamaSutra.com:** This site is one of the best places on the Internet to find out about game design in the real world. Registration, required before accessing the articles, is free and well worth it.
- **news://rec.games.design:** This newsgroup is tops for keeping abreast of techniques that are being used to solve problems in video game design and programming. Please read the official FAQ before posting.
- **http://www.GDMag.com:** This is the Web site of *Game Developer Magazine,* the world's foremost magazine dedicated to game design. Articles that do not quite cut it for the magazine find their way to the Web site.
- **http://www.GarageGames.com:** The *Torque* game engine has been mentioned a few times in this book, and here is where you will find the development team behind the engine. The site also provides a download page for games created using the engine.
- **http://www.HappyPuppy.com:** One of the most popular game sites on the Internet, HappyPuppy has areas dedicated to all aspects of video game design, as well as general links to publishers, studios, and jobs.
- **http://www.computerandvideogames.com/edge/forum/:** This is the forum site for the industry's premier multiformat video game review and industry news magazine. Boards cover everything from last year's best games to next year's big hits, as well as offering solid advice from industry professionals. Their writers have the same *EDGE* magazine, tongue-in-cheek approach to video games.
- **http://www.GamesRadar.com:** Part of the Future Publishing group's network of sites, GamesRadar is geared toward the best information available to gamers, game designers, journalists, and other industry professionals.

- **http://videogames.suite101.com:** This link is a repository for game design information, links, articles, books, and online courses.

Download Sites

Please remember, when downloading from any site, and in particular those oriented toward the mass-market, that you should deploy adequate anti-virus protection. Any software deemed to have mass appeal will also, unfortunately, often be an attractive host for all manner of digital parasites, so, as always, please make sure your protection is high quality and up-to-date.

- **http://www.GameSpy.com:** The GameSpy network is the first place to go for game-specific downloads. Registration is free, and there is an advertiser-sponsored queuing system for downloads. To bypass this, visitors can pay a nominal fee for no-wait downloads, which is worth it if you are going to be downloading the most recent, popular demos.
- **http://www.Download.com:** Part of the excellent CNet family of sites, this is one of the best places to download software, source code, and libraries of all kinds, and not just video game-related tools.

Sounds and Graphics

- **http://www.CoolText.com:** This is a great site for creating logos using customizable effects. Even better than Microsoft WordArt, it can also produce buttons. The graphics are primarily for use on Web sites, but could be used equally well in presentation-pack documentation or customized for use in the Official Design Document. The downloads are royalty-free, but acknowledgment is appreciated.
- **http://www.Freetextures.com:** Here, you will find free textures.
- **http://www.The3DStudio.com:** This Web site has some nice textures and textured models for use in 3DMAX or compatible applications.
- **http://www.3DLinks.com:** You will find help here for model or concept art creation. Also, 3DLinks provides pointers to the best 3D graphics sites on the Internet.
- **http://www.vectorg.com/cga/CGA.htm:** This is the Computer Game Artists Association Web site.

Miscellaneous

The following links are for general game development–related Web sites that just don't seem to fit in anywhere else being very broad in their remits.

- **http://www.theesa.com:** The Entertainment Software Association Web site (formerly the IDSA—International Digital Software Association).
- **http://www.igda.com:** The Independent Game Developers Association Web site.
- **http://www.game-developer.com:** Home of the Game Developer Search Engine.

Index